1965

The New Orpheus

Essays toward a Christian Poetic

The New Orpheus

Essays toward a Christian Poetic

Edited by NATHAN A. SCOTT, JR.
ASSOCIATE PROFESSOR OF THEOLOGY AND LITERATURE
THE UNIVERSITY OF CHICAGO

SHEED AND WARD - NEW YORK

Library of Congress Catalog Card Number 64–13566

Manufactured in the United States of America

For M.H.

Contents

Introduction

WITHIN THE FORUM of contemporary criticism, it might be somewhat premature at the present time to announce the emergence of a new movement that is distinguished by the influence upon it of a Christian theological perspective. And, even if this nascent impulse has already become so vigorous as to justify some such announcement, the more sensitive ones among those in whom it finds expression would doubtless be embarrassed by any sudden election to membership in a special "school" or "party." For nothing is more repugnant to the Christian consciousness than the "groupist" outlook and the mischief that is created in cultural life by a politics of exclusion. But however much resistance we may rightfully offer in this connection to the huckster of *Tendenz,* it has been difficult not to notice a fresh critical effort being undertaken over the past several years. It, to be sure, has not bristled with the kind of urgent topicality that might have made it a subject of debate in the *Partisan Review*. Yet, quietly and steadily, and apparently without any great sense of collaboration, many critics of our period, being Christians, have been attempting to discover wherein it is, if in any respect at all, that there may be said to exist the possibility of a Christian theory of literature. And many others, though without this kind of theoretical interest, have addressed themselves to the work of practical literary interpretation and, in thus refusing to sever their aesthetic preoccupations from their various existential and theological commitments, have helped to exert a wholesome adverse pressure on that *mystique* of "the text" which has so largely governed the criticism of the last thirty or forty years.

So, however cautiously we ought to plot the rising curve of this new insurgency, it does begin to be a significant fact in the literary life of our time. And one measure of its vitality may just be the malice with which it is occasionally spluttered out against by an unsophisticated (or dishonest) secularism which pretends to be aghast at the intrusion of theological perspectives into the literary order, as though literature could itself in any way be segregated from the larger life of the mind.

The most immediate "efficient" cause of this collection doubtless arises out of what I have felt to be the inconvenience involved in depending upon a library "reserve" shelf when, in alternate years in the Divinity School of the University of Chicago, I invite a group of graduate students to join me in canvassing the literature of contemporary Christian criticism. And, in putting together this book, I have hoped to provide a convenient survey instrument for future students of my own and for other students working generally in the field of modern criticism and, in a more specialized way, in the particular area that is here in view. But the more important "final" cause of this volume concerns my desire to call the work of recent Christian critics and theorists to the attention of the general public (both within and outside the theological community) that "keeps up" with the best conversation going on in the literary criticism of our period.

Those who already have some acquaintance with the richness and variety of the Christian achievement in recent criticism may, of course, want to enter a demurrer, at this point or at that, when they notice the omission of some piece of work which they highly regard. But the purpose of this collection has been not so much to record that achievement as to suggest it, and thus, inevitably, there was much of great value that no effort could be made to include.

The categories under which the material is arranged do not wholly exclude one another, and some of the essays might easily have been assigned another place within the total design. But, despite a certain roughness of differentiation in the five subject-headings, they do serve to focus the major themes on which recent Christian reflection in the field of poetics has tended to center. And, among these, it is the first—the problem of how a general Christian aesthetic is to be constituted—that has received the least attention. Catholic scholars of Roman allegiance have generally tended merely to weave and to re-weave fresh synopses and syntheses of the sentences in Aristotle and Aquinas bearing on the arts, or—as in the case of Maritain's great book of 1953, *Creative Intuition in Art and Poetry*—this mode of thought is merely complicated by some infusion (in not too great an amount to upset the Scholastic decorum) of Romanticist aesthetic, of, say, Plato-*cum*-Longinus-*cum*-Coleridge-*cum*-Brémond. Anglicans, in their perennial fascination with the mystery of the Incarnation, often seem to be promising what in fact they never get round to delivering—namely, a systematic theory of art that is consistently elaborated on the premises of an Incarnational theology. And—omitting the important exception of the Dutch Reformed theologian, the late Gerardus van der Leeuw[1]—Protestant thinkers have as yet produced virtually nothing at all of commanding importance in the field of general aesthetics. So van der Leeuw's magisterial treatise on *Sacred and Profane Beauty* is perhaps the lone contemporary example of an enterprise of systematic aesthetical thought that is *radically* Christian in perspective. But the four essays that are here included in this area may suggest something of the direction in which it will be most profitable to move—and most especially is this true of the brilliant piece by the Swiss Calvinist, Denis de Rougemont, which, like van der Leeuw's work, has the salutary effect of reminding us that genuinely Christian work in the philosophy of art must be deeply grounded in the rich stuff of Biblical thought and of kerygmatic theology.

What is theologically decisive for the writers whose essays comprise the IInd Part of this book is perhaps most fully hinted at in Allen Tate's essay on Dante where the two dimensions of the Christian *kerygma* that seem to have been brought most immediately into play are the doctrines of Creation and of the Incarnation. And these, apparently, are for Mr. Tate significant aspects of the Chris-

[1] *Vide* Gerardus van der Leeuw, *Sacred and Profane Beauty: The Holy in Art,* trans. by David E. Green; Preface by Mircea Eliade (New York: Holt, Rinehart and Winston, 1963).

tian testimony, because they both put us in mind of the fact that the existent world is itself our only "glass of vision" into ultimate reality. That is to say, the doctrine of Creation, in denying both that the world is identical with God and that it is in some way an emanation of a "World Soul," tells us that all creatures bear to God or to what is Radically Significant a relation that is identical with that which a work of art bears to its maker. The world of God's creatures, in other words, though it stands over against Him, is not an illusion, for it was *made* by Him and can therefore furnish the imagination with valid images of what is ultimately real. And the doctrine of the Incarnation tells us not only that the world is *capax Dei* but that it was indeed an adequate theatre for the drama in which God's Son took the leading part. And one judges that both these aspects of the Christian testimony are focal for Mr. Tate's understanding of the artist's vocation, since both the doctrine of Creation and the doctrine of the Incarnation, in reassuring us of the essential stoutness and reliability of the realm of finite, contingent reality, have the effect of legitimizing the whole transaction whereby the artist's imagination mingles constitutively with the world.

Mr. Tate's essay on Dante, and his companion-piece on Poe[2] which is not reprinted here, suggest, in other words, that he finds today the basic norm for poetics to be a theological norm. For these essays provide clear evidence that he believes with T. E. Hulme that the supposition that a poem must always be "moaning or whining about something or other," that the poet must always be flying off "into the circumambient gas," exhibits a deep illness of the mind, the kind of illness of which Poe is for him a major exemplar. The "angelic imagination" which "tries to disintegrate or to circumvent the image in the illusory pursuit of essence" is, in short, in his view a diseased imagination which is in need of the kind of tonic that is contained in the sobriety and sanity of the

[2] *Vide* Allen Tate, "The Angelic Imagination: Poe as God," *Collected Essays* (Denver: Alan Swallow, 1959). This essay originally appeared in Mr. Tate's *The Forlorn Demon* (Chicago: Henry Regnery Co., 1953).

Christian realist attitude toward creation. And the "angelic imagination" is to be contrasted with the "symbolic imagination" (whose great exemplar is Dante) which knows that the only kind of wisdom attainable by the human creature is that which is won through a series of maneuvers by the analogical mind whereby the finite world is itself apprehended as our one way into what is ultimately real. The "symbolic imagination," like Hulme's "classical" imagination, is always holding back: it never forgets that man is mixed up with earth: it never flies off "over abysses . . . up into the eternal gasses": it refuses to "go blindly into an atmosphere too rarefied for man to breathe for long."[3] No, the symbolic imagination—which is for Mr. Tate the normative type of artistic imagination—is instructed by the essential insights that are enshrined in the doctrines of Creation and of the Incarnation: it refuses therefore to "circumvent the image in the illusory pursuit of essence"—and thus it furnishes a criterion of health for the diagnosis of all those tendencies toward "angelism" which constitute the characteristic illness that besets modern literature. And it is much the same kind of realism that distinguishes the understanding of the nature of the Christian vision that lies behind the essays by Malcolm Ross and Fr. Lynch.

The IIIrd Part of the book takes us into the area where the Christian critic is today surest of himself and where he has done his most significant work. Here the task is that of demonstrating what it is in the nature of literature and in the nature of the critical act that gives the theological critic his enfranchisement, that certifies his peculiar effort and gives cogency to the special perspective that he brings to bear on the issues of practical and theoretical criticism. And in the essays by Professor James, Fr. Ong, and myself a fairly representative statement emerges of the kind of case that is being made. Professor Buckley's essay, however, offers what very much needs to be heard—namely, a cautionary word against

[3] T. E. Hulme, "Romanticism and Classicism," *Speculations,* ed. by Herbert Read (London: Kegan Paul, Trench, Trubner & Co., Ltd., 1936), p. 120.

excessive reliance on all programmatic schemes: the proof of the criticism, in other words, will be not so much in the theoretical rationale by which it justifies itself as in its actual performance in relation to the works of art which it undertakes to open up and interpret. "If it is delicate, experienced, and above all *concerned* with literature, the Christian sensibility will inevitably make moral and theological use of its experience of art; but it will do so interiorly and unobtrusively. . . . And if it is not [delicate, experienced, and . . . *concerned* with literature], no amount of formulation or abstraction can bring it any closer to art. . . ." And, finally, the essays by T. S. Eliot and W. K. Wimsatt with which Part III concludes move beyond the question as to how a theological criticism constitutes itself to the question that concerns the relation between the literary space and the moral space and how the two are at once to be held together and kept separate.

In the essays that comprise Part IV an effort is being made at correlation of belief and some of the fundamental forms or genres with which poetic criticism deals. Finally, in Part V some representative statements are offered of the various types of response and judgment that are noticeable today amongst Christian critics who are attempting to reckon with what is distinctively devious and vagrant and yet promising (as Professor Wilder wants very much to insist) in the account of human existence that is given by the literary imagination in the modern period. And the five Parts, it is hoped, taken all together, form a basic introduction to the problems, the methods, and the aims of Christian poetics, as the discipline is being presently conceived by many scholars and critics representing various and diverse forms of churchmanship, Catholic (Roman and Anglican) and Protestant.

N. A. S., Jr.

University of Chicago
12 August 1963

Part I
THE PROBLEM OF A CHRISTIAN AESTHETIC

Dorothy Sayers

Towards A Christian Aesthetic*

It will be immediately obvious how deeply this paper is indebted to R. G. Collingwood's Principles of Art, *particularly as regards the disentangling of "Art Proper" (expression and imagination) from the "pseudo-Arts" of "amusement" and "magic." The only contribution I have made of my own (exclusive of incidental errors) has been to suggest, however tentatively, a method of establishing the principles of "Art Proper" upon that Trinitarian doctrine of the nature of Creative Mind which does, I think, really underlie them. On this foundation it might perhaps be possible to develop a Christian aesthetic which, finding its source and sanction in the theological centre, would be at once more characteristically Christian and of more universal application than any aesthetic whose contact with Christianity is made only at the ethical circumference.*

I AM TO SPEAK to you to-night about the Arts in this country—their roots in Christianity, their present condition, and the means by which (if we find that they are not flourishing as they should) their mutilated limbs and withering branches may be restored by re-grafting into the main trunk of Christian tradition.

This task is of quite peculiar difficulty, and I may not be able to carry it out in exactly the terms which have been proposed to me. And that for a rather strange reason. In such things as politics, finance, sociology and so on, there really is a philosophy and a

* This essay was delivered by Dorothy Sayers as an Edward Alleyn Lecture in England in 1944.

Christian tradition; we do know more or less what the Church has said and thought about them, how they are related to Christian dogma, and what they are supposed to *do* in a Christian country.

But oddly enough, we have no Christian aesthetic—no Christian philosophy of the Arts. The Church as a body has never made up her mind about the Arts, and it is hardly too much to say that she has never tried. She has, of course, from time to time puritanically denounced the Arts as irreligious and mischievous, or tried to exploit the Arts as a means to the teaching of religion and morals—but I shall hope to show you that both these attitudes are false and degrading, and are founded upon a completely mistaken idea of what Art is supposed to be and do. And there have, of course, been plenty of writers on aesthetics who happened to be Christians, but they have seldom made any consistent attempt to relate their aesthetic to the central Christian dogmas. Indeed, so far as European aesthetic is concerned, one feels that it would probably have developed along precisely the same lines had there never been an Incarnation to reveal the nature of God—that is to say, the nature of all truth. But that is fantastic. If we commit ourselves to saying that the Christian revelation discovers to us the nature of *all* truth, then it must discover to us the nature of the truth about Art among other things. It is absurd to go placidly along explaining Art in terms of a pagan aesthetic, and taking no notice whatever of the complete revolution of our ideas about the nature of things that occurred, or should have occurred, after the first Pentecost. I will go so far as to maintain that the extraordinary confusion of our minds about the nature and function of Art is principally due to the fact that for nearly 2,000 years we have been trying to reconcile a pagan, or at any rate a Unitarian, aesthetic with a Christian—that is, a Trinitarian and Incarnational—theology. Even that makes us out too intelligent. We have not tried to reconcile them. We have merely allowed them to exist side by side in our minds; and where the conflict between them became too noisy to be overlooked, we have tried to silence the clamour by main force, either by brutally subjugating Art to religion, or by shutting them up in separate prison cells and forbidding them to hold any communication with one another.

Now, before we go any further, I want to make it quite clear that what I am talking about now is aesthetic (the philosophy of Art) and not about Art itself as practised by the artists. The great artists carry on with their work on the lines God has laid down for them, quite unaffected by the aesthetic worked out for them by philosophers. Sometimes, of course, artists themselves dabble in aesthetic, and what they have to say is very interesting, but often very misleading. If they really are great and true artists, they make their poem (or whatever it is) first, and then set about reconciling it with the fashionable aesthetic of their time; they do not produce their work to conform to their notions of aesthetic—or, if they do, they are so much the less artists, and the work suffers. Secondly, what artists chatter about to the world and to each other is not as a rule their art but the technique of their art. They will tell you, as critics, how it is they produce certain effects (the poet will talk about assonance, alliteration and metre; the painter about perspective, balance and how he mixes his colours, etc.)—and from that we may get the misleading impression that the technique *is* the art, or that the aim of art is to produce some sort of "effect." But this is not so. We cannot go for a march unless we have learnt, through long practice, how to control the muscles of our legs; but it is not true to say that the muscular control *is* the march. And while it is a fact that certain tricks produce "effects"—like Tennyson's use of vowels and consonants to produce the effect of a sleepy murmuring in "The moan of doves in immemorial elms," or of metallic clashing in "The bare black cliff clanged round him"—it is not true that the poem is merely a set of physical, or even of emotional effects. What a work of art really is and does we shall come to later. For the moment I only want to stress the difference between aesthetic and Art, and to make it clear that a great artist will produce great Art, even though the aesthetic of his time may be hopelessly inadequate to explain it.

For the origins of European aesthetic we shall, of course, turn to Greece; and we are at once brought up against the two famous chapters in which Plato discusses the Arts, and decides that certain kinds of Art, and in particular certain kinds of poetry, ought to be banished from the perfect State. Not all poetry—people often talk as though Plato had said this, but he did not: certain kinds he wished to keep, and this makes his attitude all the more puzzling, because, though he tells us quite clearly why he disapproves of the rejected kinds, he never explains what it is that makes the other kinds valuable. He never gets down to considering, constructively, what true Art is or what it does. He only tells us about what are (in his opinion) the bad results of certain kinds of Art—nor does he ever tackle the question whether the bad moral results of which he complains may not be due to a falseness *in* the Art, i.e. to the work's being pseudo-Art or inartistic Art.

He seems to say that certain forms of Art are inherently evil in themselves. His whole handling of the thing seems to us very strange, confused and contradictory; yet his aesthetic has dominated all our critical thinking for many centuries, and has influenced, in particular, the attitude of the Church more than the Church perhaps knows. So it is necessary that we should look at Plato's argument. Many of his conclusions are true—though often, I think, he reaches them from the wrong premisses. Some of them are, I think, demonstrably false. But especially, his whole grasp of the subject is inadequate. That is not Plato's fault. He was one of the greatest thinkers of all time, but he was a pagan; and I am becoming convinced that no pagan philosopher could produce an adequate aesthetic, simply for lack of a right theology. In this respect, the least in the Kingdom of Heaven is greater than John the Baptist.

What does Plato say?

He begins by talking about stories and myths, and after dismissing as beneath consideration the stories and poems which are obviously badly written, he goes on to reject those which are untrue, or which attribute evil and disgusting behaviour to the gods, or which tend to inculcate bad and vulgar passions or anti-social behaviour in the audience. After this (which sounds very much like what moralists and clergymen are always saying nowadays) he leaves the subject-matter and goes on to certain *forms* of poetry and art—those forms which involve *mimesis*—the mimetic arts. Now *mimesis* can be translated "imitation," or "representation"; and we can at once see that certain forms of Art are more mimetic than others; drama, painting and sculpture are, on the whole, mimetic—some natural object or action is represented or imitated (though we may find exceptions in modernist and surrealist paintings which seem to represent nothing in Heaven or earth). Music, on the other hand, is not mimetic—nothing is imitated from the natural world (unless we count certain effects like the noise of drums in a martial piece, or trills and arpeggios representing the song of birds or the falling of water, down to the squeaks, brayings, twitterings and whistlings of cinema organs). In the Third Book of the *Republic,* Plato says he will allow the mimetic arts, provided that the imitation or representation is of something morally edifying, that sets a good example; but he would banish altogether the representation of unworthy objects, such as national heroes wallowing about in floods of tears, and people getting drunk, or using foul language. He thinks this kind of thing bad for the actors and also for the audience. Nor (which seems odd to us) are actors to imitate anything vulgar or base, such as artisans plying their trades, galley-slaves or bos'ns; nor must there be any trivial nonsense about stage-effects and farmyard imitations. Nothing is to be acted or shown except what is worthy to be imitated, the noble actions of wise men—a gallery of good examples.

We may feel that Plato's theatre would be rather on the austere side. But in the Tenth Book he hardens his heart still further. He decides to banish *all* mimetic art—all representation of every kind; and that for two reasons.

The first reason is that imitation is a kind of cheat. An artist who knows nothing about carpentering may yet paint a carpenter so that, if the picture is set up at a distance, children and stupid people may be deceived into thinking that it is really a carpenter. Moreover, in any case, the realities of things exist only in Heaven in an ideal and archetypal form; the visible world is only a pale reflection or bad imitation of the heavenly realities; and the work of art is only a cheating imitation of the visible world: therefore representational art is merely an imitation of an imitation—a deceptive trick which tickles and entertains while turning men's minds away from the contemplation of the eternal realities.

At this point some of you will begin to fidget and say, "Hi! Stop! Surely there is a difference between mimicry intended to deceive and representation. I admit that there are such things as tin biscuit boxes got up to look like the works of Charles Dickens, which may deceive the unwary, and that very simple-minded people in theatres have been known to hiss the villain or leap on the stage to rescue the heroine—but as a rule we know perfectly well that the imitation is only imitation, and not meant to take anyone in. And surely there's a difference between farmyard imitations and John Gielgud playing Hamlet. And besides—even if you get an exact representation of something—say a documentary film about a war, or an exact verbal reproduction of a scene at the Old Bailey—that's not the same thing as *Coriolanus* or the trial scene in *The Merchant of Venice;* the work of art has something different, something more—poetry or a sort of a something . . ." and here you will begin to wave your hands about vaguely.

You are, of course, perfectly right. But let us for the moment just make a note of how Plato's conception of Art is influenced by his theology—the visible world imitating, copying, reflecting a world of eternal changeless forms already existent elsewhere; and the artist, conceived of as a sort of craftsman or artisan engaged in *copying* or imitating something which exists already in the visible world.

Now let us take his second reason for banishing all representational art. He says that even where the action represented is in itself good and noble, the effect on the audience is bad, because it leads them to dissipate the emotions and energies that ought to be used for tackling the problems of life. The feelings of courage, resolution, pity, indignation and so on are worked up in the spectators by the mimic passions on the stage (or in pictures or music) and then frittered away in a debauch of emotion over these unreal shadows, leaving the mind empty and slack, with no appetite except for fresh sensations of an equally artificial sort.

Now, that is a real indictment against a particular kind of art, which we ought to take seriously. In the jargon of modern psychology, Plato is saying that art of this kind leads to phantasy and day-dreaming. Aristotle, coming about fifty years after Plato, defended this kind of art: he said that undesirable passions, such as pity and terror were in this way *sublimated*—you worked them off in the theatre, where they could do no harm. If, he means, you feel an inner urge to murder your wife, you go and see *Othello* or read a good, gory thriller, and satisfy your blood-lust that way; and if we had the last part of his *Poetics,* which dealt with comedy, we should probably find it suggested, in the same way, that an excess of sexual emotion can be worked off by going to a good, dirty farce, or vulgar music-hall, and blowing the whole thing away in a loud, bawdy laugh.

Now, people still argue as to whether Plato or Aristotle was right about this. But there are one or two things I want you to notice. The first is that what Plato is really concerned to banish from his perfect state is the kind of art which aims at mere entertainment—the art that dissipates energy instead of directing it into some useful channel. And though Aristotle defends "art for entertainment," it is still the same kind of art he is thinking about.

The second thing is that both Plato and Aristotle—but especially Plato—are concerned with the moral effect of art. Plato would allow representational art so long as he thought that it had the effect of canalising the energies and directing them to virtuous action—he only banishes it, on further consideration, because he has come to the conclusion that *no* representational art of any kind —not even the loftiest tragedy—is successful in bracing the moral constitution. He does not tell us very clearly what poetry he will keep, or why, except that it is to be of what we should call a lyrical kind, and presumably, bracing and tonic in sentiment, and directly inculcating the love of the good, the beautiful and the true.

Thirdly: Plato lived at the beginning, and Aristotle in the middle of the era which saw the collapse and corruption of the great Greek civilization. Plato sees the rot setting in, and cries out like a prophet to his people to repent while there is yet time. He sees that the theatre audience is in fact looking to the theatre for nothing but amusement and entertainment, that their energies are, in fact, frittering themselves away in spurious emotion—sob-stuff and sensation, and senseless laughter, phantasy and day-dreaming, and admiration for the merely smart and slick and clever and amusing. And there is an ominous likeness between his age and ours. We too have audiences and critics and newspapers assessing every play and book and novel in terms of its "entertainment value," and a whole generation of young men and women who dream over novels and wallow in day-dreaming at the cinema, and who seemed to be in a fair way of doping themselves into complete irresponsibility over the conduct of life until war came, as it did to Greece, to jerk them back to reality. Greek civilisation was destroyed; ours is not yet destroyed. But it may be well to remember Plato's warning: "If you receive the pleasure-seasoned Muse, pleasure and pain will be kings in your city instead of law and agreed principles."

And there is something else in Plato that seems to strike a familiar note. We seem to know the voice that urges artists to produce works of art "with a high moral tone"—propaganda works, directed to improving young people's minds and rousing them to a sense of their duties, "doing them good," in fact. And at the same time, we find—among artists and critics alike—a tendency to repudiate representational art, in favour of something more austere, primitive and symbolic, as though the trouble lay *there*.

It is as though, in the decline of Greece, and in what is known as the "Decline of the West," both Plato and we agreed in finding something wrong with the arts—a kind of mutual infection, by which the slick, sentimental, hedonistic art corrupts its audience, and the pleasure-loving, emotional audience in turn corrupts the arts by demanding of them nothing but entertainment value. And the same sort of remedy is proposed in both cases—first, to get rid of "representationalism"—which, it is hoped, will take away the pleasure and entertainment and so cure the audience's itch for amusement; secondly, to concentrate on works which provide a direct stimulus to right thinking and right action.

What we have really got here is a sort of division of art into two kinds: *Entertainment-art,* which dissipates the energies of the audience and pours them down the drain; and another kind of art which canalises energy into a sort of mill-stream to turn the wheel of action—and this we may perhaps call *Spell-binding Art.* But do these two functions comprise the whole of Art? Or are they Art at all? Are they perhaps only accidental effects of Art, or false Art—something masquerading under the name of Art—or menial tasks to which we enslave Art? Is the real nature and end of Art something quite different from either? Is the real trouble something wrong with our aesthetic, so that we do not know what we ought to look for in Art, or how to recognize it when we see it, or how to distinguish the real thing from the spurious imitation?

Suppose we turn from Plato to the actual poets he was writing about—to Aeschylus, for instance, the great writer of tragedies. Drama, certainly, is representational art, and therefore, according to Plato, pleasure-art, entertainment-art, emotional and relaxing art, sensational art. Let us read the *Agamemnon.* Certainly it is the representation by actors of something—and of something pretty sensational: the murder of a husband by an adulterous wife. But it is scarcely sensational entertainment in the sense that a thriller novel on the same subject is sensational entertainment. A day-dreaming, pleasure-loving audience would hardly call it entertainment at all. It is certainly not relaxing. And I doubt whether it either dissipates our passions in Plato's sense or sublimates them in Aristotle's sense, any more than it canalises them for any particular action, though it may trouble and stir us and plunge us into the mystery of things. We might extract some moral lessons from it: but if we ask ourselves whether the poet wrote that play in order to improve our minds, something inside us will, I think, say "No."

Aeschylus was trying to tell us something, but nothing quite so simple as that. He is saying something—something important—something enormous—. And here we shall be suddenly struck with the inadequacy of the strictures against "representational art." "This," we shall say, "is not the copy or imitation of something bigger and more real than itself. It is bigger and more real than the real-life action that it represents. That a false wife should murder a husband—that might be a paragraph in the *News of the World* or a thriller to read in the train—but when it is shown us like this, by a great poet, it is as though we went behind the triviality of the actual event to the cosmic significance behind it. And, what is more, this is *not* a representation of the actual event at all—if a B.B.C. reporter had been present at the murder with a television set and microphone, what we heard and saw would have been nothing like this. This play is not anything that ever happened in this world—it is something happening in the mind of Aeschylus, and it had never happened before."

Now here, I believe, we are getting to something—something that Plato's heathen philosophy was not adequate to explain, but which we can begin to explain by the light of Christian theology. Very likely the heathen poet could not have explained it either—if he had made the attempt, he too would have been entangled in the terms of his philosophy. But we are concerned, not with what he might have said, but with what he did. Being a true poet, he was true in his work—that is, his art was that point of truth in him which was true to the eternal truth, and only to be interpreted in terms of eternal truth.

The true work of art, then, is something *new*—it is not primarily the copy or representation of anything. It may involve representation, but that is not what makes it a work of art. It is not manufactured to specification, as an engineer works to a plan—though it may involve compliance with the accepted rules for dramatic presentation, and may also contain verbal "effects" which can be mechanically accounted for. We know very well, when we compare it with so-called works of art which *are* "turned out to pattern" that in this connection neither circumcision availeth anything nor uncircumcision, but a new creature. Something has been created.

This word—this idea of Art as *creation* is, I believe, the one important contribution that Christianity has made to aesthetics. Unfortunately, we are apt to use the words "creation" and "creativeness" very vaguely and loosely, because we do not relate them properly to our theology. But it is significant that the Greeks had not this word in their aesthetic at all. They looked on a work of art as a kind of *technē,* a manufacture. Neither, for that matter, was the word in their theology—they did not look on history as the continual act of God fulfilling itself in creation.

How do we say that God creates, and how does this compare with the act of creation by an artist? To begin with, of course, we say that God created the universe "out of nothing"—He was bound by no conditions. He can create only within that framework and out of that material which the universe supplies. Admitting that, let us ask in what way God creates. Christian theology replies that God, who is a Trinity, creates by, or through, His second Person, His Word or Son, who is continually begotten from the First Person, the Father, in an eternal creative activity. And certain theologians have added this very significant comment: the Father, they say, is only known to Himself by beholding His image in His Son.

Does that sound very mysterious? We will come back to the human artist, and see what it means in terms of *his* activity. But first, let us take note of a new word that has crept into the argument by way of Christian theology—the word *Image.* Suppose, having rejected the words "copy," "imitation" and "representation" as inadequate, we substitute the word "image" and say that what the artist is doing is *to image forth* something or the other, and connect that with St. Paul's phrase: "God . . . hath spoken to us by His Son, the brightness of this glory and *express image* of His person."—Something which, by being an image, *expresses* that which it images. Is that getting us a little nearer to something? There is something which is, in the deepest sense of the words, *unimagin-*

able, known to Itself (and still more, to us) only by the image in which it expresses Itself through creation; and, says Christian theology very emphatically, the Son, who is the express image, is not the copy, or imitation, or representation of the Father, nor yet inferior or subsequent to the Father in any way—in the last resort, in the depths of their mysterious being, the Unimaginable and the Image are *one and the same.*

Now for our poet. We said, when we were talking of the *Agamemnon,* that this work of art seemed to be "something happening in the mind of Aeschylus." We may now say, perhaps, more precisely, that the play is the *expression* of this interior happening. But *what,* exactly, was happening?

There is a school of criticism that is always trying to explain, or explain away, a man's works of art by trying to dig out the events of his life and his emotions *outside* the works themselves, and saying "these are the real Aeschylus, the real Shakespeare, of which the poems are only faint imitations." But any poet will tell you that this is the wrong way to go to work. It is the old, pagan aesthetic which explains nothing—or which explains all sorts of things about the work *except* what makes it a work of art. The poet will say: "My poem is the expression of my experience." But if you then say, "What experience?" he will say, "I can't tell you anything about it, except what I have said in the poem—the poem *is* the experience." The Son and the Father are *one:* the poet himself did not know what his experience was until he created the poem which revealed his own experience to himself.

To save confusion, let us distinguish between an *event* and an *experience.* An event is something that happens to one—but one does not necessarily experience it. To take an extreme instance: suppose you are hit on the head and get concussion and, as often happens, when you come to, you cannot remember the blow. The blow on the head certainly happened to you, but you did not *experience* it—all you experience is the after-effects. You only experience a thing when you can express it—however haltingly—to your own mind. You may remember the young man in T. S. Eliot's play, *The Family Reunion,* who says to his relations:

> You are all people
> To whom nothing has happened, at most a continual impact
> Of external events . . .

He means that they have got through life without ever really *experiencing* anything, because they have never tried to express to themselves the real nature of what has happened to them.

A poet is a man who not only suffers "the impact of external events," but experiences them. He puts the experience into words in his own mind, and in so doing recognizes the experience for what it is. To the extent that we can do that, we are all poets. A "poet" so-called is simply a man like ourselves with an exceptional power of revealing his experience by expressing it, so that not only he, but we ourselves, recognise that experience as our own.

I want to stress the word *recognise.* A poet does not see something—say the full moon—and say: "This is a very beautiful sight—let me set about finding words for the appropriate expression of what people ought to feel about it." That is what the literary artisan does, and it means nothing. What happens is that then, or at some time after, he finds himself saying words in his head and says to himself: "Yes—that is right. *That* is the experience the full moon was to me. I recognize it in expressing it, and now I know what it was." And so, when it is a case of mental or spiritual experience—sin, grief, joy, sorrow, worship—the thing reveals itself to him in words, and so becomes fully experienced for the first time. By thus recognizing it in its expression, he makes it his own—integrates it into himself. He no longer feels himself battered passively by the impact of external events—it is no longer something happening *to* him, but something happening *in* him, the reality of the event is communicated to him in activity and power. So that the act of the poet in creation is seen to be threefold—a trinity—experience, expression and recognition; the unknowable reality in the experience; the image of that reality known in its expression; and power in the recognition; the whole making up the single and indivisible act of creative mind.

Now, what the poet does for himself, he can also do for us. When he has imaged forth his experience he can incarnate it, so to speak, in a material body—words, music, painting—the thing we know as a work of art. And since he is a man like the rest of us, we shall expect that our experience will have something in common with his. In the image of *his* experience, we can *recognize* the image of some experience of our own—something that had happened to us, but which we had never understood, never formulated or expressed to ourselves, and therefore never known as a real experience. When we read the poem, or see the play or picture or hear the music, it is as though a light were turned on inside us. We say: "Ah! I recognize that! That is something which I obscurely felt to be going on in and about me, but I didn't know what it was and couldn't express it. But now that the artist has made its image —imaged it forth—for me, I can possess and take hold of it and make it my own, and turn it into a source of knowledge and strength." This is the *communication of the image in power,* by which the third person of the poet's trinity brings us, through the incarnate image, into direct knowledge of the in itself unknowable and unimaginable reality. "No man cometh to the Father save by Me," said the incarnate Image; and He added, "but the Spirit of Power will lead you into all truth."

This recognition of the truth that we get in the artist's work comes to us as a revelation of new truth. I want to be clear about that. I am not referring to the sort of patronising recognition we give to a writer by nodding our heads and observing: "Yes, yes, very good, very true—that's just what I'm always saying." I mean the recognition of a truth which tells us something about ourselves that we had *not* been "always saying"—something which puts a new knowledge of ourselves within our grasp. It is new, startling, and perhaps shattering—and yet it comes to us with a sense of familiarity. We did not know it before, but the moment the poet has shown it to us, we know that, somehow or other, we had always really known it.

Very well. But, frankly, is that the sort of thing the average British citizen gets, or expects to get, when he goes to the theatre or reads a book? No, it is not. In the majority of cases, it is not in the least what he expects, or what he wants. What he looks for is not this creative and Christian kind of Art at all. He does not expect or desire to be upset by sudden revelations about himself and the universe. Like the people of Plato's decadent Athens, he has forgotten or repudiated the religious origins of all Art. He wants entertainment, or, if he is a little more serious-minded, he wants something with a moral, or to have some spell or incantation put on him to instigate him to virtuous action.

Now, entertainment and moral spell-binding have their uses, but they are not Art in the proper sense. They may be the incidental effects of good Art; but they may also be the very aim and essence of false Art. And if we continue to demand of the Arts only these two things, we shall starve and silence the true artist and encourage in his place the false artist, who may become a very sinister force indeed.

Let us take the amusement-art: what does that give us? Generally speaking, what we demand and get from it is the enjoyment of the emotions which usually accompany experience without having had the experience. It does not reveal us to ourselves: it merely projects on to a mental screen a picture of ourselves as we already fancy ourselves to be—only bigger and brighter. The manufacturer of this kind of entertainment is not by any means interpreting and revealing his own experience to himself and us—he is either indulging his own day-dreams, or—still more falsely and venially—he is saying "What is it the audience think they would like to have experienced? Let us show them that, so that they can wallow in emotion by pretending to have experienced it." This kind of pseudo-art is "wish-fulfilment" or "escape" literature in the worst sense—it is an escape, not from the "impact of external events" into the citadel of experienced reality, but an escape from reality and experience into a world of merely external events—the progressive externalisation of consciousness. For occasional relaxation this is all right; but it can be carried to the point where, not merely art, but the whole universe of phenomena becomes a screen on which we see the magnified projection of our unreal selves, as the object of equally unreal emotions. This brings about the complete corruption of the consciousness, which can no longer recognise reality in experience. When things come to this pass, we have a civilisation which "lives for amusement"—a civilisation without guts, without experience, and out of touch with reality.

Or take the spell-binding kind of art. This at first sight seems better because it spurs us to action; and it also has its uses. But it too is dangerous in excess, because once again it does not reveal reality in experience, but only projects a lying picture of the self. As the amusement-art seeks to produce the *emotions* without the experience, so *this* pseudo-art seeks to produce the *behaviour* without the experience. In the end it is directed to putting the behaviour of the audience beneath the will of the spell-binder, and its true name is not "art," but "art-magic." In its vulgarest form it becomes pure propaganda. It can (as we have reason to know) actually succeed in making its audience into the thing it desires to have them—it can really in the end corrupt the consciousness and destroy experience until the inner selves of its victims are wholly externalised and made the puppets and instruments of their own spurious passions. This is why it is dangerous for anybody—even for the Church—to urge artists to produce works of art for the express purpose of "doing good to people." Let her by all means encourage artists to express their own Christian experience and communicate it to others. That is the true artist saying: "Look! recognize your experience in my own." But "edifying art" may only too often be the pseudo-artist corruptly saying: "This is what you are supposed to believe and feel and do—and I propose to work you into a state of mind in which you will believe and feel and do as you are told." This pseudo-art does not really communicate power to us; it merely exerts power over us.

What is it, then, that these two pseudo-arts—the entertaining and spell-binding—have in common? And how are they related to true Art? What they have in common is the falsification of the consciousness; and they are to Art as the *idol* is to the Image. The Jews were forbidden to make any image for worship, because before the revelation of the threefold unity in which Image and Unimaginable are one, it was only too fatally easy to substitute the idol for the Image. The Christian revelation set free all the images, by showing that the true Image subsisted within the Godhead Itself—it was neither copy, nor imitation, nor representation, nor inferior, nor subsequent, but the brightness of the glory, and the express image of the Person—the very mirror in which reality knows itself and communicates itself in power.

But the danger still exists; and it always will recur whenever the Christian doctrine of the Image is forgotten. In our aesthetic, that doctrine has never been fully used or understood, and in consequence our whole attitude to the artistic expression of reality has become confused, idolatrous and pagan. We see the Arts degenerating into mere entertainment which corrupts and relaxes our civilisation, and we try in alarm to correct this by demanding a more moralising and bracing kind of Art. But this is only setting up one idol in place of the other. Or we see that Art is becoming idolatrous, and suppose that we can put matters right by getting rid of the representational element in it. But what is wrong is not the representation itself, but the fact that what we are looking at, and what we are looking *for,* is not the Image but an idol. Little children, keep yourselves from idols.

It has become a commonplace to say that the Arts are in a bad way. We are in fact largely given over to the entertainers and the spell-binders; and because we do not understand that these two functions do not represent the true nature of Art, the true artists are, as it were, excommunicate, and have no audience. But there is here not, I think, so much a relapse from a Christian aesthetic as a failure ever to find and examine a real Christian aesthetic, based on dogma and not on ethics. This may not be a bad thing. We have at least a new line of country to explore, that has not been trampled on and built over and fought over by countless generations of quarrelsome critics. What we have to start from is the Trinitarian doctrine of creative mind, and the light which that doctrine throws on the true nature of images.

The great thing, I am sure, is not to be nervous about God—not to try and shut out the Lord Immanuel from *any* sphere of truth. Art is not He—we must not substitute Art for God; yet this also is *He,* for it is one of His Images and therefore reveals His nature. Here we see in a mirror darkly—we behold only the images; elsewhere we shall see face to face, in the place where Image and Reality are one.

David Jones

Art and Sacrament

AN ENQUIRY CONCERNING THE ARTS OF MAN AND THE CHRISTIAN COMMITMENT TO SACRAMENT IN RELATION TO CONTEMPORARY TECHNOCRACY

THE CONTRIBUTORS to this collection of essays* have been asked to write down something touching the problems or dilemmas experienced in their daily tasks or avocations. Further, they have been asked to do this as persons of a certain persuasion. The problems they discuss are of necessity common to all men living in our present society, but they discuss these same common problems as persons who subscribe to the dogma of the Roman Church. That dogma is said to concern only propositions of faith and propositions of morals.

Hence, when asked to attempt some contribution round and about the subject of what are today called "the arts," a serious doubt arose in my mind. For recalling the ancient distinction between Ars and Prudentia it seemed that propositions of faith and morals must fall entirely under the head of Prudentia. So, in one way, I felt there was nothing to say; except in the sense that a feather-weight who happened also to be a Welsh Calvinistic-Methodist might, in writing of his life and work, refer to chapels

* Mr. Jones' reference is to the volume *Catholic Approaches* (London: Weidenfeld and Nicolson, 1955) in which this essay first appeared. David Jones, *Epoch and Artist.* New York: Chilmark Press, Inc., 1964. Copyright by David Jones, 1959.

and deacons as well as to boxing-rings and trainers. What he wrote might indeed be full of interest, but it could not be a dissertation on the Calvinistic-Methodist art of boxing, for there is no such thing. Thus we speak of the "art of strategy" but we do not speak of a "Catholic strategy" any more than we speak of a Catholic science of hydraulics, a Catholic vascular system, or a Catholic equilateral triangle. We do not speak so because we see that that would be no less absurd than if we spoke of the iniquity of five degrees of frost or of the pious intentions of corrugated zinc.

There are then no such things as the Catholic arts of painting and engraving or the Catholic art of writing proses or poems; but these happen to be mainly the arts of which I have any contactual experience, or at which I try my hand from time to time. Apart from my having no inclination to do so, no purpose would be served were I to attempt to write of my experiences as a Catholic who happens to be a sort of artist, or as an artist who happens to be a Catholic of sorts, *à la* the imaginary Methodist boxer above cited. So if I am to contribute anything at all it seems that I must launch out on those fog-bound and tricky waters, into that sea of discussion concerning the nature of art *qua* art. I fear it will turn out to be a very unrewarding trip indeed; the ocean is very extensive. Moreover to venture upon it at all in a brief essay is rather like setting out in a rowing-boat to explore the Seven Seas over the week-end. So don't hope for much more than a wetting and a realization of the magnitude of the proverbial troubles at sea.

In those waters (though there is no such thing as "Catholic art" in the sense above indicated), certain charts of Catholic and pre-Catholic provenance will be found relevant to our task of trying to make a landfall or two. This is because the postulates of our religion presuppose that man is such and such a creature and the kind of creature presupposed will be found to involve the nature of art. Which in turn brings us up against the apparent nature of the technocracy in which we live and of which we are a part. I say "apparent nature" advisedly and for the following reasons. In periods of civilizational change it must always have been difficult, for persons whose perceptions of the permanent values had been formed by reference to analogies familiar to themselves and to their fathers, to perceive those same values operating in the new forms and attitudes of thought which the civilizational change had brought about. We must also remember that no metamorphosis since prehistoric times is in any way comparable to the metamorphosis that we are now undergoing.

But even with all this fully in mind and very much to the fore of our minds, we still may not sufficiently discount our own biases and these may lead us to misinterpret and misapprehend the situation. Even so, we must record our dilemmas. Should they date badly and turn out to be period aberrations, thus affording amusement to the next generation, so much the better. The cracks we thought we detected in the fabric were more apparent than real, so all is well.

However that may be, it is with much diffidence and a fear that the approach may be unrewarding that I ask such stale-sounding questions as: "What is the nature of the thing called art?" What sort of thing is it? What can we posit of it? What is its function? How does it function? How is it positioned with regard to the thing called "human nature?" That is to say, how does this activity stand *vis-à-vis* the creature said by Christians to be a rational animal with a supernatural end? What sort of distinction is intended when philosophers speak of Ars and Prudentia? How comes it that this distinction is made? We nominate variously things or qualities or activities only in order to clarify in our minds some otherness which we sense or know or have reason to suppose exists. Sometimes we nominate things differently because they appear to us to be different in kind, sometimes we do so to mark a difference of degree. In the case of Ars and Prudentia the distinction is clearly not one of degree but of kind. So here are two kinds. But kinds of what? Clearly a future distinction faces us, for "art" describes a *quality* of a certain kind. It is not comfortable to compare an activity with a quality. Moreover though "prudence" is a virtue of quality the word "quality" is insufficient to convey what we mean when we speak of Prudentia.

It is worth nothing that *prudentia* is a contraction of *providentia* and that in English "providence" is still related to the Divine Providence. So we use Prudentia for convenience to denote, as it were, the tutelary genius who presides over the whole realm of faith, morals, religion, ethic; she is thought of as Holy Wisdom. Hence the rhetorical expressions found in Maritain describing her as "Queen of the Moral Virtues" and "noble and born to command," etc.

It is a commonplace that those sanctified persons whom the Church bids us honour as specially blessed are those who have responded most sensitively not only to the express demands but to the subtlest inclinations of this mistress. It is perhaps less often observed, though it requires observing, that those who reject the postulates of supernatural religion are no less bound than are the men of religion by the allurements of *a* Prudentia; indeed this binding is most marked.

We all know that the enticements of Prudentia are apt to become remote or to pall. Her bright trinkets (which are never merely decorative, but always palladic and of the nature of insignia) by which we may have been particularly held, may now seem to us no more than amulets of superstition. We may then experience something of the meaning of the words they chant each Good Friday evening: *Quomodo obscuratum est aurum, mutatus est color optimus.*[1]

But if we abandon this Prudentia it is only to be committed to another. Her charms are substantial and unelusive. Her get-up is woven of the immediate and the contingent. She assures us that she is unconcerned with morals, yet there is about her a familiar tang, and no wonder, for she uses Black Market products, concocted of crude ethic and raw morals, certain important ingredients, suspending agents and solvents being omitted from the stolen prescriptions.

[1] "How is the gold become dim and the finest colour changed." *Lamentations* iv, I. Tenebrae for Holy Saturday, 1st Nocturn, Lesson 2.

She induces us to do this rather than that. She is full of do's and don'ts. She is on intimate terms with a number of party-leaders, and before we know where we are she induces us to become party-members; and the party is of necessity a prudential society concerned with oughts and ought nots. So that, no less than the saints or the men of dogmatic religion or the men of ethic or the men of primitive cults or the enlightened world-improvers of yesterday or their disillusioned inheritors of today, we *all* are committed to a Prudentia of sorts.

If this is so, if there can be no possibility of us escaping from what is denoted under the term Prudentia (the pseudo-Prudentias and bogus Prudentias, which the majority of us in fact follow, being here included) then there seems little or no purpose in posing the kind of questions which so often are posed touching Prudentia and Ars as though these were two comparable qualities in opposition to each other or two jurisdictions or figures in a hierarchy having claims against each other. I do not believe that such conceptions make sense and this essay is partly written to indicate some of the grounds of that objection. I have already, I hope, indicated some of the difficulties. My approach can be in no sense systematic, but taken as a whole these meanderings may indicate something of the nature of the problem as I conceive it to be. It may not matter so much what maze we tread or how we fumble with or drop the thread so long as our thread is Ariadne's that she got from the artifex-son[2] of the bride of Jove.

The zoological description of man as a creature of the highest order of the class *mammalia* of the genus *homo* of the species *sapiens* is of interest to us, for simply as a definition it takes us some distance (if only by a mere accident of labelling)[3] toward

[2] The thread that Ariadne gave to Theseus to guide him through the labyrinth was given to her by Hephaestus who, it will be remembered, was a tutelar figure for all the arts, and, being the son of Zeus and Hera, was a kind of Logos.

[3] It *is* an accident of labelling, in that for the zoologist a distinction is made between *homo sapiens* and *homo Neanderthalis;* whereas, seeing the latter was *homo faber* he must, theologically speaking, have been "sapiential,"

the definition proposed by theology. For theology supposes man to be, first and foremost, a sapiential mammal. Further that this *sapientia*, by which man proceeds, implies, by a further chain of reasoning, that this mammal has an end other than that of the other mammals, or, as they say, this creature, because he is endowed with rationality (i.e., has a "rational soul") must have a supernatural end. In catechismal terminology this is expressed by asserting that the natural end of man (i.e. the end conformable to man's nature) is eternal felicity.

Though we may reject as too assumptional this theological proposition, we may still find it has a bearing on whatever may happen to be our own view of the matter; seeing that none of us can escape having some view. Just as those who believe that "The proper study of mankind is man" may (as someone else observed) come to the opinion that the study most proper to man is God, so those who believe there is such a creature as man may find it hard to continue in that belief without coming to the opinion that the proper end of that creature is God.

If there is such a thing as a creature distinct among the primates on account of having a *sapientia* which the other primates have not, then such a creature is a prudential creature, a creature responsible to Prudentia. The existence of such a creature is by no means unquestioned by many and by some it is denied, but here we are supposing the existence of this creature. It is here understood to be a creature whose informing principle or soul is rational; a creature who is unlike any other corporeal creature in having a measure of freedom of will and hence committed, of its nature, to what is labelled "faith and morals." If this seems too ecclesiastical a label we should not let that put us off, for it suffices to say that the contents of the parcel thus labelled are (however described) indispensable once we have to deal with a creature that is in any sense a "free agent." And Man is either in some sense and to some degree a free agent or he does not exist. That is to say there is no

---

especially when it is remembered that his fabrications were connected with rites for the dead.

creature answering to the description, Man, used in the following sense: A creature able, owing to its nature, to will or do anything not totally subject to a pure determinism (as, e.g., the reflexes of its own instincts). A creature which is not only capable of gratuitous acts but of which it can be said that such acts are this creature's hall-mark and sign-manual.

These last words, even as I write them, pull me up with a jerk. For without intention or plan of argument and while in the very process of somewhat tortuously considering why man (if he exists) is a creature of faith and morals and is thus the darling of Prudentia, we find ourselves unexpectedly confronted, as by an old friend at a street's bend, with man's natural activity, the activity we call "art."

A few pages back I suggested that this enquiry would resemble a voyage in uncertain waters and that we should be lucky in making a landfall or two. Perhaps the foreland that suddenly has loomed might be called "Gratuity Ness." For in observing that the chief mark of man lies in his being capable of the gratuitous we are immediately confronted with the nature of Ars. We can now call to mind what other navigators in these difficult waters have recorded in their logs. We remember a saying, usually regarded as a somewhat wild, dated and naughty saying to the effect that art is for the sake of art. And, along with this dictum, we recall another, coming from a very different sort of milieu, to the effect that "Art is the sole intransitive activity of man." On examination it is clear that these two sayings are two expressions of the same assertion, but that the latter of the two is by far the better in that it is not open to misinterpretation. It states the case in terms that do not invite attack.

It is the intransitivity and gratuitousness in man's art that is the sign of man's uniqueness; not merely that he makes things, nor yet that those things have beauty. For it must be noted and stressed that works of meticulous perfection and beauty of many kinds are commonly produced by beasts of many kinds—"so work the honey bees" and other exemplary artificers; the agger-making beaver, the ant, the nuthatch whose nest, I'm told, is something of a strong-point. There is no end to the ingenuity of certain beast-made works. These various beastly activities and contrivances of animal nature may surpass in functional inerrancy, and perhaps in some other respects, the achievements of man. For though the spider's web and the honeycomb are contrived by animate creatures their beauty can be said to be of the same order as that achieved by inanimate nature: the hoar-frost on the pane or the leaf vein. In none of the animalic making is there any evidence of the gratuitous, nor is there any evidence of "sign." This making is wholly functional, these activities are transitive.

It would seem from this that these creatures are outside faith and morals. They are irresponsible agents only, sentient creatures, willy-nilly doing the will of Providence just as does insentient creation. As stated above they make things, but for the reasons also above stated their making cannot be included under Ars. Any Incorporeal beings or "pure intelligences" (as the theologians call angels) have of necessity the same end as man; and they too are being created with power of choice. But owing to their incorporeality such beings cannot make things and so are excluded from Ars.

The animals, lacking choice, are excluded from Prudentia and, though they share man's corporeality, they are excluded from Ars, again for lack of this power of choice which man alone shares with the incorporeal intelligences.

So there is a common cause preventing the animals from being either prudential beings or artists. This common cause reversed secures for man his unique title, *poeta,* and his inescapable commitment to Prudentia.

So that it is a degree of freedom of some sort that causes man to be, of necessity, an artist and the same freedom of sorts commits him of necessity to Prudentia.

We can state it another way round: Man could not belong to Prudentia except as an artist and he could not be an artist but for that tie-up with Prudentia.

So that it is here supposed that man is a creature whose end is extra-mundane and whose nature is to make things and that the things made are not only things of mundane requirement but are of necessity the signs of something other. Further, that an element of the gratuitous adheres to this making.

It is said in *The Shorter Oxford English Dictionary* that the word "art" from *artem* has, probably, at root, the meaning of something fitted together, because here the Latin element *ar-* means "to fit." The dictionary goes on to say that art means (1) skill (2) human, as opposed to "natural," skill. This seems in agreement with what has been said above that art describes an activity. That activity is one of fitting together. Art concerns a means or process, a means by which is achieved a "perfect fit."

One could say that the "end" of Ars *is* that "perfect fit." Or we might, for convenience' sake, say that Ars has no end save the perfecting of a process by which all sorts of ends are made possible. It *is* that process. It is concerned with perfecting a means. In so far as art has an end that end is a "fitting together" and the word art means a fitting together.

That is why I assert that the much misinterpreted tag that art is for art's sake is, in that sense, true. It is of course totally untrue if used in any other sense. If, for example, we meant by it that the excellence of the art, or fitting together, exemplified in any given instance, mitigated some evil consequence, we should be displaying just that sort of confusion with regard to Ars and Prudentia which we have been considering in the foregoing paragraphs.

When we say of so-and-so that "he perfected that work" we mean always that someone has, in some sense or other, fitted certain things together. It is the fitting together that we praise, the process of perfecting.

We may find the resultant form unsympathetic, we may deplore or detest both the intention and the result, but that does not prevent us from recognizing that a manipulation and juxtaposing of "shapes" (of some sort) has "created" a "form" (of some sort). The *materia* used, i.e. the "shapes," employed may be simple, or complex in the extreme. They may be of material substances or they may be of immaterial concepts given tangible visual or audible expression, and the resultant "form" which these "shapes" in juxtaposition created will vary accordingly. Thus a piece of turned iron, pierced at intervals and formed at one end to handle, by which we regulate the opening of a casement-window is neither less or more contrived by Ars than are those juxtaposings of concepts that take material expression under the shapes of arranged lines of words, spaces, commas, points, by which poets regulate the openings of casements for us to enjoy and suffer the sights they would show us.

In all cases whoever it was who "perfected that work," whether the work in question was a door-handle or the Venus of Melos, did so by "a fitting together" of some sort, by the exercise of an intransitive activity. That is to say the activity whereby those two material things, the image and the door-furnishing, were achieved is of its nature an intransitive activity. But there is also a passing over to an object, so a transitivity. "Female-imageness" has been achieved and "door-handle-ness." Two made things have been added to the world; the one showing forth certain female attributes and the other providing a convenient means of opening or shutting a door. So the various "ends" of those two makings are very dissimilar. But none of these ends could be achieved without the coming into play of the intransitive activity of art. That intransitivity is the same in both instances. But that intransitive activity has, in both instances, passed over to an object, has affected something else and has thus been employed in a transitive sense.

Bowling at a wicket in a cricket-match is an art, so we must posit intransitivity of bowling because intransitivity adheres to art. But there is a passing over to an object, a transitivity. The immediate object is the discomfort of a batsman and there are remoter objects: the winning of a match, prestige and such-like vanities. There is also something far more profound, a showing-forth of some kind. On the analogy of "door-handle-ness" and "female-image-ness," here, presumably, "cricket-ness," the haecceity of cricket rather than of some other ball-game, is shown forth, recalled and perpetuated by, in and through, the art of bowling. Yet, in spite of these several transitivities, "passings over to" and the achievement of various ends, the art in bowling remains intransitive. So that though bowling is not cricket, cricket could not *be* without bowling and bowling involves the intransitivity native to Ars.

Persons at cricket-matches are sometimes heard to exclaim "Beautiful!" of a ball. Beauty is rightly regarded as a quality that may or may not adhere to the bowler's achievement; but did not the intransitivity of an art abide in bowling, such ejaculations would lack all meaning. As it is, all is well, the cricket-fan's exclamation corresponds to a reality. It is an excellent example of the dictum, *Id quod visum placet*. The beauty seen by those who can tolerate this game is an objective beauty which the activity of art has made to shine out under the form of bowling. So that while the showing forth of the haecceity of cricket may have occasioned the plaudit, what is applauded is the beauty seen to be resident in an art. Not that "art" and "beauty" are the same thing (a confusion liable to occur), but that in this instance the beauty derives direct from man's art. It is then, in the last analysis, the intransitive activity of art that is the cause of such ejaculations as "A beautiful ball, sir!" or "Very pretty." Shy-making and embarrassing exclamations, but nevertheless valid as corresponding with a reality which, having been seen, has pleased.

No doubt my analogies may sometimes break down, but my concern is to indicate as best I can the problems that confront us when we address ourselves to a consideration of the nature of Ars by attempting a comparison of various disparate arts. The more disparate the better for our purpose. For it would be inconclusive and even misleading to consider only arts such as painting and music. For the common factor in these is not so hard to trace. But when we consider the whole field of making, of all that is *per artem,* it is much harder. For within that field are things as dissimilar as: the Diesel engine, boot-making, English prose, radar, horticulture, carpentry and the celebration of the Sacred Mysteries. Our present life involves us in all these things or activities and as each of these things or activities involves an art or arts we must either seek for a common factor or suppose that no such factor exists. But as a "desire and pursuit of the whole" is native to us all, the latter alternative is difficult of acceptance. It is too Jekyll and Hydish to afford us satisfaction.

With regard to the gratuitous quality which is said to adhere to Ars it is well to remember that theologians say that the creation of the world was not a necessary, but a gratuitous, act. There is a sense in which this gratuitousness in the operations of the Creator is reflected in the art of the creature. It has become a modern English usage to speak of such and such as being "for fun"; and when a painter, referring to a work, uses some such expressions as, "That's real fun" we all know that he is not referring to anything funny. On the contrary he is referring to a felicitous quality in the painting. It is a serious matter. We can better appreciate the nature of this kind of "fun" or "play" when it is Holy Wisdom herself who says *ludo*. In the famous passage in the Book of Proverbs she is made to say *ludens in orbe terrarum*. She was with the Logos when all things were formed, "playing before him at all times" and as the Knox translation puts it: "I must play in this world of dust, with the sons of Adam for my play-fellows."

When it is remembered that the name, Holy Wisdom, is sometimes used as another name for Prudentia we may sense a further tie-up between the activity of Ars and this tutelary figure, the Directrix of the Virtues.

When Mrs. A. declares of Mr. Z's day's work as a painter, "I don't call that work, I call it play," she is not only being more complimentary than she intends, but unwittingly bearing witness to that "play" which Sapientia herself asks of all the works of man.

Having touched on some reasons for supposing man to be a prudential animal whose nature is to practise an intransitive activity to which adheres a gratuitous quality, we must now touch upon some reasons why man must be considered a sign-maker and why his art is sign-making.

It is round and about this matter that my thoughts mainly hover. For it is here that any maker of works is faced with immediate and contractual problems regarding our present civilizational phase. So that it is only after this long preamble that I arrive at the point where I can try to fulfil what might be described as the conditions governing the contributions to this book of essays, viz. that some aspect of their personal, professional, vocational, or day-by-day "problems" should be touched upon.

I would apologize for this preamble were it not that I have found that in conversation or correspondence over this business of "art" one has to try to state some things about the nature of man, however ill-equipped and reluctant one is to do so, before one can begin to discuss the problems attaching to man as sign-maker, the nature of his *signa* and the surprising and far-reaching implications of the ideas denoted under the term "sacrament."

The terms "sacrament" and "sacramental" are apt to give off over-tones and under-tones that for a number of disparate reasons have a kind of narrowing effect. Thus, for Christians and especially for the Catholic Christian, those terms carry a specialized meaning and a special aura surrounds them. On the other hand, for secularized man in general, and especially for post-Christians or anti-Christians, such terms are suspect or uncongenial. So that in various opposing ways the wide significance and primary meaning is obscured. Hence I think a purpose is served in deliberately reminding ourselves (whatever our predilections or prejudices) that man is unavoidably a sacramentalist and that his works are sacramental in character. Even if we reject the postulates touched upon with respect to man's nature and regard him as differing only from other sentient creatures, notably the higher primates, in being of more advanced or more specialized development, we still cannot very well deny that this creature has, for about fifty millenniums (perhaps for immeasurably longer) made works, handled material, in a fashion that can only be described as having the nature of a sign.

We have ample archaeological evidence to show us that palaeolithic man, whatever else he was, and whatever his ancestors were, was a sacramental animal. We know, for instance, that this creature juxtaposed marks on surfaces not with merely utile, but with significant, intent; that is to say a "re-presenting," a "showing again under other forms," an "effective recalling" of something was intended. The name Lascaux alone is sufficient to indicate what I mean. But, on second thoughts, Lascaux may indicate something that I don't mean. For it is not the astonishing delineative skill, the realistic renderings or the acute observation—after all parrots record and repeat sounds and apes imitate gestures and for all I know might be taught to draw like academicians—nor yet is it the superb formal beauty of these works that I wish to bring to my own attention or to that of the reader. Rather it is something that has no *necessary* connection with these perfected skills; such perfections are *not* the determining mark. The merest rough, bungled incision or the daubed-on red ochre, the most elementary "cup-markings" on the stone at the burial-site (and Homo Neanderthalis appears to have done this much) provide perhaps more fool-proof examples of what I mean. For here, with the barest minimum of skill and without any, or much, shining out of the *splendor formae,* we would appear already to be in the domain of sign (sacrament), of anamnesis, or anathemata. We are with beasts of a sort, but not, it would seem, perishing beasts. And, if not, then with beasts that share at least something with the incorporeal intelligences ". . . *cum angelis . . . sine fine . . .*"

For it is on account of the anthropic sign-making that we first suspect that anthropos has some part in a without-endness. Our suspicions may be first aroused by some "find" from the Pliocene System and they may be heightened when we see some such work as the Demeter of Cnidus or hear sung the *Lauda Sion,* or see a reproduction of Agostino di Duccio's Twins, as corporeal as heavenly, in relief at Rimini, or read the "Chapel Peryllous" passage in Malory, or hear the gramophone record of Joyce's incomparable *Anna Livia* read by himself, or look at facsimiles of Ravenna mosaics. Nevertheless the multiplicity of artistic perfections in such and in innumerable other such works as these does not make such works either less or more anthropic signs than are the scratchings on the earliest known palaeolith. If we smell a rat because of the marks on the eolith or on the elk-bone we smell only that same rat whenever we approach these subsequent *signa* of man. We know that that rat's hole is well earthed, pungent with corporeality, warm with "this flesh," brightened with built fires, chill also "*et opertam mortis caligine,*"[4] located in a tangled no-man's-land where anthropos and anthropoid, because of the mortal smog and our own caliginousness, appear sometimes hard to distinguish. But we suspect also, from that rat-smell, that that rat's hole in the forward area must have some liaison with a trench system organized in very great, or rather in infinite, depth. That is to say our rat-odour is not althogether a finite odour. It has, if one may employ a cornered and somewhat patented term, the "odour of sanctity." It smells of the "sacred."

This word no less than the word "sacrament" needs (so I think) to be rescued both from certain antipathetic biases and from a certain kind of appropriativeness. The latter being partly responsible for the former. Certainly there is the time-honoured distinction between the "sacred" and the "profane." It is a distinction valid enough and useful enough in certain contexts—just as is the distinction between "religious" and "secular." But properly speaking and at the root of the matter, Ars knows only a "sacred" activity. I believe this must be so once we grant that the notion of "sign" cannot be separated from this activity of art. Why, granted the sign-making nature of man's art, must those signs be "sacred"? Is "sacredness" implicit in "sign"?

I think it to be so if we assent to what philosophers say about "being," *esse*. I understand them to say that for anything to be real it must have *esse*. I am very conscious of the dangers of employing weapons borrowed from the gun-rack of formal philosophy when

[4] Book of Job x, 21, "and covered with the mist of death," quoted from the Dominican Little Office, Matins of the Dead, 3rd Nocturne, Lesson 9.

one is untrained in the use of such arms; but at least perhaps we can distinguish the stock from the barrel. When philosophers tell us that the "bad" is a deprivation of some "good" and is thus a negative quality only, we all can apprehend something of what is meant. We know that the "bad" is real enough in the common speech sense of the word "real," but that in a deeper sense the bad must be a deprivation of some reality. And in everyday speech we in fact employ this philosophical usage; as when a painter says of a painting which he does not like: "It is so bad, it simply does not exist" or "My dear, it just isn't there," or "It's nothing." These are but three examples from everyday jargon. We know what is meant just as we guess what is meant by those vivid and measured words: *Bonum et ens convertuntur*.

A sign then must be significant of something, hence of some "reality," so of something "good," so of something that is "sacred." That is why I think that the notion of sign implies the sacred.

Unless this reasoning fails to make necessary distinctions and so is faulty, it would appear that the activity called art is, at bottom, and inescapably, a "religious" activity, for it deals with realities and the real is sacred and religious. But, to be on the safe side, I shall put the matter in other terms, thus:

(1) We are told, or we conclude, that man is a "moral" being, which means for reasons already discussed that he is a "religious" being.

(2) We know that we make things. We know this for certain and without reflection. To make things is our day by day activity. We infer from this that man is a maker. On reflection we feel able to define man as a maker of things. On investigation we find that this has been his characteristic unbroken activity for some tens of milleniums, perhaps for much longer.

If what we are told or conclude is true (as stated in (1) above) and unless we are deluded with respect to what we "know" (as stated in (2) above), then it follows as of absolute necessity that there adheres to man's making a "religious" something.

I understand that more than one opinion has prevailed with

regard to the etymology of the word *religio,* but a commonly accepted view is that, as with *obligatio,* a binding of some sort is indicated. The same root is in "ligament," a binding which supports an organ and assures that organ its freedom of use as part of a body. And it is in this sense that I here use the word "religious." It refers to a binding, a securing. Like the ligament, it secures a freedom to function. The binding makes possible the freedom. Cut the ligament and there is atrophy—corpse rather than *corpus.* If this is true, then the word *religio,* no less than the words *prudentia, ars* and *signum,* means nothing, makes no sense, unless we presuppose a freedom of some sort.

But there is a similar difficulty in using the word "religious" as there is in using the words "sacred" and "sacrament," indeed the difficulty is much greater. As the words "religion" and "religious" are, quite properly and by universal consent, used normally to denote moral systems, ritual practices, observances and states of mind, it is necessary that I should indicate as clearly as I am able, what is meant by my particular use of the word "religious" *vis-à-vis* the art of man, otherwise I shall have only myself to blame for being misunderstood. We all understand clearly what is meant when we say that *religio* is that which binds man to God. But when we say that the activity called art is of its nature bound to God, because it is an inescapably "religious" activity we have to think much harder in order to explain what we mean.

I shall now have a shot at explaining what I mean by "religious" in this sense and in this context: Were we trying to discover what is meant by, e.g., the assertion: "Nature is beautiful" we would I think be better advised to begin by considering the patterns made by the germ-cells of a formidable disease than by considering the female torso, the green hills or the dog-rose; because unless we are so effectually clear-headed as to be impervious to associations these associations may easily become red herrings and there are red herrings enough in any case. So in this present instance of trying to state in what sense *ars* implies *religio* I think it safer to choose an art that is relatively free of any "artistic" associations, an art that is not included under such terms as "the Arts," and one which is normally thought of as "a doing" rather than "a making," and one which is at all points governed by urgent, hard, practical, this-world necessities. What about strategy? According to my reasoning, *in so far* as strategy partakes of *ars*, then it must in some sense partake of this *religio*. I argue that it does partake of art because man-as-strategist is concerned with a positioning, and so a juxtaposing, of certain several parts with a view to establishing a certain whole.

That is to say a number of existing shapes (which themselves may or may not require re-shaping) are shifted about; by which activity a form, not previously existent, is created.

In so far as form is brought into being there is reality. "Something" not "nothing," moreover a new "something," has come into existence. And if, as we aver, man's form-making has in itself the nature of a sign, then these formal realities, which the art of strategy creates, must, in some sense or other, be *signa*. But of what can they possibly be significant? What do they show forth, re-present, recall or, in any sense, reflect? It would seem that the forms which strategy shows forth can be typic only of that archetypal form-making and ordering implicit in the credal clause *per quem omnia facta sunt*. That is to say they partake in some sense, however difficult to posit, of that juxtaposing by which what was *inanis et vacua* became radiant with form and abhorrent of vacua by the action of the Artifex, the Logos, who is known to our tradition as the Pontifex who formed a bridge "from nothing" and who then, like Brân in the *Mabinogion*, himself became the bridge[5] by the Incarnation and Passion and subsequent Apotheoses.

Although these forms, in the case of strategy, are conditioned very

[5] Hence the Welsh proverb: "He who would be head, let him be the bridge," *A fo ben bid bont*, still in actual use in Wales. It derives from the myth of Bendigeidfran who bridged the Irish Sea with his own body for his army to march upon. It seems a startling foreshadowing of what was achieved by the Incarnation. At the same time it offers from remote Celtic antiquity a theme familiar to us in the Roman title Pontifex Maximus and the title Servus Servorum Dei.

narrowly by the exigencies of a situation, nevertheless they come into being by the operations of a mind free to judge. The mind of the strategist may judge wrongly but it judges, and the "virtue of art" is said to be "to judge." So that insofar as any god-likeness can be predicated of the strategist, that likeness derives from the fact that the art implicit in strategy is, like all other art, a sign of the form-making activities universally predicated of the Logos. It is then the form-making which is also a sign-making that causes man's art to be bound to God. Implicit in the activity called art, and belonging to the very essence of that activity, there is that which makes it a ligament. As we have said above, it is the whole purpose of a ligament to bind in order to secure freedom of action; and that to sever a ligament is to make impossible any further action or freedom to act. Attempt to sever the concept, *ars,* from what is implied under the root meaning of *religio* and there is no *ars,* there is an empty term only or, at most, a convenient label.

Should any reader have followed me thus far I would again remind that reader, in case I have left any ambiguity as to the sense in which I here employ the terms "religio" and "religious," that I do not here use those terms in their more accustomed sense as pertaining to pieties, dispositions of the will, explicit acts of worship, states of mind or soul. On the contrary I employ the terms here solely with reference to the nature of *art*. So that neither the kind of art nor the uses to which it is put, whether evil or good, nor the intentions of the men practising these multifarious arts can affect either one way or the other the "religiousness" which is implicit in all art as such.

It was in order to convey this that I chose the art of strategy as my example. For strategy in so far as it partakes of art, offers less occasion for those particular misunderstandings which would tend to arise had something more recognizably an art, and immeasurably more typical, been chosen: for example had poetry, dancing, painting, sculpture, song or architecture been chosen.

But having made some attempt to indicate certain characteristics that are implicit in the activity of art we are now free to consider some more explicit manifestations of those same characteristics by which we recognize that the art of man is essentially a sign-making or "sacramental" activity. We have come through a tangled wood of attempted definitions and have been hampered by unavoidable explanations, but now perhaps we are more free to deploy in the open and can see better how the front shapes.

As it is the sign-making or "sacramental" character of art that is our chief concern, I shall, in the following pages, confine myself to a more explicit consideration of what that may mean, and especially what it may mean to us today in view of our civilizational trend.

As was stated at the beginning, the contributors to these essays are Catholics, so that the reader will fully understand that certain events are taken as having actually occurred in time and at a certain site, and that these events have necessarily very important bearings on man and on his activities. And if, as we have seen, man is man-the-artist, then these events have a bearing on the nature of art, otherwise they would not be mentioned here.

I believe it to be relevant to this matter of art that during the period of the early Roman Emperors a cult arose in the Aramaean lands which demanded as a condition of membership the acceptance of a belief involving certain of the arts. The arts involved were not recognized as arts and the members of that cult were passionately concerned with a state of mind and soul and not at all with what we ordinarily call "the arts." Indeed, for some centuries they were, for well-known reasons, indifferent or hostile to those arts. But none of this disposes of the fact that it was a central belief of this new society that certain outward signs and manual acts were obligatory. Admittance into that society was under the sign of water and continued membership involved the signs of the quasi-artefacts of bread and wine. So in spite of the fact that this cult was explicitly concerned with the inward man, with spiritual and moral regeneration and with a life beyond this world, its members were committed from the beginning to the use of material signs. More than that, those signs were not regarded as mere symbols, they were regarded as integral to the belief and in the words of a very eminent member of that new society, they were regarded as a sacred tradition to be handed on because it was a *traditio* "received of the Lord."[6]

Now the crucial question is: Why did the Lord employ art-forms and establish a tradition commanding the continued employment of those forms?

This, at first reading, may sound to be a question of strictly theological provenance. Theologians can tell us why the Eucharist was instituted, that is to say, they can give us a theologian's answer, but as far as I am aware that answer would not cover our query in the sense in which it is asked. Nor does the theological disagreement that divides non-Catholics from Catholics concerning the Eucharist touch upon our query. Moreover the fruitful discussion within the Roman Communion, which has tended to elucidate more clearly the nature of the relationship between the Supper, Calvary and the Mass, has not in any way been directly concerned with our query either.[7] For in all their disputes, theologians, both Protestant and Catholic, *take it for granted* that a sign-making of some sort was initiated in the Upper Room and that that sign-making was, in some sense, meant to be repeated. So that our query is anterior to, or apart from, those strictly theological questions. It is, in fact, an anthropological rather than a theological question, for we are not here considering the truth about the Sacrament but are noting only that *men make sacraments*.

The Notices for the Week may read: Sunday within the Octave of Corpus Christi, Sung Mass, 11 a.m. or they may read: Lord's Day next, Breaking of Bread at 11 o'clock. In both cases we are

[6] I Corinthians xi, 23

[7] Although it would be true to say that the astonishing sense of integration and wholeness which in the 1920s was given to this triple relationship by Maurice de la Taille, S.J., seemed, for the present writer, to shed a sort of reflected radiance upon the sign-world in general. Perhaps it was that his French understanding of an artistic wholeness made his theological propositions so coherent and enlivening and, as I say, illuminating beyond their immediate context.

notified of an intention to re-present, recall or show forth something under certain signs and by manual acts, so an "art-work" is notified in both cases. In the latter case the minister might rebut the suggestion that he was committed to sign or sacrament. In the former case the minister might (having his mind on "Sacraments" with a capital S) be anxious to agree with that rebuttal as far as the other rite was concerned, and they might both be a little jumpy over the term "art-work." Nevertheless, if you attended either of those two assemblies, on the *Dies Dominica* following, you would, without any doubt at all, witness, or participate in, an art-work. The kind or amount of "ritual" employed would in no sense affect the matter, nor would the extreme discrepancies of doctrine, nor the fact that one of those rites was, in your belief, sufficient in all respects and the other, in some respects, deficient. You would, in both those assemblies, witness corporeal creatures doing certain manual things with material elements and proclaiming that these things were done for a signification of something. You would be witness of something not dissimilar from what you witness in the kitchen where the cook is making a cake patterned with icing-sugar. If the cook should say: "This is for Susan's birthday—don't you think it a work of art?" you may or may not agree with the cook's notion of beauty but you would not be able to deny the "art." For leaving aside the art of cooking and the supererogatory art of icing, in so far as the cake is "made for Susan's birthday" it is "made over" in some sense. By every possible test it belongs to Ars. It belonged to Ars, or rather it was pre-ordained to Ars, from the first movement of the cook's mind to make something that should be significant of Susan's birth.

We might almost say it belonged to art *ante omnia saecula,* though perhaps that is going a bit far and we don't want to be a sitting bird for the guns of unsporting metaphysicians. But certainly all the conditions, determining what is art from what it is not, are more than fulfilled. There is making, there is added making, there is explicit sign, there is a showing forth, a re-presenting, a recalling and there is gratuitousness and there is full intention to make this making thus. Moreover this particular making signifies a birth. It recalls a past event and looks back at some anniversaries and looks forward to future anniversaries, it is essentially celebrative and festal: it would be gay. For as Poussin said of another art: "The goal of painting is delight." And this is universally true of all art no matter how difficult it is to posit the delight. But this making, though joyful and celebrative of a birthday, recalls also, by implication, a day, or many days, of at least some degree of acute pain, perhaps of great anguish, and, perhaps, even of death. So that this making covers, in a rudimentary way, or contains in embryo, all that is shown forth in the greatest imaginable art-works. I mean no art can compass more than that attempted in the line of the Sequence for Easter Day: *Mors et vita duello conflixere mirando.*

It was pure good fortune that we stumbled on this example in the kitchen, for indeed we might have searched further and fared far worse. For probably there are not many arts that would so simply and conclusively show forth to us the nature and function of Ars.

I don't know what the reader may be thinking by the time this point is reached, but I think there is now some likelihood of answering my questions as to why, in the Cenacle, certain signs were instituted, or, as is said above, certain art-forms were employed and their continuance commanded. It may be felt by some that such a question is idle and uncalled for on the grounds that the whole world knows that human beings "naturally" require and employ signs, rites, commemorative acts and the like. Others might agree with this objection and add that it is evidently God's will that man should behave thus because he was made thus; which is but another way of saying that these things are "natural to him." This last is true enough but I put the question only to discover whether it would be a more clearly stated truth if we added seven words and said "natural to him in virtue of his being an artist." This merely makes what is implicit explicit.

It is difficult to see that anything other than man being an artist could account for these things being "natural" to him. His moral nature would not require these things of him. His contemplative nature does not require them, nor his speculative intelligence. The philosophers assure us that art belongs not to the speculative but to the practical intelligence. Some deeply religious minds seem to regard these things, these signs and outward showings, as being necessary only because of an infirmity and because we require them as aids toward a spiritual state. They speak as though this sign-making were adjuvant only and a kind of concession to us because we have bodies. But this would appear to imply that the body was itself an infirmity or a kind of deprivation. Whereas the body is not an infirmity but a unique benefit and splendour, a thing denied to angels and unconscious in animals. We are committed to body and by the same token we are committed to Ars, so to sign and sacrament. If we are forbidden to think of the body as an infirmity how can these arts and sacraments be thought of as aids only to an infirm condition? I suspect that we have here the clue to that frustration which afflicts and makes at cross purposes all argument between those who aver that sacraments are necessary and those who aver otherwise.

The latter urge that a condition of the interior man, a state of grace, is what matters. The former tend to say that while this is true enough, nevertheless certain sacraments are appointed as channels to that end. But unless they can show that sacrament, as such, apart from a particular use of certain specific sacraments is something to which man is of his nature unavoidably committed they are apt to appear worsted in the argument. The notion that sacrament is something added rather than something radical and inescapable is allowed to infiltrate their defences. The red herring of "ritualism" is often permitted to vitiate the argument. The question of "ritualism" belongs to another discussion altogether, and can only confuse the present issue. It suffices here to say that "form" is inevitable and right and "formalism" is always an abuse and that "ritual" is right and inevitable and "ritualism" is always an abuse. And indeed both words, formalism and ritualism, are used always in a derogatory sense.

But sign and sacrament are to be predicated not of *some* men and their practices but of *all* men and their practices. If it is a question of calcination then one man is the kettle and the other the pot. Those who live in glass houses should not throw stones and in this matter the whole human race is housed in glass. In this respect the Plymouth Brethren and the Arval Brethren are in the same predicament; for it is a predicament of being human. None of us must allow ourselves to get away with the idea that we can avoid sacrament. To do so we should either have to suppose ourselves to be incorporeal intelligences or hippopotamuses or other such creatures of the Artifex, the Son. But try as he may no man can be like either of these, for along with his rational soul he has corporeality. It is impressive that the Doctor of Angelology should describe this body as a "substantial advantage." And this advantage is said to be on account of the body being a sensory organ. So that again we are face to face with Ars.

A man can not only smell roses (some beasts may do that, for lavender is said to be appreciated in the Lion House) but he can and does and ought to pluck roses and he can predicate of roses such and such. He can make a *signum* of roses. He can make attar of roses. He can garland them and make anathemata of them. Which is, presumably, the *kind* of thing he is meant to do. Anyway, there's no one else can do it. Angels can't nor can the beasts. No wonder then that Theology regards the body as a unique good. Without body: without sacrament. Angels only: no sacrament. Beasts only: no sacrament. Man: sacrament at every turn and all levels of the "profane" and "sacred," in the trivial and in the profound, no escape from sacrament.

Some man known to the reader may indeed appear to escape from all that is commonly or vulgarly meant by the "sacramental," but no sooner does he put a rose in his buttonhole but what he is already in the trip-wire of sign, and he is deep in an entanglement of signs if he sends that rose to his sweetheart, Flo; or puts it in a vase by her portrait; and he is hopelessly and up to his neck in that entanglement of Ars, sign, sacrament, should he sit down and write a poem "about" that sweetheart. Heaven knows what his poem will really be "about"; for then the "sacramental" will pile up by a positively geometric progression. So that what was Miss Flora Smith may turn out to be Flora Dea and Venus too and the First Eve and the Second also and other and darker figures, among them no doubt, Jocasta. One thing at least the psychologists make plain: there is always a recalling, a re-presenting again, anaphora, anamnesis.

If, in the Cenacle, forms of words were used and manual acts employed involving material substances, these things can have been done only by virtue of the doer being a man along with us; more explicitly, by his being man-the-artist along with us. What was done would have been neither necessary nor possible unless man is man-the-artist.

It looks then as though, whatever may be said for some religious beliefs, the Christian religion is committed to Ars in the most explicit, compelling, and integral manner. It is incumbent upon all Christians to believe, and it is a central dogma of the Catholic Church, that the Redemption of the World was accomplished once for all at a certain date in time and a specified site, that is, on Calvary. Now that event, it might be argued, does not commit Christians to signs, but commits them only to a belief that such and such took place historically for their supernatural benefit. I was indeed about to use an argument which has a kind of affinity to this argument to the extent of saying that Calvary did not involve Ars whereas the Supper did, and that what was done on the Hill was a "doing" only, whereas what was done in the Cenacle was a "making" (*poiesis*). But brief reflection will show that Calvary itself (if less obviously than the Supper) involves *poiesis*. For what was accomplished on the Tree of the Cross presupposes the sign-world and looks back to foreshadowing rites and arts of mediation and conjugation stretching back for tens of thousands of years in actual pre-history. Or, to speak in theological terms, the Tree of the Cross presupposes the other Tree, and stretches back to the "truly necessary sin of Adam" and the "happy fault," so that St. Thomas in the Good Friday hymn could write: *Ars ut artem falleret.*

It has been and is argued by many that the actual lifting up of the *Signum* on the Hill put an end to all need of further *signa.* This sounds convincing until we consider what was done at the Supper, when it seems no longer tenable. For in the Cenacle the Victim himself did something and said something which no matter how it is theologically interpreted and no matter what its interrelatedness to what was done on the Hill, was unmistakably and undeniably a sign-making and a rite-making and so an act of Ars; moreover an act to be, in some sense, repeated. The exact implications touching what it is that is to be repeated have been and are debated among Christians. But according to the belief of the Catholic Church the sign-making instituted in the Upper Room is to be so closely associated with what was done on the Hill that the benefits of those doings are said to be chiefly (but far from exclusively) mediated through a continuation of that sign-making. But even if we are Christians holding an opinion at the furthest possible remove from this Catholic belief we are still committed to the notion of sign. And in any case, apart from this Christian commitment, we are committed to sign in virtue of being men.

But the records describe how the redeemer "on the day before he suffered" involved the redeemed in an act of Ars. As it was the whole world that he was redeeming he involved all mankind, from before Swanscombe Man to after Atomic Man, in that act. If the very mean or channel of redemption is intricated in Ars we conclude that Ars and Man are inseparable. It is impossible to deny that Ars was involved in what was done at the Supper and it is no less impossible to deny that what was done was done in anticipation of the events of the morrow. It would appear, to me, impossible that at the Redemption of the World anything should have been done which committed man to any activity not utterly inalienable from his nature. In such a context the extraneous in inconceivable.

It is said of the eucharistic signs that they are a showing forth of something "in an un-bloody manner." That particular instance from the domain of theological definition might, *mutatis mutandis,* be used to help us understand better something of the function, in general, of Ars as a shower-forth.

The everyday things, the food and drink common to a given civilization milieu, yet already typic and significant owing to some milleniums of association with rite, cultus, *disciplinae* (thus saturated with Ars) were, in the supper-room, declared to signify such and such. So far from there being any abrogation of Ars there was a deliberate employment of Ars by the gratuitous institution of a new and impletive rite. That rite was concerned wholly with communicating spiritual things, so the context is entirely theological. It would therefore be presumption in me to touch upon such matters except to point out that the means whereby those spiritual things are said, by the theologians, to be communicated, involves Ars. Now anything involving Ars is within the purview of this essay. So that no matter how incompetent we may be to speak of theological things and no matter how much we lack spiritually we are forced to consider these sacrosanct signs when Ars is the subject under consideration.

For those of us who are unable to subscribe to Christian belief this act can be seen as a further example of the truth that Ars is inalienable from Man and Man from Ars; but for those of us who can so subscribe, then this act may be seen not only as an example but as an unique, most compelling and ratifying example of that same inalienability. An example moreover compelling those in the latter category to a corresponding manual act owing to the unequivocal words "Do this for an anamnesis of me."

But leaving Christians and their obligations altogether aside and speaking, for a while, as one unconcerned for the truth or untruth of the Christian documents, main tradition or divergent theologies, it remains true that in the signs referred to we have not only an element of art but some indication of the *kind* of activity that we predicate of Ars at her most abstract. This much should be as evident to those who imagine themselves to be antipathetic to the signs as to those who claim a love of them. A non-Christian person would rightly observe that these signs equally involve Ars whether the intention of the sign-makers is un-Catholic or Catholic. But such a person would also observe that in the latter case something further was involved. He would note that the intention in this case envisaged an abstract art *par excellence;* for nothing could be less "representational" or more re-presentative or further from "realism" or more near reality than what is intended and posited in this latter instance. He would note an extreme objectivity in the view that sign and thing signified are regarded as having a true identity. He would note the rejection of the opinion held elsewhere that such an identification overthrows the nature of a sign. He would not be at all concerned for the truth or otherwise of these views, he would note only that there was, in those views, a something which found some kind of analogy in other arts.

The bell would chime rather than toll. The answering chimes might be very faint but still audible. If he were a person of first-hand acquaintance with the visual art of painting or the aural art of poetry he might well be aware of certain analogous intentions. Not analogies that could be at all pressed but still analogies of a sort. For the painter may say to himself: "This is not a representation of a mountain, it *is* 'mountain' under the form of paint." Indeed, unless he says this unconsciously or consciously he will not be a painter worth a candle. It is indeed the "pith and knot of the matter." This applies also to the poet. Such an observer might recall also what Cézanne is reported to have said: "We must do Poussin again after Nature." This saying has, in some obscure way (a faint chime), reminded me always of the language of a synodic definition.

In this essay, then, our concern is not with the truth or otherwise of a given theology, that is outside my scope and would not be relevant. What is here relevant is that such a theology exists and that it can be seen as affording, by analogy, a remarkable example of the activities of Ars. I repeat, I speak only by analogy.

At this point I must apologize for having to introduce some autobiographical matter: When, in 1919, I re-commenced my studies as an art-student, my fellow-students and I wasted a good deal of our time (I hope art-students are still so occupied) discussing, not without heat, the "nature of art." As the opinion "There's nothing like leather" was our opinion also, we meant by "art" the arts of painting, sculpture, etc. For one reason or another certain queries touching what Christians did or did not assert with regard to the eucharist were at that time much in my mind, and though I in no way connected these queries with the queries concerning the arts, I sometimes found myself thinking of the two matters together, though still unrelatedly.

The question of analogy seemed not to occur until certain Post-Impressionist theories began to bulk larger in our student conversation. Then, with relative suddenness, the analogy between what we called "the Arts" and the things that Christians called the eucharistic signs became (if still but vaguely) apparent. It became increasingly evident that this analogy applied to the whole gamut of "making." The reader may associate the word "Post-Impressionism" only with a particular school of painting, he may regard its manifestations as deplorable. Or, if he should happen to be himself a young art-student of today, he may possibly regard the word as indicating an outmoded phase of aesthetic experiment. However that may be, there was implicit in Post-Impressionist *theory* something which being true must remain true and cannot be gainsaid. It was that something which opened the eyes of us to what, many years back, I had occasion to describe as "the unity of all made things." For one of the more rewarding notions implicit in the Post-Impressionist idea was that a work is a "thing" and not (necessarily) the impression of some other thing. For example, that it is the "abstract" quality in any painting (no matter how "realistic") that causes that painting to have "being," and which alone gives it the right to be claimed an art-work, as a making, as *poiesis,* along with the triple spiral in the New Grange tumulus, Palestrina's music for the *Improperia,* the columns of the Parthenon, the arranged disorder of Julia's love-knots, the taut hemp knot for a tackle, any liturgical act, or the thatching of a roof.

When in 1920 or '21 I first made the acquaintance of Eric Gill he had long since come to his own conclusions regarding some of these matters which had, this way or that, occupied the groping minds of many of us. These various stirrings were part of a general movement, at the core of which was that conviction, well expressed by James Joyce; "practical life or 'art' . . . comprehends all our activities from boat-building to poetry." Round about 1923 there was available John O'Connor's translation of Maritain, and that, from the pen of a formal philosopher, provided certain reassurances and further data with regard to some matters which had occupied our thoughts as makers of things. It seemed to some of us at that period that important classifications made by Maritain (and some others) would have a correspondingly clarifying effect upon all subsequent discussion of the nature of Ars. In this we were over-optimistic. We did not sufficiently take into account the tide of subjectivism against which such objective views were struggling. For example, the rewarding speculations of T. E. Hulme can hardly be said to have made his book a best seller. But then neither is that brief chapter, of about thirty lines only, in which Aristotle[8] contrasts "making" (*poiesis*) with "doing" (*praxis*), a "best seller"; yet it contains so much for those concerned with the kind of thing that art is; it is a foundational fragment.

To return from this autobiographical digression: I regard the for-or-against-the-abstract argument that is so very much publicized today as an unfortunate evasion of a real issue. Instead of an enhanced understanding of that issue and a real clarification of the mind touching the whole field of "making," we have a concentration of certain arts only and a tiresome misunderstanding concerning those arts. For though the Post-Impressionist theories indicated an approach that was most salutary, they also provided ammunition for an unrewarding and somewhat unreal battle. That ammunition has been most improvidently expended in the war of theories concerning "abstract art" and "representational art"; and in the resultant inter-party strife. None of all this is surprising, for warring

[8] See *The Nicomachean Ethics,* Bk. VI, ch. 4, 'Of Art'.

aesthetic theories are normal enough and, given our civilizational situation, are expected in a most aggravated form. Nevertheless no matter what the situation, we cannot escape the obligation of asserting as axiomatic that all art is "abstract" and that all art "re-presents."

I am very far from thinking that the acceptance of this "axiom" (as I regard it) would affect, or enable us to resolve, the actual quandaries and contradictions that face us today in the whole domain of "making." For those difficulties are deeply intricated with our present civilizational phase and with the bewildering developments of a technocracy which is causing an unprecedented metamorphosis in human society all over the world and at every level. I think only that *if* the axiom is indeed axiomatic then no matter what the situation we must needs hold to it. This would apply even if for all practical purposes the axiom was without effect and even if, to all appearance, it seemed without meaning. The holding to it would not be in the nature of holding to a lost cause or adhering to a discredited proposition, or a refusal to admit the actualities of a situation. It would, on the contrary, be a holding to something which sooner or later would be seen to cast light on that situation.

"All art re-presents." I have hyphenated re-presents for a good reason, but must now show the reason. If I wrote, e.g., of Hogarth's highly realistic painting called "The Shrimp Girl" that it "represented such and such" I should not convey at all what the work in fact *is*. If I wrote "re-presented such and such" there is a slight gain and "re-presented such and such under other forms" is still more of a gain, but more amplification is required to cover fully what is indicated under the shorthand, hyphenated term "re-present." I shall therefore attempt a fuller statement sticking to Hogarth's "Shrimp Girl" as my example partly because it is a picture of which I am fond, also because no one can cavil as to its merits; but more because it is highly visual and, as they say, "faithful to the appearance of nature." It is a charming record of an apparently charming subject, so all that could be desired by the most popular and unsophisticated standards.

My fuller statement of what that painting is and does might read somewhat as follows: It is a "thing," an object contrived of various materials and so ordered by Hogarth's muse as to show forth, recall and re-present, strictly within the conditions of a given art and under another mode, such and such a reality. It is a *signum* of that reality and it makes a kind of anamnesis of the reality. What that reality strictly is it is hard to say owing to its complexity. Superficially what is here shown forth under the form of paint is, I suppose, a female street-vendor's mortal flesh and poor habiliments seen under our subtle island-light in the gay squalor that was eighteenth century low-life England. Or had this "sketch" been made in Calais, no matter, or had the girl not been a fish-girl but a model dressed up to look like one—still no matter, for whatever the accidents of the flesh and blood "reality" this reality did but supply the raw material for whatever concept the sight of it set in motion in the mind of the painter.

And here we have a very subtle relationship indeed. That is why I say above that the "reality" shown forth is too complicated to posit with any precision or fullness. Goodness knows what that "reality" was in Hogarth's mind. Though the fact that he claimed to have discovered something he called "the line of beauty," and wrote an analytical treatise attempting to prove it and to thereby establish a canon of aesthetics based on formulae of proportions, should be sufficient to warn us that that "reality" was complex and that the conveyance of it in paint involved a lot besides verisimilitude to the accidents of nature. So we can say only one thing for certain: that whatever the material and immaterial elements of that "reality" may have been, the workings of Hogarth's art gave to the world a *signum* of that reality, under the species of paint.

It is this objective sign that we can apprehend and enjoy in the National Gallery provided we have the right dispositions. By which I mean that sometimes we are too tired to appreciate anything and sometimes our mood is such that we can appreciate only other *signa,* Cosimo Tura's or Braque's. But we are not here concerned with the subjective. That beauty is "in the eye of the beholder" no doubt indicates a subjective truth, but in another and more objective sense it is very far from the truth.

Here then is a *signum,* a made thing having such and such significance and totally independent of our fluctuating reactions or of our inability to react at all. It came into existence just about two hundred years ago by virtue of the intransitive activity called art. By the particular working of Hogarth's genius a reality is offered to us. So long as there is not a serious disintegration of the "matter" (the paint) we have whatever is denoted under "Shrimp Girl" really present under the form of paint, remembering that "Shrimp Girl" is but a label only for a complex of realities. Not, needless to say, "really present" in the particular sense used by the theologians, but in a certain analogous sense. I can speak only by analogy and it may be I speak ill-advisedly, but I know of no other way of giving sufficient emphasis, especially in view of our culture-situation and for a number of other reasons.

I have already greatly exceeded the number of words proposed for this essay and have done no more than indicate the nature of Ars as instanced in: strategy, a birthday-cake, a religious rite and a well-known picture. I argue that these exceedingly diverse examples bear witness to the nature of the thing we call art and the nature of the creature we call man and the inseparability of the one from the other. I have tried to show how, in some sense or other, what we have found in each of these four examples must be sought for in all the makings of man. It is here argued that the artist is not, to use a most expressive Americanism, "out on a limb," but that judging from widely differing data, the activity of art, far from being a branch activity, is truncal and that the tree of man, root, bole, branches and foliage, is involved, of its nature, in that activity.

I had hoped in the light of these suggestions or propositions to consider in some detail the difficulties that face us in regard to our present culture-phase. But the length entailed forbids this. In the remaining pages I can do no more than hint at or suggest the general nature of the dilemma as I see it to be: How are we to reconcile man-the-artist, man the sign-maker or sacrament-maker, with the world in which we live today? It would appear that there is a dichotomy which puts asunder that which our nature demands should be joined together. We hear a great deal, from persons of all sorts, about incompatibilities, separations, divorces and nullities. But there is also another sort of divorce that characterizes the phase of civilization in which we live and which thus affects the thoughts and lives of all of us, whether we are aware of it or not. The divorce of which I speak is far more difficult of analysis than those divorces affecting the nature of the marriage bond between man and woman and, if I may say so without being altogether misunderstood, is anterior in importance. For the very notion of a "Sacrament" binding two persons is devoid of meaning unless the nature of man is sacramental, and, as we have argued, without *ars* there is no possibility of *sacramentum.*

But this divorce with which we are here concerned is a dichotomy to be observed in the actual civilization of which we are a part. It is a situational problem. However one tries to express it one leaves much unsaid or one puts it in such a way as to invite valid objections. But something may perhaps be indicated by saying that there have been always frictions, estrangements and contradictions within man himself owing to the wedding within himself of the "utile"[9] and the sacramental and that the fruit of this wedding was, to a lesser or greater degree, observable through the whole gamut of man's making, but that now these estrangements take on the nature of actual and agreed separations.

Sometimes it looks as though a general separation had, by common consent, been made absolute and that the marriage contract certifying that man himself *is* this wedding had been nullified. Whereas we had supposed this union to be indissoluble and cer-

[9] I realize that the word "utile" is here open to objection, but I use it here as a shorthand term to indicate what is vulgarly and generally understood by "merely utilitarian" or "simply functional."

tainly had judged it to be consummated. Otherwise we could not account for the large and identifiable progeny issuing from that union over a period of some fifty milleniums. Nor indeed could we otherwise account for the work of our own hands, still less for the work of those hands referred to in the rubric, *Ambabus manibus accepit calicem.*[10]

I should like to make it doubly clear that nothing is intended in these pages beyond an enquiry. In my view the most we can do is ask questions concerning a situation. That much is also the least we can do, or rather that much is forced on us once we become aware of certain dilemmas in our own hands. My own questionings have naturally arisen in connection with such plastic and graphic arts as I have tried to practise. If one is making a picture or making a writing it is *inevitable* that all these questions of "sign," of "showing forth again under forms," of the validity of the signs employed, of whether these are available and effectual etc., will be part of one's daily problems. Some of these particular problems I touched upon in the Preface to *The Anathemata*. But in this present instance I have attempted rather to suggest a more general inquiry concerning this whole business of Ars as such, in relation to man, more particularly in relation to man today and especially in relation to what, as Catholics, we know to be our inescapable commitments to signs or sacraments. Other men are, in fact, implicitly committed, but we are committed in the most explicit manner possible.

Because the Church is committed to "Sacraments" with a capital S, she cannot escape a committal to sacrament with a small s, unless the sacramentalism of the Church is to be regarded as a peculiar and isolated phenomenon. We know that such a view is not to be entertained and that the sacramental quality is evidenced in the past works of man over the whole period of his existence so far known to us. It is argued in these pages that this is the very quality by which "man" is distinguished from "animal" and from "angel" and I have tried to state why I think this to be so. I have said

[10] See the Mass rubric directing the celebrant to take hold of the chalice with both hands.

further that many of us find ourselves asking of ourselves: To what extent is the civilizational trend depriving us of this normality? It must be left to the reader to ask whether or not, in his or her view, it is the trend of our technocracy to increasingly put asunder what is joined together in man-the-artist. Should the answer be at all in the affirmative, then to that exact extent, and no more, there is ground for dilemma and for further scrutiny because it means that more and more human beings, through no fault of their own at all, are alienated from the mere notion of sacrament with a small s.

Were this alienation to become more complete, then the persons affected would have to regard the postulate of the Church with respect to Sacraments as something to be accepted on authority only, something which the rules happened to say must be done. Something which, though foreign to all their ways and habits of thought, was, for mysterious and inexplicable reasons demanded of them in the name of religion. Or, alternatively, they would have to reject those postulates as being not only incompatible with their lives, works and habit of thought but as belonging to an out-moded conception of man's nature and requirements, and as no longer even comprehensible except as a survival of by-gone practices. My own sympathies would most decidedly lean to the latter of the two alternatives were I not persuaded that, in spite of any appearances, man remains, by definition, man-the-artist. But that conviction will furnish no lorica or padding against the dilemmas and quandaries. Indeed, it is that conviction which strips off all defensive armour, so that the sharp contradictions and heavy incongruities may at least be felt. Vulnerability is essential, or we may not notice the dichotomy even if it exists.

I said, ah! what shall I write?
I inquired up and down
(he's tricked me before
with his manifold lurking-places).
I looked for his symbol at the door.
I have looked for a long while
at the textures and contours

I have run a hand over the trivial intersections.
I have journeyed among the dead forms causation projects from pillar to pylon. I have tired the eyes of the mind regarding the colours and lights.
I felt for his wounds
in nozzles and containers.
I have wondered for the automatic devices . . . I have tested the inane patterns without prejudice. I have been on my guard to not condemn the unfamiliar . . . for it is easy to miss him at the turn of a civilization. . . .

These few lines are fragments of a fragment abandoned in *c.* 1938. They are quoted not because I think they are of much intrinsic worth but because they may perhaps further indicate those dilemmas which occasioned their composition, dilemmas which show themselves to underlie some of the problems discussed in this present essay of enquiry.

As a postscript I venture to ask the reader to consider what Maurice de la Taille said was done on Maundy Thursday by Good Friday's Victim, I quote: "He placed Himself in the order of signs."

Denis de Rougemont

Religion and the Mission of the Artist

RECENTLY I WAS ASKED to speak on "The Mission of Art as a Creative Expression of the Human Spirit." I would not have agreed, but for the bearing of the subject upon a conference of ecumenical study, bringing together some artists and writers, and some Protestant, Anglican, and Orthodox theologians.* It seemed to me that this title, as it was proposed specifically by Christians, and not by vague or hazy humanists, merited a serious *mise au point.*

To me, the expression, "Mission of Art," rings false. Art, with a capital letter, is one of those official allegories which we have inherited from the nineteenth century and from Romanticism (with its admiration for Wagner and Baudelaire), who were condemned and fined by our forebears. This allegory marks the existence of a sort of "religion of Art," born of the romantic sects and brotherhoods—the preRaphaelites, the symbolists, etc.—which in our time has lost its sacred vigor; but which subsists nevertheless under the form of a very widespread prejudice, amongst the Philistines, the middle class (la bourgeoisie), in Hollywood, and in inaugural addresses. Art, with a capital letter, is something ideal, something

* International Conference on Christianity and Art, convened at the Ecumenical Institute, Chateau de Bossey, Celigny, Switzerland, May, 1950. Translated, with the author's permission, by Stanley Romaine Hopper.

distinguished, vaguely *en rapport* with the Infinite, not useful for anything; respectable, interesting women more than men; the business of certain specialists allowing escape from the too real cares of daily life, elevating souls and softening mores—in short, resembling closely the conception which most of our contemporaries have of the Christian religion. It is not serious if we admit with Talleyrand that "whatever is exaggerated is lacking in seriousness." No serious artist says that he makes "Art," unless it is to defend himself against the tax collector or the suspicious policeman.

On the other hand, the word "art" is a serviceable term, which denotes the ensemble of artistic activities and the objects which result from them.

In either case, whether it is a question of romantic exaggeration or of a generic term, it is evident that Art, with or without the capital, cannot have any "mission." Neither a false god nor a word can have a mission. Only man is capable of receiving one.

In the next place, I have some doubt about the adjective, "creative," as it appears in the title as proposed.

The use of the verb, "to create," in relation to human activity is, I believe, rather recent. This manner of speaking of the human act, by comparing it, or even equating it, to the divine act, not only comes from a synergist doctrine which demands examination, but coincides historically with the impoverishment or loss in the modern epoch of the belief in a Creator God. I am not at all sure that man is capable of creating, in the true sense of this term: that is, of producing an absolute mutation, an absolute novelty in the universe. That which is currently called today a "creation" is in reality only a slightly different arrangement of elements already known according to laws known or knowable. Therefore it is a *composition*. Before Romanticism, we were content to say that a musician composed an opera, that a painter composed a picture. But today, we say that he "creates" a symphony, that he "creates" forms. No one can prove that a man creates something, because no one can know the totality of existent things with their structures and their rapports. We shall limit ourselves, therefore, to the classical term, "composition," when speaking of works of art.

So much having been said, let us consider now what is the mission—if there be one—of the men who compose books, pictures, scores, statues, pleasure grounds, poems; and, first of all, what is the nature of their activity, and what are its proper ends.

I

All sorts of people make things, objects, and instruments. *Homo faber* designates a great part of humanity: workers, artists, scholars, legislators, and craftsmen.

Let us ask what difference there is between the man who makes a poem, a score of music, a picture, a façade, and the man who makes a machine, an equation, a law, a shoe, a chemical product, or a photo.

For about two centuries now, we have become accustomed to answering this question in an apparently simple manner. We think that artists make useless objects (or, as we say in French, *gratuits*), and that others make objects necessary to our daily lives, genuinely useful, such as automobiles, statistics, tools. We cannot do without razors, says the modern man, but if necessary we can—and even without much sacrifice—do without pictures, or statues. Art products are a luxury, and the other products are necessities. All our education leads us to believe this, and if we are required to justify this habitual belief, our professors have recourse to certain interpretations of Kant, according to which an object of art would have its end in itself, and would serve no end, therefore, but that of being contemplated—which is to say, honored with a glance on the way to the dining room.

But these criteria of utility or necessity, on the one hand, and of gratuitousness or uselessness, on the other, are inconsistent and absolutely superficial. They teach us nothing concerning the nature of the work of art. But they do teach us something about the nature and attitude of the society which accepts them: the knowledge that this society has lost the sense of the sacred. Many civilizations have existed, and perhaps will exist, for which a stone or a piece of wood, sculptured or painted in a certain manner, have been infinitely more "useful" than an electric razor is for us. These objects have been regarded as eminently useful, because they contained a power, an exalting or terrifying quality, a meaning. They were taken seriously by the peoples who believed that the meaning of life, the fear of death, the sense of dread before the sacred power, are serious things. Whereas we consider as serious, and, therefore, useful, whatever permits us, for example, to go more swiftly, though it matters little from what motive or toward what end.

The fact that even in theory we hold the work of art to be destitute of direct utility, proves simply that art does not respond to the most potent desire of modern man; that modern man should be able, therefore, to dispense with it; that he has in truth no need of it (as we call useful that which we need); and that he believes he should respect it only by virtue of a kind of prejudice. From which, it may be said in passing, we should be able to deduce the utter vanity of the actual attempts made to vulgarize art to give it publicity. It is the need for art which should be awakened. To this end, we should change the total attitude, the entire orientation of modern man—before setting out to distribute reproductions of Van Gogh!

If therefore I set aside the criterion of utility, or lack of utility, as being relative, variable, and subject to change in meaning according to the religious condition of a society, I find myself once more before the initial question—in what respect does artistic activity distinguish itself from the other activities of man?

I would venture the following answer: that, as distinct from all other products of human action, *the work of art is an object of which the raison d'etre necessary and sufficient, is* TO SIGNIFY, *organically, and by means of its own structure.*

Whether it consists in a structure of meanings, or forms, or sounds, or ideas, the work of art has for its specific function the bribing of the attention, the magnetizing of the sensibility, the fascinating of the meditation, the ensnaring—and at the same time it must orient existence toward something which transcends sounds and forms, or the words so assembled. It is a trap, but an oriented trap.

It is true, of course, that an equation is an object which has no function other than that of signifying. Nevertheless, its structure remains entirely analyzable and reducible to its elements which are susceptible of being grouped in other ways—as the equal sign shows—without destroying the signification: which is not the case with the work of art.

It is true that a machine may very well fascinate us, or even a face, or a waterfall. However, these objects were not made for this purpose—for this alone, by the deliberate act of man.

But if, in searching for the nature of the work of art, I define it as a *calculated trap for meditation,* we see that the understanding of its nature is tied up with that of its end: a trap is made in order to capture something. In the work of art, nature and aim, essence and end, are inseparable. It is a question of a single and identical function, which is, to signify something by sensible means.

II

It will perhaps be thought that I am holding beauty rather cheaply in all this, and that my definitions will run counter to some classical definitions in much the same way as they run counter to our current and commonplace ideas. In fact, there are those who insist that beauty should be the aim of art, and that the proper function of the artist should be that of "creating beauty," as it is said. I confess that I am not at all sure about this. And I will make, on this point, three remarks of unequal importance.

The first is a simple statement of fact that I throw into the discussion without presuming to judge it. *The principal artists of our epoch,* such as Picasso or Braque, Joyce or Kafka, Stravinsky, T. S. Eliot or André Breton, *do not try to make beauty,* and without any doubt they will refuse to say that beauty is the aim of their work.

Whether the work be beautiful or ugly, charming or odious, for sense and spirit it matters little: their aim is to express or to describe realities at any cost, and even at the price of ugliness, if necessary. The academic artists alone, the false artists, still try to make something "beautiful or flattering."

My second remark is of a much more serious nature. It seems to me that "beauty" *is not a biblical notion or term.* The Scriptures speak to us of truth, justice, freedom, and love, but very little or not at all of beauty. They do not tell us that God is Beauty, but that God is Love. Neither does Christ say that He is the Beauty, but that He is the Way, the Truth, and the Life. This way is not beautiful, but rough and painful. The truth is not beautiful, but liberating. This life does not open into beautiful harmonies, but passes by the narrow gate of death.

Is it necessary to think, as one has written, that in the Bible there is a question of a "terrible lacuna"? A lacuna which the Greek ideal would have filled through amalgamating itself into the Christian tradition, then distinguishing itself anew at the time of the Renaissance? Or must we, on the contrary, ask ourselves whether our notion of beauty is not subject to serious revision?

Finally, my third remark, which is entirely independent of the first two, will take the form of a confession. I find myself incapable of making any use of the *concept* of beauty in itself. Obviously, it happens that as frequently as anyone else I exclaim, "How beautiful it is!"—before the most varied things, such as a landscape or a building, a human being or a work of art, an airplane, a sporting exploit, a fruit, an heroic act, a sentiment. . . . But this enumeration, by virtue of its heteroclitic character, shows that beauty is not a specific property of the work of art. We can describe anything as beautiful. It is a subjective qualification, a term convenient but vague, an exclamation. If I exclaim that a work is beautiful, it is easy to see that this "beauty" which I attribute to it resolves itself upon analysis into very diverse realities. In saying, "how beautiful it is!" I wish to say, I ought to say, "How well it is made!" "How true are its proportions!" "How much more free or strong one feels for having seen this!" "How it excites the passions, or is of inexhaustible interest!" or simply, "How I love it!" because one calls, "beautiful," whatever one loves with intensity. Thus, after all, behind the word, "beauty," we find again justice, or truth, or freedom, or love.

To put by the Greek concept of beauty, is not, therefore, to deny art. To declare that the Bible scarcely speaks of beauty, is not for a single instant to say that the Bible excludes art; and, similarly, to state that the modern artists do not seek beauty in itself and primarily, does not signify that they are bad artists. Very much to the contrary, all this is tantamount to saying that art is something other than a search for beauty, and that those who make a work of art assign to themselves a very different aim.

I believe that the aim (conscious or not) of all true art is to make objects which signify; therefore, it is to make one attentive to the meaning of the world and of life.

Naturally, what the artist succeeds in signifying does not need to be understood by him prior to the work itself. There is not first of all a certain meaning, and then afterward a determination to illustrate it by a work. But rather it is by the work, and in it alone, that a certain meaning manifests or reveals itself. The critics or the public, or sometimes the artist himself, will try afterward to "disengage" this sense, and to isolate it from the work by an effort of translation or abstraction. But in reality the meaning is tied to each detail, just as it is tied to the work as a whole—if it is good—and it truly exists only within it. If it were possible to express this meaning by some other means, the work would lose its *raison d'être*.

We will qualify, therefore, as a "great work," that work which commands attention the most imperiously and for the longest time, that which carries farthest man's meditation upon his destiny and upon the order of things. And we shall call "lasting," that work which will play its role as a trap most efficaciously for many generations and peoples. The current expressions, "I have been captured by this work," or "It is very taking," appear to me accurate and revealing, from this point of view.

III

If such, then, is the nature and end of the work of art, we may now consider under what conditions an artist is able to fulfill his particular mission.

There are two things that I should like to indicate at the outset and in the simplest manner possible: the artist fulfils his mission

(1) in so far as he is a good *craftsman*

(2) in so far as his works *signify* in an efficacious manner.

Which calls, naturally, for some explication.

The good craftsman is he who has a mastery over his means, who follows well the rules of his particular game, who, in short, constructs, exactly and craftily, his traps for the sensibility, reflection, and imagination. Let us call all this—that is, the ensemble of the processes of the craft and the rules of composition—*rhetoric*. This is the part of the "artificer," artificial *and* skillful at the same time. But it is precisely respect for the skills, the love of their proper uses and their laws, which from the outset distinguishes the true artist from the amateur—any person who feels himself inspired or moved, and thinks he can replace rhetoric with sincerity. I am not certain whether it is Laforgue or Valéry who has written: "The bourgeois are those who believe that there is something in the world more important than a convention." Or let us cite Baudelaire: "It is clear that the rhetoric and the prosodies are not arbitrarily contrived tyrannies, but a collection of rules required by the organization of spiritual being itself, and at no time have the prosodies and rhetorics prevented originality from putting itself forward distinctly. On the contrary, to understand how they helped in the hatching of originality would be infinitely more true."

Sincerity has scarcely any import in art. It certainly has none when it is a question of the craft of the artist, because this craft is, by definition, made up of artifices. On this point the moderns have committed a strange error, when, after Romanticism and some of its byproducts, they have believed that they must betake themselves, as they say, "to the school of Nature," and so accept no longer any guide other than sincerity, or even naiveté. I put it as a fact, that a man possessed by the need to express himself, or to express something by means of a work of art, is absolutely incapable of expressing sincerely what he wants to express, unless he has first of all mastered his rhetoric. When Jean-Paul Sartre gives his disciples the precept of not "writing," that is to say, of explaining oneself it matters not how and without trying to "write well," he gives the formula for modern philistinism, and deprives his disciples all the more of the means for really expressing their message. Let us remark also, *a propos* of this term "message" which we especially abuse—and not only in Christian surroundings—that it is impossible "to deliver a message," in so far as we have not mastered its means of expression to the point of being able to adapt them, to make them serve, to orient them—and this even unto the least detail—in the direction and according to the *sense* of that which we wish to communicate. To express a message of truth, but "no matter how," is almost certainly to express something altogether different from the message in question—*i.e.,* the disorder of language, the absence of inner coherence, and finally, non-truth itself. It is to forget that what we first of all perceive in the work of art are the means—the words, the colors, or the forms, the sounds and their rapports or groupings. To be sure, even if one knew all the rules of the game and if one applied them with care, one could never be sure of winning; in other words, the artist is never *sure* that the public perceives truly what he has wished to say—but at least it is necessary to make the odds in his favor.

Of course it is possible to object that the public perceives in a work, first of all, not the technical means in themselves, but rather the author's style. If I have not mentioned style as the third condition whereby the artist fulfils his mission, it is because in my view the style is born of the conflict between the first condition—the craft, the means—and the second—that which the artist wishes to signify, the message. If there is no style in a work, it is because there is no drama between the means of expression and that which one wishes to express, between technique and signification, between rhetoric and message. And if there is no drama, it is because one of the two terms is strongly deficient, or even absent. In the latter case there would then be no *art* properly so-called. There is only an almost empty form—and that is academicism—or a formless message, and that is the daily communication, without art, precisely. Or further: if the means are not put in question (or to the question) by a very exacting signification, one will fall into what we call "pure rhetoric," into eloquence and formalism. If, on the other hand, the signification that one wishes to express is too intense and imperious for the means at our command, we shall fall into obscurity, or into an inarticulate cry.

Let us come then to the second condition—the signification, or the message.

On this point I will be brief and will limit myself to a few formulas. I think that an artist (it being granted that he is a good craftsman) fulfils his mission, in proportion as his work elicits in the spectators, readers, or hearers, a sense of liberation; manifests the true, that is to say, renders a truth sensible; evokes the order of the world of the laws of man's destiny; builds or reveals the structures in the sensations, imagination, ideas; and finally, induces to greater love.

A single remark upon this point: it is evident that a classical work of art, a work of Bach, for example, creates order in man, evokes the order of the world, renders its laws comprehensible and even lovable. But some entirely different works, which seem to have no purpose other than that of evoking the present disorder, chaos, and absurdity, the "sound and fury" of a tale "signifying nothing" —I am thinking of certain parts of Joyce's work, or *The Waste Land* of T. S. Eliot, or the stories of Faulkner, the painting of Picasso—these works, dialectically, nostalgically, in revolt and defiance, carry still a witness to the lost order of the world—because art, all art worthy of the name, never has had and never can have any other object.

Such being the two conditions which an artist must fulfil to be equal to his mission, it becomes clear that criticism, the evaluation of the works of art, ought, on the one hand, to bear upon the skill and the means, and, on the other, upon the meaning and the value of the realities bribed and revealed by those means. That is to say, criticism ought to be at one and the same time *technical,* on the one hand, and on the other metaphysical or ethical—which is to say, in the end, *theological.*

IV

I realize full well that in speaking of a theological criticism of the works of art, I shall shock not only the great majority of my contemporaries, on the public side, and some artists, but also the theologians. The latter will say that it is not their business, that they must occupy themselves with the dogmas of the Church. With that I agree. Note that I do not say that this theological criticism would necessarily be the business of the theologians. They are often badly prepared by a strongly didactic turn of mind—most of them are saddled with some teaching obligation—and in that particular case it is a question of developing first of all a power of comprehension, and of nourishing it with a living experience of art. But perhaps one may propose that those who devote themselves to the criticism of art—and every artist more or less is of this number—might at least make an effort to go beyond the stage of a total lack of theological culture where we see them today.

It is within this perspective that I am going to run the risk of suggesting neither a scale of judgment, nor a doctrine, nor a canon for the arts, but a theme for meditation which perhaps would be of such a nature as better to sustain and to justify the judgments which one brings to bear upon works of art—and this, through making ourselves more attentive to the spiritual situation of the artist.

What does the artist really do, after all? In the exaggerated language which we have inherited from Romanticism, without reflecting at all upon the import of the words, we customarily say in the twentieth century

(1) that the artist *creates*
(2) that he *incarnates* in his works certain realities
(3) that he *is inspired.*

I say again, these three verbs are used improperly, and deserve justly the greatest severity on the part of the theologians. But the exorbitant misuse itself suggests a possibility of faithful and sober usage. The three everyday verbs that I have just cited—to create, to incarnate, to inspire—irresistibly evoke the attributes of the Holy Trinity.

If we are able to say of the artist that he creates, it is not merely the consequence of a Promethean or Luciferian overestimate of the human powers. In composing with what he has learned from the world, and with that which he is internally, a work external to himself, man imitates symbolically the act of the Creator forming the world and forming Adam. And certainly we must question whether this human work adds anything to the world, in spite of the fact that it is something which was not here before. Man is only able to rearrange that which God has created *ex nihilo.* But in the artist's love for the work which he detaches from himself—not in the work in itself—there is a parable of the fatherly action, an attempt to love the creation as the Father has loved it.

Why has God separated the world from Himself? Why and how does He love it? In what way is this object of His love distinct from Him, and what autonomy does it enjoy? These questions and many analogous ones arise and fix themselves in the mind which pauses before the mystery of the First Person. Thus, to meditate upon the mystery of the Father, would be to lead at one and the same time to the best understanding of the act of the artist, and to its limits or its relativity.

In the second place, we have seen that the artist, in composing a work of art, tends to signify something which would not be perceptible otherwise. Let us not say that he incarnates a reality, for it is not a question of the flesh. But he renders this reality intelligible, legible, audible, by physical means. What takes place then, from the side of the spectator, the reader, the auditor? It happens that the expression veils that which is expressed, while manifesting it at the same time to our senses. Because that which is expressed is not separable from the means of expression, or is so by abuse only. That which reveals is at the same time that which conceals. The meaning of a picture, for example, is not distinct from the colors, forms, proportions, and style, by which, but also in which, it exists. It is possible, therefore, to see them and not to see it. In the eyes of reason the means remain essentially heterogeneous to the reality which they express—why those and not some others?—and yet we would know nothing of it without them. . . . I do not press the matter. I am obliged here to limit myself to indicating the possible point of departure of a dialectic which would find its model, and perhaps its norms, in the doctrine of the Second Person of the Trinity, and in a meditation on its mystery.

In the third place, the artist is currently credited with being inspired. The most determined adversaries of Romanticism, such as Valéry, have never denied that the primitive impulsion of a work of art might be a "gift of the gods"—a single verse, for example, or the vision of a form, on which the operations of the technique afterward develop themselves. The inspiration, whether it operates at each moment or whether it intervenes only at the start and in a single instant, is an undeniable fact of experience. But from whence does it come? What Paul Valéry calls "the gods," without compromising himself, would be for certain other people the Holy Spirit, and for others still a message from the unconscious. Sometimes, we imagine that this instantaneous vision has revealed in a lightning flash the existence of a secret way, which it remains only to follow; and sometimes we have the impression that we invent the way while advancing upon it. This problem, let us observe, torments not only the artist, but also, and more consciously still, the physicist of today. Do I invent, he says to himself, or is it rather that I discover a reality? Do I project into the cosmos the forms of my spirit, or is it rather that I espouse by the spirit some of the objective forms of the real? And the man who receives a call sometimes subsists in this doubt to the point of anguish. Do I surrender to some obscure determination of my desire, or is it rather that I really respond to a summons received from somewhere else? Where does the voice come from? Who speaks? Myself, or the Other? Such is the predicament which the intervention of the Holy Spirit creates in man.

Once again it is my purpose here merely to suggest some possible direction for thought. I limit myself to submitting this notion: that Christian meditation upon the act and the work of the artist can deepen, inform, and instruct itself within the framework of a meditation upon the doctrine and mystery of the Trinity; and that Christian meditation will find in the vocabulary and dialectical arguments employed for nearly twenty centuries by trinitarian theologians the whole of a theory which introduces us better than any other to the human mysteries of the act of art.

I will add one last suggestion. We know that the greater part of the heresies have resulted in interpretations sometimes excessive and sometimes deficient in some particular point of trinitarian doctrine. May we believe that the deviations or excesses represented by such or such an artistic school reflect these heresies, or perhaps come from them, unknown even to those who represent them? And would we not have there the principle for a theological critique of the development of the arts? It is certain that if this were the case, we should be able at last to go beyond the stage of arbitrary judgments upon tastes and colors, or upon the import, moral or not, of the works of art, judgments which are based ordinarily upon the mode of the day before yesterday, or upon bourgeois prudence, or upon a revolt against them. It seems to me that some attempts along this line would be worth the labor of the risk—and by laymen first of all.

V

By way of conclusion, I shall try to summarize in two sentences the conception of art which I hold and upon which the preceding pages are based.

Art is an exercise of the whole being of man, not to compete with God, but to coincide better with the order of Creation, to love it better, and to reestablish ourselves in it. Thus art would appear to be like an invocation (more often than not unconscious) to the lost harmony, like a prayer (more often than not confused), corresponding to the second petition of the Lord's prayer—"Thy Kingdom come."

W. H. Auden

Postscript: Christianity and Art*

ART IS COMPATIBLE with polytheism and with Christianity, but not with philosophical materialism; science is compatible with philosophical materialism and with Christianity, but not with polytheism. No artist or scientist, however, can feel comfortable as a Christian; every artist who happens also to be a Christian wishes he could be a polytheist; every scientist in the same position that he could be a philosophical materialist. And with good reason. In a polytheist society, the artists are its theologians; in a materialist society, its theologians are the scientists. To a Christian, unfortunately, both art and science are secular activities, that is to say, small beer.

No artist, qua artist, can understand what is meant by *God is Love* or *Thou shalt love thy neighbor* because he doesn't care whether God and men are loving or unloving; no scientist, qua scientist, can understand what is meant because he doesn't care whether to-be-loving is a matter of choice or a matter of compulsion.

To the imagination, the sacred is self-evident. It is as meaningless to ask whether one believes or disbelieves in Aphrodite or Ares as to ask whether one believes in a character in a novel; one can only say that one finds them true or untrue to life. To believe in Aphrodite and Ares merely means that one believes that the

* From *The Dyer's Hand,* by W. H. Auden. © Copyright 1962 by W. H. Auden. Reprinted by permission of Random House.

poetic myths about them do justice to the forces of sex and aggression as human beings experience them in nature and their own lives. That is why it is possible for an archaeologist who digs up a statuette of a god or goddess to say with fair certainty what kind of divinity it represents.

Similarly, to the imagination, the godlike or heroic man is self-evident. He does extraordinary deeds that the ordinary man cannot do, or extraordinary things happen to him.

The Incarnation, the coming of Christ in the form of a servant who cannot be recognized by the eye of flesh and blood, but only by the eye of faith, puts an end to all claims of the imagination to be the faculty which decides what is truly sacred and what is profane. A pagan god can appear on earth in disguise but, so long as he wears his disguise, no man is expected to recognize him nor can. But Christ appears looking just like any other man, yet claims that He is the Way, the Truth and the Life, and that no man can come to God the Father except through Him. The contradiction between the profane appearance and the sacred assertion is impassible to the imagination.

It is impossible to represent Christ on the stage. If he is made dramatically interesting, he ceases to be Christ and turns into a Hercules or a Svengali. Nor is it really possible to represent him in the visual arts for, if he were visually recognizable, he would be a god of the pagan kind. The best the painter can do is to paint either the Bambino with the Madonna or the dead Christ on the cross, for every baby and every corpse seem to be both individual and universal, *the* baby, *the* corpse. But neither a baby nor a corpse can say *I am the Way,* etc.

To a Christian, the godlike man is not the hero who does extraordinary deeds, but the holy man, the saint, who does good deeds. But the gospel defines a good deed as one done in secret, hidden, so far as it is possible, even from the doer, and forbids private prayer and fasting in public. This means that art, which by its nature can only deal with what can and should be manifested, cannot portray a saint.

There can no more be a "Christian" art than there can be a Christian science or a Christian diet. There can only be a Christian spirit in which an artist, a scientist, works or does not work. A painting of the Crucifixion is not necessarily more Christian in spirit than a still life, and may very well be less.

I sometimes wonder if there is not something a bit questionable, from a Christian point of view, about all works of art which make overt Christian references. They seem to assert that there is such a thing as a Christian culture, which there cannot be. Culture is one of Caesar's things. One cannot help noticing that the great period of "religious" painting coincided with the period when the Church was a great temporal power.

The only kind of literature which has gospel authority is the parable, and parables are secular stories with no overt religious reference.

There are many hymns I like as one likes old song hits, because, for me, they have sentimental associations, but the only hymns I find poetically tolerable are either versified dogma or Biblical ballads.

Poems, like many of Donne's and Hopkins', which express a poet's personal feelings of religious devotion or penitence, make me uneasy. It is quite in order that a poet should write a sonnet expressing his devotion to Miss Smith because the poet, Miss Smith, and all his readers know perfectly well that, had he chanced to fall in love with Miss Jones instead, his feelings would be exactly the same. But if he writes a sonnet expressing his devotion to Christ, the important point, surely, is that his devotion is felt for Christ and not for, say, Buddha or Mahomet, and this point cannot be made in poetry; the Proper Name proves nothing. A penitential poem is even more questionable. A poet must intend his poem to be a good one, that is to say, an enduring object for other people to admire. Is there not something a little odd, to say the least, about making an admirable public object out of one's feelings of guilt and penitence before God?

A poet who calls himself a Christian cannot but feel uncomfortable when he realizes that the New Testament contains no verse (except in the apochryphal, and gnostic, *Acts of John*), only prose. As Rudolf Kassner has pointed out:

> The difficulty about the God-man for the poet lies in the Word being made Flesh. This means that reason and imagination are one. But does not Poetry, as such, live from there being a gulf between them?
>
> What gives us so clear a notion of this as metre, verse measures? In the magical-mythical world, metre was sacred, so was the strophe, the line, the words in the line, the letters. The poets were prophets.
>
> That the God-man did not write down his words himself or show the slightest concern that they should be written down in letters, brings us back to the Word made Flesh.
>
> Over against the metrical structures of the poets stand the Gospel parables in prose, over against magic a freedom which finds its limits within itself, is itself limit, over against poetic fiction (*Dichtung*), pointing to and interpreting fact (*Deutung*). (*Die Geburt Christi.*)

I hope there is an answer to this objection, but I don't know what it is.

The imagination is a natural human faculty and therefore retains the same character whatever a man believes. The only difference can be in the way that he interprets its data. At all times and in all places, certain objects, beings and events arouse in his imagination a feeling of sacred awe, while other objects, beings and events leave his imagination unmoved. But a Christian cannot say, as a polytheist can: "All before which my imagination feels sacred awe is sacred-in-itself, and all which leaves it unmoved is profane-in-itself." There are two possible interpretations a Christian can make, both of them, I believe, orthodox, but each leaning towards a heresy. Either he can say, leaning towards Neoplatonism: "That which arouses in me a feeling of sacred awe is a channel through which, to me as an individual and as a member of a certain culture, the sacred which I cannot perceive directly is revealed to me." Or he can say, leaning towards pantheism: "All objects, beings and events are sacred but, because of my individual and cultural limitations, my imagination can only recognize these ones." Speaking for myself, I would rather, if I must be a heretic, be condemned as a pantheist than as a Neoplatonist.

In our urbanized industrial society, nearly everything we see and hear is so aggressively ugly or emphatically banal that it is difficult for a modern artist, unless he can flee to the depths of the country and never open a newspaper, to prevent his imagination from acquiring a Manichaean cast, from *feeling,* whatever his religious convictions to the contrary, that the physical world is utterly profane or the abode of demons. However sternly he reminds himself that the material universe is the creation of God and found good by Him, his mind is haunted by images of physical disgust, cigarette butts in a half-finished sardine can, a toilet that won't flush, etc.

Still, things might be worse. If an artist can no longer put on sacred airs, he has gained his personal artistic liberty instead. So long as an activity is regarded as being of sacred importance, it is controlled by notions of orthodoxy. When art is sacred, not only are there orthodox subjects which every artist is expected to treat and unorthodox subjects which no artist may treat, but also orthodox styles of treatment which must not be violated. But, once art becomes a secular activity, every artist is free to treat whatever subject excites his imagination, and in any stylistic manner which he feels appropriate.

We cannot have any liberty without license to abuse it. The secularization of art enables the really gifted artist to develop his talents to the full; it also permits those with little or no talent to produce vast quantities of phony or vulgar trash. When one looks into the window of a store which sells devotional art objects, one can't help wishing the iconoclasts had won.

For artists, things may very well get worse and, in large areas of the world, already have.

So long as science regards itself as a secular activity, materialism is not a doctrine but a useful empirical hypothesis. A scientist, qua scientist, does not need, when investigating physical nature, to bother his head with ontological or teleological questions any more than an artist, qua artist, has to bother about what his feelings of sacred awe may ultimately signify.

As soon, however, as materialism comes to be regarded as sacred truth, the distinction between the things of God and the things of Caesar is re-abolished. But the world of sacred materialism is very different from the world of sacred polytheism. Under polytheism, everything in life was, ultimately, frivolous, so that the pagan world was a morally tolerant world—far too tolerant, for it tolerated many evils, like slavery and the exposure of infants, which should not be tolerated. It tolerated them, not because it did not know that they were evil, but because it did not believe that the gods were necessarily good. (No Greek, for example, ever defended slavery, as slave owners in the Southern States defended it, on the grounds that their slaves were happier as slaves than they would be as freemen. On the contrary, they argued that the slave must be subhuman because, otherwise, he would have killed himself rather than endure life as a slave.)

But, under religious materialism, everything in life is, ultimately, serious, and therefore subject to moral policing. It will not tolerate what it knows to be evil with a heartless shrug—that is how life is, always has been and always will be—but it will do something which the pagan world never did; it will do what it knows to be evil for a moral purpose, do it deliberately now so that good may come in the future.

Under religious materialism, the artist loses his personal artistic liberty again, but he does not recover his sacred importance, for now it is not artists who collectively decide what is sacred truth, but scientists, or rather the scientific politicians, who are responsible for keeping mankind in the true faith. Under them, an artist becomes a mere technician, an expert in effective expression, who is hired to express effectively what the scientific politician requires to be said.

Part II

THE NATURE OF THE CHRISTIAN VISION

Malcolm Ross

The Writer as Christian*

WE HAVE BEEN HEARING a good deal lately about *a Christian revival in literature.* Clearly poets like T. S. Eliot, W. H. Auden, and the late Dylan Thomas, novelists like Mauriac, Bernanos, and Graham Greene—to mention only the better known names—constitute a unique constellation, a constellation which took shape slowly and is only now being observed for what it is. These writers are Christian writers, in the exact sense. They are not merely Christians who happen to write. Their art is consciously dedicated to the realization of a specifically Christian vision of reality.

This is not to say, of course, that a writer steeped in Freud or Einstein or Sir James Frazer is therefore not a Christian writer. Christian art at its highest has never been, in the exclusive sense, pure. It is quite possible that a Christian today might find almost as much use for Freud and Einstein as St. Thomas Aquinas once found for the pagan Aristotle. W. H. Auden is a fine example of the capacity of the Christian artist in our time to digest and to employ the findings of the new psychology. T. S. Eliot's Christian universe is compounded, among other things, of the new anthropology and the new physics. I would even say that it is precisely this capacity to meet, to grasp and to put in order the magnificent chaos of secular thought which characterizes a genuinely Christian art in our time or in any other time.

* Reprinted from *Faculty Papers* with the kind permission of the author and The National Council of the Episcopal Church.

It is necessary, however, to distinguish the specifically Christian ordering of experience in art from that literature of mythic religiosity now so prevalent. For there are literary critics who will pin the label "religious," and even "Christian," on any work of art which is not incarcerated within the sheer four walls of a materialistic determinism. Nowadays if any man so much as guess out loud that mysteries may lie beyond the range of telescope and microscope, he is acclaimed at once as a seer, mystic, prophet, saint.

And the conventional literary historian, trained in the fine art of reducing everything to neat categories, movements, patterns, schools, types, has, by his very method, helped to obliterate the real distinctions which must be observed between a specifically Christian literature and that undogmatic religiosity of feeling and vision so common in current writing.

True, it is no longer easy to isolate the specifically Christian work. No serious writer is able any longer, surely, to work within the limits of a flat naturalism. Even radical social change no longer seems enough to satisfy the artist's thirst for meaning or his craving for security. He has come to seek a metaphysical rather than a merely sociological kind of security. His sense of the mystery of the universe has deepened. So has his sense of the mystery of selfhood. He is no longer comforted when he says to himself, "I think, therefore I am." He is anxious. His little umbrella of science no longer protects him against what seems to be the unpremeditated, unpredictable storm of being. This, precisely this, is the human situation as it is revealed in the lightning flash of our moment in time. The Christian writer today must be fully aware of just this situation, just this predicament.

It is in terms of final ends that we must draw our distinction between a Christian and a non-Christian art. In his pursuit of the mystery the Christian artist will use every means at his disposal. He is not afraid to look into the subconscious world of desire and myth. He is not disturbed by Frazer's dying corn god; nor is he dismayed by the time-space concept of Einstein. The universe of Einstein will serve him as well now as the Ptolemaic universe once served him. The Christian has come to know symbolic knowledge for what it is. And he can use it.

The Basic Distinction

The basic distinction between the Christian and the non-Christian religious artist in our time lies just here. The Christian is able or should be able to use the new symbols provided him by physics, anthropology, psychology. The non-Christian is used by these symbols. And it is just this point of distinction which the literary historian so often misses. For instance, Professor William Tindall, in his book *Forces in Modern British Literature,* has a chapter which he calls "The Hunt for the Father." The Freudian notion that all religion, and religiosity, is nothing else but the sublimated need for symbols of parental authority and protection is made here to apply equally to Eliot, Auden, Yeats, Joyce, Lawrence, Kafka— and even to George Bernard Shaw. By this elastic formula, authentic Christianity is equated with various degrees of jungle myth, the Lamarckian theory of creative evolution, with all forms of idealism, and even, in the case of James Joyce, with a forthright if painful rejection of Christianity.

Now it is true that in all these writers one may detect degrees of religious impulse and feeling. In only two of them, Eliot and Auden, is the specifically Christian note to be found. By different paths Lawrence and Shaw arrive at a kind of nature worship, the adoration of the blood-stream or the life force, as the case may be. Yeats concocts his own myth from many diverse elements. But the mythology of Yeats is an alternative to Christianity, just as William Blake's mythology was an alternative to Christianity, just as Huxley's romantic Hinduism is an alternative to Christianity.

A Christian writer like Eliot, as anxious as any of his contemporaries to break through the naturalistic surfaces to deeper levels of knowledge and experience, can afford, as these others do, to exploit the primitive myth, the content of the dream, the symbols of physics or of theosophy, and yet be able to create an art which is radically different from the art of Yeats, or Lawrence, or Kafka, or Joyce. Why? What distinguishes the symbol-making of the Christian artist from the symbol-making of these others?

Christianity is a dogmatic religion. It demands a certain precision of belief. Christian art bears the stamp of dogma. Not in any obvious way, however; and that the Christian artist is not enslaved, is not driven to any flat conformity seems quite evident when you remember that writers as different from each other as Dante and Chaucer and Milton and Dostoievski and Eliot are Christian writers. The Christian artist has worked in wholly disparate cultural moments. Because he created the Gothic style he is not therefore a Gothic artist. Later he created the baroque. The fact is that the Christian tradition is the charitable captor of all traditions. It is all things to all men. It cannot, therefore, be defined in terms of its externals. Any definition by externals would miss entirely the fertile and chameleon-like freedom of Christian art.

The central dogma of Christianity is the dogma of the Incarnation. In this dogma, respecting as it does both the divinity of the Word and the humanity of the flesh, is contained the whole principle of the Christian aesthetic. The implications of this are endless. Certainly some of them are these: While the flesh is frail, and while nature itself has suffered the wound of sin, the Incarnation redeems the flesh and the world, laying nature and reason open once more to the supernatural. In other words, the Incarnation creates the sacramental vision of reality. The flesh, the world, things are restored to dignity because they are made valid. Existence becomes a drama which, no matter how painful it still may be, is nevertheless meaningful. No detail in the drama is without its wholly unique reality. No thing is insignificant.

The Christian Symbol Is Historical

Not only is the dogma of the Incarnation sacramental in its implications for the artist's knowledge of nature. It is also sacramental in its implications for history. As all serious students of the subject have noted, the Christian symbol is inevitably historical. Nothing distinguishes the Christian aesthetic so sharply from the aesthetic of the modern Freudian myth-maker as Christianity's insistence on the historical. The Incarnation occurs in time. It reveals the action of God in history. Pagan myth is never historical but cosmic—a kind of natural revelation. It commemorates the harvest, the alternation of the seasons, the desires and fears of man naked in the grip of natural forces. The dying corn god who is born again in spring belongs to this order of myth. But for the Christian, the death and resurrection of Christ is not a cosmic myth. It is an historical event, which, however, absorbs sacramentally the cosmic into the historical. Thus Easter absorbs into its structure the rebirth of nature in spring, the ancient Jewish feast of the Passover with all its sense of the role of Providence in history, and the resurrection of Christ which completes history by defining its end. In short, Christianity absorbs the cosmic, the biological, and the psychological myth into the historical symbol. Yet each level of meaning in the new pattern retains its own uniqueness, its own proper truth. For the artist, then, the symbolism of Christianity is an assurance of wholeness.

I have, of course, been describing the essence of Christian art at its height and in its depth. In any approach to the contemporary Christian revival one must be aware simultaneously of the authentic sacramental Christian tradition and of the wounding of that tradition at its very heart by both Reformation and Counter-Reformation. The wound is not easily healed. Nor can the Christian writer any longer proceed as though there had been no wound *or* as though nothing since the wound has been valid and in health. Whether he be Catholic or Protestant the contemporary Christian writer is forced to take account of the break in his own tradition and also of the brilliant and vital growth of secular traditions which may seem to be, but intrinsically are not, alien to his own.

Let us admit that with Protestantism there occurred in poetry an abdication of the physical and natural order, a retreat to "the

Paradise within" which by the twentieth century was a paradise swarming with serpents. Its symbol is no longer the tree of knowledge but the psychoanalyst's couch. But surely there were gains, too, in all this. Man's knowledge of himself has deepened. And while it is true that Protestantism delivered nature to the naturalist it is also true that nature was thereby opened to enquiry as it never had been before. On the other hand, Catholicism, forced back on the defensive by the double assault of the Reformation and the new science, while able to conserve sacramental dogma as dogma, was, until recently, unable to insert this dogma persuasively either in the natural order or in the social order. For if Protestantism abandoned sacramentalism in principle it is, I think, fair to say that Catholicism for a long while and to a large extent abandoned it in practice. Sacramentalism is an act—not just an idea about an act. It is an act which seeks to universalize itself. Nor is it properly an act in support of obsolete forms of knowledge or of obsolete forms of political and social organization. One clear piece of evidence for the view that Catholicism did not always act sacramentally at the level of history is the famous papal statement that the tragedy of the nineteenth century was the loss of the working class to the Church.

The Essence of Christian Art

If sacramentalism is the life of Christian art, and I think it is, its cultivation in our time must be made strenuous. If Christian art is to be wholly revelant today it must not be merely pious. Above all it must not be archaic, yearning nostalgically for the ages of faith. Is there anything more emblematic of retreat and even of defeat than the construction in the twentieth century of a Gothic church? (As though to engage in Christian worship one should withdraw into a distant age and shun the skills, the materials, the medium of this time and this place!) For a sacramentalist, surely, a new Gothic church is irrelevant. And it is therefore almost irreverent.

A fully sacramental Christianity must be able to penetrate and reinfuse the historical order—not as it was, not as it might have been if there had been no Renaissance, no Reformation, no French revolution, no class struggle—but the historical order as it is, as it has actually become.

The Chaos of Secularism

If secularism has brought about chaos, let us at least admit that this is a magnificent chaos! And if knowledge is indeed to be re-ordered again by Christianity, let us admit that no scrap or particle of knowledge can be ignored or dismissed. For sacramentalism must seek to take into itself its very opposite—it can have no op-posite—it can exclude nothing. Even the spiritual, intellectual, and aesthetic fruits of the Protestant revolt against the sacramental principle must be sacramentally possessed, or there is no sacra-mentalism. The whole literature of interior spiritual struggle from Bunyan to Kafka must be repossessed. Nothing must be wasted.

The test I would make of the contemporary Christian revival in letters is a simple one. It is this: Assuming that this new Christian literature is dogmatically Christian—which it is—is it fully rele-vant? If it turns out to be nothing more than pious paper Gothic it is worth very little indeed.

I think the relevance of contemporary Christian literature must be considered not only in terms of the idiom in which the Chris-tian writer addresses us but also in terms of the actual dilemma of modern man. What, using the word in its broadest sense, char-acterizes modern secular culture? Pre-eminently two things: frag-mentation and alienation. Never as now has man known so much about the workings of nature. And yet the very science by which he knows nature threatens to destroy him. Never as now has man known so much about the workings of the self. But what he has come to know frightens him. Never as now has man known so much about the workings of society. But he is lost in society, overwhelmed by it. The diabolical newspaper headline has for him now the same fatalistic force as the muttering of the witchdoctor once had for the most primitive savage. In short, modern man feels himself to be separate from, alienated from the universe. He feels separate from, alienated from himself. And thus he is, genuinely, beside himself. The universe, the society, the self—these have all become objects of knowledge, alien to each other and alien to the knower. The situation is the very reverse of the sacramental knowledge of reality. It is a situation which has been described before—many times. The point is, how is it to be corrected?

It is precisely to this situation that contemporary Christian art must address itself if it is to be relevant, if it is to be, in the deepest sense, Christian. One must recognize at once that such a situation presents enormous technical and semantic difficulties for the Christian artist. The long process of fragmentation and alienation that has gone on in our culture for over two hundred years has been destructive not only of the sacramental world-view but of the very language in which the Christian sense of reality was expressed. The traditional frame of reference within which the Christian poet once worked has largely vanished. Milton could count on his readers knowing the Scriptures. In the seventeenth century no man of twenty years would guess, as a student of mine recently guessed, that Moses was the husband of the Virgin Mary! And as late as Crashaw and Herbert, Catholic and Anglican poets could count on their readers knowing the shape and the substance of the liturgy of the Church, with all its wealth of image and symbol.

It has been generally observed that one of the difficulties of a poem like T. S. Eliot's *Ash Wednesday* is this: Eliot here depends for his most significant effects upon an understanding of liturgy and ecclesiasticism not possessed in our day by any save professional Churchmen and scholars. The poem may indeed communicate without being understood. Any sensitive reader of poetry, I think, is aware of the intensity and the integrity of this poem. Nevertheless it is paper Gothic, although a very superior kind of paper Gothic. The way of the Christian artist nowadays cannot be this way. A sacramental re-entry into the experience, the knowledge, the sensibility of our time can scarcely be effected by any effort, however fervent, to restore a Christian idiom appropriate to another and vastly different cultural moment. No one has realized this more sharply than Mr. Eliot himself. In the *Four Quartets* this kind of difficulty is in large part overcome. As Miss Helen Gardner has pointed out, while the *Four Quartets* abounds in liturgical images and allusions these are used to deepen and enrich effects already articulated by other means. This is not paper Gothic. The building is modern, functional. And yet it retains, without being at all archaic, cross, candle, incense.

Four Quartets

The great achievement of Eliot's *Four Quartets* is, of course, in the sacramental re-possession of nature and time, things, and history. In these poems the sacramental act is consummated through, and by means of, contemporary sensibility and contemporary knowledge. Mr. Eliot is fully aware, for instance, of the distinction we must now make between clock time and the baffling interior time of the stream of consciousness which cannot be measured at all by the tick of the clock. He is aware, too, of the idea of the continuum, of the sense we now have of reality as a flow, a stream without beginning or end. In these poems the concepts of beginning and end become concepts of value, purpose, destiny, rather than merely chronological concepts. And the intuition of eternity is made to possess and to illuminate the personal and the historical levels of the time process. In the *Four Quartets,* then, Eliot seeks to bring back into a pattern of meaning nature, history, the person. In *Dry Salvages*, the third of the *Four Quartets,* you get a fine illustration of the recovery of authentic Christian symbol. The river and sea of this poem are actual river and sea. You could get wet in them, you could drown in them. They exist in their own unique right. Was there ever a keener sense of salt water than here:

> The whine in the rigging,
> The menace and caress of wave that breaks on
> water

> The distant rote in the granite teeth
> And the wailing warning from the approaching
>   headland
> . . . .
> And under the oppression of the silent fog
> The tolling bell . . .

Yet this is not descriptive nature poetry; this is not Masefield. In Eliot the river is a river. But it rises, through psychological and anthropological allusion to ethical and spiritual levels of meaning for the life of the person, just as Eliot's sea, actual and sensuously known at one level, is also at another level the symbol of the motion and the intention of history. And beneath its chaotic and complex rhythm beats "the unhurried ground swell, measuring time that is not our time," and touching both exterior nature and interior man with inscrutable but perpetual benediction.

I would say that Eliot as a Christian sacramentalist has, in the *Four Quartets,* overcome the fragmentation of contemporary culture by re-absorbing the natural or cosmic myth in the historical symbol. And I would say that he has done so in the terms proper to our moment in time. Nor does the achievement of Eliot stand alone. Auden works in the same direction and not the least important of his contributions to a modern Christian symbolism is the fusion in his best poetry of the Anglican sacramental sense with the distinctly Protestant thought of writers like Kierkegaard and Niebuhr. In varying degrees this recovery of sacramental power, of wholeness, is apparent in the work of Dylan Thomas, Graham Greene, François Mauriac.

The Challenge to Christian Symbolism

May I conclude my very general remarks on this problem of Christian symbolism by offering still another generalization? The recovery of the sacramental symbol of contemporary Christian writers is as yet by no means complete. I believe that despite the achievements which I have mentioned, there is some real danger that this promising cultural movement may be dissipated and lost again. I shall try to explain what I fear in terms of Eliot. Is it not the case that while Eliot has caught the necessary analogical relationship between nature, history, and man and has therefore helped to heal the rupture between these orders, that he has not at all overcome the disease of alienation? Is it not true that while he is sensitive to the motion of history he does not understand at all the content of history? He knows man, but not men. He does not enter into the concrete, the practical historical situation. Is this why the people of his *Cocktail Party* are so trivial, so ludicrously unrepresentative? Is this why he makes his lady saint die a sacrificial death at the hands of barbarous natives in some outpost of Empire? Here is nothing, surely, but ecclesiastical Kipling! Here is Christian sacrifice put in a Jungle-book vacuum. How irrelevant this is to the sacrificial demands made on the Christian by the intolerable practicalities of our specific moment in time! The corporate sense, the sense of living community, is absent in Eliot. It is absent in Auden. In Mauriac I would say that there is a feeling for the content of history and no feeling for its motion. Dostoievsky was the last major Christian artist to possess fully the sacramental knowledge of man alive in a society that moves. Dostoievsky in *The Brothers Karamazov* realizes symbolically the Christian fact of communion, and he places it in the living core of the historical process.

Without a recovery of this corporate sense, I suspect that Christian art can advance no further because it will have failed to cure the disease of alienation. The artist must do more now than absorb the cosmic myth into the historical symbol. He must insert himself into the historical process. He must stop hunting for the accidental social hierarchies of the lost ages of faith. He will be aware that within history only partial fulfillments of the Christian perspective are possible. But he must also be aware that without such partial fulfillments his art, and history itself, will vanish. This is the challenge for him now.

Allen Tate

The Symbolic Imagination
The Mirrors of Dante*

IT IS RIGHT even if it is not quite proper to observe at the beginning of a discourse on Dante, that no writer has held in mind at one time the whole of *The Divine Comedy:* not even Dante, perhaps least of all Dante himself. If Dante and his Dantisti have not been equal to the view of the whole, a view shorter than theirs must be expected of the amateur who, as a writer of verses, vainly seeks absolution from the mortal sin of using poets for what he can get out of them. I expect to look at a single image in the *Paradiso,* and to glance at some of its configurations with other images. I mean the imagery of light, but I mean chiefly its reflections. It was scarcely necessary for Dante to have read, though he did read, the *De Anima,* to learn that sight is the king of the senses and that the human body, which like other organisms lives by *touch,* may be made actual in language only through the imitation of *sight.* And sight in language is imitated not by means of "description"— *ut pictura poesis*— but by doubling the image: our confidence in its spatial reality is won quite simply by casting the image upon a glass, or otherwise by the insinuation of space between.

I cannot undertake to examine here Dante's double imagery in

* This essay and "The Angelic Imagination" were given in shorter versions as the Candlemas Lectures at Boston College, February 10–11, 1951. Reprinted from *Collected Essays* by Allen Tate by permission of the publisher, Alan Swallow.

all its detail, for his light alone could lead us into complexities as rich as life itself. I had almost said richer than life, if by life we mean (as we must mean) what we ourselves are able daily to see, or even what certain writers have seen, with the exception of Shakespeare, and possibly of Sophocles and Henry James. A secondary purpose that I shall have in view will be to consider the dramatic implications of the light imagery as they emerge at the resolution of the poem, in Canto XXXIII of the *Paradiso*. These implications suggest, to my mind, a radical change in the interpretation of *The Divine Comedy,* and impel me to ask again: What kind of poem is it? In asking this question I shall not be concerned with what we ordinarily consider to be literary criticism; I shall be only incidentally judging, for my main purpose is to describe.

In *Purgatorio* XXX Beatrice appears to Dante first as a voice (what she says need not detain us here), then as light; but not yet the purest light. She is the light of a pair of eyes in which is reflected the image of the gryphon, a symbol of the hypostatic union, of which she herself is a "type." But before Dante perceives this image in her eyes, he says: "A thousand desires hotter than flames held my eyes bound to the shining eyes. . . ."[1] I see no reason to suppose that Dante does not mean what he says. *Mille disiri più che fiamma caldi* I take to be the desires, however interfused by this time with courtly and mystical associations, of a man for a woman: the desires that the boy Dante felt for the girl Beatrice in 1274 after he had passed her in a street of Florence. She is the same Beatrice, Dante the same Dante, with differences which do not reject but rather include their sameness. Three dancing girls appear: Dante's allegory, formidable as it is, intensifies rather than impoverishes the reality of the dancers as girls. Their dance is a real dance, their song, in which they make a charming request of Beatrice, is a real song. If Dante expected us to be interested in the

[1] Quotations in English from *The Divine Comedy* are from the translation by Carlyle, Okey, and Wicksteed, in the Temple Classics edition. Here and there I have taken the liberty of neutralizing certain Victorian poeticisms, which were already archaic in that period.

dancers only as the Theological Virtues, I see no good reason why he made them girls at all. They are sufficiently convincing as the Three Graces, and I cannot feel in the pun a serious violation of Dante's confidence. The request of the girls is sufficiently remarkable: *Volgi, Beatrice, volgi gli occhi santi*—"Turn, Beatrice, turn those holy eyes." Let Dante see your holy eyes; look into his eyes. It is extravagant to substitute for the image of the gryphon the image of Dante in Beatrice's eyes? I think not. *He is in her eyes*—as later, in *Paradiso* XXXIII, he will be "in" God. Then a startling second request by the dancers: "Of thy grace do us the favor that thou unveil thy mouth to him"—*disvele / a lui la bocca tua* . . . "that he may discern the second beauty which thou hidest"—*la seconda belleza che tu cele*. At this point we get one of the innumerable proofs of Dante's greatness as a poet. We are not shown *la seconda belleza,* the smiling mouth; we are shown, instead, in the first four *terzine* of the next canto, the effect on Dante. For neither Dante nor Homer *describes* his heroine. As Beatrice's mouth is revealed, all Dante's senses but the sense of sight are *tutti spenti;* and sight itself is caught in *l'antica rete*—"the ancient net"—a variation of *l'antica fiamma*—"the ancient flame"—that he had felt again when he had first seen Beatrice in the Earthly Paradise.

What the net is doing here seems now to me plain, after some ten years of obtuseness about it. The general meaning is, as Charles Williams holds, that Dante, having chosen the Way of Affirmation through the physical image, feels here in the Earthly Paradise all that he had *felt* before, along with what he now *knows*. Why did he put the worldly emotion of his youthful life into the figure of the net? It is not demanded by the moment; we should not have the sense of missing something if it were not there. If it is a simple metaphor for the obfuscation of sensuality, it is not a powerful mataphor; we must remember that Dante uses very few linguistic metaphors, as distinguished from analogical or symbolic objects; when he uses them they are simple and powerful. The net, as I see it, is not simply a metaphor for the "catching" of Dante by Beatrice in 1274, though it is partly *that* ancient net; it is also a net of even more famous antiquity, that in which Venus caught Mars; and it is thus a symbolic object. Moreover, if Beatrice's eyes are univocally divine, why do the three Theological Dancers reproach him with gazing at her "too fixedly"—*troppo fico*—as if he or anybody else could get too much of the divine light? He is, of course, not yet ready for the full Beatific Vision. But an astonishing feature of the great scene of the divine pageant is that, as a trope, a subjective effect, the smile of Beatrice simultaneously revives his human love (Eros) and directs his will to the anticipation of the Beatific Vision (Agapé): both equally, by means of the action indicated by the blinding effect of both; he is blinded by the net and by the light, not alternately but at one instant.[2]

To bring together various meanings at a single moment of action is to exercise what I shall speak of here as the symbolic imagination; but the line of *action* must be unmistakable, we must never be in doubt about what is happening; for at a given stage of his progress the hero does one simple thing, and one only. The symbolic imagination conducts an action through analogy, of the human to the divine, of the natural to the supernatural, of the low to the high, of time to eternity. My literary generation was deeply impressed by Baudelaire's sonnet *Correspondances,* which restated the doctrines of medieval symbolism by way of Swedenborg; we were impressed because we had lost the historical perspective leading back to the original source. But the statement of a doctrine is very different from its possession as experience in poetry. Analogical symbolism need not move towards an act of imagination. It may see in active experience the qualities necessary for static symbolism; for example, the Grave of Jesus, which for the theologian may be a symbol to be expounded in the Illuminative Way, or for the mystic may be an object of contemplation in the Unitive Way. Despite the timeless orders of both rational discourse

[2] It seems scarcely necessary to remind the reader that I have followed in the scene of the Earthly Paradise only one thread of an immense number in a vastly complex pattern.

and intuitive contemplation, it is the business of the symbolic poet to return to the order of temporal sequence—to *action*. His purpose is to show men experiencing whatever they may be capable of, with as much meaning as he may be able to see in it; but the action comes first. Shall we call this the Poetic Way? It is at any rate the way of the poet, who has got to do his work with the body of this world, whatever that body may look like to him, in his time and place—the whirling atoms, the body of a beautiful woman, or a deformed body, or the body of Christ, or even the body of this death. If the poet is able to put into this moving body, or to find in it, a coherent chain of analogies, he will inform an intuitive act with symbolism; his will be in one degree or another the symbolic imagination.

Before I try to illustrate these general reflections, I must make a digression, for my own guidance, which I am not competent to develop as searchingly as my subject demands. The symbolic imagination takes rise from a definite limitation of human rationality which was recognized in the West until the 17th Century; in this view the intellect cannot have direct knowledge of essences. The only created mind that has this knowledge is the angelic mind.[3] If we do not believe in angels we shall have to invent them in order to explain by parable the remarkable appearance, in Europe, at about the end of the 16th Century, of a mentality which denied man's commitment to the physical world, and set itself up in quasi-divine independence. This mind has intellect and will without feeling; and it is through feeling alone that we witness the glory of our servitude to the natural world, to St. Thomas' accidents, or, if you will, to Locke's secondary qualities; it is our tie with the world of sense. The angelic mind suffers none of the limitations of sense; it has immediate knowledge of essences; and this knowledge moves through the perfect will to divine love, with

[3] The difficulties suffered by man as angel were known at least as early as Pascal; but the doctrine of angelism, as a force in the modern mind, has been fully set forth for the first time by Jacques Maritain in *The Dream of Descartes* (New York, 1944).

which it is at one. Imagination in an angel is thus inconceivable, for the angelic mind transcends the mediation of both image and discourse. I call that human imagination angelic which tries to disintegrate or to circumvent the image in the illusory pursuit of essence. When human beings undertake this ambitious program, divine love becomes so rarefied that it loses its human paradigm, and is dissolved in the worship of intellectual power, the surrogate of divinity that worships itself. It professes to know nature as essence at the same time that it has become alienated from nature in the rejection of its material forms.

It was, however high the phrases [writes Charles Williams], the common thing from which Dante always started, as it was certainly the greatest and most common to which he came. His images were the natural inevitable images—the girl in the street, the people he knew, the language he learned as a child. In them the great diagrams were perceived; from them the great myths open; by them he understands the final end.[4]

This is the simple secret of Dante, but it is a secret which is not necessarily available to the Christian poet today. The Catholic faith has not changed since Dante's time. But the Catholic sensibility, as we see it in modern Catholic poetry, from Thompson to Lowell, has become angelic and is not distinguishable (doctrinal differences aside) from poetry by Anglicans, Methodists, Presbyterians, and atheists. I take it that more than doctrine, even if the doctrine be true, is necessary for a great poetry of action. Catholic poets have lost, along with their heretical friends, the power to start with the "common thing": they have lost the gift for concrete experience. The abstraction of the modern mind has obscured their way into the natural order. Nature offers to the symbolic poet clearly denotable objects in depth and in the round, which yield the analogies to the higher syntheses. The modern poet rejects the higher synthesis, or tosses it in a vacuum of abstractions.[5] If he

[4] Charles Williams: *The Figure of Beatrice* (London, 1943), p. 44.

[5] Another way of putting this is to say that the modern poet, like Valéry or Crane, tries to seize directly the anagogical meaning, without going through the three preparatory stages of letter, allegory, and trope.

looks at nature he spreads the clear visual image in a complex of metaphor, from one katachresis to another through Aristotle's permutations of genus and species. He cannot sustain the prolonged analogy, the second and superior kind of figure that Aristotle doubtless had in mind when he spoke of metaphor as the key to the resemblances of things, and the mark of genius.

That the gift of analogy was not Dante's alone every medievalist knows. The most striking proof of its diffusion and the most useful example for my purpose that I know, is the letter of St. Catherine of Siena to Brother Raimondo of Capua. A young Sienese, Niccolo Tuldo, had been unjustly convicted of treason and condemned to death. Catherine became his angel of mercy, giving him daily solace—the meaning of the Cross, the healing powers of the Blood; and so reconciled him to the faith that he accepted his last end. Now I have difficulty believing people who say that they live in the Blood of Christ, for I take them to mean that they have the faith and hope some day to live in it. The evidence of the Blood is one's power to produce it, the power to show it as a "common thing" and to make it real, literally, in action. For the report of the Blood is very different from its reality. St. Catherine does not report it; she recreates it, so that its analogical meaning is confirmed again in blood that she has seen. This is how she does it:

> Then [the condemned man] came, like a gentle lamb; and seeing me he began to smile, and wanted me to make the sign of the Cross. When he had received the sign, I said, "Down! To the bridal, my sweetest brother. For soon shalt thou be in the enduring life." He prostrated himself with great gentleness, and I stretched out his neck; and bowed down, and recalled to him the Blood of the Lamb. His lips said naught save Jesus! and Catherine! And so saying, I recieved his head in my hands, closing my eyes in the divine goodness and saying, "I will."
>
> When he was at rest my soul rested in peace and quiet, and in so great fragrance of blood that I could not bear to remove the blood which had fallen on me from him.

It is deeply shocking, as all proximate incarnations of the Word are shocking, whether in Christ and the Saints, or in Dostoevsky, James

Joyce, or Henry James. I believe it was T. S. Eliot who made accessible again to an ignorant generation a common Christian insight, when he said that people cannot bear very much reality. I take this to mean that only persons of extraordinary courage, and perhaps even genius, can face the spiritual truth in its physical body. Flaubert said that the artist, the soldier, and the priest face death every day; so do we all; yet it is perhaps nearer to them than to other men; it is their particular responsibility. When St. Catherine "rests in so great fragrance of blood," it is no doubt the Blood of the Offertory which the celebrant offers to God *cum odore suavitatis,* but with the literal odor of the species of wine, not of blood. St. Catherine had the courage of genius which permitted her to *smell* the Blood of Christ in Niccolo Tuldo's blood clotted on her dress: she smelled the two bloods *not alternately but at one instant,* in a single act compounded of spiritual insight and physical perception.

Chekhov said that a gun hanging on the wall at the beginning of a story has got to be fired off before the story ends: everything in potency awaits its completed purpose in act. If this is a metaphysical principle, it is also the prime necessity of the creative imagination. Is not St. Catherine telling us that the Blood of Christ must be perpetually recreated as a brute fact? If the gun has got to be fired, the Blood has got to be shed, if only because that is the first condition of its appearance; it must move toward the condition of human action, where we may smell it, touch it, and taste it again.

When ecclesiastical censorship of this deep insight in the laity exceeds a just critical prudence, the result is not merely obscurantism in the arts; it is perhaps a covert rejection of the daily renewal of the religious life. Twenty-five years ago the late W. B. Yeats had a controversy with the Irish bishops about the famous medieval Cherry Tree Carol, which the hierarchy wished to suppress as blasphemous. The Blessed Virgin is resting under a cherry tree, too tired to reach up and pluck a cherry. Since Christ lives from the foundations of the world, He is omnipotent in the womb, and He commands the tree to lower a bough for His Mother's convenience; which it obligingly does, since it cannot do otherwise. Here again the gun is fired and the Blood is shed. If the modern Church has lost the historic experience of this kind of symbolism, which is more tolerable, I believe, in the Latin countries than with us, it is at least partial evidence that the Church has lost the great culture that it created, and that at intervals has created the life of the Church.

I return from this digression to repeat that Dante was the great master of the symbolism, the meaning of which I have been trying to suggest. But the symbolic "problem" of *The Divine Comedy* we must not suppose Dante to have undertaken analytically; it is our problem, not his. Dr. Flanders Dunbar has stated it with great penetration: "As with his progress he perceives more and more of ultimate reality through the symbol [Beatrice], at the same time the symbol occupies less and less of his attention, until ultimately it takes its place among all created things on a petal of the rose, while he gazes beyond it into the full glory of the sun."[6] The symbolic problem, then, is: How shall Dante move step by step (literally and allegorically) from the Dark Wood, the negation of light, to the "three circles, of three colors and one magnitude," God Himself, or pure light, where there are no sensible forms to reflect it? There can be no symbol for God, for that which has itself informed step by step the symbolic progress. Vision, giving us clear visual objects, through physical sight, moving steadily upward towards its anagogical transfiguration, is the first matrix of the vast analogical structure. As Dante sees more he sees less; as he sees more light the nearer he comes to its source, the less he sees of what it had previously lit up. In the Empyrean, at the climax of the Illuminative Way, Beatrice leaves Dante and takes her place in the Rose; St. Bernard now guides him into the Intuitive Way.

For the Illuminative Way is the way to knowledge through the senses, by means of aided reason, but here the "distance" between us and what we see is always the distance between a concept and

[6] H. Flanders Dunbar: *Symbolism in Medieval Thought and Its Consummation in the Divine Comedy* (New Haven, 1929), p. 347.

its object, between the human situation in which the concept arises and the realization of its full meaning. Put otherwise, with the beginning of the *Vita Nuova* in mind, it is the distance between the knowledge of love, which resulted from the earthly love of Dante for Beatrice, and the distant "object," or God, that had made the love in the first place possible: the distance between Beatrice and the light which had made it possible for him to see her. The Kantian synthetic proposition of the entire poem, as we enter it through the symbolism of light, is: Light is Beatrice. Here the eye is still on the human image; it is still on it up to the moment when she takes her place with the other saints in the Rose, where she is only one of many who turn their eyes to the "eternal fountain." Light is Beatrice; light is her *smile;* her final smile, which Dante sees as she enters the Rose, is no longer the mere predicate of a sentence, for there is now no distance between the smile and what had lit it. Although, in so far as it is a smile at all, it is still the smile at the unveiling of the mouth, it is now the smile without the mouth, the smile of light. And thus we arrive at the converse of the proposition: Beatrice is light. Now Dante's eye is on the light itself, but he cannot see it because Beatrice, through whose image he had progressively seen more light, has disappeared; and he can see nothing. There is nothing to *see*. For that which enables sight is not an object of vision. What has been seen is, in what is surely one of the greatest passages of all poetry, "the shadowy prefaces of their truth." Illumination, or intellect guided by divine grace, powerful as it is, halts at the "prefaces." But the Unitive Way leads to the Presence, where both sight and discursive thought cease.

Whether Dante should have tried to give us an image of God, of that which is without image and invisible, is an unanswerable question. Is it possible that we have here a break in the symbolic structure, which up to the end of the poem has been committed to the visible? At the end we are with Love, whose unpredicated attribute is the entire universe. Has Dante given us, in the "three circles, of three colors and one magnitude," merely the trinitarian and the doctrinal equivalent of the ultimate experience, instead of an objective symbol of the experience itself? In the terms of Dante's given structure, such a symbol was perhaps not possible; and strictly speaking it is never possible. If he was going to give us anything he doubtless had to give us just what he gave; he gave it in an act of great artistic heroism. For in the center of the circles he sees the image of man. This is the risk, magnified almost beyond conception, of St. Catherine: the return of the supra-rational and supra-sensible to the "common thing." It is the courage to see again, even in its ultimate cause, the Incarnation.

If we will look closely at the last four lines of the *Paradiso,* and double back on our tracks, I believe that we will see that there is no break in the dramatic structure—the structure of the action.[7] For the poem is an action: a man is acting and going somewhere, and things are happening both to him and around him; otherwise the poem would be—what I may have given the impression of its being—a symbolic machine. In the space of an essay I cannot prepare properly the background of the suggestion that I am about to offer. For one thing, we should have to decide who "Dante" is, and where he is in the action that he has depicted—questions that nobody seems to know much about. For what it may be worth, I suggest that the poet has undertaken to involve a fictional character named Dante—at once the poet and not the poet of that name—in a certain action of the greatest possible magnitude, the issue of which is nothing less, perhaps something greater, than life or death. In this action the hero fails. He fails in the sense that he will have to start over again when he steps out of the "poem," as he surely must do if he is going to write it.

Thus I see *The Divine Comedy* as essentially dramatic and, in one of its modes, tragic. Are we to suppose that the hero actually attained to the Beatific Vision? No; for nobody who had would be

[7] By "dramatic" I mean something like *practic,* a possible adjective from *praxis,* a general movement of action as potency which it is the purpose of the poem to actualize. In the Thomist sequence, *potentia: actio: actus,* "dramatic" would roughly correspond to the middle term.

so foolish as to write a poem about it, if in that spiritual perfection it could even occur to him to do so. The poem is a vast paradigm of the possibility of the Beatific Vision. No more than its possibility for the individual person, for "Dante" himself, is here entertained. What shall we make of his failure of memory, the slipping away of the final image, which he calls *tanto oltraggio*—"so great an outrage?" It would be a nice question to decide whether something had slipped away, or whether it had ever been fully there. The vision is imagined, it is *imaged;* its essence is not possessed. I confess that it is not an argument from the poem to say that had Dante claimed its possession, he would have lost that "good of the intellect" which we forfeit when we presume to angelic knowledge; and it was through the good of the intellect that he was able to write the poem. But it is an external argument that I believe cannot be entirely ignored.

The last *terzina* of the last canto tells us: *All' alta fantasia qui mancò possa*—"To the high fantasy here power failed." What power failed? The power to write the poem, or the power to possess as experience the divine essence? Is it a literary or a religious failure? It is obviously and honorably both. It makes no more sense to say Dante achieved his final vision as direct experience than to say that Sophocles married his mother and put out his own eyes; that the experience of the *Oedipus Rex* represents the personal experience of Sophocles. What Dante achieved is an *actual* insight into the great dilemma, eternal life or eternal death, but he has not hedged the dilemma like a bet to warrant himself a favorable issue. As the poem closes, he still faces it, like the rest of us. Like *Oedipus,* the fictional Dante learns in humility a certain discipline of the will: we may equate up to a point the dark-blindness of Oedipus and the final light-blindness of Dante; both men have succeeded through suffering in blinding themselves to knowledge-through-sense, in the submission of *hybris* to a higher will.[8] The fictional Dante at the end steps out of the frame and becomes

[8] Oedipus does not achieve this of course until the end of *Oedipus at Colonus.*

again the historical Dante; Oedipus steps out of his frame, his fictional plot is done, he is back in the world of unformed action, blind and, like Dante, an exile. Shall Oedipus be saved? Shall Dante? We do not know, but to ask the question is to point to a primary consideration in the interpretation of *The Divine Comedy,* particularly if we are disposed, as some commentators have been, to believe that Dante the man used his poem arrogantly to predict his own salvation.

If Dante does not wholly succeed in giving us in the "three circles, of three colors and one magnitude," an image of the Godhead, I think we are ready to see that it was not necessary; it was not a part of his purpose. Such an image is not the "final cause" of the poem. The poem is an action; it is an action to the end. For the image that Dante gives us of the Godhead is not an image to be received by the reader as essential knowledge in his own "angelic" intelligence, as an absolute apart from the action. It is a dramatic image; the image is of the action and the action is Dante's. To read Canto XXXIII in any other way would be perhaps to commit the blunder that M. Gilson warns us against: the blunder of thinking that Dante was writing a super-philosophical tract, or a pious embellishment of the doctrine of Thomas Aquinas, instead of a poem. The question, then, is not what is the right anagogical symbol for God; it is rather what symbol for God will serve tropologically (that is, morally and dramatically) for the tragic insight of the poet who knows, through the stages of the Three Ways, that the Beatific Vision is possible but uncertain of realization. Dante sees himself, Man, in the Triune Circles, and he is in the Seraphic Heaven of Love. But at the end desire and will are like a "wheel moving equally"; motion imparted to it at one point turns it as a whole, but it has to be moved, as the wheel of our own desire and will must be moved, by a force outside it. The wheel is Dante's last symbol of the great failure. Since it must be moved, it is not yet at one, not yet in unity, with the divine will; it obeys it, as those other wheels, the sun and stars, moved by love, obey.

I take it that the wheel is the final geometrical projection of the *visual* matrix of analogy; it is what the eye sees, the material form, and what in its anagoge it eventually aspires to become. We must remember that Beatrice's eyes are spheres, no less than the physical universe itself, which is composed of concentric spheres. The first circles that Dante shows us are in Canto III of the *Inferno,* Charon's—"for round his eyes were wheels of flame." The last, the Triune Circles, are the anagoge of the visual circle, and are without extension; they are pure light, the abstraction or sublimation of flame. Flame burning in a circle and lighting up a circle, and what it encloses, are the prime sensible symbols of the poem. Only Satan, at the geometrical center of the world, occupies a point that cannot be located on any existing arc of the cosmos. This is the spherical (or circular) expression of Satan's absolute privation of light-as-love which in the Empyrean turns the will-wheel of Dante with the cosmic spheres. These are the will of God as love; and if we ignore the dramatic structure, and fail to look closely at the symbolic, we shall conclude that Dante is at one with the purpose of the universe. But, as we have seen, the symbolic structure is complicated by the action, and in the end the action prevails. That is to say, Dante is *still moving.* Everything that moves, says Dante the Thomist in his letter to Can Grande, has some imperfection in it because it is, in the inverse degree of its rate of motion, removed from the Unmoved Mover, the Triune Circles, God. By a twist of this argument, which, of course, as I shall presently indicate, is specious, Satan himself has no imperfection: he too lies immobile—except for the fanning wings that freeze the immobile damned in Giudecca—as the Still Point in the Triune Circles is immobile. If Dante's will is turning like a wheel, he is neither damned nor saved; he is morally active in the universal human predicament. His participation in the love imparted as motion to the universe draws him towards the Triune Circles and to the immobility of peace at the center, as it draws all creatures; but a defection of the will could plunge him into the other "center."

Now Dante is astonished when he sees in the Primum Mobile a reversal of the ratio of speed of the spheres as he had observed it on earth, through the senses. "But in the universe of sense," he says to Beatrice, "we may see the circlings more divine as from the center they are more removed." In the spiritual universe the circlings are more divine the nearer they are to the center. It is a matter of perspective; from the earth outward the revolutions of the spheres are increasingly rapid up to the ninth, the Primum Mobile, whose speed is just short of infinite; the Primum Mobile is trying to achieve with all points of its surface a simultaneous contact with the Still Point of the Empyrean. What he sees in the Primum Mobile is this perspective visually reversed; instead of being the outer "crust" of the universe, the Primum Mobile is actually next to the central Still Point, whirling with inconceivable speed. God, the Still Point, is a non-spatial entity which is *everywhere* and *nowhere*. The Ptolemaic cosmos, which had been Christianized by the imposition of the angelic hierarchy of Dionysius, has been, in a way not to be completely visualized, turned inside out. The spheres, which began their career as an astronomical hypothesis, are now no longer necessary; they are replaced in the ultimate reality by nine non-spatial gradations of angelic intelligence, in three triads, the last and ninth circle of "fire" being that of the simple angels, the "farthest" removed in the non-spatial continuum from the Divine Love.

Where then is the earth, with Satan at its exact center? I think we must answer: Where it has always been. But "where" that is we had better not try to say. At any rate neither Satan nor the earth is at the spiritual center. His immobility thus has no perfection. In the full spiritual reality, of which the center of the material universe becomes an outermost "rind," beyond space, Satan does not exist: he exists in the world of sense and in the human will. The darkness of hell, from the point of view of God (if I may be allowed the expression), is not an inner darkness, but an outer. So, in the progress from hell to the Empyrean, Dante has come from the inner darkness of man to the inner light of God; from the outer darkness of God to the outer light of man.

This anagogical conversion of symbol that I have been trying to follow in one of its threads is nowhere by Dante merely *asserted;* it is constantly moving, rendered moment by moment as *action.* Like most good poets, great or minor, Dante wrote better than he had meant to do; for if we took him at his word, in the letter to Can Grande, we should conclude that the *Paradiso* is a work of rhetoric calculated "to remove those living in this life from a state of misery and to guide them to a state of happiness." It seems probable that persons now enrolled among the Blessed got there without being compelled to see on the way all that Dante saw. Were we reading the poem for that kind of instruction, and knew not where else to find it, we might conclude that Dante's *luce intellectual,* with its transformations in the fourfold system of interpretation, is too great a price to pay even for salvation; or, at any rate, for most of us, the wrong price. It would perhaps be a mistake for a man to decide that he has become a Christian at the instance of Dante, unless he is prepared to see all that Dante saw—which is one thing, but always seen in at least two ways.

A clue to two of the ways is the mirror symbol. As we approach it, the kind of warning that Dante at intervals pauses to give us is not out of place. For if the way up to now has been rough, we may expect it from now on to be even rougher. The number of persons, objects, and places in *The Divine Comedy* that are reflections, replies, or manifestations of things more remote is beyond calculation. The entire natural world is a replica *in reverse* of the supernatural world. That, I believe, we have seen so far only on the dubious authority of my own assertion. But if Dante is a poet (I agree with M. Gilson that he is) he will not be satisfied with assertion as such, even with the authority of the Church to support it. The single authority of poetry is a difficult criterion of actuality that must always remain beyond our reach. And in some sense of this actuality Dante has got to place his vast two-way analogy (heaven like the world, the world like heaven) on the scene of action, and make it move. Let us take the stance of Dante at the beginning of *Paradiso* XXVIII, and try to suggest some of the ways in which he moves it:

as in the mirror a taper's flame, kindled behind a man, is seen by him before it be in his sight or thought,
as he turns back to see whether the glass speak truth to him, and sees that it accords with it as song-words to the music;
so my memory recalls that I did turn, gazing upon the lovely eyes whence love had made the noose to capture me;
and when I turned, and my own eyes were struck by what appears in that orb whenever upon its circling the eye is well fixed,
a point I saw which rayed forth light so keen that all the vision that it flames upon must close because of its sharp point.

(One observes in passing that even in the Primum Mobile Beatrice bears the net-noose dimension of meaning.) Beatrice's eyes are a mirror in which is reflected that "sharp point," to which Dante, still at a distance from it, now turns his direct gaze. As he looks at it he sees for the first time what its reflection in Beatrice's eyes could not convey: that it is the sensible world turned inside out. For the sensible world as well as her eyes is only a reflection of the light from the sharp point. Now he is looking at the thing-in-itself. *He has at last turned away from the mirror which is the world.* What happens when we turn away from a mirror to look directly at the object which we saw reflected? I must anticipate Beatrice's famous experiment with one of my own. If you will place upon a table a box open at one end, the open end toward a mirror, and then look into the mirror, you will see the open end. Turn from the mirror and look at the box itself. You still see the open end, and thus you see the object *reversed.* If the box were reproduced, in the sense of being continued or moved *into* the mirror, the actual box would present, when we turn to it, a closed end; for the box and its reflection would show their respectively corresponding sides in congruent projection. Quantitative visualization of the cosmic reversal is not completely possible. But through the mirror analogy Dante performs a stupendous feat of the imagination that in kind has probably not been rivalled by any other poet. And it is an analogy that has been firmly grounded in action.

In conclusion I shall try to point to its literal base; for we have seen it, in *Paradiso* XXVIII, only as a simile; and if we had not had it laid down earlier as a physical fact to which we must assent, a self-contained phenomenon of the natural order, it would no doubt lack at the end that fullness of actuality which we do not wholly understand, but which we require of poetry. The self-contained fact of the natural order is established in Canto II of the *Paradiso,* where Beatrice performs a physical experiment. Some scholars have been moved by it to admire Dante for this single ray of positivistic enlightenment feebly glowing in the mind of a medieval poet. So far as I know, our critics have not considered it necessary to be sufficiently unenlightened to see that Beatrice's experiment is merely poetry.

Before I reproduce it I shall exhibit a few more examples of the mirror symbol that appear at intervals in the five last cantos. In Canto XXIX, 25– 27, form permeates matter "as in glass . . . a ray so glows that from its coming to its pervading all, there is no interval." Still in XXIX, 142–145, at the end: "See now the height and breadth of the eternal worth, since it has made itself so many mirrors in which it is reflected, remaining in itself one as before." At line 37 of Canto XXX we enter the Empyrean where Dante sees the great River of Light "issuing its living sparks"; it too is a mirror, for Beatrice explains: "The river and the topaz gems that enter and go forth, and the smiling grasses are prefaces of their truth" (i.e., of what they reflect). In Canto XXX, 85–87, Dante bends down to the waves "to make mirrors of my eyes"; and again in XXX he sees the Rose of Paradise, another mirror, in one of his great similes:

> And as a hillside reflects itself in water at its foot, as if to look upon its own adornment, when it is rich in grasses and in flowers,
> so, mounting in the light, around, around, casting reflection in more than a thousand ranks I saw all that of us have won return up yonder.

And finally the climactic reflection, the "telic principle" and the archetype of them all, in Canto XXX, 127–132:

> The circling that in thee [in the Triune God] appeared to be
> conceived as a reflected light, by my eyes scanned a little,
> in itself, of its own color, seemed to be painted with our effigy,
> and thereat my sight was all committed to it.

Where have these mirrors, which do their poetic work, the work of making the supra-sensible visible—one of the tasks of all poetry—where have they come from? The remote frame is doubtless the circular or spherical shape of the Ptolemaic cosmos;[9] but if there is glass in the circular frame, it reflects nothing until Virgil has left Dante to Beatrice's guidance in the Earthly Paradise (*Purgatorio* XXXI); where we have already glanced at the unveiling of mouth and eyes. I suggest that Beatrice's eyes in *Purgatorio* XXXI are the first mirror. But the image is not, at this early stage of Beatrice, sufficiently developed to bear all the strain of analogical weight that Dante intends to put upon it. For that purpose the mirror must be established as a literal mirror, a plain mirror, a "common thing."

He not only begins with the common thing; he continues with it, until at the end we come by disarming stages to a scene that no man has ever looked upon before. Every detail of Paradise is a common thing; it is the cumulative combination and recombination of natural objects beyond their "natural" relations, which staggers the imagination. "Not," says Beatrice to Dante, "that such things are in themselves harsh; but on your side is the defect, in that your sight is not yet raised so high."

A mirror is an artifact of the practical intellect, and as such can be explained by natural law: but there is no natural law which explains man as a mirror reflecting the image of God. The great leap is made in the interval between Canto II and Canto XXXIII of the *Paradiso*.

Dante, in Canto II, is baffled by the spots on the moon, sup-

[9] The popular "visual" translation of Aristotle's primary Unmoved Mover producing, *through being loved,* the primary cosmic motion, which is circular. The philosophical source of this idea, Book XII, Chapter 7, of the *Metaphysics,* Dante of course knew.

posing them to be due to alternating density and rarity of matter. No, says Beatrice in effect, this would be monism, a materialistic explanation of the diffusion of the divine light. The true explanation is very different: all saved souls are equally in heaven; but the divine light reaches the remoter spheres and souls according to the spiritual gifts of which they are capable in the natural world. "This is the formal principle," Beatrice says, summing up, "which produces, in conformity to the excellence of the object, the turbid and the clear."

Meanwhile she has asked Dante to consider a physical experiment to illustrate the unequal reception of the divine substance. Take three mirrors, she says, and set two of them side by side, and a third in the middle but farther back. Place a candle behind you, and observe its image reflected in each of the three mirrors. The middle reflection will be smaller but not less bright than the two others: "smaller" stands quantitatively for unequal reception of a quality, spiritual insight; "not less bright" likewise for equality of salvation. But what concerns us is a certain value of the experiment that Dante, I surmise, with the cunning of a great poet, slyly refuses to consider: the dramatic value of the experiment.

There are *three*[10] mirrors each reflecting the *one* light. In the heart of the Empyrean, as we have seen, Dante says:

> In the profound and shining being of the deep light appeared
> to me *three* circles, of *three* colors and one magnitude.

In the middle is the effigy of man. The physical image of Dante had necessarily been reflected in each of the three mirrors of Canto II; but he had not seen it. I suggest that he was not then ready to see it; his dramatic (i.e., tropological) development fell short of the final self-knowledge. Self-knowledge comes to him, as an Aristotelian Recognition and Reversal, when he turns the cosmos inside out by turning away from the "real" mirrors to the light which

[10] Only two, placed at unequal distances from the candle, are strictly necessary for the experiment; but three are necessary as pointers towards the anagoge of the Trinity in the Triune Circles.

has cast the three separate images. For the first time he sees the "one magnitude," the candle itself. And it is all done with the simple apparatus and in conditions laid down in Canto II; he achieves the final anagoge and the dramatic recognition by turning around, as if he were still in Canto II, and by looking at the candle that has been burning all the time behind his back.

I have described some motions of the symbolic imagination in Dante, and tried to develop a larger motion in one of its narrower aspects. What I have left out of this discussion is very nearly the entire poem. In the long run the light-imagery is not the body, it is what permits us to *see* the body, of the poem. The rash suggestion that *The Divine Comedy* has a tragic mode—among other modes —I shall no doubt be made to regret; I cannot defend it further here. Perhaps the symbolic imagination is tragic in sentiment, if not always in form, in the degree of its development. Its every gain beyond the simple realism of experience imposes so great a strain upon any actuality of form as to set the ultimate limit of the gain as a defeat. The high order of the poetic insight that the final insight must elude us, is dramatic in the sense that its fullest image is an action in the shapes of this world: it does not reject, it includes; it sees not only with but through the natural world, to what may lie beyond it. Its humility is witnessed by its modesty. It never begins at the top; it carries the bottom along with it, however high it may climb.

William F. Lynch, S.J.

The Theological Imagination*

Does the literary imagination have a theological dimension? The important thing is to keep our minds open to the possibility. Otherwise we are not free.

Our thinking and imagining will be more fruitful here if we remember two things: 1. over against every naive and romantic assumption to the contrary, there is no such thing as a purely spontaneous and autonomous literary image, absolutely "creative" and free of metaphysics or theology; 2. theology itself is not transcendental in the pejorative sense. For it, the "short way" and the "long way," the absolute specificity of human experience and the "meaning" of it all, are not two different things. Theology gets into the interior of our images and is not an exploiting appendage.

In this essay we introduce the vocabulary of "levels of being." The collapse of such an idea has often been disastrous in the order of subjectivity and literary sensibility. We analyze three different major images on different levels, all the way from the immediately human to the theological: the image of man, the image of time, the image of ritual movement. An attempt is made to describe the unfortunate results for the imagination when it introduces various acts of dissociation into these levels.

The Four Quartets *is a special subject. Apart from every purely conceptual and formally theological idea, its two central images of immobility and intersection are found to be eminently theological in their dimensions.*

* From *Christ and Apollo* by William F. Lynch, S.J., © Sheed & Ward, Inc., 1960.

The "Autonomous" Imagination

THERE IS AN IMPORTANT SENSE in which the life of every imagination is compact with theology, that is to say, with some theology or other. We like to think that there are such things as pure images, issuing forth from the spontaneity and creativity of the artist's mind, and we often insist that these creative images have their own autonomous rights, rights which are prior, at least in time, to any extrinsic insertion of the "thinking" mind into them as a buttressing or critical force.

But this doctrine of a purely creative image, unadulterated by any form of metaphysics or theology, is a very dubious one. John Crowe Ransom, in his essay "Poetry: A Note on Ontology," has taken one of the purest little poems of Imagism (a poetic practice which thought it could reduce the image or the thing to pure thingness) and has indicated that the strictest attempts in this direction are unsuccessful.[1] T. S. Eliot, speaking in a somewhat different vein, has expressed a similar doubt: "The process of increasing self-consciousness—or, we may say, of increasing consciousness of language—has as its theoretical goal what we may call *la poésie pure*. I believe it to be a goal that cannot be reached. I believe that poetry is only poetry so long as it preserves some 'impurity' in this sense: that is to say, so long as the subject matter is valued for its own sake."[2] This statement is used for our own purposes, but let it be hoped here that our analysis of analogical thought has been helpful with the eternal problem of "subject matter." If there is no such thing as a pure poetic image, neither in any important sense is there such a thing as pure ideas in poetry, ideas which would not have to shift and zig-zag and proportionalize themselves to images and actions, or at least take a special life from their birth out of the latter.

[1] John Crowe Ransom, "Poetry: A Note on Ontology," *Critiques and Essays in Criticism* 1920–1948, ed. Robert W. Stallman (New York: Ronald, 1949), pp. 30–46.

[2] T. S. Eliot, *From Poe to Valéry* (New York: Harcourt, Brace & Company, 1948), p. 26.

This may be all very well and good, many a reader will say, and all one would have to do by way of countering the relations we have been exploring is to admit with Freud that it is quite difficult to get over the persistent theological neurosis of the whole human race. Moreover, the objection might continue, with all this chatter about the theological penetration of our images, the theological imagination ends up in an insuperable dilemma; for it destroys the very possibility of autonomy and the somehow autonomous existence of every fact in this world. A rose is a rose is a rose and that is all there is to that. Except to add that such autonomy is not only a subjective passion of the contemporary intelligence but also has a profound factual and ontological foundation. If we cannot keep theology out of things anywhere, might run the climax of the charge, then we are ourselves Manichaeans and are discarding the very substance of the achievement of contemporary civilization.

We must not blink at the fact that this is a very strong and healthy position, and that, if anything, our own paraphrase of it has diluted rather than magnified its strength. The only real trouble is that it is generally too content to remain within its points of power. The idea of autonomy is a real and great achievement. We all realize that it has been an incalculably serviceable weapon in the development of science, literary criticism, psychology, and has even been of tremendous help in such a more theological domain as that of Church-State relations. But if the autonomous mind and imagination is content to stay within the present limits of its achievement, it will take on all the vices of the equivocal mind and imagination, and will continue to generate diseases which otherwise it would not.

Let me begin the elaboration of this criticism of the *present* status of the passion for autonomy by choosing to remain for the moment within the area of "subjectivity." By this I mean to suggest that it is better not to rush too quickly at the perennial philosophical debate which revolves around the question of the levels of being, the levels of a rose or any other "fact." Plato, I take it, was the first to speculate to the effect that for every level of cognition there is a corresponding level of being that is known. If he were speaking the later language of an analogical thinker, he might tell us, for example, that there is a fact called "society" or community, but that this fact has a gradated existence; there is a society which exists on the simplest human level of the biology and the tissues of sex; there are widening and horizontal forms of society, which achieve their existence out of the stuff of familial, economic and political life; there are also vertical forms of the same fact which drive the soul into higher and higher (or, if you will, deeper and deeper) expressions of communion.

The highest or deepest of all these you may call union with God, but I call it the Church, because the Catholic imagination does not force me to imagine that at the end I must free myself from all human society to unite myself with God. Rather, it helps me to imagine that once I have embarked on a good thing with all its concreteness (here it is society), I can and must carry it with me all the way into the heart of the unimaginable.

On the other hand it is hard to think otherwise than that the Protestant imagination sometimes seems to conceive society to be a necessary evil, to be endured on all the lower levels of being, good to the next to the last drop, but to be abandoned with indecent haste before true insight or the face of the living God. It stands over against the theological imagination as Mallarmé stands to poetry (*his* goal was to destroy it). The Protestant seems, at any rate, to wish to stand in nakedness before God outside of society and often seems to make God a silence and an abyss. But He is not a silence; even *He* could not know Himself save through the Word; and are we better than God that we can know Him save through Christ; but the Church is Christ. If some unity among men is not the final word, we may as well give up all imagining and all poetry now, and love with it. For in this hypothesis we should have to take off all imagining at the end in His presence, as Jacob took off his shoes, and love would be an end but not a way. No, the mysteries of Christianity are too complicated for that kind of simplicity. We do not use the finitude of man as a final jumping off place for our contact with the infinite; we enter more and more deeply into man, into the fact of society until we come to that depth or height which is Christ; this we can call the Christic point of society, beyond which we need not go farther. For God's "imagination" from the beginning could not and did not go farther.

Admittedly, then, there are levels of being, and certainly each level has its right to separate expression. Here the idea of autonomy can very well take an unalterable stand. But let it not then create the terms for a specious debate in terms of which it would fight monotonously for facts over against merely verbal and allegorical extensions of facts as executed by a "celestial" theology. It is true that a fact is a fact is a fact, and a rose is a rose is a rose. But the true debate is: what is the fact and what is its true dimension? We have insisted that the mysteries of Christianity are a penetration deep into the fact of man, all the way into his Christic center; and that where many dig into the same center a Church is made. It is not at all a matter of constructing levels outside of the fact. The levels are proposed as deeper borings into actuality. If the maturer biblical exegetes of an earlier age were using our language and had our controversies on their hands, they might very well have said that every spiritual exegesis of a fact is not an extrinsic appendage but a deeper boring into the literal level of exegesis. But we will have more of that problem. Our business now is to recall that we agreed to a temporary abandonment of the real truth of the levels of the Christian mysteries. The question we might first ask ourselves is this:

What happens, we might say in a purely clinical way, if, in effect, every theory of levels of being is surrendered? What are the results in the way of pure subjectivity? What are the subjective diseases generated by this new situation?

What first happens—and it has already happened—is a flattening out of the orders of human sensibility, the orders of what we might call human reaction to facts. "Flattening out" is a mild phrase, for some critics have described the new situation under the words *no sensibility* or *no reaction at all*. It was this condition which Eliot undertook to project in *The Waste Land*. There is much talk in certain sections of that poem, but the talk is (deliberately) chatter and meaningless. There is "the hot water at ten./ And if it rains, a closed car at four." And there is "nothing again nothing," no knowing and no remembering. And there is again the lady who indulges in the biology and the tissues of sexual society; sensibility is dead in the upper levels of her soul; the once deeper fact is not there to delight or torture her with its echoes in other levels of her self. "When lovely woman stoops to folly and/Paces about her room again, alone,/She smooths her hair with automatic hand,/And puts a record on the gramophone." And there is the immersion in time: *Hurry up please its time.*

The Surfaces of Life

In the remaining pages of this essay I shall ask the reader to share my musings over various aspects of the flattened-out fate of three broadly important "facts." They are: 1. The general image of man himself, whether he is a multi-dimensioned reality or no; 2. the phenomenon of time, and how slowly we should fly to "eternity" before we give up the probing of the levels of time; and 3. the phenomenon of ritual movement, whether again we do not abandon this natural instinct for ritual with indecent haste in the name of the dubious glory of isolated sensibility. I fervently wish that other writers would explore the status of other facts among us. This kind of task must be as endless as life and facts themselves, and I have only chosen these three as examples, though they are rather central. To go on from there, with detail and insight, would seem to me to be one of the important functions of a creative criticism that could get very close to being poetry itself.

1. Dissociation in Man

It is with complete deliberation and forethought that I choose in the following pages to deal with the dissociative habit in so far as it occurs in two Christian writers like Eliot and Greene. For we who believe in a Christian way are a little too apt to think that the problem of dissociation and the inability to move in a related way through the various levels of being occur only outside ourselves. I would hold that this is somewhat naive and that we will be helped rather than hurt by an increased awareness of the degree to which we are ourselves vulnerable to the rather overwhelming imaginative ills of our time.

As for Eliot, there is one central point at which I am compelled to question him, and this is done with as much grace and courtesy as a great writer commands. For he has himself tried notably to reconstruct our damage in his later poetry, and there is the suspicion abroad that he has failed in several notable respects. But grace is demanded in saying this for the simple reason that we have all failed. (Allen Tate, for one, has noted how much Catholic poets have also broken down in the face of the problem of sensibility.)

In *The Waste Land* Eliot was giving us an ironic picture of the desert of our time, but in *The Cocktail Party* it has seemed to me that he is unhappily giving us a bit of a waste land of his own. My criticism is somewhat indirect and amounts to saying that this is a good play but it would have been nice if the author had written an entirely different piece. At any rate, my suggestion is that the play has as its problem the desert of human love, and there are two solutions to two human thirsts in it. One woman is sent back by her psychiatrist to the monotony and dross of her human love, and the other takes up a divine and contemplative vocation. But the psychiatrist speaks truer than he knows in saying that each is but another form of loneliness, an inferior and a superior desert. One is tempted to wish that it had been the same woman who had taken up the two vocations in the one act and the one situation.

One has no right seriously to ask that the writer should have written another play, but this second would have been the real problem of the people; we do not have the right to give to the latter a solution which is only tolerable, if deceptively, as a solution for intellectuals. As levels of being, the finite and the infinite are very frequently in dissociation among us, and we do not help the matter by introducing a Christian act of dissociation.

Or let us look at the case of Graham Greene. In *The Heart of the Matter* Scobie is a classical example of the defeat and radical torment of man. All Scobie does is stand outside of the finite, totally outside of himself, and desperately pray that God will accept his damnation as a pleasing gift. (It is very much like Kafka's way of salvation, and the frequent Protestant cry that the finite lives under the condemnation of the absolute; in all this one must again note our eternal attraction toward the idea of non-being). But then came Greene's novel *The End of the Affair*. In *The Heart of the Matter* he had been sketching the situation of much of the modern imagination, not his own. Now, however, he seems bent on a recoup, and that in Catholic terms, and he too fails to put things together (again, who are we to accuse him? but analyzing him may help us to understand ourselves).

In this novel we were given a subtle if unconscious demonstration of the Manichaean way. I would briefly suggest that in it there are two decisive halves, one which represents the failure and breakdown of human love, the other its achievement on the divine plane and without any relation to the human. The divine love is in no way achieved in the same act as the human; the latter does not lead to the divine; the divine, once achieved, does not fortify the human. This is said despite the difficulty that the affair is adulterous and of itself has no such relation. For the tones of the book are such that the liaison is not primarily adulterous, but to be taken as the attempt of man as such to find love. The second half of *The End of the Affair* is consumed by a long Augustinian dialogue with God on the part of the woman. This is a solution, indeed, this divine love, but it is not a solution which passes through the eye of a Beatrice, or the life of time. It leaps out of time. It is not a human way. One has the feeling that Greene has written a Catholic novel that is more Catholic than Catholicism.

2. *Dissociation In Time*

One lesson we can draw from all this is that, in all our attempts to analyze and correct the gradations of the collapse of sensibility in our time, we must all appraise ourselves lest, always partially blind to our own involvement in the contemporary story, we overshoot the mark. Dissociation is not helped by anything but true association, and we always have to question exactly when we have the latter. And as it is possible that we are only at the beginning of the way up, we may not get it very often. In talking of the *Four Quartets,* let us turn from the problem of human relations to that of time and human sensibility about it. The remarkable imagination of Eliot is now dealing with this very sharp area of trouble. No one is better equipped to reproduce the problem for the blood stream of the mind through the resources of poetry. The problem seems to be that we are immersed in time and are flattened down to its dimensions:

Time past and time future/ Allow but a little consciousness.
To be conscious is not to be in time . . .
Distracted from distraction by distraction

Men and bits of paper, whirled by the cold wind
That blows before and after time,
Wind in and out of unwholesome lungs
Time before and time after.
Eructation of unhealthy souls
Into the faded air, the torpid
Driven on the wind that sweeps the gloomy hills of London . . .

Ridiculous the waste sad time
Stretching before and after.

. . . as, when an underground train, in the tube, stops too long
between stations
And the conversation rises and slowly fades into silence
And you see behind every face the mental emptiness deepen
Leaving only the growing terror of nothing to think about;
Or when, under ether, the mind is conscious but conscious of nothing—

Men's curiosity searches past and future
And clings to that dimension. But to apprehend
The point of intersection of the timeless
With time, is an occupation for the saint.

Or else the poet knows also that men are already swept in the temporal sequence of their diseases, into new generations who have the taste of the abyss of anxiety, who know the terror of a larger time, the time of the sea and the time of an incredible history of the race before and after:

> The distant rote in the granite teeth,
> And the wailing warning from the approaching headland
> Are all sea voices, and the heaving groaner
> Rounded homewards, and the seagull:
> And under the oppression of the silent fog
> The tolling bell
> Measures time not our time, rung by the unhurried
> Ground swell, a time/Older than the time of chronometers . . .

These are some of the problems of the poem, the flatness of the small time and the terror of the new; and the question of the poem, though it is not a conceptual question, seems to be, what about it, what shall we do, what else is there, what else is there?

If I at all question the answers (they are not conceptual answers, but come from the refined bloodstream of a great Christian poet), it is not before considerable hesitation. For the time of Eliot is most certainly not the time of Baudelaire or Proust or Poe. His sense of time is ever so much more subtle. He knows that only through time is time conquered. He knows that the moment, as lived by men for good or evil, is more than an isolated moment; rather, it carries the weight of tradition and all the past and future,

> Not the intense moment
> Isolated, with no before and after,
> But a lifetime burning in every moment
> And not the lifetime of one man only
> But of old stones that cannot be deciphered.

He knows that time is the preserver, and that if we know more than the past it is the past we know for all that. Like St. Paul ("Leaving behind the things that are past") he also has the sense that all things are new,

Fare forward, travellers! . . .
You are not the same people who left that station
Or who will arrive at any terminus . . .

And the nature of language itself, and of poetry, must participate in the same surge of the same history, so that Dante's figure of Casella can also be seen in this modern version of a divine comedy, chasing the poet relentlessly on and away from his momentary conquest of time:

Every phrase and every sentence is an end and a beginning.
Every poem is an epitaph. And any action
Is a step to the block, to the fire, down the sea's throat
Or to an illegible stone; and that is where we start.[3]

But here perhaps is the beginning of my difficulty. For it is hard to say no to the impression, if I may use a mixture of my own symbols and his, that the Christian imagination is finally limited to the element of fire, to the day of Pentecost, to the descent of the Holy Ghost upon the disciples. The revelation of eternity and time is that of an *intersection,*

But to apprehend
The point of intersection of the timeless
With time, is an occupation for the saint—

It seems not unseemly to suppose that Eliot's imagination (and is not this a theology?) is alive with points of *intersection* and of *descent*. He seems to place our faith, our hope, and our love, not in the flux of time but in the *points* of time. I am sure his mind is interested in the line and time of Christ, whose Spirit is in his total flux. But I am not so sure about his imagination. Is it or is it not an imagination which is saved from time's nausea or terror by points of intersection?[4] There is his concern for

[3] All poetic citations from T. S. Eliot are in: T. S. Eliot, *The Complete Poems and Plays* 1909–1950 (New York: Harcourt, Brace & Company, 1956).

[4] I would call attention to this use of the intersection of time and eternity in Karl Barth, *The Epistle to the Romans,* pp. 29 and 60.

. . . the hardly, barely prayable
Prayer of the one Annunciation.

There is the dubiously temporal fascination of the poem for

. . . the still point of the turning world . . .

I can only say, there we have been: but I cannot say where.
And I cannot say, how long, for that is to place it in time.

To be conscious is not to be in time . . .

Everything that is good is annunciation and epiphany (and we may note here the altogether understandable poetic passion for epiphany

hints and guesses,
Hints followed by guesses . . .

The moments of happiness—not the sense of well-being
Fruition, fulfillment, security or affection,
Or even a very good dinner, but the sudden illumination—

in our day); there are

right action is freedom
From past and future also.

Here the impossible union
Of spheres of existence is actual,
Here the past and future
Are conquered and reconciled . . .

For most of us there is only the unattended
Moment, the moment in and out of time,
The distraction fit, lost in a flash of sunlight,
The wild thyme unseen, or the winter lightning
Or the waterfall, or music heard so deeply
That it is not heard at all, but you are the music
While the music lasts.

. . . This is the use of memory:
For liberation—not less of love but expanding
Of love beyond desire, and so liberation
From the future as well as the past.

There seems little doubt that Eliot is attracted above all by the image and the goal of immobility, and that in everything he seeks for approximations to this goal in the human order. "Love is itself unmoving." There is the violin, and we are the music while the music lasts, and the perpetual stillness of the Chinese jar, and the caught measure of the dance that does not seem to advance as the dance should. There is the detachment, as this poem understands it, of St. John of the Cross. Above all, there is this definition of love as "itself unmoving." Now this latter definition may be all very true, and capable of sharp substantiation from, let us say, St. Thomas. But it is also only partially true, according to the partialities of all human language, and capable of sharp addition, also from St. Thomas. For he tells us that God is act, and that everything is perfect in so far as it is in act.

At this point, one may very well ask what right we have to impose an abstract metaphysics upon the spontaneous images of the poet. But to this we have already given several answers in passing. For in the first place there is no such thing as an abstract metaphysics; it is composed of images, but these are composed according to the metaphysics of the analogy of being; in the second place and more importantly, I do not believe that there is such a thing as a purely spontaneous poetic image, free of the participating creativity of metaphysics and theology. Actually, there is no point in the soul so innocent that it is untouched by metaphysical and theological instincts and conflicts; therefore, our images are always and already going one way or the other. There is only a doubtful refuge from this fact in the aesthetic of modern poetry.

The readers of Eliot will have to find out what shapes and directions their own imaginations take. One hypothesis I would lay down about his is that, with relation to time and its problems, his own poetic images show a tendency to keep bouncing and leaping off this line in the direction of "eternity" and all its analogues. It does not evince a native inclination to pursue the possibilities of the line itself. Some possible evidence has been adduced for the validity of this impression. With a little less certainty on the writer's part, one last item will be suggested. Though in another context the poet tells us that here and now does not matter, he tells us even more strongly, and in a more conclusive part of the poem, that our precise place and moment is the precious thing. Nothing more than this would seem to come closer to some of the main propositions of our own essays.

> There are other places
> Which also are the world's end, some at the sea jaws.
>
> Or over a dark lake, in a desert or a city—
> But this is the nearest, in place and time,
> Now and in England.
>
> Here, the intersection of the timeless moment
> In England and nowhere. Never and always.

It is the word "nearest" that is interesting here. What does it mean? It could possibly mean that this place and time where we stand is nearest to us. But this would surely be a tautology, pretty much like saying that the nearest is the nearest is the nearest. Very likely what is being said is that it is the nearest to "eternity." Whereas, if we accept a dramatic and constructive view of time, it would seem much truer to say that it is nearest to the next moment in time. This is not meant to be subtle or ironic, for the matter is as simple as can be and as simple as that. But, you might very well say, is it not better to leap off the line into any approximation of eternity, or at any rate meet it vertically at the point of the line, than to continue on our horizontal pain with the rest of the "time-ridden faces?" Perhaps it would be, but actually it is impossible. And here I would recall some of the poem's opening lines,

> What might have been is an abstraction
> Remaining a perpetual possibility
> Only in a world of speculation.

No, what we must do is go along with the time-ridden faces. For they are at least on the right track and dealing with the right fact. We are constitutionally committed to the structures of temporality, and the major reason for most of the pain therein, for the boredom and the terror, is that at the moment we are historically committed to but one level of it. Jumping out of our human facts will not help at all, and will produce nothing but further strains. The only answer, as in every case, would seem to be to deepen the fact and its possible levels, to enter more deeply into it. And that will be done only by adding the dimension of Christic time. What that means may be gathered from the materials about the identity of process involved in the humanistic and Christic penetrations of time that are scattered throughout the *Spiritual Exercises of St. Ignatius.*

The phases of the life of man are the mysteries of man. The phases of the life of Christ are the mysteries of Christ. But it is the time of man which He re-explored. As St. Gregory tells us, the first Adam was constituted in grace and insight *at the point of achievement* of both, but the new Adam takes as his instrument, not the point of achievement, but the whole temporal process. Eliot says that the poetry, the process, does not matter, but the poetry and the process does matter (we have said that poetry is an action) and, like the age of Christ itself over against the first age of man, it must be considered a superior instrument. God is ironic, and He will not be beaten at His own game, and His game is time.

Thus his victory over Satan is internal and complete, not a victory that is extrinsic and Manichaean. His Son is the Sun, but the course of this Sun is through man. Above all, He is a bridegroom (*et ipse tamquam sponsus procedens a thalamo suo*) and an athlete (*exultavit ut gigas ad currendam viam*) running with joy (*desiderio desideravi*) through the whole length and breadth of the human adventure (*a summo caelo egressio ejus usque ad summum ejus*). He marches to the ultimate of the finite (*usque ad mortem*). Wherefore he has been exalted and every knee shall bow to Him, of all the things that are in heaven or on earth or under the earth. And this is not merely a mark of an external reward for suffering and obedience; it is the perfect sign and accomplishment of the mysteries or stages of human life, that they are, on a level more intense than ever before, an intrinsic path to the infinite. We miss the point if we only say that Christ is the gate and do not also add that man is the gate. It is our recurring mystery of more than one level in the one act and in the one fact. The single taste is the only taste which can water the waste land. Dissociated tastes, examples of which I have essayed in the case of Eliot, can only produce on the one hand a further disgust for the mysteries of man and on the other the most tenuous gnostic contacts with the mysteries of God. We have begun to settle for this kind of contractual arrangement.

But John Donne had not yet so settled. This is the way he contemplates the sick room where he may die:

> I joy that in these straights I see my west;
> For though their currents yield return to none,
> What shall my west hurt me? as west and east
> In all flat maps (and I am one) are one,
> So death doth touch the resurrection.[5]

And he reaches great identities in one single taste, the taste of the sweat of man and the blood of Christ:

> Look Lord, and find both Adams met in me;
> As the first Adam's sweat surrounds my face,
> May the last Adam's blood my soul embrace.[6]

3. Dissociation, Ritual, and Ritual Drama

Let me give a third example of a fact which, if reduced to but one level of existence, can produce the most disturbing repercussions in the human person. I am thinking of the instinctive drive in the soul toward ritual. This drive toward common movement and ritual existence is one of the most powerful movements in the soul of man. If it is choked off and denied on the deepest and religious levels of existence, as indeed it has been, it will concentrate the

[5] "Hymn to God My God, In My Sickness," *The Complete Poetry and Selected Prose of John Donne,* ed. Charles M. Coffin (New York: Random House, Modern Library, 1952), p. 271.

[6] *Ibid.,* pp. 271–272.

whole of itself on the most superficial levels of life, the immediately social, and will end in becoming an absolute, a parody of itself and of its own dignity. Whereas, if we were really united at the bedrock of our natures, most of the pressures toward the kind of conformism that all men really hate would be enormously lessened.

The fact is that these pressures come from the inside of us and are not really being satisfied at the more vital points of the soul. Romantic rebellion is always the too obvious counterpole to the kind of cheap, overgrown ritualism which besieges us, but it is no solution; in fact it only intensifies the difficulty. The thought I have in mind, not at all a reproachful but an analytical thought, is that it has been the collapse of the idea of the Church in our civilization that has driven us into our present social rites. Gimmick ritual has necessarily been substituted for the real thing. But this process is true not only of the world of technology and the mass media; it is also terribly true for many developments within the contemporary literary imagination as they occur within the souls of the intellectuals.

One thing we may be sure of. The achievements and the distortions within man's search for common movement will go on to the end of time. And so will the conversation about and the work toward a religious and ritual theatre. None of us, I dare say, can really believe any longer the facile judgment that ritualism was an early and primitive beginning for the theatre in the West, that we now know too much, now feel too much, are now too human, have too great a burden of sophistication, to recover earlier situations. We are all getting a bit weary of settling essential matters by mere tricks of vocabulary, and this use of words like "primitive" and "sophisticated" happens to be one of the tricks. The rhythm of the facts changes too easily for that. What was primitive becomes sophisticated a generation later, and vice versa.

The historical fact not often enough noticed is that *Quem Queritis,* the simplest and earliest piece in the liturgical theatre of the tenth century, was already surrounded by a context of symbolism, movement and architecture that had taken a thousand years of sophistication and toil for the West to produce. Now we have somewhat the opposite general situation: our plays are for the most part highly "sophisticated" pieces that appeal only to the "intellectual" areas of society, but they could hardly have a more miserable and more primitive context, architecturally and socially, within which to operate. There is no general style of life, in the highest and best sense of that phrase, which the theatre can call upon outside of itself as one of its natural resources. So far as real movement and manners are concerned, our playwrights are completely on their own, for the simple but tragic reason that we too are on our own, unless indeed we wish to submit to the style of no-style—that there be no ritual in life.

An interesting example of the dramatist's problem is presented by *He Who Must Die.* My own reaction to this superb piece of craftsmanship was one both of admiration and deep uncertainty. It was more than uncertainty of the top of the head; it belonged more to the whole body, which found it difficult to enter into the movement and the action, into this powerful modern retelling of the life and passion of Christ and His friends. The more I searched out the reasons for the uncertainty, in the picture itself, in *The Greek Passion,* the novel by Nikos Kazantzakis from which it was drawn, and in *The Odyssey: A Modern Sequel,* Kazantzakis' remarkable rendition of the Ulysses theme, the more I felt that the collapse of movement was his, not mine. The action was being used in the name of ideas, and the two never quite came together. And the ideas themselves were both brilliant and fraudulent, always giving the impression of having been put together and manipulated by a *composer.* The top of the writer's head was in final command. The realism was powerful, but always black and white and therefore contrived.

The real is thus manipulated in the name of superficial parallels to the Gospel story. The priests are either martyrs or villains, the people either haves or have-nots. (I was confirmed in this interpretation when I read Kazantzakis' theory that the artist has the power and right to make, mould, manipulate, destroy reality, in

Book XVII of *The Odyssey*.) In the name of Christ the immaculately "white" characters of the movie-book are always leaving the "black" characters, always desperately giving something up, abandoning it, leaving it, running, running, running. The final clue for both the movie and the novel must come from the brilliant poem. The clue is Ulysses, for Christ and the good priest, and all their friends, are Ulysses; not the Greek Ulysses trying to find his valiant way home, but the new Ulysses creating the new ritual of no ritual at all, breaking away from every father and every home, even from hope, and finally, even from freedom itself. In the end all things indeed come home again; but into the home of the head of Ulysses whose head has created them all and receives them again, with compassion because even compassion is a nice idea. The religious drama ends in the perfect parody of ritual, in the lonely head of Ulysses. It is the brilliant rite of Narcissus. Nobody else is there. This is one of the great temptations of the intellectual as he tries to create a new ritual drama.

The thought occurs, before turning to Archibald MacLeish's *J.B.*, that one of the greatest obstacles to any possible effective restoration of biblical-ritual drama among us is the constant insistence on the imposition of "modern sensibility" within the action. There is a good sense in which this can and must be done, but the project also has its fraudulent senses, especially when it means, rather apodictically, that we are what we are, we feel what we feel, and that is that and let no one raise any questions. This is historicism at its purest. Sensibility, our sensibility, is so precious a commodity that everything gets used for its purposes and is to be reduced to its shape.

Certainly in the case of *J.B.* the cart of sensibility and thought is way out in front of the horse of the action. If, almost to the point of parody, one wanted an encyclopedia of the thoughts and systems of modern man, Jung, Bergson, Freud, Husserl, the existentialists, The Golden Bough, Joyce, Dostoevsky, Marx, he will find it all in the Ulysses-Christ of Kazantzakis. The same thing goes on in *J.B.*, though in a narrower and less competent way. The air is oppressive with the thoughts and speculation of the author, who is using the story of Job as a vehicle. It is a new Job we are given, a thoroughly Romantic one, as many critics have pointed out. In the contest with God he turns out much more handsomely than God. Though nothing is left to him, there is Life and Love, a few leaves of forsythia, his wife, and the potential coals and fires of his own heart. So that thus far we have on our hands the creative mind of Kazantzakis and the enduring, understanding heart of MacLeish, both pretty much alone. There is little room here for the choral dance or the choral song.

I do not intend to quarrel here about the question of God, who is doubtfully believed in but much talked about within this religious play. My own concern is with the general assumption in the air that if *J.B.* is not very good theology, it does at least explore the human experience as the theologians do not. If this were true we could all be critically happy about the play because it is a reasonable certainty that an art which really follows the lines of human experience will be following the lines of light and the Holy Spirit, and will willy-nilly get to God. There were a few lines in the televised performance of *Child of Our Time* in which the boy who has just told the priest that he does not believe in God is given the answer that the priest is not concerned with his present disbelief but that if he will go and do everything the other boys in the home are doing for a few months the priest would then gladly discuss the problem. This would be something more substantial than the few forsythia leaves which alone are left in the ashes of civilization and which alone prevent the suicide of Mr. and Mrs. J.B. Mr. MacLeish is a very reputable fighter for ideas but in this case the ideas are too artificial to find a body. That man is magnificently best in his worst moments, that *he* can love if Reality cannot, that light can come only from the coals of our own heart, that man will go endlessly on, these are "splendid" ideas, but they cannot get a grip on reality, and the only ritual they will ever evoke is the lonely movement of thought in the head of an isolated poetry.

Even the language, therefore, gets tenuous and unsubstantial.

Forsythias are not very much reality. Names like Mrs. Murphy and Mrs. Boticelli do not evoke real images, and surely neither of them is in the audience for such a play. There is a preciosity communicated even to the real things: "the time of the wild goats," "God the boiling point of water," "blond in all that blood that daughter," "you know Muff, my purple poodle," "sticks and stones and steel are chances," "can the seven bones reply."[7]

These "realities" mean something if and only if one knows what the writer is saying and thinking in the order of something that is almost pure argument. If one doesn't follow the argument—which is as likely as not—then he will find the greatest difficulty in locating the lines of significance of Mrs. Murphy and Mrs. Boticelli, the forsythia, or death as "a bone that stammers . . . a tooth among the flints that has forgotten." Do not believe for a moment in the new dichotomy that has been offered to us, on the one hand of a Christian theology that is transcendental and on the other hand a new poetic and non-theological experience that is in touch with reality. It is already a good number of years since Lionel Trilling did us the great service of pointing out that it is the liberal imagination which is transcendental and out of touch with the gripping lines of experience. Perhaps *J.B.* should have begun where it ended, with an exploration of the love of Mr. and Mrs. J.B., to see if it has the actuality of love uncapitalized.

It is not necessary to be complicated about this whole matter. Perhaps what I am saying is that we need a lot more dancing in common before we do any more thinking. We must also begin to ask the fundamental question, what makes a playwright and what should his basic training be.

Certainly he must make himself more than a "thinker," more even than a poet as we now understand the term. Such a restriction would be theatrically fatal. He should know a good deal, and this in terms of his own blood stream, about the dance and ritual in the oldest and widest senses of these terms. He should be an actual man of the theatre, as Shakespeare probably was and Kazantzakis,

[7] Archibald MacLeish, *J. B.* (Boston: Houghton, 1958).

MacLeish, even Eliot, probably are not. He should be a man who delights in the coronation of a queen or the inauguration of a president, who delights generally in a public style of life for man. He should know history and not think that his private mind can alone create a theatre. He should be deeply aware of the eternal rhythms of the heart of the *people,* the strength these rhythms have for salvation (as they were caught, for example, at the end of *Cabiria*). He must, finally, come to an intimate knowledge of the work of the choreographers and the musicians, and not leave his own skills in isolation from theirs.

Let us therefore end this discussion of ritual where we began. We could very well end by borrowing a term from the psychologists. The term is that of *displacement.* By every instinct in them men desperately need to think and move together, ritually. One of the sources of modern anxiety is surely that people get into too many situations where they do not know what people will think or do next. If these ritual needs collapse on the deeper levels of the body and spirit, then they will break out (and have) on the cheaper levels of both.

The solution should rather lie in the direction of the deepening of the fact, or the rediscovery of its levels. Here our case is ritual. The rhythms of a song are a ritual, but they are being reduced to a crooning dream, one of the cheapest of all gnostic creations. The rhetoric of great human speech is a ritual, but I have heard it too often torn to the tatters of "meaningful fact" by fine actors who were intent on showing that they could enter into each line and syllable and movement of the body, thus giving personality and modernity to every fact. The lines were no longer allowed to float out in the air as ritual victories. Judith Anderson has done this sad thing to Medea and Laurence Olivier has done it to both Oedipus and Richard III.

Afraid of the victory of conformity, we let it remain in its present degenerate state, and we eagerly seek the recompenses of the victories of "personality" on the levels of art and the spirit. The artist becomes the isolated, romantic hero, instead of taking up the task of building, on those other levels of the fact, higher and deeper rituals wherein alone personality will be achieved and our cheaper conformities or etiquettes restore themselves to sense through not having to exhaust this magnificent energy at a single point. The dance is always formal, but David danced before the ark in freedom. It is an amazing fact that the rigidities of the perfect sonnet rhythms create the possibility of freedom for its individual musical phrases. Surely too, it is interesting that it is in the higher reserve of the divine liturgy that we have suddenly the sense of freedom, of having escaped from society. And let this last phrase be perhaps our last and best example of the truth that we have given up the penetration into all the levels of factuality. I should correct the words "escaped from society," but will not. Let them stand as they are, as a symbol that the language of the solipsist, of the romantic hero, has taken over in these highest matters, so that I as a Catholic am trapped into the use of them when I am talking of my most social, my most ritual, my freest moment. Not to speak of music, rhetoric, the dance, the sonnet, the liturgy, we hardly have the most ordinary vocabulary left in terms of which we might speak of fidelity to the forms of our literal human reality all the way through the whole line of being without abandoning these forms for some final gnostic and non-human temptation.

Perhaps it would be good to close this essay with a brief remark on this problem of vocabulary. Is there a proper and satisfactory vocabulary we can use to clarify the whole import of that crucial question of levels of being which we have placed at the very center of the relations between theology and the imagination? Probably not, because the presence of such a satisfactory language among us would itself be an indication that we were in conscious possession of these critical dilemmas and of possible ways out of them. Nevertheless we must begin. We on our part shall begin with an outline of the vocabulary of the fourfold level of biblical exegesis, not with the great hope that it will resolve everything but with the confidence that, if interpreted rightly and for us, it does supply *some* clues for an escape out of what ails us. Furthermore, we should stress that, if the questions it helped the human mind to confront are far from dated, the language itself of biblical exegesis may be quite old-fashioned for the purposes of the contemporary imagination; it is in great need of adaptation. I think that we would be more sympathetically placed toward his vocabulary and his whole way of thinking if we were to suppose that the biblical exegete was trying, in so far as this was possible, to put himself in the place of God and to follow the operations of His "imagination" as the latter was working out a unique supernatural history for men.

Part III

MOORINGS FOR A THEOLOGICAL CRITICISM

Nathan A. Scott, Jr.

The Modern Experiment in Criticism: A Theological Appraisal*

OURS IS A TIME in which, both life and thought being up against tremendous odds, we are all likely, in some degree or other, to be "crisis"-hunters, finding evidences of our general brokenness here, there, and everywhere. And, in my method of getting under way an estimate of the modern experiment in criticism, I do not myself propose to be an exception to the obsession of our age with *Tendenz,* since I suspect that any such estimate, from whatever point of view it may be undertaken, must begin by observing that criticism too is today in something like a situation of crisis. The crisis that I have in mind is one that arises out of what is central and decisive in the doctrines of modern poetics, and it was given a kind of desperate announcement a few years ago when Allen Tate bluntly raised the question which it is a peculiarity of our generation to be anxious about—namely, "is literary criticism possible?"[1]

It would not, of course, at first appear that the man of letters in our time feels himself to be at such an extremity, for one of the patron saints of the modern movement has assured us that the con-

* Reprinted from *Modern Literature and the Religious Frontier,* by Nathan A. Scott, Jr., by permission of Harper & Row.

[1] The reference is to Mr. Tate's essay "Is Literary Criticism Possible?" which appears in his book *The Forlorn Demon: Didactic and Critical Essays* (Chicago, Henry Regnery Co., 1953).

temporary critic is "among the most presentable instances of modern man" and that in depth and precision his work is "beyond all earlier criticism in our language." And on all sides today we are frequently given similar testimonies of how unparalleled in any previous age are the vigor and trenchancy of criticism in our own time. So, with a zeal that is itself certainly unparalleled in any previous time, the contemporary movement is anthologized almost annually; and the editors of the journals in which it has gained expression frequently engage their colleagues in symposia the aim of which is to indicate the gains that have been made and the solid ground on which we may now take our stand. But in all this stock-taking I think we may sense a certain anxious uncertainty as to whether anything has been achieved at all and as to whether, in the presence of the great works of the past and of the modern period, we are yet able really to penetrate the ontological intransigence of the aesthetic fact. And it is just possible that, despite the actual impressiveness of the achievement of modern criticism, this anxiety is a consequence of the doctrine which it has promoted and which has had the ironical effect of calling into question the very possibility of criticism itself. Indeed, what I want to propose is that, if we will reconsider the basic premises of modern poetics, we may be put in mind not only of what in part our present distresses in criticism derive from but also of the special kind of testimony about contemporary criticism that it may be necessary for a theorist to make whose fundamental bearings are of a theological sort.

When we seek for the principal motives that underlie the general movement of criticism in our period, we cannot, of course, for long escape the recognition that, among them at least, has been the intention of many of its most distinguished representatives to offer some resistance to the reductionist tendency of modern scientism, particularly when it broaches upon those transactions with reality that are peculiar to the humanistic imagination. I can think of no single doctrine or emphasis that is subscribed to by all those writers who at one time or another have been held accountable for "the new criticism," but certainly by far a greater number of them are of a single mind in their apprehensiveness about the deeper cultural implications of the reigning positivism than they are on any other single point. And it has been their unwillingness to give their suffrage to the absolute hegemony of empirical science which has been a decisive influence upon their approach to the fundamental issues in theory of literature. Ours has been a time in which it has been generally supposed that the only responsible versions of experience that can be had are those afforded us by the empirical sciences and in which, therefore, the common impulse has been to trivialize the arts by regarding them as merely a kind of harmless play which, at best, is to be tolerated for the sedative effect that it has upon the nervous system. But even this assignment hardly constitutes a satisfactory charter for the artist, since, in the ministry of health to the nervous system, he is not likely to compete successfully with our modern doctors of psychology. So, in the last analysis, our culture has been incapable of finding for the arts, and especially for literature, a valuable or an irreplaceable function. And the result has been that the major strategists of modern criticism have felt it incumbent upon themselves to revindicate the poetic enterprise by doing what the culture was unable to do—namely, by seeking to define that unique and indispensable role in the human economy that is played by imaginative literature and that can be pre-empted by nothing else.

This contemporary effort to specify the nature of the autonomy which a work of literary art possesses has involved a careful analysis of what is special in the linguistic strategies of the poet. And the aim has been to establish that poetry is poetry and not another thing, for it has been recognized that in a culture as dominated by scientific procedure as is our own the common tendency is to hold all forms of discourse accountable to those critical canons that are really appropriate only to scientific modes of discourse—which, of course, then makes it possible for nonscientific modes of statement to be quickly dismissed on one pretext or another. So the tack that the contemporary movement in criticism has taken has been one that involves the denial that the poet is any sort of expositor at all. He is, we have been told, not an expositor, not a Platonist, not an allegorist, not a merchant in the business of ideas; on the contrary, he is a certain kind of technician, a certain kind of maker, who constructs out of language special sorts of things, such things as we call dramas and novels and poems. As the doctrine runs, what is distinctive about the language of imaginative literature is that, in contrast to the ordinary forms of discourse, it does not involve the reduction of words to the level of being merely conceptual signs. The mind is not led to appropriate the meaning of the individual components of a literary discourse by way of seeking those referents that are extrinsic to the discourse and to which its component terms presumably point. And our immunity from any compulsion to relate the language of the poem to an external reality has, in recent criticism, been understood in terms of the organic character of poetic structure. Which is to say that the contemporary critic has come to see poetic meaning not as a function of the relationships between the terms of the poem and some reality which is extrinsic to them, but rather as a function of the interrelationships that knit the terms together into the total pattern that forms the unity of the work. Our way of stating this distinctive character of poetic language is to say that its terms function not ostensively but reflexively, not semantically but syntactically—by which we mean that, unlike the situation that obtains in logical discourse in which the terms "retain their distinctive characters despite the relationship into which they have been brought,"[2] in poetic discourse they lose their distinctive characters, as they fuse into one another and are modified by what Cleanth Brooks calls "the pressure of the context."[3] It is, indeed, this whole phenomenon to which Mr. Brooks has appropriately applied the term *irony,* a concept that he has insisted upon by way of emphatically remarking the radical extent to which the terms and "statements" of a literary work bear

[2] Ernest Cassirer, *Language and Myth,* trans. Susanne K. Langer (New York: Harper & Brothers, 1946), p. 91.

[3] Cleanth Brooks, "Irony as a Principle of Structure," in *Literary Opinion in America,* ed. Morton Dauwen Zabel (New York: Harper & Brothers, 1951), pp. 730–731.

the pressure of the total context and have their meanings modified by that context. And it will be remembered that in a brilliant passage in *The Well Wrought Urn* he suggests that they ought even to be read as if they were speeches in a drama, since, as he says, if they are to be justified at all, it will not be by virtue of their "scientific or historical or philosophical truth, but [they will, rather, be] justified in terms of a principle analogous to that of dramatic propriety."[4]

Now it is in terms of this organic character of poetic structure that our generation has come to understand the resistance of literary art to the discursive paraphrase. It does not yield a series of paraphrasable abstractions because no set of terms of which a poetic work is constituted refers to anything extrinsic to the work: they refer, rather, to the other terms to which they are related within the work. And thus the perception of the meaning of the work awaits not an act of comparison between the component terms and the external objects or events which they may be taken to symbolize, but, rather, an act of imaginative prehension that will focus upon "the entire pattern of internal reference . . . apprehended as a unity."[5] The coherence of a work of imaginative literature is to be sought, in other words, not in any set of logically manageable propositions into which it may be paraphrased but rather in the living pattern of interrelated themes and "resolved stresses"[6] that the work contains.

There is, however, one inescapable fact that such a formulation of poetic meaning may at first appear to neglect, and it is the incorrigibly referential thrust that words do have. They like to function ostensively; that is to say, they insist upon pointing to things: it

[4] Cleanth Brooks, *The Well Wrought Urn* (London: Dennis Dobson Ltd., n.d.; originally published in New York by Reynal and Hitchcock in 1947), p. 188.

[5] Joseph Frank, "Spatial Form in Modern Literature," in *Criticism: The Foundations of Modern Literary Judgment,* ed. Mark Schorer et al. (New York: Harcourt, Brace and Co., 1948), p. 383. Mr. Frank's essay contains some very acute observations on the "reflexive" character of poetic language.

[6] Brooks, *op. cit.,* p. 186.

makes no difference whether the things are actual or ideal; what counts is that they are extrinsic to the words themselves, for the words are not happy unless they are performing a semantic function. And, this being their habit, it would seem that they would be intractable before the poetic purpose. But this problem is recognized by contemporary theorists who, indeed, have come to regard the poetic labor as involving in part an effort to deliver the word from its ordinary logical bonds and its inherent mediateness. As Ezra Pound once remarked, the poet "takes words ordinarily having conventional objective meanings, and by forcing them into a new and independent structure objectifies fresh meanings. . . . The function of the artist," said Mr. Pound, "is precisely the formulation of what has not found its way into language, i.e. any language, verbal, plastic or music."[7] And it is precisely this effort of the poet to perform not simply an act of denotation but the far more difficult act of evocation, of capturing and conveying the full, living body of the world and of objectifying fresh experience of it—it is precisely this effort that very often commits him to the daring project of liberating words from the logical form into which they conventionally fall, so that they may be free to enter into the characteristic structures of poetic form in which they are affected by, and in turn affect, the total context established by the work. This is why you do not discover the meaning of a poem by taking an inventory of the various terms of which it is constituted and then by adding up the various meanings which these terms have in conventional usage. And when contemporary criticism insists upon the foolishness of such a procedure, it does so because it is sensitive, perhaps above all else, to the marvelous violence of the action that is performed upon terms once they are drawn up into the poetic process, so that each alters under the aspect of the other and enters relationships that are completely irreducible to logical form. It is the mystery that T. S. Eliot had in mind when he remarked upon "that per-

[7] Ezra Pound, "Epstein, Belgion and Meaning," *The Criterion,* Vol. IX, No. XXXVI (April, 1930), p. 471.

petual slight alteration of language, words perpetually juxtaposed in new and sudden combination," which takes place in poetry.

So we may say, then, by way of summary, that the redefinition in our time of the nature of literary art has led to the view that the given work exists in and through its language. What we have immediately before us is a patterned mosaic in language which is, in the phrase by which M. Denis de Rougemont speaks of the work of art in general, "a calculated trap for meditation"[8]—and as such it effectively insists that before it we perform an act of rapt and "intransitive attention."[9] One might even say that for the modern sensibility the poetry in the poem resides "not [in] some intrinsic quality (beauty or truth) of the materials"[10] with which the poet builds his poem, but rather in the completeness of the unity or "composition" that he contrives out of the stuff of language. What we begin with, as Mr. Eliot has told us, is simply "excellent words in excellent arrangement."[11]

Now this redefinition in modern criticism of "the mode of existence of a literary work of art" has in turn led to a redefinition of the creative process. For so rigorous has been the stress put upon the autonomy of poetic language that language itself has often very nearly been regarded as the enabling cause of literary art. It is assumed that art is a virtue of the practical intellect and that the poet's vision is not fully formed until it has become objectified in language. Indeed, the executive principle of the cre-

[8] Denis de Rougemont, "Religion and the Mission of the Artist," in *Spiritual Problems in Contemporary Literature,* ed. Stanley R. Hopper (New York: Harper & Brothers, 1952), p. 177.

[9] *Vide* Eliseo Vivas, "A Definition of the Esthetic Experience," in *The Problems of Aesthetics,* ed. Eliseo Vivas and Murray Krieger (New York: Rinehart and Co., 1953), pp. 406–411. It is to Professor Vivas that we are indebted for the definition in contemporary aesthetics of the poetic experience in terms of "intransitive attention." This concept receives further elaboration in his book *Creation and Discovery* (New York: Noonday Press, 1955).

[10] Cleanth Brooks, *Modern Poetry and the Tradition* (Chapel Hill: University of North Carolina Press, 1939), p. 43.

[11] T. S. Eliot, "Preface to the 1928 Edition," *The Sacred Wood* (London: Faber and Faber Ltd., 1934, 4th ed.), pp. ix–x.

ative process is considered really to derive not from the poet's metaphysic or his special perspective upon the human story but rather from the medium to which his vision is submitted and by which it is controlled. It is regarded as a truism that whatever it is that the poet "says" about reality in a given work is something the content of which he himself did not fully possess until the completion of the work. For, as Murray Krieger has put it, "the poet's original idea for his work, no matter how clearly thought out and complete he thinks it is, undergoes such radical transformations as language goes creatively to work upon it that the finished poem, in its full internal relations, is far removed from what the author thought he had when he began."[12] The medium alone, in other words, objectifies the poet's materials and gives them their implications. This axiom of the contemporary movement in criticism is expressed with especial directness by R. P. Blackmur, when he remarks in his essay on Melville:

> Words, and their intimate arrangements, must be the ultimate as well as the immediate source of every effect in the written or spoken arts. Words bring meaning to birth and themselves contained the meaning as an imminent possibility before the pangs of junction. To the individual artist the use of words is an adventure in discovery; the imagination is heuristic among the words it manipulates. The reality you labour desperately or luckily to put into your words . . . you will actually have found there, deeply ready and innately formed to give an objective being and specific idiom to what you knew and did not know that you knew.[13]

Whatever it is, in other words, that is in the completed work is there by virtue of the language which controls the creative process and which produces the "new word" that Yvor Winters declares the authentic work of literary art to be. The poet does not have a version of the human situation to express, some imperious preoccu-

[12] Murray Krieger, *The New Apologists for Poetry* (Minneapolis: University of Minnesota Press, 1956), p. 23.

[13] R. P. Blackmur, "The Craft of Herman Melville: A Putative Statement," in *The Lion and the Honeycomb* (New York: Harcourt, Brace and Co., 1955), p. 138.

pation to voice, or some difficult report to make; no, he has none of this: indeed, as Mr. Eliot tells us, there is no good reason for supposing that he does "any thinking on his own" at all, for it is not his business to think—not even poets as great as Dante and Shakespeare. No, all the writer need have is his medium, and, if he knows how to trust it and how to submit to it, it will do his work for him: it will, as Mr. Blackmur says, bring the "meaning to birth."

Now, to be sure, what I have offered thus far is patently an abridgment of the advanced poetics of our time, but perhaps this account is at least sufficiently complex to provide some indication of the sources of the crisis that I earlier remarked as having arisen in contemporary criticism. It is clear certainly that we are being asked by many of the most distinguished theorists of our day to regard the work of literary art as a linguistic artifact that exists in complete detachment from any other independently existent reality. The fully achieved work of art, as the argument runs, is a discrete and closed system of mutually interrelated terms: the organic character of the structure prevents the constituent terms from being atomistically wrenched out of their context and made to perform a simple referential function, and it also succeeds in so segregating the total structure from the circumambient world as to prevent its entering into any extramural affiliation. "A poem should not mean but be," says Mr. MacLeish, and thereby, in this famous line from his poem "Ars Poetica," he summarizes, with a beautiful concision, the mind of a generation.

But, then, if the work of literary art exists in complete isolation from all those contexts that lie beyond the one established by the work itself, if it neither points outward toward the world nor inward toward the poet's subjectivity, if it is wholly self-contained and cut off from the general world of meaning, why then it would seem that nothing really can be said about it at all. And in this unpromising strait are we not all chargeable with "the heresy of paraphrase"? Mark Van Doren suggests in his book *The Noble Voice* that "Any great poet is in a sense beyond criticism for the simple reason that he has written a successful story," that "criticism is most at home with failure," and that in the presence of the great success it must be "as dumb as the least instructed reader."[14] This is hardly an inspiriting conclusion for the practising critic to reach; yet it is, in a way, the conclusion that has been enforced upon him by the new poetics of our period. For the curious irony that has arisen out of the contemporary movement in criticism is a result of the fact that, on the one hand, it has striven for a concept of literary art that would permit responsible discussion of it as art rather than as something else; but, on the other hand, it has succeeded in so completely segregating art from everything else till, in its presence, it has condemned itself, at least in principle, to silence. And this is, I believe, the reason for the noticeable anxiety in the critical forums today about whether anything has really been achieved at all. Much has been achieved, of course, in the establishment of a fund of substantiated judgments about literary texts, but the point is that this achievement has had no sanction in the body of principle to which our generation has come to subscribe, for that body of doctrine has tended ultimately to represent the aesthetic fact as unavailable for critical discussion. And thus it should perhaps, after all, not be surprising that the same distinguished critic who some years ago told us that the contemporary achievement surpassed "all earlier criticism in our language" is, in a more recent essay, to be found wondering why it is that critics don't go mad; and one of his equally distinguished friends often ruminates upon the "burden" that he and his colleagues in criticism today must bear.

The distresses and distempers that lead our most sensitive practical critics today to reflect upon the inhumanly difficult nature of their labors are, in other words, a result of their betrayal by the inadequate concept of literature that has descended to them from the main strategists in modern theory. There are many points at which this concept might now be put under some pressure, but that upon which I want to focus on this present occasion is the under-

[14] Mark Van Doren, *The Noble Voice* (New York: Henry Holt and Co., 1946), pp. 181–182.

standing of the creative process that has been promoted in our time, for here, I think, we may get as good a purchase as any other upon our present dilemmas. And when this aspect of modern theory is examined, it becomes evident to how great a degree its legislation about the nature of the poetic object has determined its understanding of the process by which that object is made. What it has wanted to insist upon is the indissoluble unity of form and content in the work which gives it the kind of autonomy that prevents its being translated into any other mode of statement. And this concern has in turn led contemporary theorists to minimize the controlling effect upon the creative process of the writer's ideas and beliefs. For it has been supposed that were any great tribute to be paid to these factors we should be quickly on the way toward reinstating the heresy of didacticism, with its notion that the literary work is merely a rhetorical communication of independently formulable ideas.

So great stress has been put upon the directive role of the medium in the creative process, and we have been reminded of how radical must be the transformations of the poet's ideas, once these ideas undergo the modifications necessitated by the exigencies of a developing linguistic structure. What we are asked to understand is that nothing really exists in imaginative literature, except as it is organized by the medium which is language. Indeed, whatever does exist is itself created by the language, for, as I. A. Richards says, it is the "means of that growth which is the mind's endless endeavour to order itself"[15]—or, as Mr. Blackmur puts it in the passage which was quoted earlier, "Words bring meaning to birth and themselves contained the meaning as an imminent possibility before the pangs of junction." The medium, in other words, is a kind of intelligent agency which in some mysterious way puppetizes the poet and does the job for which, in its innocence, common sense has traditionally held him responsible.

I am aware that at this point I am to some extent exaggerating

[15] I. A. Richards, *The Philosophy of Rhetoric* (New York: Oxford University Press, 1936), p. 131.

the contemporary testimony, but its own exaggerations in this matter are, I think, sufficiently great to make my characterization intelligible. In any event I am reassured by the coincidence that I discover between my own reaction and that of the English critic D. S. Savage, who suggests in the Preface to his book *The Withered Branch* that this "dizzy elevation" of the medium in contemporary criticism clearly leaves something important out of account.[16] And there is, I believe, no finer recent statement of what is unaccounted for than that which Jacques Maritain gives us in his great book *Creative Intuition in Art and Poetry*.[17]

In this book, which grew out of his Mellon Lectures that were given during 1952 in the National Gallery in Washington, M. Maritain brings to a point of culmination nearly forty years of study in the arts and in aesthetics. And in one of its aspects the book has it as a major concern to call into question the modern notion that the creative process in art is merely an *operational* process and that the artist is merely a special sort of technician. "As to the great artists," he says, "who take pleasure in describing themselves as mere engineers in the manufacturing of an artifact of words or sounds, as Paul Valéry did, and as Stravinsky does, I think that they purposely do not tell the truth, at least completely. In reality the spiritual content of a creative intuition, with the poetic or melodic sense it conveys, animates their artifact, despite their grudge against inspiration."[18] And this must be so, because, as M. Maritain insists, the activity which produces poetic art does not begin until the poet permits himself to be invaded by the reality of "Things" and until he himself seeks to invade the deepest recesses of his own subjectivity—the two movements of the spirit being

16 D. S. Savage, *The Withered Branch* (New York: Pellegrini and Cudahy, n.d.), p. 12.

17 In the following account of this book that I give I have liberally raided two of the pages in an article of mine ("Maritain in His Role as Aesthetician") that appeared in *The Review of Metaphysics* in March, 1955 (Vol. VIII, No. 3).

18 Jacques Maritain, *Creative Intuition in Art and Poetry* (New York: Pantheon Books, 1953), p. 62.

performed together, as though one, "in a moment of affective union." When the soul thus comes into profound spiritual contact with itself and when it also enters into the silent and mysterious depths of Being, it is brought back to "the single root" of its powers, "where the entire subjectivity is, as it were, gathered in a state of expectation and virtual creativity."[19] And the whole experience becomes "a state of obscure . . . and sapid knowing."[20] Then

> after the silent gathering a breath arises, coming not from the outside, but from the center of the soul—sometimes a breath which is almost imperceptible, but compelling and powerful, through which everything is given in easiness and happy expansion; sometimes a gale bursting all of a sudden, through which everything is given in violence and rapture; sometimes the gift of the beginning of a song; sometimes an outburst of unstoppable words.[21]

And only when this point in the artistic process has been reached may *operation* begin. For the artist to initiate the processes of *operation* at any earlier point is for him "to put the instrumental and secondary before the principal and primary, and to search for an escape through the discovery of a new external approach and new technical revolutions, instead of passing first through the creative source . . . "[22] Then what is produced is but "a corpse of a work of art—a product of academicism."[23] "If creative intuition is lacking," he says, "a work can be perfectly made, and it is nothing; the artist has nothing to say. If creative intuition is present, and passes, to some extent, into the work, the work exists and speaks to us, even if it is imperfectly made and proceeds from a man who has the habit of art and a hand which shakes."[24]

At "the single root" of the poetic process, then, there is a profound act of creative intuition. And in this cognitive act, says M. Maritain, the soul "suffers things more than it learns them," experiencing them "through resonance in subjectivity." The thing that is cognitively grasped is simply "some complex of concrete and

[19] *Ibid.*, p. 239.
[20] *Ibid.*
[21] *Ibid.*, p. 243.
[22] *Ibid.*, p. 223.
[23] *Ibid.*, p. 63.
[24] *Ibid.*, p. 60.

individual reality, seized in the violence of its sudden self-assertion and in the total unicity"[25] that is constituted by "all the other realities which echo in this existent, and which it conveys in the manner of a sign."[26] And it is the richness of this imaginative prehension that gives life and power to the mathematic of poetic form.

M. Maritain is a good Thomist, and he does not therefore need to be reminded that art is "a virtue of the practical intellect" and that it requires "all the logic and shrewdness, self-restraint and self-possession of working intelligence."[27] Indeed, he insists upon the essential relation between art and reason, since it is reason that discovers the necessities in the nature of the medium that must be observed in order for the work to be brought into existence. But he also insists that the reason and the calculation that are in the poet "are there only to handle fire,"[28] and that to grant them anything more than this purely instrumental function, simply for the sake of adherence to a puritanical formalism and a spurious austerity, is to be guilty of a gratuitous dogmatism.

Now many of us will doubtless find it difficult to accept M. Maritain's argument in this book in its entirety, for there are phases of his psychology—particularly those that bear upon his doctrine of the spiritual preconscious—that will surely strike us as exceedingly cumbersome and perhaps even slightly obscurantist. And I have adduced his testimony here not because it perfectly answers all of the questions that he raises. But, at a time when it is too much our habit to regard the medium as the single factor controlling the poetic process, M. Maritain's formulation of the problem has the very great merit of eloquently reminding us again of the actual primacy in the process of *poetic vision.* He discloses to us, that is, a stratagem for declaring once again that it is not language which brings "meaning to birth" and which enables the mind "to order itself"—not language, but *vision.*

[25] *Ibid.,* p. 126.
[26] *Ibid.*
[27] *Ibid.,* p. 246.
[28] *Ibid.,* p. 218.

Eliseo Vivas also helps us to some extent, I believe, with our difficulties when he reminds us that what is in part distinctive about the artist is his "passion for order."[29] "Really, universally," said Henry James, "relations stop nowhere, and the exquisite problem of the artist is eternally but to draw, by a geometry of his own, the circle within which they shall happily *appear* to do so."[30] That is to say, the artist wants to give a shape and a significance to what Mr. Vivas calls "the primary data of experience." He wants to contain the rich plenitude of experience within a pattern that will illumine and give meaning to its multifarious detail and its bewildering contingency. But, of course, he cannot discover such a pattern unless he has a vantage point from which to view experience and by means of which his insights may be given order and proportion. Which is to say that he can transmute the viscous stuff of existential reality into the order of significant form only in accordance with what are his most fundamental beliefs about what is radically significant in life, and these beliefs he will have arrived at as a result of all the dealings that he has had with the religious and philosophical and moral and social issues that the adventure of living has brought his way. The imaginative writer's beliefs, to be sure, are very rarely highly propositional in character: they do not generally involve a highly schematized set of ideas or a fully integrated philosophic system. He customarily has something much less abstract—namely, a number of sharp and deeply felt insights into the meaning of the human story that control all his transactions with the world that lies before him. And it is by means of these insights that he discovers "the figure in the carpet."

Graham Greene, in his criticism, has often liked to observe that "Every creative writer worth our consideration, every writer who can be called in the wide eighteenth-century use of the term a poet, is a victim: a man given to an obsession,"[31] or to what he some-

[29] Vivas, *Creation and Discovery,* p. 117.

[30] Henry James, *The Art of the Novel: Critical Prefaces* (New York: Charles Scribner's Sons, 1934), p. 5.

[31] Graham Greene, *The Lost Childhood* (New York: Viking Press, 1952), p. 79.

times calls a "ruling passion." And I take it that when he speaks in this way he has in mind the poet's habit of loyalty to some discovered method of construing experience, to some way of seeing things, by means of which he grapples and comes to terms with the tumultuous and fragmentary world that presses in upon him. That is to say, I assume that Mr. Greene has in mind the act of consent which the poet gives to some fundamental hypothesis about the nature of existence which itself in turn introduces structure and coherence for him into the formless stuff of life itself. And it is indeed, I believe, this act that constitutes the real beginning of the poetic process: the rest is simply a matter of the kind of knowledgeable experimentation within the limits of his medium that the expert craftsman engages in till he discovers what he wants to say gaining incarnation within a given form.

Now I am aware that I must appear to be advocating a view of the poetic process which, in point of fact, I do not hold at all. For in much that I have just now said it may seem that I have been implying that, before even initiating the purely literary task, it is necessary for the poet to do an enormous amount of thinking. I have attributed to the writer's metaphysic or his beliefs a decisive role in the creative process, and thus it would seem that I believe it necessary for the writer to engage in a great deal of abstract thinking before that process can even be initiated. But this I do not think is true at all. I do not, of course, want to associate myself with that tendency in modern literary theory which supports the supposition that the writer is not a thinker at all. This is a notion which T. S. Eliot has, I suppose, done more than anyone else to foster, and it is simply another instance of the confusion which his criticism, great as it is, occasionally contains. In his famous essay on "Shakespeare and the Stoicism of Seneca" he tells us, for example, that the poet does not "think" but that he makes poetry out of thought and that, therefore, he cannot *as poet* be said to "believe" in the system of thought that lies behind his poetry. In the particular case with which he is dealing, he tells us that Shakespeare did not really "think"; that he simply took the muddled and incompatible ideas of Seneca and Machiavelli and Montaigne and made poetry out of them. And Mr. Eliot having—and properly so—the enormous prestige in our time that he has, it is not surprising that our generation should have become for a time so convinced that Shakespeare was not a profound thinker, if he was a thinker at all; that he merely assimilated and felicitously reexpressed well-worn truisms. Or, again, in the case of Dante, he tells us that Dante did not "think" either; that he simply took the magnificent formulations of St. Thomas and used them as the foundation of his poem. But surely there is great confusion here, for, as Fr. Martin Jarrett-Kerr has remarked, "If . . . we start from the initial conviction that one of the first marks of the major poet or novelist is the possession of a *fine mind,* we must refuse to concede that Shakespeare or Dante did not think but had their thinking done for them."[32]

Mr. Eliot's error here results, I suspect, from the supposition that to acknowledge the poet as a thinker is in effect to say that the poetic process originates in a highly developed *system* of ideas, and this is, of course, not at all the case. What I have been calling the writer's beliefs are rarely if ever the highly propositional things that Mr. Eliot, in denying them the importance which I have given them, seems to think they are. For what the writer generally has is not a *system* of belief but rather *an imagination* of what is radically significant.

So, in insisting upon the writer's necessary dependence upon his beliefs, I am not at all intending to suggest that the poet or the novelist must, first of all, be a philosopher or a theologian—though, on the other hand, I am not at all in accord with Mr. Eliot's contention that the poet is not really a thinker at all, a contention which is, by the way, significantly contradicted by Mr. Eliot's own career in poetry. There is a distinction somewhere in St. Thomas which illuminates, I think, the nature of the poet's relation to his beliefs. St. Thomas distinguishes between *cognitio per modum cognitionis*

[32] Martin Jarrett-Kerr, C.R., *Studies in Literature and Belief* (New York: Harper & Brothers, 1955), p. 5.

—knowledge, that is, in the manner of or by means of the intelligence or the discursive reason—and *cognitio per modum inclinationis,* knowledge, that is, in the manner of or by means of inclination. And what I would suggest is that the poet holds his "first principles" or his beliefs or his metaphysic *per modum inclinationis* —that is, inclinatorily. Which is to say that his beliefs point in the direction of a coherent philosophy of life toward which his sensibility has an irresistible inclination and in which it finds its necessary sanction. The contrast between the two modes of cognition is, to be sure, not an absolute contrast, and what it is therefore proper to say is that it is the *tendency* of the poet to hold his beliefs *per modum inclinationis,* though there are some writers, Mr. Eliot among them, who also hold their beliefs *per modum cognitionis.* But in whatever manner they may be held in the individual case, what I am now insisting upon principally is the precedence and the primacy of the act by which the poet searches experience and finds therein an ultimate concern that gives him then a perspective upon the flux and the flow.

Now whatever it is that concerns the poet ultimately, that constitutes his "ruling passion" and the substance of his *vision,* is something to which the critic can be attentive only as it is discoverable in the work. By now surely we have all taken to heart the lesson of Messrs. Wimsatt and Beardsley on "The Intentional Fallacy," and we understand the irrelevance of any essay in literary criticism that is based upon some process of armchair psychoanalysis which seeks to elevate the biographical category of the artist's conscious intention into a category of aesthetic discrimination.[33] But the designation of "intentionalism" as fallacious becomes itself a fallacy if it is made to support the view that a work of literary art is "a merely formal structure devoid of embodied meanings and values."[34] For such aesthetic objects, though "they may be found in the realm of pure design or pure music,"[35] simply do not exist in

[33] W. K. Wimsatt and Monroe Beardsley, "The Intentional Fallacy," *The Sewanee Review,* Vol. LIV (Summer, 1946), pp. 468–488.

[34] Vivas, *op. cit.,* p. 172.

[35] *Ibid.*

the realm of literature where surely a main part of the critic's task involves the discovery of "the actual operative intention which, as telic cause, accounts for the finished work"[36] and which can be defined only in terms of the vision of the world which it serves.

The authentic work of literary art, says M. de Rougemont, is a trap for the attention, but he also says that it is an "oriented trap." It is a trap, in the sense that, having the kind of autonomy that modern criticism has claimed for it, it "has for its specific function . . . the magnetizing of the sensibility, the fascinating of the meditation";[37] as Mr. Vivas would put it, it can command upon itself an act of "intransitive attention." But the trap is "oriented": it *focuses* the attention, that is, upon something which transcends the verbal structure itself, this simply being the circumambient world of human experience, in those of its aspects that have claimed the poet's concern. And thus it is that the autonomy of the work is no more an absolute thing than is the intransitivity of the reader's attention, for both are qualified by the implicative relations that branch out indefinitely from the aesthetic fact toward the world by which that fact is surrounded.

Here it is, then, that we may discover the point of entry into the literary work that we have. For it is analysis of the sort that we have been conducting that reveals that the work is not a closed system and that it does not have that quality of "aseity" which Scholastic theologians have considered the Godhead to possess, by reason of the self-derived and eternally independent character of its being. The work is not wholly self-contained and utterly cut off from the reader, because, in the creative process, the aesthetic intentions of the artist are not segregated from all that most vitally concerns him as a human being but are, on the contrary, formed by these concerns and are thus empowered to orient the work toward the common human experience. This experience has, of course, to be grasped in and through the structures by means of which it is aesthetically rendered. But to stress the fact that poetic art signifies *by means of its structure* need not, I think, commit us

[36] *Ibid.*, p. 164.
[37] De Rougemont, *op. cit.*, p. 176.

to a formalism so purist as to require the view that the autonomy of the work is absolute. For, as I have been insisting, great literature does, in point of fact, always open outward toward the world, and that which keeps the universe of poetry from being hermetically sealed off from the universe of man is the poet's vision that it incarnates, of spaces and horizons, of cities and men, of time and eternity. This is why those modern theorists who tell us that the literary work is merely a verbal structure and that its analysis therefore involves merely a study of grammar and syntax—this is why they so completely miss the mark. They forget that writers use language with reference to what they know and feel and believe and that we can therefore understand their poems and novels only if we have some appreciation of how their beliefs have operated in enriching the meaning of the words that they employ. The poem-in-itself, in other words, as merely a structure of language, is simply a naked abstraction, for the real poem, the real novel, is something that we begin to appropriate only as we seek some knowledge of the context of belief and the quality of vision out of which it springs and with reference to which the words on the printed page have their fullest and richest meaning.

Now we have, I think, arrived at the point in our argument at which it is finally possible for me to say that the aspect of poetic art to which I have been referring by the terms *vision* and *belief* is precisely the element which we ought to regard as constituting the religious dimension of imaginative literature. When I speak of the religious dimension of literary art, in other words, I do not have in mind any special iconic materials stemming from a tradition of orthodoxy which may or may not appear in a given work. For were it to be so conceived, it might indeed then be something peripheral and inorganic to the nature of literature itself; whereas the way of regarding our problem that I now want to recommend is one that involves the proposal that the religious dimension is something intrinsic to and constitutive of the nature of literature as such. And I am here guided in my understanding of what is religious in the orders of cultural expression by the conception of the matter that has been so ably advanced by the distinguished

Protestant theologian Paul Tillich. In all the work that he has done in the philosophy of culture over the past thirty years, the persistent strain that is to be noted is one that arises out of his insistence upon what might be called the coinherence of religion and culture. He likes to say that "Religion is the substance of culture and culture the form of religion."[38] He has remarked, for example:

> If any one, being impressed by the mosaics of Ravenna or the ceiling paintings of the Sistine Chapel, or by the portraits of the older Rembrandt, should be asked whether his experience was religious or cultural, he would find the answer difficult. Perhaps it would be correct to say that his experience was cultural as to form, and religious as to substance. It is cultural because it is not attached to a specific ritual-activity; and religious, because it evokes questioning as to the Absolute or the limits of human existence. This is equally true of painting, of music and poetry, of philosophy and science. . . . Wherever human existence in thought or action becomes a subject of doubts and questions, wherever unconditioned meaning becomes visible in works which only have conditioned meaning in themselves, there culture is religious.[39]

And Professor Tillich has acknowledged that it is to the theoretical comprehension of this "mutual immanence of religion and culture" that his philosophy of religion is primarily dedicated. "No cultural creation," he says, "can hide its religious ground,"[40] and its religious ground is formed by the "ultimate concern" to which it bears witness; for that, he insists, is what religion is: it "is ultimate concern."[41] And since it is religion, in this sense, that is truly substantive in the various symbolic expressions of a culture, the task of criticism, in whatever medium it may be conducted, is, at bottom, that of deciphering the given work at hand in such a way as to reveal the ultimate concern which it implies. For, as he says, in the depth of every cultural creation "there is an ultimate . . . and [an] all-determining concern, something absolutely serious,"[42] even

[38] Paul Tillich, *The Protestant Era* (Chicago: University of Chicago Press, 1948), p. 57.

[39] Paul Tillich, *The Interpretation of History* (New York: Charles Scribner's Sons, 1936), p. 49.

[40] Tillich, *The Protestant Era,* p. 57.

[41] *Ibid.,* p. 59.

[42] *Ibid.,* pp. 58–59.

if it is expressed in what are conventionally regarded as secular terms.

It should, of course, be said that, in these definitions, Professor Tillich is not seeking to *identify* religion and culture; but he does want to avoid the error that T. S. Eliot has cautioned us against "of regarding religion and culture as two separate things between which there is a relation."[43] For what he recognizes is that the whole cultural process by which man expresses and realizes his rational humanity is actually governed by what are his most ultimate concerns—his concerns, that is, "with the meaning of life and with all the forces that threaten or support that meaning . . ."[44] And, in passing, it is, I think, worth remarking that it is this profoundly realistic approach to the problem of cultural interpretation that enables Professor Tillich to see that in our own period the most radically religious movements in literature and painting and music may gain expression in strangely uncanonical terms—in despairing maledictions and in apocalyptic visions of "the abyss" of disintegration that threatens the world today. For, as he would say, in the very profoundity with which *Wozzeck* and the *Guernica* and *The Waste Land* express the disorder of the times there is an equally profound witness to the spiritual order that has been lost, so that these great expressions of the modern movement in art are rather like a confused and uncertain prayer that corresponds to the second petition of the Our Father.[45]

We are now, then, brought to the point at which we must regather our bearings by a final act of recapitulation. We have said that the work of literary art is a special sort of linguistic structure that traps the attention intransitively; but we have also argued that the intransitivity of the reader's attention is not absolute, since

[43] T. S. Eliot, *Notes Towards the Definition of Culture* (New York: Harcourt, Brace and Co., 1949), pp. 31–32.

[44] James Luther Adams, "Tillich's Concept of the Protestant Era," Editor's Appendix, *The Protestant Era,* p. 273.

[45] M. de Rougemont says that "art would appear to be like an invocation (more often than not unconscious) to the lost harmony, like a prayer (more often than not confused), corresponding to the second petition of the Lord's Prayer—'Thy Kingdom come.'" *Vide op. cit.,* p. 186.

the autonomy of the object which captures his attention is not itself absolute. The literary work is a trap, but it is a trap that is *oriented* toward the world of existence that transcends the work—and the work is *oriented* by the *vision,* by the belief, by the *ultimate concern* of which it is an incarnation: its orientation, that is to say, is essentially religious. And this is why criticism itself must, in the end, be theological. The prevailing orthodoxy in contemporary criticism, to be sure, generally represents hostility toward the idea of metaphysical and theological considerations being introduced into the order of critical discourse. But, as Leslie Fiedler has remarked:

> The "pure" literary critic, who pretends, in the cant phrase, to stay "inside" a work all of whose metaphors and meanings are pressing outward, is only half-aware. And half-aware, he deceives; for he cannot help smuggling unexamined moral and metaphysical judgments into his "close analyses," any more than the "pure" literary historian can help bootlegging unconfessed aesthetic estimates into his chronicles. Literary criticism is always becoming "something else," for the simple reason that literature is always "something else."[46]

Our abdication from the reigning poetics of our time is, however, only partial, for the religious dimension of literature, as we have defined it, must be regarded as something which, in so far as it is really a datum for critical inspection and assessment, exists in the language of the work. For the only thing that lies before the critic is a composition in language, and it is, presumably, his skill in the supervision of language that primarily distinguishes the literary artist; surely it would be wrong-headed to assume that the thing that makes him an artist is the profundity or the novelty of his vision: no, he makes good his vocational claim in the republic of letters by the extent of the success with which he shapes the substance of experience, in accordance with his vision of what it is that makes it ultimately meaningful. And he can give a significant form or shape to experience only in so far as he takes the highest kind of advantage of the medium in which his art is wrought.

[46] Leslie Fiedler, "Toward an Amateur Criticism," *The Kenyon Review,* Vol. XII, No. 4 (Autumn, 1950), p. 564.

So it may then, I think, be taken for granted that whatever it is that *orients* a work of literary art or that constitutes the *ultimate concern* that it embodies is something that will disclose itself in the ways in which the writer brings the resources of language into the service of his project. And thus we shall want very carefully to preserve all that has been gained in modern criticism as a result of its methodological researches into the problem of how the language of imaginative literature is to be understood and talked about. But for the critic to insist upon remaining merely a kind of grammarian is for him to forgo many of the most interesting and significant discriminations that literary criticism can make. For, though the literary work is a special sort of linguistic structure, that which holds the highest interest for us is the special seizure of reality which this structure is instrumental toward. It is, in other words, the nature of literature itself that compels the critic finally to move beyond the level of verbal analysis to the level of metaphysical and theological valuation. On this level, of course, he can establish the propriety of his judgments only by reference to his own insight, his own scale of values, his own sense of what is important in art and in life. And, as the English critic, the late S. L. Bethell, remarked:

> . . . if he is a Christian worthy of the name, his whole outlook will be coloured by his religion; he will see life in Christian terms, and, though he may ignore an atheist writer's professed atheism, he will still judge his degree of insight into character by his own insight, which will have been formed in part by his Christian experience. And the non-Christian critic—let us be clear about this—will also judge a writer's insight into character (or into anything else, of course) by the standard of his own insight, however derived. There is no "impartial criticism" in this sense, or rather there is no critical neutrality; there are only Christian critics and Marxist critics and Moslem critics—and critics who think themselves disinterested but who are really swayed unconsciously by the beliefs they have necessarily acquired by being members of a particular society in a particular place and time.[47]

And, as Bethell observed with great shrewdness,

[47] S. L. Bethell, *Essays on Literary Criticism and the English Tradition* (London: Dennis Dobson Ltd., 1948), pp. 24–25.

the last are really the least impartial, for, believing themselves impartial, they are open to every unconscious influence upon their judgment, while the "doctrinaire" critic may keep his doctrine well in view and, if not entirely avoiding prejudice, may at least give his readers fair warning of what to expect.[48]

But now at this point the question may well be raised as to whether my use of these quotations from Bethell is calculated to suggest that we are justified in trying to guarantee literary art by the quality of belief that it possesses. And, were this question to be put to me, my impulse, as a Christian, would, I think, be to say, with Professor Roy W. Battenhouse, that "the good poet should be able, like Adam in the Garden, to name every creature correctly. Apprehending the form of each thing that is brought before him, he should be able to assign it its proper place."[49] But, of course, this capacity, which so influentially determines the outcome of the artistic process, is itself very largely dependent upon the artist's metaphysical or religious orientation—so that, as a Christian, I should again feel prompted to say, with Mr. Battenhouse, that

> if it is true that the light with which an artist sees inclines to affect the justness of his observations, the presence of full light cannot but clarify the issues of proportion and order. With inadequate lighting, the artist will not see certain things he ought to see; it will be all too easy for him to draw disproportionately what he does see. To put it another way the artist who takes up his location in Plato's cave has not the same chance as he who sets up shop by Christ's open tomb.[50]

In principle, I should, in other words, expect the Christian reader at least—all other things being equal—more enthusiastically to give his suffrage to a literature that was Christianly *oriented* than to one which was not. But now, not as a matter of principle but as a matter of fact, the Christian reader lives in a period whose characteristic quality, at least ever since the Renaissance, has been defined, as Erich Heller has reminded us, not merely by a dissociation of faith from knowledge but by what has been the profounder sev-

[48] *Ibid.*, p. 25.

[49] Roy W. Battenhouse, "The Relation of Theology to Literary Criticism," *The Journal of Bible and Religion,* Vol. XIII, No. I (February, 1945), p. 20.

[50] *Ibid.*

erance of faith from sensibility. "It is this rift," says Mr. Heller, "which has made it impossible for most Christians not to *feel,* or at least not to feel *also* as true many 'truths' which are incompatible with the truth of their faith."[51] They have, in other words, been in very much the same position that the father of the possessed child was in whom the Synoptist records as having cried out: "Lord, I believe; help thou mine unbelief" (Mark 9:24). And, this being the case, the Christian reader will actually respond to the various constructions of the human story that he encounters in literature with a latitudinarianism that will, at least in part, be akin to that which any other sensitive reader in our time brings to bear upon his dealings with literary art: that is to say, what he will require is that the view of life that is conveyed by the given poem or novel commend itself as a *possible* view, as one to which an intelligent and sensitive observer of the human scene *might* be led by a sober consideration of the facts of experience. And, though he will agree with Mr. Eliot that to judge a work of art by artistic standards and to judge it by religious standards ought perhaps to "come in the end to the same thing,"[52] he will recognize, as Mr. Eliot does, that, in our time, this is an end at which most of us will have great difficulty in arriving.

But, hesitant as the Christian critic in our time ought to be in defining for himself a program whose rigor would have the effect of delimiting the range of his sympathies and of isolating him from the actualities of the literary life, we may yet, I think, put to him the question as to what in general will be his approach to the literature of our own period. Here we must remember, as Professor Amos Wilder has so well said, that "the most significant art of the twentieth century—Stravinski, Picasso, Joyce, Kafka, Pound, Eliot—is that which comes immediately out of the epochal convulsions of the time, out of full immersion in the condition of man today."[53] And, this

[51] Erich Heller, *The Disinherited Mind: Essays in Modern German Literature and Thought* (Philadelphia: Dufour and Saifer, 1952), p. 125.

[52] Eliot, *op. cit.,* p. 29.

[53] Amos N. Wilder, *Modern Poetry and the Christian Tradition* (New York: Charles Scribner's Sons, 1952), p. 176.

being the case, we should not be surprised that "the fountains of spiritual renewal" in literature, as Professor Wilder says, have often broken forth "outside the churches in uncanonical witness, prayer and celebration."[54]

The crypto-religious character of many of the basic impulses in modern literature has, of course, often been remarked upon, and we must remain mindful that the artist's failure to canalize these impulses in the direction of explicit Christian affirmation is, very frequently, not to be construed in terms of his own agnosticism and intransigence, but, rather, in terms of the Christian community's failure to present itself to him as something with which he might really make common cause. This is why "the protagonists of traditional values, the witnesses of the older covenants and charters of our common life, the saints in the sense of the dedicated and disciplined individuals who assume the costs of nonconformity, the martyrs or scapegoats of the general crisis"—this is why all these are often "found in secular guise, unordained except by the authenticity of their utterance."[55] And the recognition of these ambivalences and dislocations by the Christian critic must be the starting point, I believe, of any transaction into which he may enter with the world of modern art.

The great effort of the Christian critic in our day should have as its ultimate aim a reconciliation between the modern arts and the Church, between the creative imagination and the Christian faith. The immense obstacles on the side of art and on the side of the Church that hinder this achievement are, however, not to be minimized. The great misfortune is that those modern writers who have experienced most profoundly the intellectual and spiritual predicaments of the time and whose return to Christianity would therefore be most arresting are often those who are most acutely sensible of the failure of institutional Christianity—and especially of Protestantism—to give due place to "the yea-saying impulse of the biblical faith and its moment of creative play."[56] It is felt "that

[54] *Ibid.*, p. 268.
[55] *Ibid.*
[56] *Ibid.*, p. 243.

a Christian so sterilizes his heart that there is no concern left for art and the rich play, the riot and fecundity of life."[57] It is the rejection of a Christianity (and generally a Protestant Christianity) that is felt to be ascetical and world-denying which forms the rule among modern writers rather than the exception: Yeats and Joyce and Wallace Stevens and many others have refused the Gospel, very largely, one feels, because of the failure of its interpreters to express what Professor Wilder feels to be the genuine element of antinomianism in the Gospel itself.[58] He puts the issue with great clarity in his book *The Spiritual Aspects of the New Poetry:*

> For the poets the scandal of Christ is his asceticism. The very medium of their art as poets; indeed, the very element of their experience as men, is the gamut of human living, emotions, drama. "Man's resinous heart" and the loves, loyalties, the pride, the grief it feeds—these are the stuff of poetry and the sense of life. And the Cross lays its shadow on this; it draws away all the blood from the glowing body of existence and leaves it mutilated and charred in the hope of some thin ethereal felicity. The wine of life is changed to water. . . . The "dramatic caves" of the human heart and imagination are renounced for some wan empyrean of spiritual revery. The very word "spiritual" has come to signify inanity and vacuity. The refusal of religion by the modern poet, and by more than moderns and by more than poets, goes back to the apparent denial of human living by religion, to the supposed incompatibility of life with Life and of art with faith.[59]

That this is the major hindrance on the side of art to a reconciliation between the creative imagination and the Church one may very quickly discover by a perusal of one of the most interesting spiritual documents of our period, the *Partisan Review* symposium, *Religion and the Intellectuals* (1950), in which the general testimony of many of the most influential literary figures of our day tends to confirm Professor Wilder's assessment.

There are also serious hindrances on the side of the Church to a *rapprochement* between art and faith. There are many religious

[57] Amos N. Wilder, *The Spiritual Aspects of the New Poetry* (New York: Harper & Brothers, 1940), pp. 197–198.

[58] *Vide* Wilder, *Modern Poetry and the Christian Tradition,* Chapter X.

[59] Wilder, *The Spiritual Aspects of the New Poetry,* p. 196.

people who suppose their own conservative and unaroused attitudes toward modern life to be based upon valid Christian principles, when they really derive from a protected social situation in which it has been possible for them to shut their eyes to the dislocations of the age to which history has committed both them and ourselves. They face with defensiveness and hostility much of modern literature in which these stresses and strains are reflected, and they insist upon the excessiveness of its alarmism and its irrelevance to the world in which they choose to believe that they live. It is their habit to speak of many of the major writers of this century—Pound and Gide, Joyce and Lawrence, Kafka and Faulkner—as if the difficulties presented by their work were merely frivolous and as if the inclination of their vision toward a tragic perspective were a consequence merely of their morbidity or even of the disorder in their personal lives. And they mistake their censoriousness with respect to the modern artist for a genuinely Christian position. A more sophisticated version of the same unfriendliness to the modern arts arises out of the extreme disjunctions between the natural order and the order of revelation that are insisted upon in those currents of Protestant thought stemming from Crisis-Theology. In this theological framework the arts, as a department of human culture, are comprehended in terms of their issuance from the natural order, all of whose fruits are, of course, to be viewed, as a matter of principle, with a deep suspicion and skepticism.

The difficulties, in other words, that hinder reconciliation in our day between the modern artist and the Christian Church seem to be, as Professor Wladimir Weidlé has suggested in his penetrating essay *The Dilemma of the Arts,* difficulties of "mutual incomprehension."[60]

One thing, however, is, I believe, fairly certain, and that is that the Christian community will not succeed in relating itself creatively to the modern artist if it attempts to do so by laying down its law,

[60] Wladimir Weidlé, *The Dilemma of the Arts,* trans. by Martin Jarrett-Kerr, C.R., (London: S.C.M. Press Ltd., 1948), Chapter VI.

by hedging him about with rules and programs to be followed and carried out. Its proper course is perhaps most clearly set forth in a set of distinctions that Professor Tillich has made central to his philosophy of culture. Those who are familiar with his thought will recall that there are three terms for which he has a great liking: he often speaks of "autonomy," of "heteronomy," and of "theonomy," and it will at this point be helpful for us to put ourselves in mind of what is at issue in the distinctions that he draws between these terms. In each case, it will be noticed, the suffix derives from the Greek *nomos,* meaning usage or the law of human life; so the three terms stand for different versions of what the nature of that law is.

The prefix of the first, autonomy, derives from the Greek *autos,* meaning "self"; and thus the term points to that view of the law of life which suggests that man is himself the source of it and that the culture which he creates is not therefore to be measured by reference to any ultimate principle transcendent to the rational and the human. The prefix of the second term, heteronomy, derives from the Greek *heteros,* meaning "that which is other than, different from, alien to, strange"; so, when Professor Tillich uses this term, he has in mind those ecclesiastical and political communities that relate themselves to the enterprises of culture by hedging them about with laws and authoritative criteria that are not organic to their nature. Finally, the prefix of the third term has its origin in the Greek word *theos,* meaning "god," and Professor Tillich employs the concept of theonomy to designate that view of culture which understands the divine law to be "at the same time, the innermost law of man himself,"[61] which regards the transcendent as being not a dimension external to, and therefore to be imposed upon, man's cultural life but rather as the inescapable spiritual ground of all our art and philosophy and science. Autonomy, in other words, represents the attempt to cut the ties of a culture with its transcendent ground, with anything ultimate and unconditional; heteronomy represents "the attempt of a religion to

[61] Tillich, *The Protestant Era,* pp. 56–57.

dominate autonomous cultural creativity from the outside,"[62] while a theonomy is "a culture in which the ultimate meaning of existence shines through all finite forms of thought and action; the culture is transparent, and its creations are vessels of a spiritual content."[63]

Now Professor Tillich's excellent point is that the way of heteronomy can never be the way of a truly radical Christianity. The Church's method of addressing culture must, to be sure, involve a criticism of "self-complacent autonomy," but always, he insists, the Christian community, when it is alive to the full implications of an Incarnational faith, will remember that "in the depth of every autonomous culture an ultimate concern, something unconditional and holy, is implied." And the genius of authentically Christian humanism is most truly expressed when, in its dealings with what is called "secular culture," it so takes this body of witness up into itself that the distinction between the sacred and the secular ceases to exist.

It will, I believe, be along this way—the way of "theonomy"—that a reunion of art and religion, if it is to occur at all, will be achieved. But, of course, what will be chiefly required is an infinite degree of tact and humility in the Christian critic, and thus a reconciliation between art and faith in our day would be, as Professor Weidlé has said,

> the symptom of a renewal of the religious life itself. When frozen faith melts again, when it is once more love and freedom, then will be the time that art will light up again at the new kindling of the fire of the spirit. There seem to be many indications that such a future is possible; and in any case it is the only future still open to art. There is one way alone—and there is no other—because artistic experience is, deep down, a religious experience, because the world art lives in cannot be made habitable save by religion alone.[64]

[62] *Ibid.*, p. xvi.
[63] *Ibid.*
[64] Weidlé, *op. cit.*, p. 125.

Vincent Buckley

Criticism and Theological Standards*

THE DICTUM WITH WHICH Eliot begins his paper, "Religion and Literature," has been taken by several subsequent critics as a declaration of principle; and it is worth while repeating that dictum:

Literary criticism should be completed by criticism from a definite ethical and theological standpoint. . . . In ages like our own, in which there is no such common agreement, it is the more necessary for Christian readers to scrutinize their reading, especially of works of the imagination, with explicit ethical and theological standards.

As I have already suggested, Eliot's own concern here is a pastoral one. He wants Christian readers to "scrutinize their reading" in terms which will help them to protect themselves from corrupting influences: it seems that a Christian, by taking theological thought, can add a cubit to the stature of his sensibility, and turn it thereby into a fortified tower. But if Eliot's concern is largely pastoral and protective, that of his followers[1] has tended to be affirmative to the point of aggression. The principle in whose defence they attack is common to them and to Eliot; and not one of them seems to have been any more successful than he in putting it to illuminating use in works of actual criticism.

* From *Poetry and Morality* by Vincent Buckley, published by Chatto and Windus Ltd., London.

[1] I refer to those Anglican critics who are often called the School of Christian Discrimination, from the title of Bro. George Every's book.

The declaration of the principle raises an important issue, the issue of poetry and belief. Most Christians who have considered this problem cannot be satisfied either by I. A. Richard's talk of pseudo-statements or by the contention of such men as Erich Heller that, since the poet usually means what he says, poetry puts on us the duty of agreeing or disagreeing with him. The talk of pseudo-statements is unsatisfactory because good poets do indeed mean what they say, and consider the saying it important enough to demand a lifetime's dedication. But Heller's position is unsatisfactory for a twofold reason: Whatever the poet means or intends to say, the critical reader must ultimately be concerned with what the poem as a whole says; and in fact every critical reader knows that the kind of response elicited in him by poetry is not at all of the kind which asks to be expressed in terms of agreement and disagreement. These reservations made, we find the central question still unresolved. In fact, I have seen no persuasive solution to the problem of poetry and belief; and I do not intend to attempt a solution of my own. What is interesting, however, about the statements of Eliot's Christian followers is the fact that they raise the question not for a theoretical but for a practical reason. They raise it not as an abstract problem but as a question of the practical duties and rights of the critic. Consequently, their work amounts to an attempt to answer not the question: What is poetry in relation to truth? but the less exasperating question: What is a criticism based on truth in relation to a literature seldom based on truth?

Eliot has defined the purpose of criticism as "the elucidation of works of art and the correction of taste." And we may assume that his Anglican disciples agree. But "purpose" here means "social purpose," and refers to a social activity and use. The actual process of criticism may be defined as a more-or-less formal guidance of the reader, even of a hypothetical reader, to the kind and quality of life embodied in a poem or novel. It is therefore a communal matter and, as Leavis never wearies of stressing, it is almost inevitably phrased so as to elicit agreement, modification or enlightened dissent.

It is here, of course, that the difficulty arises with a criticism which claims to be Christian. Christianity is a dogmatic religion, and one which illuminates the whole of man's experience. To the non-believer, therefore, a Christian criticism will seem to be a kind of aesthetic dogmatism making for its own powers of interpretation claims which derive from, and represent, the claims of Christianity itself. To the Christian, on the other hand, it will often seem to be the truest kind of criticism because it derives from a true vision of man. On the one hand it is seen as a particularly demanding and even aggressive ideology thrusting out from the ruck of contemporary loyalties; on the other it is seen as the belief which prescribes the norm for human conduct, and so for art itself.

It is difficult, then, to separate one's attitude to a "Christian criticism" from one's attitude to Christianity itself. Yet it seems foolish to resent the claims of Christianty in the literary field. It is not simply one ideology among others: It has a special relevance to literature because, beyond all other ideologies, it is incarnational; and it has a special force in proving that relevance, because it is realistic about human limitations. But it is precisely at the point where we admit these claims that confusion is so likely to arise. It arises through the assumption that it is Christianity as such which makes claims for its own relevance in literary criticism, and seeks to prove that relevance. But it is Christians, not Christianity, who concern themselves with literature, who make claims and attempt to prove them. And it is sheer impertinence for any or all of such critics to claim that their criticism represents Christianity.

The question, then, is whether a specifically Christian criticism is possible; and underlying that is the further question whether theological formulations have any relevance at all to works of the imagination. Certainly, whenever those formulations are invoked, they are invoked as a standard, an unyielding norm, something objective by recourse to which the critic may test the validity of his own and his subjects' point of view. So. S. L. Bethell writes:

Dr. Leavis has more than once stated that literary criticism involves ethical considerations, and it is obvious that we cannot discuss a writer's "insight" without having some standard by which to assess it. But Dr. Leavis has nowhere said that theological considerations are also necessary; indeed he would seem to believe the contrary. Yet, even apart from the fact that there are insights which are spiritual without being ethical, does not the acceptance of an ethical position in itself involve at least some relation to the systems of theology? If the critic elects to take his stand on "ethics" without any philosophical examination of the matter, there will always be a chance that his ethics may consist of personal predilections or the assumptions of his own social group.[2]

I think the contention is a helpful one; the warning given in the last sentence is particularly apt. But, taking this passage as a whole, is it not a curiously abstract statement for a practising critic to rest on? Is it not, in fact, a most evasive statement? The term "theology" appears quite elusive under Bethell's pen; at one moment it is linked with "considerations," at another with "systems"; and we are never told in what sense of the word theology is especially relevant to literature. Ethics, too, bear "some relation to the systems of theology," but we are never told what relation. Mr. Bethell's very prose, in fact, reflects the difficulty of his position. And that difficulty arises only because he is concerned to press for a criticism which is specially, specifically, overtly Christian: Christian not only in its inspiration but also in its intention and its terms.

Such a case always seems to be argued in terms of the application of special Christian categories. And I should consider such terms as dangerously inappropriate as the attitude which lies behind them. Whatever criticism is, it is not an "application" of anything; it is certainly not the application of "categories." Nor is it the relating of works to an overt standard which remains independent of both work and critic. This attitude is too mechanical, this language too systematised, for such a delicate operation as that of criticism, which is an act of reverence—controlled and selective reverence—

[2] *Essays on Literary Criticism and the English Tradition* (Dennis Dobson, London, 1948), p. 13.

towards the thing criticised. It is therefore not a matter of application, but of a full response—a kind of response which involves not only intelligence but the whole affective personality, and involves it even when the final judgment is a rejection of the values embodied in the work being assessed. It seems to me a fallacy to believe that this response can be made fully conscious, fully articulated, fully fitted into the appropriate critical formulae. To attempt to make it so articulated is, in the end, to drive a wedge between these "two qualities"—intelligent and affective—of the judging person, and to remove him further from the work of art itself. He will tend to become detached in the least happy sense of that word.

There is more to it than that. I cannot see (and I speak as a Christian) why anyone should want to apply principles explicitly at all. Of course, it is the whole person who responds to a poem or novel; and if that person is a believing Christian, then it is a believing Christian who judges; one can't, without great harm to oneself and to poetry, pretend to be something one is not. But it is not only as a believing Christian that one judges. If it were, then Christianity would be something exclusive; and all intellectual intercourse between Christians and non-Christians would become virtually impossible. But it is not. One's sensibility may be permeated with Christian values, one's vision of the world may be pervasively religious; but I see no reason why this should cut one off from full imaginative participation in the work of any artist, so long as that art has human significance and is complete within its chosen terms. Yet this, paradoxically, is what Bethell's position leads to. To invoke a "standard" is to elect to stand apart from the work of art which one is measuring against it.

If we regard Christianity, and the literary criticism deriving from it, not as exclusive but inclusive, we shall have to decide at what point it becomes relevant to literary judgment. Eliot himself speaks, we may notice, of "completing" literary criticism with ethical and theological criticism; he envisages two operations of the critical intelligence, and not one. What he does is to point forward from literary criticism, which may be assumed to have its own procedure and value, to a kind of study which we may call religious-cultural criticism. Yet Eliot does not in fact undertake such a study; and Leavis accuses him, with a good deal of justice, of substituting theological considerations for literary rather than completing one with the other. The same is true of his followers, and they have been criticised for it. R. G. Cox, for example, in reviewing Bethell's book, interprets his subject's positive position as follows: "His most plausible point seems to be that since all criticism will show the influence of the critic's personal beliefs it is better for these to be explicit rather than unconscious."[3]

Yes, for clarity of mind, for balance of approach; but not everything in the critic's responsiveness can be made conscious, let alone explicit; and certainly it cannot be made so explicit as to merit the name of "beliefs." In any case, why should the consciousness of one's beliefs lead to any talk of interpretation, of standards, of categories, and the rest? It is a strange picture, that of a reader determinedly holding his beliefs formulated and ready in his mind while he strives to surrender his sensibility in active responsiveness to a poem or novel. We can inject the colouring of sense into such a picture only if we suppose that the explicit beliefs become operative, grow to the stature of criteria, after the work of responding is over and the work of its formulation begun.

Those really are the *practical* questions, especially for those who regard Christian belief as relevant to literature: In what way is it relevant? And at what point in our response to a work does it become relevant?

In what way? Is it relevant as a standard of moral orthodoxy to which the moral meaning of a work can be referred? Surely not; the activity involved in such a work of reference cannot help being one of undue abstraction; and the more plausibly a moral meaning can be abstracted and held up against a standard, the more we will tend to abandon the moral stature of the work as a whole. Too much is left out. Criticism at this depth is valuable only if it

[3] *Scrutiny,* Vol. XV, No. 3, p. 229.

insistently points back to the work, to the fleshed context from which it is abstracting. And while the "standard" remains the important consideration, while our eye is on conformity to a standard, our critical dealings with the actual work will be in danger of becoming a kind of legerdemain.

Surely Christianity is relevant as a form (I should prefer not to say "way") of life guiding and enlivening our own native responses: guiding *because* it enlivens them. If that is so, then it need not involve the erection of a "standard," which is permanently and unalterably "there"; and anyone observing the process of our critical judgment from the outside would be hard put to it to see it as a specifically Christian criticism.

There is another consideration. Of course, as a man grows in his view of life he will tend to neglect certain kinds of literary work, and the less he will tend to find literature in itself, as a way or guide of life, completely satisfying. This is not to say that he will develop *special* interests, or become the sophisticated rider of ever more exclusive hobby-horses. But he *will* be selective, and it is the living of his way of life, his being vitally informed by his vision, which will be the agent of selection. Literature may be a meeting-place of many human activities, the nodal-point at which theological and social and musical and psychological realities have their most synoptic and concentrated union. But no man can live by literature alone; and it is what he does live by that will so largely determine his instinct for the works which will be of the greatest value for him. On the other hand, this seems to me as much an instinct or sense as a conscious choice. The point I should want to make is that the intellectual basis of his way of life will not wholly determine his reading, nor ought it to determine in advance his response to what he does read.

Christianity is relevant. But at what point does it become relevant? The fallacy of such men as Bethell, Bro. George Every, and even Fr. Martin Jarrett-Kerr, is to make it relevant as a sort of extra preoccupation while actually reading. Christianity thereby becomes an interest directing the person of the critic towards formulating while he should be responding.

But we may for the moment assume a different position. It may be that Christianity, considered as a special inspiration or aid, assumes value only after the work of responding is over. Then it would lead to a special formulation (presumably of a kind other than the literary-critical), which we should call by a separate name. Certainly this seems a proper continuation of the critical faculty, and an immensely useful one, *if it can be done*. The only doubt which arises is a doubt as to its possibility; I cannot myself recall any really illuminating demonstration of it.

One feels in any case that, if it were possible, if it came to be done, it would concern not any separate work or body of work, but a whole stream or tendency, and that its value would consequently be of a nearly sociological kind, of a sociology with a theological ground. Where an individual work or writer is in question, such a sociological use would be useful only to the extent that it was the product of a total and responsive reading. The only true sociologists of literature would be the best critics. And if that is true, then the "sociological" conclusion would be implicit in any case in the actual response, the process of literary criticism itself; it would be an abstraction and formalisation not from a work of art apprehended in sociological terms, but from a criticism already done, whether mentally or in writing. It would have only a limited point for readers as experienced as oneself, but most point for a class of readers insufficiently responsive to the implications of works of art. If one's experience of a writer is as full as possible, there is no reason for attempting to "complete" it by formulating it into terms foreign to the experience itself. If it is delicate, experienced, and above all *concerned* with literature, the Christian sensibility will inevitably make moral and theological use of its experience of art; but it will do so interiorly and unobtrusively, changing it into an element of personal growth founded on Christianity. And if it is not, no amount of formulation or abstraction can bring it any closer to art; one's application of explicit standards could have merely a pastoral intention and effect.

This is what, I suggest, Eliot does in his later writings. It is also what Bethell, Every, and Nicholson do. Their function is to provide clues to literature for the benefit of their co-religionists. In exercising their function they make varying claims for what they are doing, and offer to account for it in varying terms. Bethell and Every, for example, obviously regard themselves as practising critics, using Christian beliefs as a standard of immediate critical judgment. Nicholson, on the other hand, claims to be not a critic but a moralist: the claim which Eliot makes for himself in the opening pages of *After Strange Gods*. As Nicholson says: "This book is not an attempt to measure modern literature by a Christian yardstick. It is not, fundamentally, *literary* criticism at all. It is rather an enquiry into the assumptions as to the nature and purpose of Man which underlie much of modern writing. . . ."[4]

But it is impossible to find the underlying assumptions of a literature unless you assume that they do not merely "underlie" it, but are actually in some way embodied in it. Nicholson does make this assumption, and he acts on it; consequently his work must be judged as literary criticism, because it searches not behind but within the works with which it concerns itself.

Two things become quite evident in Nicholson's book. The one is that he *does* use critical procedures; and the other is that Christianity is for him not an enlivening form of life, not even a standard, but a kind of specialty, an additional intellectual hobby.

We notice, for example, that in his remarks on various writers, Christian references and approximations in literature become of special interest, not as demonstrating anything about the quality of the literature or even of its author's unconscious beliefs, but in and for themselves. Here is the hobbyist's mentality, at its crudest and least responsive to literary values.

What happens in the case of the relatively sensitive critic such as Fr. Martin Jarrett-Kerr is a lapse at crucial moments into

[4] *Man and Literature* (S.C.M. Press, London, 1943), p. 5.

sophisticated special pleading. It happens, for example, in the book on Lawrence which he published under the name Fr. Tiverton —at that point where, in considering Lawrence's view of sex, he digresses to give an account of the orthodox Christian attitude to sex, to defend that attitude, and to show how Lawrence at once misunderstood it and unconsciously approximated to it. Here we find, not a "specialty," a boyish preoccupation with counting references, but a lapse of attention. Fr. Tiverton's general account, in another context, might be just and useful but, in the context of a specifically literary study, it interrupts the free action of the sensibility and tilts towards a kind of special pleading.

What I am attempting to provide, by the use of these examples, is not a series of anecdotes discreditable to one school of critics, but empirical evidence that an ethical and theological criticism of literature which *completes* literary criticism is very difficult to conceive, and that the people who have attempted it in the last two decades have fallen into the pit of divided intention. In each case the intentions have become divided either because the possibilities have not been clearly seen or because the interest has not been kept pure. Nicholson wants to be a moralist on a simple pastoral level, and becomes a bad and tendentious critic with a hobbyist's attitude to his central standard. Fr. Jarrett-Kerr wants to be a literary critic, and becomes at crucial moments an open advocate for his own beliefs. Bethell wants to be a critic, but becomes a polemical theorist at a fairly unsatisfactory level. All three of them suffer from using theology as an intellectual interest and not as the guarantee of inward sensitive life.

What is wrong, for example, with the digression by Fr. Tiverton to which I have just referred? It is a fairly long digression and, on the whole, a fairly just one. But it is not just in this context; it belongs elsewhere, and its status as a digression is no status at all. However informative it may be, it can only have the effect in this place of distracting attention from the reality of the creative works which are its very *raison d'etre*. It distracts the attention of the reader, and it distracts the attention (or gives evidence of a prior distraction) of the author as well; for it impairs the exercise of sensibility by removing it from any object other than the due process of an argument.

Fr. Tiverton might well reply: "Yes, but what has sensibility to do with it? I use and test my sensibility when I am in actual contact with the novels. Writing about them is another thing. There I have the right to formulate any intellectual position which will be of use to me." Certainly one can understand that his temptation was very strong. But a better critic would not have yielded to it. What the digression shows is a divided intention: an intention to see that Lawrence is understood in the most satisfactory terms possible, and an intention that Christianity should not be misunderstood. The use of the second intention detracts from the effectiveness of the first, which it is the critic's business to ensure. If the reality of the texts one is writing about may be forgotten while a digression on a quite different level is embarked on, the responsiveness of the sensibility is diminished; and the sensibility should be as active in its own way during the business of writing as during that of reading. It *should* be active, because its activity is the only guarantee of critical aptness.

It seems apparent, then, that the Christian critics who have followed Eliot's lead have failed dismally to justify the existence of "Christian discrimination." The failure may be partly due to the fact that not one of them is a good enough critic. But there are other reasons. Although their overt aims differ, from Bethell to Fr. Jarrett-Kerr, and from these two men to Nicholson, they have each suffered from a division of aims, a failure to assess them properly before writing. And that failure, in turn, comes from a reluctance to see in what sense theology is relevant to literature, and so in what sense a Christian criticism is possible at all. They have all yielded, in fact, to the temptation to take a short-cut, vaulting on their way the stile of "theological considerations."

My own feeling is that the more it declares its own Christian nature the less good a Christian criticism will do. Bethell is rightly concerned to stress that ethical insight is not to be divorced from the Christian view of man and his destiny; but he reveals the hollowness of his own critical attitude when he refers to that view as "theological considerations." Nor does he once give any justification for believing that a specific writer's literary value is connected with his theological wisdom. I agree with him (I suppose he would agree with me) that there *is* a connection. But it is a connection of such a delicate kind that we merely bedraggle it when we try to dress it in a formula.

Christianity is in general relevant to English literature not only because of the historical development of that literature but also because of the historical nature of Christianity. The contention is too large to defend or even to explain here; and it can be indicated best by the brief statement that literature is incarnational, and so is Christianity. But it is not relevant simply as a body of doctrine. Indeed, the body of doctrine is simply *not there* for the critic to use unless it exists in him not merely as doctrine but as discrimination. It can only exist in him as a force in his affective personality as well as a force in his intelligence. It is foolish to try to separate sensibility from conscience; but in the best critics conscience is energised to such an extent that it becomes transformed into terms of sensibility. This is certainly true of critics of the stature of Arnold, Eliot, and Leavis; and Dr. Johnson's weakness as a critic may possibly be attributed to the fact that conscience in him was often not energised in this way.

There is another fact. Christianity should not be used merely as an objective "standard" not because it is too small, but because it is too huge. The attempt to "complete" literary criticism "by criticism from a definite ethical and theological standpoint" arises from the desire to have an artist who will offer us an account of life which is totally Christian, a world which is at once orthodox and complete: and that is impossible. No creative artist exhausts art or Christianity; there is not one, as Eliot recognises, who does not actually deviate from Christianity. The life of Christianity is the life of the Church, and this is infinitely greater and more embracing than the whole tradition of literature. All an artist can offer is his personal response to the growth of his personal wisdom, even where the final offering invites us to speak of it in terms of "impersonality," of self-transcendence. It may be that this response will be more satisfying the more firmly it is rooted in a communal traditional wisdom of a religious kind; but in so far as it is art, it is personal, it is one man's voice. The task of the critic is to the same extent communal and personal. He cannot ask that the artist conform to his own puny grasp of the truth. Nor can he expect the artist to give us a truth sufficient to live by, any more than he can expect ratification of what is special, exclusive, in the faith he already lives by.

So much can be said, by way of indicating that Christianity is more relevant to literary criticism the more inward and unobtrusive it is: by way of indicating, too, how ill-advised have been the attempts of Eliot's followers to promote a school of Christian discrimination. Yet it must be added that, although their shortcomings have been amply recognised, in *Scrutiny,* for example, their good intentions have not. They are accused time and time again of the crudest propagandist motives and the most dishonest manoeuvres to produce a shoddy result.

The *Scrutiny* writers are no more to blame than anyone else, and they have been faced with considerable provocation. But I raise the matter in the belief that a critic who proceeds, however unobtrusively and responsibly, in the light of a Christian vision, is apt to be suspect among his fellow critics. It may be that they feel his claim, however implicit, to be informed by an orthodoxy is also a claim to a disproportionate advantage over them in the possession of critical balance. And the point is that, although Christianity is relevant, its relevance may not always be admitted.

There are two cases which strike one as significant. We have, for example, D. J. Enright reproaching Walter Stein with claiming too much for Christianity: "The only point in saying this is that it reminds us that most of this controversy is at the heart of it a controversy about religion. . . ."[5]

[5] D. J. Enright: "Literature and Belief": *Essays in Criticism,* Vol. VI, No. 1, p. 64. It is interesting that Enright, quite unfairly, applies the term "tub-thumping on a high level" to Stein's article.

Enright may not have intended it, but the clearest implication of his remark is that any proffering of Christian insight as an aid in criticism can only lead to controversy, because it must lead to a debate about the truth of Christianity as a system. So what should be personal insight is reduced towards intellectual system, and what is offered as an aid is treated as an occasion for argument. Is the Christian claim (however it is advanced) so inordinate as this, that it inevitably stimulates not agreement but its opposite? Does the first mention of Christian insight inevitably tend to undermine the "common pursuit of true judgment"?

It would seem so. Leavis, whose attacks on the school of Christian discrimination are otherwise just, fleers at Eliot for having a definite dogmatic belief behind his criticism:

> Mr. Eliot has no need to talk hesitantly about "the need for a religious sense"; he adheres to a religion, and can point to his Church and recite its dogmas.
>
> Nevertheless, those of us who find no such approach to tradition and orthodoxy possible can only cultivate the sense of health they have.[6]

Leavis is probably right in believing that Eliot's use of his dogmatic belief has harmed his criticism. But that is not the present point. The first sentence of his statement, particularly in its tone, in the imputation of sectarianism to Eliot, is markedly unfair. It is not on the ground of his capacity to recite dogmas that Eliot has ever claimed attention for his remarks. He refrains from doing so even in that most unsatisfactory book, *After Strange Gods*. He hardly ever invokes dogma at all; and when he does so, as in his essay on Baudelaire, he does not invoke anything which one would be content merely to recite. He nowhere rests his case on conformity of that kind; and the picture of him which these words evoke is a ludicrously inexact one. What is wrong with the essay on Baudelaire is not that it has dogma behind it, but that the dogma is too subjectively held, and that it leads to a repellent and rather unbalanced conclusion.

I am sure Leavis would agree. And with *his* final sentence, one

[6] *Scrutiny*, Vol. III, No. 2, p. 185.

can only agree in turn. Literary criticism is as much a personal matter, as much the product of a personal sense of life and value as literature itself. It may be added that Christians differ as widely from one another in their "sense of health" as non-Christians do. But the question remains: How is Christianity relevant? and Who will recognise the relevance of a literary insight informed by a doctrinal belief?

Certainly any critic who rests his criticism consciously on his own "sense of health" should be careful to ensure that that sense is as active and expansive as it can be and that it reflects as fully as possible the light of objective truth. Doctrine may be admissible in criticism only as sensitive judgment, but it *is* admissible. It is no answer to say that we can only judge by results; for if Christianity is as urgently controversial as Enright seems to feel it is, surely there will be disagreement about results as well. I am not supporting the "Christian discriminators," who have obviously shown up very badly. But I suggest that we may have Christian critics of the most honest and responsible kind, whose criticism will be as apt to enforce—not, it must be remarked, inculcate—a total insight as Leavis' own criticism is. How far they would be likely to differ from Leavis, or from Eliot, is a separate matter. And certainly they will not work through the "application" of "categories," or the mere invoking of a "standard"; but we cannot confine them, either, to a sort of sociology, to picking up and arranging the crumbs from the table of the real critic.

Note—Leavis also goes on to indicate what is the root of our dissatisfaction with Eliot's concern for doctrine: "One may at any rate venture that health—even religious health—demands a more active concern for other things than formal religion than Mr. Eliot now shows or encourages." Of course he is right. My point about his previous remark is simply that the use of the word "recite," the emphasis revealed in the use of "*his* Church" and "*its* dogmas" is sign of a dislike of doctrine as such.

G. Ingli James

The Autonomy of the Work of Art: Modern Criticism and the Christian Tradition*

I

IT IS NOT QUITE as fashionable as it was to speak of the autonomy of the work of art. It is likely to be assumed that one belongs to a critical tradition which has become increasingly suspect during the last decade or so. This tradition—initiated according to some[1] by I. A. Richards, according to others[2] by the French Symbolists and their nineteenth-century English exponents—tries to treat the poem as utterly self-contained and self-explanatory and appears to imply that the one true critical method is to present the reader with poems which, as far as possible, have been cut adrift from their historical and biographical context. Yet it is possible to speak of the work of art as autonomous and not to subscribe to these views at all, just as it is possible to say of a human being that he is an individual, unique, without meaning to suggest that he is completely self-enclosed, divorced from other human beings and from any particular time and place. Indeed, it is my

* First printed in *The Sewanee River,* Volume LXX, Number 2 (Spring, 1962).

[1] See e.g., Helen Gardner, *The Business of Criticism* (Oxford, 1959), and George Watson, "A Modern Literary Heresy" (the *Listener,* Oct. 16, 1958).

[2] Notably Frank Kermode, in *Romantic Image* (London, 1957).

main contention that it is precisely when we do think of the person in this way (autonomous yet not existing in a vacuum) that we are likely to think of the poem in this way too. But this is to anticipate. My first suggestion is simply that it might be helpful to try to distinguish, in a way that does not seem to be usual, between two doctrines of the autonomy of the work of art: the one, as I shall suggest, healthy and sane, the other not so; yet the two standing to each other rather as heresy does to orthodoxy, the heresy developing one aspect of the truth to the exclusion of everything else and to the point where all that it says is life-denying. Such a distinction, I think, might be particularly helpful at the present time, when a significant number of writers seem to be preoccupied with the problem of how to disengage themselves from the kind of aesthetic monism which, as Prof. Kermode and others have shown, the modern movement in literature has inherited from the Romantic-Symbolist tradition, without going over to the opposite extreme of treating the poem as though it were merely a function of something outside itself.

This opposite view—that of art as subservient to an end outside itself—is something which both the doctrines of which I am speaking reject. They are united in their hostility to any suggestion that a poem exists to express something which has been conceived of prior to the poem and can be stated adequately in the literal language of abstract ideas. The poet, they maintain, can say what he has to say only in and through the verbal devices—the metaphors, similes and so on—which he employs; the poem is not a means but an end in itself, autotelic; to use Valéry's analogy: dancing (something done for its own sake), not walking (something done with a purpose). Hence, of course, the reluctance of modern poets and critics to say what the poem "means"; their frequent resort to Mallarmé's remark, "Ce n'est point avec des idées, mon cher Degas, qu'on fait des vers. C'est avec des mots," and to Eliot's dictum that we should study poetry as poetry—the implications of which have been systematically elaborated by the American New Critics into a denunciation of what they describe, in their polysyllabic way, as the paraphrastic and biographical heresies and the intentionalist and affective fallacies. Hence too the unprecedented insistence in our own time on the distinctiveness of the language of poetry, and on the importance of practical criticism ("the words on the page"). Both doctrines, in other words, have helped to promote some of the most resounding slogans and characteristic emphases of contemporary criticism. And they have done so in the course of constructing a modern apology for poetry. Each has asserted, in a hostile environment—a scientifically-minded world all too ready to assume that what cannot be explained in purely rational terms either doesn't exist, or is unimportant, or is best left alone—that our deepest and most important experiences cannot be contained without residue in the generalizing, conceptualizing language of the discursive reason. Only poetry, with its oblique modes of writing, is somehow capable of rendering them.

Both doctrines, then, represent a reaction against a rationalistic view of life and art, and both conceive of poetry as the embodiment of our experience of what transcends definition and classification. But having said this it is necessary to distinguish. For although they confront a common enemy, and although their defences sometimes look very much alike, they are in fact conducting the campaign from very different positions, and make uneasy allies. The one, for example, can justifiably be said, I think, to belong to what is fundamentally the Christian tradition of thought and belief; the other is incompatible with it. And in order to substantiate this I want to turn now, for a while, from criticism to theology and from the twentieth century A.D. to the fourth.

II

It has been argued that there occurred during the Trinitarian controversies of the first four centuries A.D. a decisive break with Greek rationalism. This argument is familiar enough, no doubt, to theologians and to philosophers of certain schools, but it merits the attention also of those whose immediate interest is in the methods and assumptions of modern criticism.[3] The Greek mind, it has been pointed out, manifests an ineradicable bias towards the universal. Throughout the classical era the individual was dismissed as something incapable of becoming the object of knowledge, save as a particular instance of a universal rule. In the Greek view it was only as a member of a class that the singular could be thought or known, with the result that ὑπόστασις, the word which finally came to be used of a concrete individual thing, was generally regarded as synonymous with οὐσία, the word signifying the characteristic nature of a thing (that which we describe when we assign to the known a class name, indicating in general terms *what* it is).—It is not difficult to understand what Gilson and others mean when they say of the Greeks that they gave us a philosophy of essence, the product of reason; that they delighted in concepts, purely intellectual constructions, and measured all by them, and that it was from another source that the idea of "existence" was introduced into Western thought.

The only way of replying to the Greek attitude, of course, is to claim that conceptual knowledge is not the only kind; that there is something we may call "personal knowledge" wherein we know individuals in the full flavour of their individuality. Thus the intimate knowledge one has of a person one loves is knowledge not of an *it,* a lifeless, classifiable object, but of a unique, unrepeatable individual. Here, it might be said, in the realm of what Buber speaks of as I-thou relationships, where knowledge is based not so much on external observation as on what Marcel terms "participation," the individual is known. And one could add that it is not only when we are confronted with persons that this kind of knowledge is possible, though doubtless it is only then that it is fully developed. In the world of inanimate objects, too, we know what it is to be

[3] For a much fuller and more adequate discussion of the momentous nature of what took place in the realm of fourth-century Trinitarian theology, see the following, to which I am deeply indebted: C. C. J. Webb, *God and Personality* (London, 1919), especially Lecture II; L. Hodgson, *The Doctrine of the Trinity* (London, 1943), especially Lecture IV; J. V. Langmead Casserly, *The Christian in Philosophy* (London, 1949).

vividly aware of the unique and to experience something analogous to a personal relationship. A man may value a tree not for the use he can make of it but for its own sake; he may gaze at it without purpose, contemplating and admiring it in its concrete individuality.

Now this claim—that personal experience, because it is experience of the unique, escapes the abstractions and generalizations of conceptual thought—is not the monopoly of Christian believers. But it would nevertheless appear to be the case that the kind of departure it involves from the Greek philosophical tradition first occurred during the Trinitarian disputes of the Patristic age. The problem which faced the Christian Fathers during these disputes was how to find a terminology which would do full justice both to the unity of the Godhead and its revealed diversity. What they were struggling to convey was the fact that in their experience the three individuals of the Trinity were one, yet not one simply in the way that three particulars, three instances of a universal rule are one. The formula finally accepted, in which οὐσία was employed to signify the unity, and ὑπόστασις to underline the diversity, solved the problem by making a new distinction between these two terms; ὑπόστασις, in effect, was redefined: what it now represented was the individual considered, at last, as capable of being known. And οὐσία now represented not merely the specific unity in which three members of the same class partake, but the unity of three individuals in perfect communion or interpermeation. The full significance of what had happened is best understood when we recall that the word to which Latin theology turned in its search for an equivalent to the redefined ὑπόστασις, was *persona,* previously a legal and dramatic term. *Persona,* in other words, here began to take on, for the first time, something of the significance which the word *person* now has when we speak (as we so often do in our controversies with those who seek to diminish man to a mere unit or specimen) of the freedom and dignity of the human person and of the importance of personal relationships. Implicit in the Trinitarian doctrine was the recognition that the relation between the members was *the* personal relationship of which we have imperfect analogues on earth, and that in such relationships, in which we participate in the life of another, we know the individual.—It is difficult not to agree with those who claim that in analysing and elucidating the nature of divine personality men had here illuminated, though without fully realizing it, the nature not only of human personality but of all the individual entities of earthly experience and the manner in which they are known.[4] The foundation had been laid for the assertion that when we are fully responding to life we know the singular, the unique.

It was obvious from the very beginning, of course, that personal experience was a mystery. By its very nature it eluded the clear, univocal language of rational discourse. Such language, in which we tie classifying labels to experience, neither conveys nor demands a personal response; it is addressed to a passive audience and might be described as monologue. Personal experience requires something more like dialogue and imposes a profound strain on words, availing itself of metaphor, analogy and paradox, verbal devices which, because of the ambiguity they involved, had seemed to the Greek philosophical mind to be a dangerous perversion and failing of language.[5] In the doctrine of the Trinity, with its paradoxical insistence on one yet not one but three, three yet not three but one, such linguistic techniques presented themselves more obviously perhaps than ever before as the means of arriving at and recording insights incapable of being expressed in literal, conceptual terms. Had the Fathers been aware of all the implications of what they had done, they might well have subscribed to some such statement as the following:

> . . . the old Rhetoric treated ambiguity as a fault in language, and hoped to confine or diminish it; the new Rhetoric sees it as an inevitable consequence of the power of language and as an indispensible means of most of our important utterances—especially in Poetry and Religion.

[4] It should be noted, however, that Karl Barth has argued that the term *persona* as used in ancient and medieval theology has no direct connection with the modern terms "person" and "personality."

[5] See W. B. Stanford, *Ambiguity in Greek Literature* (Oxford, 1939) p. I.

This, of course, is not from the fourth century but from I. A. Richards' *Philosophy of Rhetoric,* published in 1936, and serves to bring me back to modern literary theory and its characteristic contention that there is a kind of knowledge which only literature can convey. It is to just such a doctrine that the Christian tradition of thought and belief tends. And what I am suggesting is that behind a great deal of contemporary criticism there lie those notions of person and personality which were first explicitly offered to the human mind in the context of Christian theological discussion. If we think of the work of art as autonomous, it is often the case, I believe, that we do so out of a recognition that our deepest and most important experiences are profoundly personal, and that personal experience—being experience of the unique—can be embodied only in the oblique, indirect methods of imaginative literature. In other words, we think of literature as being autonomous in the same way as a person—in the Christian sense of the word—is autonomous.[6]

This, as I say, is what I think much modern criticism (the best of it in my opinion) actually does—for example when it speaks of a poem's organic unity. M. H. Abrams, in his book *The Mirror and the Lamp,* argues that this involves thinking of a poem on the analogy of a plant, and that consequently one of the basic metaphors or analogies underlying critical thought from the Romantic period to the present day may be described as biological. But the notion of organic unity does not derive, ultimately, from biology; biology itself is here indebted to the realm of the personal.[7] If we speak of a plant—or a poem—as an organic whole it is because we think of it on the analogy of a person—an individual, incapable

[6] There is a very relevant and most interesting discussion of the relation between poems and persons, and also of the notion of literature as dialogue, in two essays by Walter J. Ong, S.J.: "A Dialectic of Aural and Objective Correlatives," *Essays in Criticism,* VIII (1958), 166–181, and "The Jinnee in the Well-Wrought Urn," *Essays in Criticism,* IV (1954), 309–320.

[7] It is interesting to note that certain of the Fathers, in their attempt to elucidate the kind of unity existing within the Trinity, were led to find an analogy in the root, the tree and the fruit.

of being accounted for by logical analysis or reduced to a mechanical association of parts. The organic theory of poetry is, fundamentally, not so much biological as personalist aestheticism. And whereas I am not suggesting that an explicit recognition of this fact is a necessary condition of good criticism, I do think that it enables us to understand more fully the procedures of such criticism and to distinguish them more sharply from those of another kind, one which also talks of the autonomy of the work of art, but in a very different sense. It is to this second interpretation of what it means to be autonomous that I now want to turn.

III

From the very beginning Christianity has recognized that to be a person is to be unique but not alone: individuals, in the Christian view, can respond to one another, can enter into a relationship—indeed must do so if they are to know the other as an individual and to realize their own individuality.[8] As John MacMurray has put it in his recent book,[9] "there can be no man until there are at least two men in communication." Each human being, that is to say, is unique, but all are akin; so that whereas a person is not to be treated as a mere unit in an impersonal system, a cog in the machine, neither is he to be thought of as existing in solitary confinement. Similarly, although he is not to be considered merely as a function of his environment, nevertheless he does belong to a particular time and place and perform a certain job; but he "absorbs" his environment, as it were,[10] without ceasing to be himself, and he informs his role with his own personality.

[8] This emerges very strongly in the work of C. C. J. Webb and of those Anglican theologians who, like Prof. Hodgson, follow him in developing what D. M. Baillie terms a "social" interpretation of the Trinity, as opposed to writers like Barth who tend to emphasize a different aspect of the doctrine. For a discussion of these two divergent trends in modern Trinitarian theology, see Baillie's *God Was In Christ* (paper covered edition, London, 1961), Chap. VI.

[9] *Persons in Relation* (London, 1961).

[10] The phrase is Fr. Langmead Casserley's, *op. cit.*, p. 209.

It is possible, however, to take a very different view of what it means to be an individual: to believe that man can realize his own unique personality only by refusing to recognize himself as belonging to any group and by cutting himself free, as far as possible, from the limitations of his own time and place. Behind such a view of course there lies the conviction that there are only two alternatives open to man: either he exists as one of a group and thereby dissolves himself in the collectivity, or he exists in isolation and is truly an individual. The third alternative, viz., that in personal relationships man can achieve what we call community —a unity in which the members do not submerge their individuality in the mass, but in which each is perfectly himself—is rejected as impossible.

In our own time this rather cheerless view has found powerful advocates, and this is hardly surprising, for it is the product, at least in part, of the sick hurry, the superficial contacts and consequent breakdown of a sense of community in modern life. In such a world, in which the crowd that flows up and down King William St. seems to be an anonymous mass of standardized, unresponsive faces, it is no wonder that some have suggested that the only way to discover and preserve one's identity is to withdraw into the innermost recesses of the private self. But too much emphasis must not be placed on the external conditions of modern life. Primarily it is the breakdown of religious belief which accounts for the feeling that the only alternative to a collectivized mode of living is lonely isolation. For not only does the man who believes in a personal God not, for that very reason, find himself completely alone; he is also aware of his kinship with the others; the other, no matter how alien he may seem, is in fact a fellow creature.[11] Contemporary urban civilization, in other words, may not be particularly conducive to personal relationships, but the Christian knows, if his belief is alive, that community is possible; knows indeed that it already exists, waiting to be realized. And

[11] This is true even of Kierkegaard, though Kierkegaard considers that in order to enter into a relationship with God it is necessary to renounce relationships with other human beings.

consequently his reaction is not to contract out of society but to reach out and recall men to the norm: a unity in which each of the members finds, not forfeits, his individuality. But for the man who rebels against depersonalization and yet has never experienced anything approaching a personal relationship, either with man or with God, there is at best only the hope that such a unity may be possible, and at worst the conviction that only in isolation is one really able to *be,* to *exist.*

The emergence of this predicament is to be seen very clearly in the poetry of Arnold; in *Empedocles on Etna* for example. Empedocles, like Arnold, is confronted with a world in which "littleness united is become invincible" and there appears to be no room for the growth of the human spirit; and the point is that only two courses seem to offer themselves. Either he must remain a prisoner of his environment or he must retreat to the freedom of isolation. Arnold, of course, knows that neither alternative makes for life. The two extremes, in fact, closely resemble each other. On the one hand the individual is suffocated by the dehumanizing pressure of the mass, on the other by the rarefied atmosphere of an existence devoid of human contacts. Hence Empedocles' cry: "Thou canst not live with man or with thyself."

Like Auden, Arnold is aware that "We must love one another or die"; like Lawrence, he recognizes that "We have our very individuality in relationship. . . . It is in the living touch between us and . . . other lives, other phenomena, that we move and have our being." And it is his hope that he may discover what Auden and Lawrence speak of ("Ah, love, let us be true to one another!"). But lacking any experience of that "living touch," and deprived too of his Christian belief, he knows, in his darkest moments, that he can be certain only of the twin poles of the Empedoclean dilemma. In his own words, "the dialogue of the mind with itself has commenced"; and this, as Buber has remarked, in another context, is not genuine dialogue; it is monologue disguising itself ingeniously for a while as dialogue. Empedocles commits suicide.

The so-called existentialists of our own day have advanced one stage further. Like Empedocles they discount the possibility of community; but they do not commit suicide, for the simple reason that they have abandoned personal relationships as an ideal in a way that Arnold never did. Faced with the choice between man-in-the-mass and self-contained man, they are willing to settle for the latter. Needless to say, I am not referring here to such writers as Jaspers, Marcel and Buber, each of whom, in his own way, insists on the mutual relation between man and man. I am thinking rather of those atheist existentialists whose protest against the reduction of the individual to an "object" takes the form of individualism pure and simple. Thus Heidegger and Sartre reject the idea of a human essence, a human nature common to all men. They see in such a notion nothing but a threat to the freedom and existence of the individual, an attempt to subordinate him to a conventionalized mode of life and consequently to prevent him from being true to his unique self. It is their unshakeable conviction that anything which joins men together engulfs them, and that the Christian idea of man as free but finite—an individual, but created according to a single pattern in the Mind of the Creator—is an illusion. To be a person—to exist—means, therefore, to them to exist in isolation. Sartre, for example, does not deny that each man belongs to a particular time and place and plays a certain role, and to that extent may be decribed as *a* Frenchman, *a* ticket collector, and so on. But he suggests that man can differentiate himself from every respect in which he is a "somewhat"; he has the power of "reducing to nothing" (*néantir*) or of "nullifying" (*néantiser*) the historical, economic and political factors which at any given moment constitute what he describes as his "situation." And it is in and through this act of negation that he achieves, in Sartre's view, self-transcendence—ceases to be a mere item in the world, lifeless and inert (*être-en-soi*) and becomes a free, conscious individual (*l'être-pour-soi*). In short, Sartre and Heidegger assert the freedom and dignity of the human person, but at the cost of condemning him to a liberty which, because it is infinite, is unbearable; there are no bounds beyond which he may not pass. They want, in Buber's words, "to derive the essence of human existence from the experience of a nightmare." They would even try to persuade us that the air which Arnold found so unbearably thin is in fact bracing and invigorating. To this there is no answer other than the one Empedocles gives to Apollo:

> Thou keepest aloof the profane,
> But the solitude oppresses thy votary!
> The jars of men reach him not in thy valley—
> But can life reach him?
> Thou fencest him from the multitude—
> Who will fence him from himself?
> He hears nothing but the cry of the torrents,
> And the beating of his own heart.
> The air is thin, the veins swell,
> The temples tighten and throb there—

But this, of course, to Sartre, would seem only weakness, a failure to meet the challenge of life.

IV

Now it seems to me that it is something very much like Sartre's notion of personality that underlies what I have called the second doctrine of the autonomy of the work of art. Behind, that is to say, the modern view that literature conveys what cannot be conveyed in any other way, there is sometimes the conviction that the deepest and most important experiences are those enjoyed not by one individual responding to another but by the radically solitary man who can communicate only with himself. Such experiences, obviously, elude the language of abstraction and generalization; they can find expression, if at all, only in art—an art which is autonomous in the same way that such an isolated, self-sufficient person is autonomous.

Sartre himself is well aware of imaginative literature as an indispensable means of saying what he has to say. In common with the other major existentialists he is primarily interested in the use of language, not for what Leavis has described as the lucid arrangement of ready-minted concepts but for the exploration of concrete situations. For the same reason that Kierkegaard is preoccupied with paradox and Marcel refuses to write systematic works, Sartre turns to the novel, the short story and the drama. And in this, as in so many other ways, existentialism reveals important affinities with contemporary criticism. There is involved in both cases a protest against what Gerard Manley Hopkins, with his intense awareness of the individually distinctive and unique, denounced as the attempt to dissolve existence into a "world of formulas." Each in its own way affirms that existence is a mystery and that the mystery is, in Marcel's phrase, "not to be degraded to a problem." It is hardly surprising, though not perhaps sufficiently remarked, that if a reader of modern British and American criticism turns to the continental existentialists he will encounter, time and again, attitudes which are strikingly familiar, even to the point of identical key words and phrases. Thus Ian Watt, in his study of the novel, observes that whereas Fielding is concerned to assign the individual to his moral and social species, so that we know his characters from the outside—standing back from them as it were and identifying the specimen, Richardson's literary objective is the individual, the personality, with the result that he employs all the resources at his command to involve us in the events and feelings described. Richardson, he points out, "does not analyse Clarissa . . . she is defined by the fulness of our participation in her life!" Inevitably one is reminded of such comments when considering Buber's analysis of knowledge into third-person and second-person relations, or Marcel's notion of knowing by participation as opposed to knowing superficially. And the similarity is even more remarkable when we remember that modern literary theory and practice have tended, at least until very recently, to favour the kind of novel in which the author eliminates himself from the scene by projecting himself into the life and situations of one or more of the characters and tells the story from the point of view of a participant.[12] As Watt says, "This is the kind of participation which the novel typically induces: it makes us feel that we are in contact not with literature but with the raw materials of life itself as they are momentarily reflected in the minds of the protagonists."[13] But if it does make us feel this, it is because we share with the existentialists a mistrust of the systematizing intellect. If one considers that the writer who asks us to survey life is somehow inferior to the writer who invites us to experience it, it is because of a conviction that life cannot be fully known unless we cease to regard it "objectively," from a distance, and become personally involved in it, and this because the world we know is one of unique personages and events.

But nothing is more striking than the way in which the contrast between Christian and atheist existentialism illuminates a similar divergence in modern criticism's reaction against rationalism.—When we recognize that the work of art is sometimes spoken of as autonomous in the same way, and for the same reason, that Sartre treats a person as autonomous, and at other times in a quite different sense, it helps us, I think, to understand more fully, and evaluate more precisely, some of the more salient features of the contemporary critical scene. In the first place, it throws new light on something to which Prof. Kermode drew attention in his book *Romantic Image*. Prof Kermode pointed out that the modern view of art as autotelic has been accompanied by two other assumptions: first, that the artist is necessarily isolated; and secondly, that there occurred, during some specific historical period, a far-reaching catastrophe (Eliot's famous "dissociation of sensibility," for example), since when art and the artist have been permanently on the defensive against a world irrevocably given over to mechanistic, rationalistic modes of thinking. Now it is perfectly true that one frequently meets these assumptions, but they are held by those

[12] "In a bird's-eye view of the English novel from Fielding to Ford, the one thing that will impress you more than any other," Joseph Warren Beach suggested, "is the disappearance of the author." *The Twentieth Century Novel* (New York, 1932), p. 14.

[13] Ian Watt, *The Rise of the Novel* (London, 1957), pp. 272 and 193.

who are thinking of art, and the artist, as autonomous in the Sartrian sense. It is when one considers that the only alternative to mass civilization is a withdrawal into the solitary self, and sees art as the product of such a withdrawal—it is then that one believes that the artist must inevitably be alienated from society. And it is then, too, that one is likely to look back into the past in order to try to find some moment when things seemed to go so irretrievably wrong that the individual would never again be able to find and be his true self in society. The point in creating such a myth—a myth of a pregnant historical disaster[14]—is, of course, that it both expresses and helps to sustain the belief that community is no longer possible, and that the blame for this is to be placed wholly on the external conditions of modern life. The individual, it implies, can no longer experience personal relationships with others, no matter how hard he tries.

Prof. Kermode suggests that this myth contains an implicit parallel with the Fall. But any resemblance to Christian doctrine is illusory. A criticism which rests on the assumption that the individual is what the Christian tradition claims him to be will speak of the role of the artist in the modern world in very different terms. To begin with, it will reject any idea of the artist as essentially isolated. The artist, it will suggest, is certainly more responsive to life than most other men, less prone to live in a world of ready-made categories and threadbare formulas; but this is not to deny his fundamental kinship with the others (for no man is an island), or to say that art must be the product of an introspective self-absorption. On the contrary, good art will be thought of as the embodied experience of a person who is himself unusually alive to reality and who demands, in his work, an equally full and living response from the reader. Such a response, it will be recognized, is not always forthcoming; the reader may turn his back on good literature; he may resent the effort involved and prefer—especially perhaps in the

[14] There seems to be a parallel here, again, with existentialism—at least in the case of Heidegger, who believes that such a catastrophe took place between the time of Parmenides and Aristotle.

modern world—to vegetate among the clichés and platitudes of the mass media, thus failing to realize himself as a unique and fully human being. In this event art will have failed to rouse him to life. But the point is that no one who is deeply committed to the Christian view of man can believe that some men—let alone the majority —lack even the latent ability to enjoy such life. The mass of men, no matter how lifeless and dead they sometimes appear, are all individuals, potentially capable of a personal response, and it is to them and to that potential, no less than to the more fully developed human being, that great art addresses itself. It speaks—in the view, let me repeat, of those who think of it as autonomous in what I call the Christian sense of the word—not merely to the artist himself, not merely to a cultural *élite* even, but to all sorts and conditions of men, whether or not they reply, and today as much as in the seventeenth century. The artist is what Wordsworth said he is: "a man speaking to men."

This, it seems to me, is not only an eminently sound way of looking at art, but also one which modern poets and critics do, to a very large extent, adopt. On the other hand, they are undoubtedly influenced too, as I have said, by very different assumptions, viz., that the time is hopelessly out of joint and that the artist cannot attempt, without loss of integrity, to communicate with other men. This, as Prof. Kermode and others have shown, is our Romantic-Symbolist heritage. For the French Symbolists, isolation is something to be embraced. The artist, in their view, must recoil from the intractable materialistic world into the depths of his self-consciousness. He must take as his emblem the dancer. One can see very clearly the connection between dancing and the Symbolist aesthetic. Here was an art form which, even more than music perhaps, could be thought of as completely autotelic. Being both wordless and inseparable from the artist it did not seem to exist merely in order to convey an abstract idea or serve a preconceived purpose. It was something done for its own, and for the artist's, sake.[15] And this was espe-

[15] Cf. John Bayley, *The Romantic Survival* (London, 1957); see especially Chap. IV.

cially so in the case of the two dancers whom Mallarmé and his French and English associates most admired: Jane Avril of the Moulin Rouge and Loïe Fuller of the Folies Bergères. These two women, who danced alone, with impassive, masklike faces, and often before mirrors, seemed to epitomize for Mallarmé all that he was struggling to achieve in literature. The effect is conveyed in these lines, on Jane Avril, from one of his poems:

> Alone, apart, one dancer watches
> Her mirrored, morbid grace;
> Before the mirror, face to face,
> Alone she watches
> Her morbid, vague, ambiguous grace . . .
>
> And, enigmatically smiling,
> In the mysterious night,
> She dances for her own delight.
> A shadow smiling
> Back to a shadow in the night.[16]

"A shadow smiling back to a shadow in the night"—"the dialogue of the mind with itself"; the kind of autonomous existence which Arnold found so desperately distressing, the Symbolist tradition proposes as an ideal. Art is to be the embodied experience of the isolated individual who communicates only with himself. As for the audience, it may look on while the poet excavates his own consciousness, but it must expect no concessions for it is not being in any way addressed.

It is the presence of this Symbolist aesthetic side by side with that other interpretation of what it means for a work of art to be autonomous which accounts, also, for the existence in modern poetry and criticism of two opposed attitudes to the question of "meaning" and, consequently, of paraphrase. To demand that art should be autonomous in the Symbolist sense is to require that it should be meaningless, since what is totally unique is by its very nature unintelligible. The writer who seriously attempts to achieve

[16] Quoted by Prof. Kermode, *op. cit.*, p. 70.

such autonomy must aim to create a completely private language and world; his poem must, literally, "not *mean* but *be*." On the other hand, not everyone who speaks of art as autonomous and who quotes MacLeish's famous phrase with approval is recommending that poetry should be void of meaning. More often than not it is a way of asserting that imaginative literature is supremely meaningful but that it cannot be reduced to, or exhausted by, any prose "meaning" which may be extracted from it. The same phrase or formula, that is to say, can mean two very different things: either that the poet must cultivate a thoroughly esoteric symbolism, or that his language, whether it is symbolic or in some other way oblique, must be intelligible—even though intelligibility ought not to be the only, or even the most important, criterion in literature.[17] —In the same way critics differ in their interpretation of the so-called paraphrastic heresy.

Everything depends upon whether literature is thought of on the analogy of Mallarmé's impersonal, self-sufficient dancer, or as something more like a human being: something which has a life of its own and is ultimately mysterious and irreducible, but which can nevertheless be known—with a knowledge which is not indeed rationalistic but does involve the activity of the discursive reason; the product, to use Wordsworth's phrase, of "Reason in her most exalted mood."

Those for whom art is an escape from the realm of essence into existence pure and simple will find any attempt to say in abstract terms what a poem is *about* pointless and offensive. Those, however, for whom a poem (like a person) demands a total response (which is not of the intellect only but in which the intellect is certainly engaged) have no need to feel inhibited about paraphrasing. They will, it is true, regard it as heretical to equate the poem with the paraphrase, but they will not go to the point of claiming that it

[17] For a particularly clear statement of this second attitude to meaning see John Coulson's essay "The Retreat from Meaning," *The Arts, Artists and Thinkers*, ed. John M. Todd (London, 1958), pp. 254–270. "The negative test," says Mr. Coulson, "is crucial: a work of art ceases to be such when it is meaningless."

should not be possible to extract prose meanings from poems, or else that such meanings have nothing to do with the poetry. And this, as far as I can see, is the very sane assumption on which the majority of modern critics proceed. In the course of doing so, however, they frequently make the kind of defensive gesture which bears witness to the strength of the opposition. Thus in a recent article,[18] Graham Hough, about to paraphrase one of Wallace Stevens' poems, feels it necessary to remark, "This is supposed to be wicked, a poem should not mean but be."

Even more significant perhaps is the habit of defending paraphrase by reference to that well-known passage in *The Use of Poetry and the Use of Criticism* in which Eliot suggests that the meaning of a poem can, in some cases at least, perform the same function as the bit of meat which the imaginary burglar always throws to the house-dog: it can keep the reader's mind diverted while the poem gets on with the job. This is how Prof. Kermode, for example, justifies his explication of a poem by Stevens. "It is painful, but I hope useful," he writes, "to mangle this great and obscure poem; it may well be an inaccurate account that is here offered, but with such verses it is true that one needs to quiet the housedog of the mind with any meat so that the poem may do its work."[19] This statement, it seems to me, confuses two quite distinct attitudes to meaning and paraphrase. On the one hand it appears, with Eliot, to suggest that the intellect plays no part in the critical appreciation of the poem; the *poetry* is intended for whatever faculties we have left over after the *mind* has been diverted by some extraneous, paraphrasable "meaning." On the other hand it is fairly obvious that this is not what Prof. Kermode believes. He knows very well that some paraphrases are less "inaccurate" than others; that some prose meanings are an integral part of, and a useful introduction to, the poem's larger, more inclusive meaning,

[18] "The Poetry of Wallace Stevens," *Critical Quarterly,* Vol. 2, No. 3, pp. 201–18.

[19] Frank Kermode, *Wallace Stevens* (Edinburgh and London, 1960), p. 45.

and some are not. And like anyone else who believes this, he attempts to make his as relevant, as accurate, as possible. But, in the shape of Eliot's memorable analogy, the anti-intellectualism of the Symbolist tradition surreptitiously invades and undermines his own account of what he is doing.

Such cases, in which a critic speaks as though he regards poetry as the embodiment of what is utterly unique and incommunicable, when in fact he does not, are fairly frequent, with the result that modern criticism is sometimes spoken of as being far more liberal and eclectic in method than most of its theoretical pronouncements seem to suggest. The explanation would seem to be that it tends to subscribe, in theory, to one doctrine of the autonomy of the work of art, but in practice to another. It tends to speak of the poem on the analogy of an individual in the Symbolist (or Sartrian) sense, but to *think* of it on the analogy of a person in the traditional, Christian sense. In other words, the two doctrines which I have tried to distinguish must not be thought of as belonging, on the whole, to two strictly different sets of critics. It is more usual to find critics—and poets—moving, apparently without any sense of incongruity, from one to the other and back again; and for all their fundamental differences the two doctrines have, as I have said, sufficient superficial resemblances for us to understand how such transitions are possible.

Hence the contradictory attitudes exhibited not only to meaning and paraphrase but also to the question of how far good criticism should take into account a poem's historical background. In what is sometimes called the battle between the scholars and the critics, the critics are by no means always consistent and united in their aims. They insist that a poem is not to be treated as a mere function of the social, political and economic conditions of the age, as though it were wholly immersed in time. But in doing so they sometimes give the impression of advocating that criticism should completely disregard the historical and biographical context, whereas at other times they do not seem to intend anything as thoroughgoing as this. And again, this is not so much, in my observation, a matter of dispute between different schools of criticism as an inconsistency into which individual critics are prone to fall. Confronted, for example, by someone whose approach to literature is aridly academic and mechanical—who treats poems as lifeless objects in a museum to be classified and related to their period rather than responded to as living things—the literary critic is likely to react in an extremist manner and dismiss as worthless all the information which scholarship seeks to provide, even although this is not his customary attitude and practice. Admittedly this is something which is more likely to happen in conversation (and acrimonious conversation at that) than anywhere else. But it involves a fundamental shift of position and therefore should not happen at all; and it would not happen, I think, if the majority of critics had a clear understanding of their underlying assumptions, and in particular of what exactly they mean by the *autonomy* of the work of art. If they consider that a poem is autonomous in the Sartrian sense, then they are perfectly consistent in treating it as though it has somehow managed to cut itself quite free from its "situation" and exist in a vacuum. If, however, they mean—as is usually the case—that it is autonomous in the way that the Christian tradition has taught us to think of a person as autonomous, then it does indeed belong to a particular time and place, though without being wholly immersed in its temporal context; like a person, it belongs to history yet transcends it; it is both "of an age" *and* "for all time." And if this is so, it follows that a knowledge of its historical and biographical background can be valuable in precisely the same way and to the same extent that one's knowledge of a person's background can be. "Background information" can enormously enrich our total understanding of both persons and poems; and without it we are liable to make the most elementary errors. It becomes a dehumanizing distraction only when we cease to use it to illuminate the living entity and begin to use the poem (or person) to illustrate our familiarity with the background—which is, of course, what pressures of all kinds, subtle and otherwise, are constantly inviting us to do.

V

Finally, if as I have suggested, most modern criticism—and certainly the best of it—is profoundly indebted to the Christian notions of person and personality, this is not, needless to say, to imply that Christian belief is either an automatic guarantee or a necessary condition of good criticism. Ideally, no doubt, a critic who is also a Christian ought to be unusually responsive, both to literature and to people. It is not that his faith ought to provide him with any external yardstick by which to measure the quality of poems and persons (and the last thing it should do is to lead him to evaluate them simply according to whether or not they profess, in the abstract, beliefs similar to his own); but it ought to sharpen his feeling for life, his ability to discriminate what is human and alive from what is impersonal and dead. But only if his faith is not simply a matter of mechanical acceptance of conventional formulas but something deeply felt and lived, modifying his whole sensibility, is it likely to do this.[20] And together with this reservation it must also be remembered that a great deal of the most sensitive and acute criticism of our time—for all that it has availed itself, as I would claim, of Christian insights—has been the work of non-believing Humanists.

To which, however, it needs to be added, I think, that Humanism, in literary criticism as in other fields, is ultimately not enough. It has limitations, which betray themselves, as a rule, when it encounters not wholeness and health but crudity and insensitivity. Confronted, in a person or a poem, with what is less than fully human, the Humanist critic will recognize the failure of another to respond to the richness and complexity of life (and to demand such a response from him); but he is constantly in danger of reacting in a bitterly hostile or contemptuous manner. For, unlike the Christian, he has nothing in the last resort to sustain him in the belief

[20] Christianity, as Vincent Buckley has said, "is more relevant to literary criticism the more inward and unobtrusive it is." *Poetry and Morality* (London, 1959), p. 224.

that all men are individuals (unique but akin), and that consequently behind every manifestation of the glib, the obtuse, the indifferent and the brutal, whether in literature or out of it, there is always a person failing to fulfil himself. Literature, in other words, is wonderfully humanizing, but only the literature of religious belief seems capable of ensuring that we retain our own human poise and dignity even in the face of those whose attitudes are so life-denying that they give the impression of not being members of the human community at all. When Lawrence said of the novel that it "can help us to live as nothing else can" he was making an exaggerated claim for secular literature; and his own tendency to fall into savage misanthropy when he contemplated "things gone dead" is some indication of how misleading such a claim is. There is, even in some of the best of our contemporary critics, a rather similar tendency, a certain lack of charity and compassion for those whom they judge (usually, quite rightly) to be only partially alive. They seem at times to resemble Jane Austen's critical Mr. Darcy, who said of himself, you may remember, "As a child I was taught what was *right,* but I was not taught to correct my temper. I was given good principles; but left to follow them in pride and conceit." Like Darcy, I feel, some of our Humanist critics appear to need humanizing; and I fancy that only religion could accomplish that.

Walter J. Ong, S.J.

The Jinnee in the Well-Wrought Urn*

I

THIS IS THE AGE which has repudiated books about the girlhood of Shakespeare's heroines. Criticism within the past few decades has made it its business to guarantee the autonomy of the work of art as constituted within its own limits. Every effort has been made to clear the art object of accretions, to focus attention on it as freed of irrelevancies concerning the author's life, his friends and his problems, or of errant speculation about the previous or subsequent history of characters, if any—from all that might be styled the personalist irrelevancies adventitious to the work of art in its own totality. The effort has been reasonably successful. The once undisputed popularity of biographical excursion has been severely curtailed. It maintains itself with effort even in concert programme notes.

The compulsions responsible for the present emphasis are many and complex, and they operate in quite diverse quarters simultaneously. The conviction that it is neither the potter who made it nor the people, real or fictional, to whose lives it is tangent, but the well-wrought urn itself which counts, has been fed indifferently out of studies of Donne or Pope or Coleridge, out of trenchant criticism working through contemporary literature, out of theory spun from clues picked up in St. Thomas Aquinas, and from in-

* Reprinted by kind permission of the author, and of the Editor of *Essays in Criticism,* in which it originally appeared (Vol. IV, No. 3).

numerable other sources. Indeed, the ability it manifests to pick up nourishment almost anywhere at all is convincing testimony to the essential truth of the conviction in question: it is in accord with facts as they are.

In a sense, the current emphasis on the work of art as such simply exploits by reaction a special weakness of nineteenth-century criticism such as Hazlitt's or Lamb's. Associated with commitments of rhetorical theory through long centuries, this weakness was not even new. But the present age found it singularly ripe for attack, and the past few decades have, by a kind of inner compulsion, set themselves to forging weapons for the anti-personalist armory. This compulsion is discernible in T. S. Eliot's submersion of the individual's subjective talent in an objective tradition (of which, to be sure, the subjective talent is simultaneously the expression), and in the attack launched by E. R. Leavis and others against a criticism based on measuring fictional characters by "real life"—by their seeming adaptability to ultra-fictional projection. The same compulsion is seen everywhere in the persistent emphasis of American criticism as represented by such work as that of Cleanth Brooks or Kenneth Burke.

But a change of heart, however carefully defined, is setting in, as a close reading of recent critical credos, such as those of Leslie Fiedler or of Richard Chase, shows. The compulsion to beat the personalist horse loses force as the impression gains ground that he has shown no unambiguous signs of life for a long while. Beating him becomes a bore, and we want something newer and more interesting to do.

However, it is not quite clear to me, nor perhaps to many others, that the horse is really dead. A phenomenon so universal and persistent as the personalist deviation in criticism, it would seem, still deserves rather more explicit consideration than it has received. It has been written off in places at which it might well have been looked into. Personalist deviationism is, after all, not merely the last infirmity of feeble sensibilities. Dr. Johnson, who is honestly admired by most objective critics and is cited by Mr. Fiedler as a practitioner commonly acknowledged as extraordinarily good, not only stands for an approach to literature that is frankly moral, in a distressingly simplified fashion, but could state bluntly to Boswell that "the biographical part of literature is what I love most." (The personalist horse does seem dead and shrunk to a heap of bones when we try to imagine a present-day critical collection with *that* for a title-page motto.)

This is not to say that the personalist approach to a work of art is to be advocated. If I may be permitted a personal deviation of my own, I myself subscribe wholeheartedly to the practice and theory of focusing primarily on the work of art itself and feel no desire to defend the personalist approach as a substitute technique. It is not defence of the personalist drift, but explanation, that is needed. The personalist deviation is here to stay, not only in programme notes but in serious discussions of literature which, apparently unaffected by recent critical trends, continue to pour from the presses. For some it may be a racking experience to own that the personalist approach is still established as the dominant approach in most classrooms. But there it is, all the same.

However objectionable, the personalist approach manifests a persistency that itself clamours for explanation. If the urn really is the issue, why is it always in peril of being overlooked or tossed aside? If you so much as whisper that there is a jinnee in the urn, most onlookers will be only too willing to drop the urn without further ado. Broken, it will let the jinnee out, and they can ask him a few questions. While decrying the tendency to behave this way, we may be excused for asking what accounts for the presence of the tendency in the first place.

II

There are countless ways in which works of art fray out into personalities and thus give the personalist distraction a foothold within the art object itself. The most obvious, that of character in literature or even in the plastic arts, is both so straight-forward and so complicated—with the curious susceptibility characters exhibit even for getting themselves psycho-analysed—that it hardly need be mentioned. But there are other footholds, some closely approximating to this. There is the autobiographical strain which persistently fertilizes fiction. Or there is the obverse autobiography of a Scott Fitzgerald, where not only are the novels cut to the measure of the author's life, but this life itself is lived to the measure of the novels—type and antitype are generated not only simultaneously but reciprocally as well.

Or there is the fact that groupings of works by author have a rough and ready viability not found in groupings by classes. The body of works by Shakespeare—plays, sonnets, and other poems all together—form a whole in a way more integrated than that formed by the body of Elizabethan sonnets or by Elizabethan drama. *Sweeney Agonistes* belongs with *Tradition and the Individual Talent* in a way it does not with Pound's *Cantos* or with a poem by Auden.

Or, again, there is the fact that the final stage of interest in a poet's work creates inevitably the poet's shrine, which is consecrated to the poet's person and thus may as well be his birthplace as something more readily connected with his works. The Shakespeare Memorial Theatre is at Stratford, not on the south bank of the Thames. Or, once more, the personalist distraction intrudes itself by reason of the sense of communion which rides through the contemplation of a work of art. At the threshold of consciousness, there hovers the awareness that others, or at least another, knows this work in the intimate way that I do. What would be an intrusion on our attention if only an object were concerned, is thus transmuted into a sharing in terms of this injection of personality, however vague it may be. One wonders if there could be any artistic experience at all if the contemplator were a human being entirely alone in the universe.

This is not all. The very genesis of works of art is often—perhaps always and necessarily—derivative from personal relations and tensions. That the muses are conceived of as persons and not as clouds or waves bears testimony to a state of mind elusive but real. Certainly the artistic impulse is at a kind of peak when the person-to-person relationship takes possession of the whole field of life in a crisis terminating ordinarily in marriage. For the great majority of persons, this is the only time anything like artistic creativity even remotely threatens in their lives. Even those whose creative activity persists testify to the earlier period of intensification of impulse and the readjustment demanded for continuation. There is Villon's verse testament executed "en l'an de mon trentiesme aage," or Mr. Eliot's pertinent remarks about those who want to continue to write poetry after their early youth. The crisis adverted to here is one which hardly exerts itself so immediately in the case of scientists.

Even where there is readjustment and the period of artistic impulse associated in one way or another with entrance upon the plenary personal relationship of marriage is past, the personal drive continues in the production of works of art. Frank accounts of artistic development, such as Stephen Spender's recent account, throughout are replete with personal relations and tensions, which, again, would have an entirely different status in the life of a mathematician or physicist or perhaps even a metaphysician.

It would be hard to disprove the statement that the impulse to produce a work of fine art simply cannot arise except within a framework of personal give-and-take, a *you-me* situation, set up within the artist's mind. The lack of artistic impulse among animals is a simple corollary of the dead quiet which Rilke found so terrifying in the animal eye. J. S. Mill's attempt to define poetry as something not heard but *over*heard is largely traceable to the impulse of the abstractionist, scientific mind to extricate poetry from the network of personality in which it is involved. But the attempt is successful, or at least titillating, precisely in so far as it removes the sensorily ascertainable audience and replaces it with a mysterious audience suggesting the bottomless depths of a pure personality, disengaged from the crudities of sense perception and existing only in the vibrant tension which makes a *me* separate from a *you*.

Creative activity is often—again, perhaps always—powered by the drive to accomplish, in terms of the production of an object of art, an adjustment or readjustment in certain obscure relationships with other persons. The state of protest in which artistic activity is so often framed is evidence of how matters stand here. Only persons are liable to protest. You cannot protest to a fact or to an object. Although you speak of protesting against it, you can only protest about it to some *one*. In a discussion of Lionel Trilling's recent book, R. P. Blackmur very properly suggests the artistic sterility of a feeling for systems—impersonal things—and the fact that existing politics is good not *for* literature, but "to *aggravate* literature." These sensitively conceived remarks underscore the value of high-potential person-to-person situations in generating the artist's product.

Even critical activity is dependent on this person-to-person situation for its coming into being. Another way of putting this is to say, as it is commonly said, that criticism is a social activity in a way in which scientific activity is not. Although in science there is question of background, there seems to be no question of a personal *mise en scène* as a condition of scientific activity in the way in which there is in critical activity. Even when questions as to who says what about whom are not obvious at the surface, issues involving such questions are likely to be found in the depths, where the wells of criticism, like those of the poem, are driven deep in the personal situation in which the critic finds himself. The goddess of criticism is a kind of in-law of the muses, and there is some question of an underground passage between the watering places to which she brings her devotees and the springs of Helicon.

III

The artistic situation differs from the scientific, against which it is helpful to set it here, precisely in centering about an externalized, man-made object. The persuasion that the object itself must be primary is thus both sound and promising. But the object is not free of involvement in tragedy simply because of its primacy as object. Although it stands solidly—or pretty solidly—on its own feet, it is none the less a harbinger of disappointment and of death. For once we have granted to the work of art the kind of autonomy which the artistic situation demands, once we have decided to allow it to slough its irrelevancies, which would dissipate its own objective being in the confusion of personal issues out of which it perhaps arose, a further question presents itself: Is it not in the last analysis cruel to face a human being with merely an object as such, a being which is less than a person? As soon as contemplation enters beyond a certain stage of awareness, is not the human being going to be unsatisfied if he cannot find another, a person, a *you* in whatever it is he is concerned with?

It seems that he is going to be unsatisfied, precisely in so far as he drives this contemplation of the object to its ultimate—in so far as he takes it in its maximum of seriousness. We consider here the case not of passing attention to a work of art but the case of plenary attention, serious and protracted and repeated. Contemplation of this sort involves love, and the question is whether it can be carried on, or how far it can be carried on, without some suggestion of reciprocity. Projected into an unpeopled void, love becomes only the ultimate refinement of self-torture. And while it is true that contemplation of a minor object of art may not involve the full psychological mechanism of love in all its complications, still, in proportion as the object of art pretends to be serious, it at least sets in motion this tremendous mechanism, which demands for full satisfaction the reciprocity of another person.

Man's deepest orientation is personal. He cannot give himself fully in an outpouring of love unless someone else is *there,* with at least the capability of giving a self in return. Otherwise, psychological disaster threatens—the disaster which takes such heavy toll of serious writers or artists.

The morass of personality which surrounds the work of art in ways only briefly hinted at here establishes the personalist aberration as a permanent threat. As contemplation enters upon a more serious stage, the human being is driven by the whole economy of what it is to be man to find opposite himself, in that which he contemplates, a person capable of reacting in turn. This drive is primordial and will not be denied. It can be deflected from the object, as it ordinarily is, by a refusal to take the object in total seriousness, by a smile, a shrug of the shoulders, by an acknowledgment, if only subconscious, that somewhere or other the poem will break down, will ultimately reach a point at which it is incapable of eliciting further love—unlike a person, who can go on eliciting love without limit.

When the personalist aberration sets in, or in so far as it sets in, the resolution of the state of tension is otherwise effected. The movement of love goes on, but persons—the characters of the novel, the artist himself responsible for the object, the peopled parlour where the Ming vase was displayed, or the woman who ran her fingers over the cool jade—will begin to haunt the attention, not as within the work of art itself but as constituted more and more in their own right. This personalization is, of course, unsatisfactory, even to the compulsion from which it derives. It is only an evanescent appeasement, for these persons do not exist in the present situation controlled by the object, and it is an existent and responsive person that human nature demands. But the personalist drive, if still frustrated, has had a kind of say.

The nature of the frustration here can be misunderstood. It turns not on the fact that the work of art is man-made but on the fact that it is an object. Drilled at least from the time of Walter Pater to focus all aesthetic questions on the man-made art object, we are likely to overlook the fact that the fundamental impasse here presents itself at a more basic level than that of art itself, and that the impulse to focus the difficulty at the level of art is only another manifestation of the tendency to keep the potential of personality around an object at a maximum. The art object, with its immediate social context, is an easier point than the natural object at which both to study and to project the personalist aberration. That for both operations we today automatically avail ourselves of the object of art rather than of the natural object testifies perhaps to the waning power of the imagination in our present culture.

In more primitive cultures, it has been otherwise. It has been otherwise in the earlier history of the culture of the West. The nature cults react to the impasse created by the person-object situation not only on the artistic, but upon the natural level as well. Hebrew and early Christian critiques of the nature cults of antiquity attack the cults precisely on such ground. In the analysis offered by the writer of the Book of Wisdom, it is man's orientation towards personality which has betrayed him in his contemplation of natural objects, so that he pretends that the objects themselves are persons, imagining "either the fire, or the wind, or the swift air, or the circle of the stars, or the great water, or the sun and the moon, to be the gods that rule the world." The pre-Hellenic nature cults are accused of pretending to close a circuit where it cannot be closed, of failing to own that the person-to-person drive must push on past the person-object situation to find a response which plays back. While the objects of nature are indeed redolent of Person, the Person must be not in, but beyond them. The error lies in the self-deception which tries to turn the object into a person instead of squarely facing the impasse.

Centuries later, this same critique is extended to the Graeco-Roman world and given additional dimension by Paul in the opening of his Letter to the Romans. Men have allowed themselves to be misled in imputing what is proper to the invisible and incorruptible God (personality as such is not visible, the human person, in so far as merely visible, being rather like an object) not only to human beings but to birds and four-footed animals and creeping things. Here the aberration of idolatry, of misplaced personalism, is presented as intimately connected with other deep psychological displacements. The deterioration of the sexual aspect of marriage in an idolatrous society is not a mere accident, for treating objects like persons and persons like objects suggests a basic imbalance sure to make itself felt in this deepest of human personal relationships.

IV

It would be difficult to assign the precise differences between the place of the artist and the art objects in contemporary society and their place in the Judaeo-Hellenistic world. It is, however, certain that the shifts that have produced the modern world have radically altered the focus of the personalist crisis. Men are less and less inclined to impregnate inanimate nature with personality, at least in any crass fashion, although it is well to recall that in Mr. Eliot's later poems, as H. Marshall McLuhan has recently pointed out, the quite convincing speakers seem to be sections of the landscape. Even apart from reflections suggested by this and the many related phenomena which everyone can think of, it would be too simple to maintain that the old apotheosis of natural objects has simply been removed and the apotheosis of the objects of human art put into its place. But it is certain that a great shift has taken place from the former to the latter kind of apotheosis.

Between Graeco-Roman times and the present, the crudity—indeed, the childishness—of almost all medieval and Renaissance purely rhetorical theory, which stands in such strange contrast to the sophistication of theological, philosophical, and even, within its limits, what we might today call the para-physical or para-medical theory of the same periods, and which lags far behind rhetorical practice, betrays the fact that through the Middle Ages and the Renaissance the object of art had not aggregated to itself any large concentration of serious intellectual issues. No especially crucial questions attached to objects of art, not because earlier ages had an adequate apparatus of theory for explaining away the questions, but rather because the object of art failed, it would seem even in the case of serious artists, to become in any urgent way the psychological crux for things. It was idolatry of nature, implemented indeed by art, but only implemented, which long remained the real threat. The idolatry of art seems only during the Renaissance to have begun to appear as something more than a mist on the horizon.

Whatever the complete details of its history, the shift in emphasis from nature to art has matured today in connection with several related phenomena. There is the elaboration of rhetorical and esthetic theory which has marked the past few centuries, there is the cult, half-explicit but quite real, of the artist who is martyr to his craft and burnt up wholly in its service, and, finally, there is the present insistence on focusing the object of art itself to the careful exclusion of its personalized periphery.

The first of these phenomena, the elaboration of theory, is simply testimony to the fact that the work of art itself is now somehow capable of focusing the central issues of human existence. The second points immediately to the personalized aspect of these issues, for in figures such as those of Kafka or Proust or Joyce—at least as they exist as symbols in men's minds, for, as to their persons, we cannot presume to frame a definitive answer—we find the human being who has given himself to the work of art so completely as to blur the distinction between himself and it, presenting himself to it, as though it were a person, in an act of total abandonment, and thus endowing it, by what must be the ultimate fiction, with the marrow of his own abrogated personality. For the devotee of the martyr-artist, the blurring here is accomplished not at the periphery of the work of art by shading this periphery out into personalities, but rather at the very centre of the work, where the personality of the artist has so annihilated itself as to be defined by nothing more than the work. The autobiographical bias in the work here does not stand in relationship to a life retained in its own right as real. The autobiography has consumed the life in its telling. The real life has been terminated in a foundation sacrifice: a human being has been put to death in order to serve as the ultimate substructure of the artistic edifice. To serve even the cause of the natural fertility which underlies the fertility of art, neither Moloch nor any other Baal could ask for more.

It is in association with such phenomena as these that the present insistence on the autonomy of the art object acquires its high seriousness. The concentration on the object is hardly a passing infatuation of a school of critics. It is a specialized focus of a persistent problem at the centre of human life. If the object of art has become less religious today in being less often explicitly directed towards an extra-temporal goal, it has also become more religious in bearing more directly the weight of religious issues. The object-person question pressing on the art object today is not a mere prop tangential to human living. It is the axis, the quiet pole that bears the weight and movement of all.

The assertion that in works of art it is the object itself which counts thus treads such crucial ground that it must be made with great honesty, which means with circumspection and humility. Not only the truth of the situation, but its awkwardness as well, must be faced. This awkwardness derives from the fact that, far-fetched as it may seem when applied to less important works of art, the principle apparently holds that in a valid but not exclusive sense, each work of art is not only an object but a kind of surrogate for a person. Anything that bids for attention in an act of contemplation is a surrogate for a person. In proportion as the work of art is capable of being taken in full seriousness, it moves further and further along an asymptote to the curve of personality.

The very insistence on the object-existence of the work of art, the insistence that it be set off from another reality, clean and self-possessed, involves an anomaly. For it is not an object, but a person who is self-possessed. It is only persons who, in their deep interiors where no other creature can enter, are cut off clean from the rest of the world, poised alone. The object situation itself is really the crux, the ultimate impossibility—a situation which by its very structure points away from itself to another world of persons, which carries in itself its own dissolution. The very way in which we envision the object-situation as clean, cut off, is derived not so much from the object as from our own personalist bias. We have forgotten the lesson of Gestalt-psychology. This is humiliating for those who must deal with objects, as we all must. But it will do no good to blink the facts and pretend that they are otherwise. And it will perhaps do no harm to understand and sympathize with the recurrent impulse—shall we say, of the undergraduate?—to get away from it all and back into the vibrant world of personalities again.

The fact is that, in the last analysis, as a matter of full, serious, protracted contemplation and love, it is unbearable for a man or woman to be faced with anything less than a person—and thus, tragically, even part-way unbearable to be faced only with other human persons, where the personal relationship is inevitably enmeshed in material situations involving objects, and where even the human being, measurable, definable, partakes of the nature of object at the same time that he is person. In all our moves, our motivation, perhaps in secret and by indirection, bears towards the counter-move, hopes to find itself really a counter-move. Our great fear is that we are not being loved. Our gaze on the object, we peep anxiously from the corners of our eyes, alert for someone's response somewhere.

This situation keeps the jinnee in the urn and promises to keep him there for good. Try as you may, he will not be exorcized. What is worse, he will always threaten to prove more interesting than the urn itself. For he is a person, or—since it is hard to be certain about jinn, themselves folklore creatures grown out of the person-object crisis and representing an ambiguous and unsatisfactory compromise, for some Moslem writers make them angelic or demonic persons, but others mere diaphanous animals—at any rate, if he is not a person, he behaves enough like one to betray the bias of the human heart.

T. S. Eliot

Religion and Literature*

WHAT I HAVE TO SAY is largely in support of the following propositions: Literary criticism should be completed by criticism from a definite ethical and theological standpoint. In so far as in any age there is common agreement on ethical and theological matters, so far can literary criticism be substantive. In ages like our own, in which there is no such common agreement, it is the more necessary for Christian readers to scrutinize their reading, especially of works of imagination, with explicit ethical and theological standards. The "greatness" of literature cannot be determined solely by literary standards; though we must remember that whether it is literature or not can be determined only by literary standards.[1]

We have tacitly assumed, for some centuries past, that there is *no* relation between literature and theology. This is not to deny that literature—I mean, again, primarily works of imagination—has been, is, and probably always will be judged by some moral standards. But moral judgements of literary works are made only according to the moral code accepted by each generation, whether it lives according to that code or not. In an age which accepts some precise Christian theology, the common code may be fairly orthodox:

[1] As an example of literary criticism given greater significance by theological interests, I would call attention to Theodor Haecker: *Virgil* (Sheed and Ward).

though even in such periods the common code may exalt such concepts as "honour," "glory" or "revenge" to a position quite intolerable to Christianity. The dramatic ethics of the Elizabethan Age offers an interesting study. But when the common code is detached from its theological background and is consequently more and more merely a matter of habit, it is exposed both to prejudice and to change. At such times morals are open to being altered *by* literature; so that we find in practice that what is "objectionable" in literature is merely what the present generation is not used to. It is a commonplace that what shocks one generation is accepted quite calmly by the next. This adaptability to change of moral standards is sometimes greeted with satisfaction as an evidence of human perfectibility: whereas it is only evidence of what unsubstantial foundations people's moral judgements have.

I am not concerned here with religious literature but with the application of our religion to the criticism of any literature. It may be as well, however, to distinguish first what I consider to be the three senses in which we can speak of "religious literature." The first is that of which we say that it is "religious literature" in the same way that we speak of "historical literature" or of "scientific literature." I mean that we can treat the Authorized translation of the Bible, or the works of Jeremy Taylor, as literature, in the same way that we treat the historical writing of Clarendon or of Gibbon—our two great English historians—as literature; or Bradley's *Logic,* or Buffon's *Natural History*. All of these writers were men who, incidentally to their religious, or historical, or philosophic purpose, had a gift of language which makes them delightful to read to all those who can enjoy language well written, even if they are unconcerned with the objects which the writers had in view. And I would add that though a scientific, or historical, or theological, or philosophic work which is also "literature," may become superannuated as anything but literature, yet it is not likely to be "literature" unless it had its scientific or other value for its own time. While I acknowledge the legitimacy of this enjoyment, I am more acutely aware of its abuse. The persons who enjoy these writings *solely* because of their literary merit are essentially parasites; and we know that parasites, when they become too numerous, are pests. I could easily fulminate for a whole hour against the men of letters who have gone into ecstasies over "the Bible as literature," the Bible as "the noblest monument of English prose." Those who talk of the Bible as a "monument of English prose" are merely admiring it as a monument over the grave of Christianity. I must try to avoid the by-paths of my discourse: it is enough to suggest that just as the work of Clarendon, or Gibbon, or Buffon, or Bradley would be of inferior literary value if it were insignificant as history, science and philosophy respectively, so the Bible has had a *literary* influence upon English literature *not* because it has been considered as literature, but because it has been considered as the report of the Word of God. And the fact that men of letters now discuss it as "literature" probably indicates the *end* of its "literary" influence.

The second kind of relation of religion to literature is that which is found in what is called "religious" or "devotional" poetry. Now what is the usual attitude of the lover of poetry—and I mean the person who is a genuine and first-hand enjoyer and appreciator of poetry, not the person who follows the admirations of others—toward this department of poetry? I believe, all that may be implied in his calling it a *department*. He believes, not always explicitly, that when you qualify poetry as "religious" you are indicating very clear limitations. For the great majority of people who love poetry, "*religious* poetry" is a variety of *minor* poetry: the religious poet is not a poet who is treating the whole subject matter of poetry in a religious spirit, but a poet who is dealing with a confined part of this subject matter: who is leaving out what men consider their major passions, and thereby confessing his ignorance of them. I think that this is the real attitude of most poetry lovers towards such poets as Vaughn, or Southwell, or Crashaw, or George Herbert, or Gerard Hopkins.

But what is more, I am ready to admit that up to a point these critics are right. For there is a kind of poetry, such as most of the work of the authors I have mentioned, which is the product of a special religious awareness, which may exist without the general awareness which we expect of the major poet. In some poets, or in some of their works, this general awareness may have existed; but the preliminary steps which represent it may have been suppressed, and only the end-product presented. Between these, and those in which the religious or devotional genius represents the *special* and limited awareness, it may be very difficult to discriminate. I do not pretend to offer Vaughn, or Southwell, or George Herbert, or Hopkins as major poets: I feel sure that the first three, at least, are poets of this limited awareness. They are not great religious poets in the sense in which Dante, or Corneille, or Racine, even in those of their plays which do not touch upon Christian themes, are great Christian religious poets. Or even in the sense in which Villon and Baudelaire, with all their imperfections and delinquencies, are Christian poets. Since the time of Chaucer, Christian poetry (in the sense in which I shall mean it) has been limited in England almost exclusively to minor poetry.

I repeat that when I am considering Religion and Literature, I speak of these things only to make clear that I am not concerned primarily with Religious Literature. I am concerned with what should be the relation between Religion and all Literature. Therefore the third type of "religious literature" may be more quickly passed over. I mean the literary works of men who are sincerely desirous of forwarding the cause of religion: that which may come under the heading of Propaganda. I am thinking, of course, of such delightful fiction as Mr. Chesterton's *Man Who Was Thursday,* or his *Father Brown.* No one admires and enjoys these things more than I do; I would only remark that when the same effect is aimed at by zealous persons of less talent than Mr. Chesterton the effect is negative. But my point is that such writings do not enter into any serious consideration of the relation of Religion and Literature: because they are conscious operations in a world in which it is assumed that Religion and Literature are not related. It is a conscious and limited relating. What I want is a literature which should be *un*consciously, rather than deliberately and defiantly, Christian:

because the work of Mr. Chesterton has its point from appearing in a world which is definitely not Christian.

I am convinced that we fail to realize how completely, and yet how irrationally, we separate our literary from our religious judgements. If there could be a complete separation, perhaps it might not matter: but the separation is not, and never can be, complete. If we exemplify literature by the novel—for the novel is the form in which literature affects the greatest number—we may remark this gradual secularization of literature during at least the last three hundred years. Bunyan, and to some extent Defoe, had moral purposes: the former is beyond suspicion, the latter may be suspect. But since Defoe the secularization of the novel has been continuous. There have been three chief phases. In the first, the novel took the Faith, in its contemporary version, for granted, and omitted it from its picture of life. Fielding, Dickens and Thackeray belong to this phase. In the second, it doubted, worried about, or contested the Faith. To this phase belong George Eliot, George Meredith and Thomas Hardy. To the third phase, in which we are living, belong nearly all contemporary novelists except Mr. James Joyce. It is the phase of those who have never heard the Christian Faith spoken of as anything but an anachronism.

Now, do people in general hold a definite opinion, that is to say religious or anti-religious; and do they read novels, or poetry for that matter, with a separate compartment of their minds? The common ground between religion and fiction is behaviour. Our religion imposes our ethics, our judgement and criticism of ourselves, and our behaviour toward our fellow men. The fiction that we read affects our behaviour towards our fellow men, affects our patterns of ourselves. When we read of human beings behaving in certain ways, with the approval of the author, who gives his benediction to this behaviour by his attitude toward the result of the behaviour arranged by himself, we can be influenced towards behaving in the same way.[2] When the contemporary novelist is an individual think-

[2] Here and later I am indebted to Montgomery Belgion: *The Human Parrot* (chapter on The Irresponsible Propagandist).

ing for himself in isolation, he may have something important to offer to those who are able to receive it. He who is alone may speak to the individual. But the majority of novelists are persons drifting in the stream, only a little faster. They have some sensitiveness, but little intellect.

We are expected to be broadminded about literature, to put aside prejudice or conviction, and to look at fiction as fiction and at drama as drama. With what is inaccurately called "censorship" in this country—with what is much more difficult to cope with than an official censorship, because it represents the opinions of individuals in an irresponsible democracy, I have very little sympathy; partly because it so often suppresses the wrong books, and partly because it is little more effective than Prohibition of Liquor; partly because it is one manifestation of the desire that state control should take the place of decent domestic influence; and wholly because it acts only from custom and habit, not from decided theological and moral principles. Incidentally, it gives people a false sense of security in leading them to believe that books which are *not* suppressed are harmless. Whether there *is* such a thing as a harmless book I am not sure; but there very likely are books so utterly unreadable as to be incapable of injuring anybody. But it is certain that a book is not harmless merely because no one is consciously offended by it. And if we, as readers, keep our religious and moral convictions in one compartment, and take our reading merely for entertainment, or on a higher plane, for aesthetic pleasure, I would point out that the author, whatever his conscious intentions in writing, in practice recognizes no such distinctions. The author of a work of imagination is trying to affect us wholly, as human beings, whether he knows it or not; and we are affected by it, as human beings, whether we intend to be or not. I suppose that everything we eat has some other effect upon us than merely the pleasure of taste and mastication; it affects us during the process of assimilation and digestion; and I believe that exactly the same is true of anything we read.

The fact that what we read does not concern merely something called our *literary taste,* but that it affects directly, though only amongst many other influences, the whole of what we are, is best elicited, I think, by a conscientious examination of the history of our individual literary education. Consider the adolescent reading of any person with some literary sensibility. Everyone, I believe, who is at all sensible to the seductions of poetry, can remember some moment in youth when he or she was completely carried away by the work of one poet. Very likely he was carried away by several poets, one after the other. The reason for this passing infatuation is not merely that our sensibility to poetry is keener in adolescence than in maturity. What happens is a kind of inundation, of invasion of the undeveloped personality, the empty (swept and garnished) room, by the stronger personality of the poet. The same thing may happen at a later age to persons who have not done much reading. One author takes complete possession of us for a time; then another; and finally they begin to affect each other in our mind. We weigh one against another; we see that each has qualities absent from others, and qualities incompatible with the qualities of others: we begin to be, in fact, critical; and it is our growing critical power which protects us from excessive possession by any one literary personality. The good critic—and we should all try to be critics, and not leave criticism to the fellows who write reviews in the papers—is the man who, to a keen and abiding sensibility, joins wide and increasingly discriminating reading. Wide reading is not valuable as a kind of hoarding, an accumulation of knowledge, or what sometimes is meant by the term "a well-stocked mind." It is valuable because in the process of being affected by one powerful personality after another, we cease to be dominated by any one, or by any small number. The very different views of life, co-habiting in our minds, affect each other, and our own personality asserts itself and gives each a place in some arrangement peculiar to ourself.

It is simply not true that works of fiction, prose or verse, that is to say works depicting the actions, thoughts and words and passions of imaginary human beings, *directly* extend our knowledge of life. Direct knowledge of life is knowledge directly in relation to ourselves, it is our knowledge of *how* people behave in general, of *what* they are like in general, in so far as that part of life in which we ourselves have participated gives us material for generalization. Knowledge of life obtained through fiction is only possible by another stage of self-consciousness. That is to say, it can only be a knowledge of other people's knowledge of life, not of life itself. So far as we are taken up with the happenings in any novel in the same way in which we are taken up with what happens under our eyes, we are acquiring at least as much falsehood as truth. But when we are developed enough to say: "This is the view of life of a person who was a good observer within his limits, Dickens, or Thackeray, or George Eliot, or Balzac; but he looked at it in a different way from me, because he was a different man; he even selected rather different things to look at, or the same things in a different order of importance, because he was a different man; so what I am looking at is the world as seen by a particular mind"—then we are in a position to gain something from reading fiction. We are learning *something* about life from the authors direct, just as we learn something from the reading of history direct; but these authors are only really helping us when we can see, and allow for, their differences from ourselves.

Now what we get, as we gradually grow up and read more and more, and read a greater diversity of authors, is a variety of views of life. But what people commonly assume, I suspect, is that we gain this experience of other men's views of life only by "improving reading." This, it is supposed, is a reward we get by applying ourselves to Shakespeare, and Dante, and Goethe, and Emerson, and Carlyle, and dozens of other respectable writers. The rest of our reading for amusement is merely killing time. But I incline to come to the alarming conclusion that it is just the literature that we read for "amusement," or "purely for pleasure" that may have the greatest and least suspected influence upon us. It is the literature which we read with the least effort that can have the easiest and most insidious influence upon us. Hence it is that the influence of popular novelists, and of popular plays of contemporary life, requires to be scrutinized most closely. And it is chiefly *contemporary* literature that the majority of people ever read in this attitude of "purely for pleasure," of pure passivity.

The relation of what I have been saying to the subject announced for my discourse should now be a little more apparent. Though we may read literature merely for pleasure, of "entertainment" or of "aesthetic enjoyment," this reading never affects simply a sort of special sense: it affects us as entire human beings; it affects our moral and religious existence. And I say that while individual modern writers of eminence can be improving, contemporary literature as a whole tends to be degrading. And that even the effect of the better writers, in an age like ours, may be degrading to some readers; for we must remember that what a writer does to people is not necessarily what he intends to do. It may be only what people are capable of having done to them. People exercise an unconscious selection in being influenced. A writer like D. H. Lawrence may be in his effect either beneficial or pernicious. I am not even sure that I have not had some pernicious influence myself.

At this point I anticipate a rejoinder from the liberal-minded, from all those who are convinced that if everybody says what he thinks, and does what he likes, things will somehow, by some automatic compensation and adjustment, come right in the end. "Let everything be tried," they say, "and if it is a mistake, then we shall learn by experience." This argument might have some value, if we were always the same generation upon earth; or if, as we know to be not the case, people ever learned much from the experience of their elders. These liberals are convinced that only by what is called unrestrained individualism will truth ever emerge. Ideas, views of life, they think, issue distinct from independent heads, and in consequence of their knocking violently against each other, the fittest survive, and truth rises triumphant. Anyone who dissents from this view must be either a mediaevalist, wishful only to set back the clock, or else a fascist, and probably both.

If the mass of contemporary authors were really individualists, every one of them inspired Blakes, each with his separate vision, and if the mass of the contemporary public were really a mass of *individuals* there might be something to be said for this attitude. But this is not, and never has been, and never will be. It is not only that the reading individual today (or at any day) is not enough an individual to be able to absorb all the "views of life" of all the authors pressed upon us by the publishers' advertisements and reviewers, and to be able to arrive at wisdom by considering one against another. It is that the contemporary authors are not individuals enough either. It is not that the world of separate individuals of the liberal democrat is undesirable; it is simply that this world does not exist. For the reader of contemporary literature is not, like the reader of the established great literature of all time, exposing himself to the influence of divers and contradictory personalities; he is exposing himself to a mass movement of writers who, each of them, think that they have something individually to offer, but are really all working together in the same direction. And there never was a time, I believe, when the reading public was so large, or so helplessly exposed to the influences of its own time. There never was a time, I believe, when those who read at all, read so many more books by living authors than books by dead authors; there never was a time so completely parochial, so shut off from the past. There may be too many publishers; there are certainly too many books published; and the journals ever incite the reader to "keep up" with what is being published. Individualistic democracy has come to high tide: and it is more difficult today to be an individual than it ever was before.

Within itself, modern literature has perfectly valid distinctions of good and bad, better and worse: and I do not wish to suggest that I confound Mr. Bernard Shaw with Mr. Noel Coward, Mrs. Woolf with Miss Mannin. On the other hand, I should like it to be clear that I am not defending a "high"-brow against a "low"-brow literature. What I do wish to affirm is that the whole of modern literature is corrupted by what I call Secularism, that it is simply unaware of, simply cannot understand the meaning of, the primacy of the supernatural over the natural life: of something which I assume to be our primary concern.

I do not want to give the impression that I have delivered a mere fretful jeremiad against contemporary literature. Assuming a common attitude between you, or some of you, and myself, the question is not so much, what is to be done about it? as, how should we behave towards it?

I have suggested that the liberal attitude towards literature will not work. Even if the writers who make their attempt to impose their "view of life" upon us were really distinct individuals, even if we as readers were distinct individuals, what would be the result? It would be, surely, that each reader would be impressed, in his reading, merely by what he was previously prepared to be impressed by; he would follow the "line of least resistance," and there would be no assurance that he would be made a better man. For literary judgement we need to be acutely aware of two things at once: of "what we like," and of "what we *ought* to like." Few people are honest enough to know either. The first means knowing what we really feel: very few know that. The second involves understanding our shortcomings; for we do not really know what we ought to like unless we also know why we ought to like it, which involves knowing why we don't yet like it. It is not enough to understand what we ought to be, unless we know what we are; and we do not understand what we are, unless we know what we ought to be. The two forms of self-consciousness, knowing what we are and what we ought to be, must go together.

It is our business, as readers of literature, to know what we like. It is our business, as Christians, *as well as* readers of literature, to know what we ought to like. It is our business as honest men not to assume that whatever we like is what we ought to like; and it is our business as honest Christians not to assume that we do like what we ought to like. And the last thing I would wish for would be the existence of two literatures, one for Christian consumption and the other for the pagan world. What I believe to be incumbent upon all Christians is the duty of maintaining consciously certain standards and criteria of criticism over and above those applied by the rest of the world; and that by these criteria and standards everything that we read must be tested. We must remember that the greater part of our current reading matter is written for us by people who have no real belief in a supernatural order, though some of it may be written by people with individual notions of a supernatural order which are not ours. And the greater part of our reading matter is coming to be written by people who not only have no such belief, but are even ignorant of the fact that there are still people in the world so "backward" or so "eccentric" as to continue to believe. So long as we are conscious of the gulf fixed between ourselves and the greater part of contemporary literature, we are more or less protected from being harmed by it, and are in a position to extract from it what good it has to offer us.

There are a very large number of people in the world today who believe that all ills are fundamentally economic. Some believe that various specific economic changes alone would be enough to set the world right; others demand more or less drastic changes in the social as well, changes chiefly of two opposed types. These changes demanded, and in some places carried out, are alike in one respect, that they hold the assumptions of what I call Secularism: they concern themselves only with changes of a temporal, material, and external nature; they concern themselves with morals only of a collective nature. In an exposition of one such new faith I read the following words:

"In our morality the one single test of any moral question is whether it impedes or destroys in any way the power of the individual to serve the State. [The individual] must answer the questions: 'Does this action injure the nation? Does it injure other members of the nation? Does it injure my ability to serve the nation?' And if the answer is clear on all those questions, the individual has absolute liberty to do as he will."

Now I do not deny that this is a kind of morality, and that it is capable of great good within limits; but I think that we should all repudiate a morality which had no higher ideal to set before us than that. It represents, of course, one of the violent reactions we are witnessing, against the view that the community is solely for the benefit of the individual; but it is equally a gospel of this world, and of this world alone. My complaint against modern literature is of the same kind. It is not that modern literature is in the ordinary sense "immoral" or even "amoral"; and in any case to prefer that charge would not be enough. It is simply that it repudiates, or is wholly ignorant of, our most fundamental and important beliefs; and that in consequence its tendency is to encourage its readers to get what they can out of life while it lasts, to miss no "experience" that presents itself, and to sacrifice themselves, if they make any sacrifice at all, only for the sake of tangible benefits to others in this world either now or in the future. We shall certainly continue to read the best of its kind, of what our time provides; but we must tirelessly criticize it according to our own principles, and not merely according to the principles admitted by the writers and by the critics who discuss it in the public press.

W. K. Wimsatt, Jr.

Poetry and Morals: A Relation Reargued*

I

THE ANCIENT QUESTION whether poetry can appear independently of morals does not lack current answers, both affirmative and negative, and both earnestly argued. The separation of the beautiful and the good, urges one school, is a "fundamental self-deception which vitiates and depraves the very center" of the artist's character, "the fountains whence his energies as a human personality spring."[1] For this unified view of values I would at the outset confess my serious sympathy. It is difficult to dissent from it with thorough complacency. On the other hand the champions of the opposite view—most notably Professors Maritain and Adler—have assured us that "The artist is necessarily autonomous in his own sphere." It is in this direction that I myself would argue, yet I should sympathize with a critic of poetry who might argue that the necessity of this view is far from clear, that the solution is too smooth and triumphant. The same view has been advanced with great delicacy (if some wavering) by the distinguished poet and literary arbiter T. S. Eliot, yet it has suffered, I believe, on the whole from seeming to

* Reprinted with permission from *Thought;* also from *The Verbal Icon: Studies in the Meaning of Poetry,* by W. K. Wimsatt, with the permission of the University of Kentucky Press.

[1] Victor Hamm, "Literature and Morality," in *Thought,* XV (1940), 278, 280.

lack relevance to an art such as poetry, made of words and ideas, and notorious for imbroglios with all sorts of moral interest. It will be the purpose of this essay to inquire how in fact the doctrine of aesthetic autonomy can apply to poetry. And first by noticing some related but distinct issues, and then some alternative solutions to the proper issue.

Poetry, said Plato, in effect, is a kind of inspired ignorance; it stands at two removes from the truth; it is furthermore at fault in that it feeds and waters the passions. He drew a decided distinction between poetic quality and moral results. "The greater the poetic charm . . . the less are they meet for the ears of boys and men who are meant to be free." The conclusion was on the whole decidedly moral. Somewhere, in some Utopian state, a truthful and moral poetry might occur. But poetry as Plato had actually known it was intolerable. "And so when we have anointed him with myrrh and set a garland of wool upon his head, we shall send him away to another city."

There, at the start of the tradition, we have at least three main propositions (or bundles of related propositions) which anyone entering upon a discussion of poetry and morals might well distinguish and number for convenient reference.

Ia. Poetry has philosophic content—images and their interpretation —possibly true and moral, usually false and immoral.

Ib. The poetic value of poetry is not the same as, or even strictly determined by, its truth or morality.

IIa. Poetry has moral power; that is, it produces moral effects on those who hear it—possibly for good, mostly for evil.

IIb. The poetic value of poetry is not the same as, or even strictly determined by, its moral effect.

III. Both philosophico-moral content and moral effect have a claim on our allegiance which is prior to the claim of poetic value.

It will be observed that the second pair of propositions, IIa and IIb, concern what poetry *does,* its persuasory and contagious *effect,* but not as such what poetry *says* or is, poetry objectively considered as a body of cognitive and analyzable meaning. The first pair of propositions, Ia and Ib, consider just this body of meaning. Ib, asserting the difference between the poetic and the moral value of meaning, is the crucial proposition which a certain school of moralists, Hamm among them, would deny. Proposition II, the rule of arbitration between poetry and morals, follows from the concept of morals. Yet the very meaning of this proposition, it is worth noting, depends largely on Ib. If Ib is not true, III can relate only to what poetry *does*. If poetry is not cognitively separable from morals, if one makes no distinction between poetic meaning and moral meaning, there can be no cognitive and intrinsic conflict: the poet in being moral is only following the rule of his craft. Not III, of course, but the vindication of its premise in Ib is the concern of the critic. Let the moralist assert that poetry *should* be moral. The critic would ask whether poetry *need* be moral in order to be poetry.

Moral critique of poetry has often forced proposition III into close conjunction with the two affective propositions IIa and IIb. From poetry, said Stephen Gosson, the English Plato of 1579, we advance to piping, "from pyping to playing, from play to pleasure, from pleasure to slouth, from slouth to sleepe, from sleepe to sinne, from sinne to death, from death to the Divel." Such complaints, it should be said at the start, are not what the theorist of poetry would discuss, nor any of the like moral and political issues which arise from propositions IIa, IIb, and III, the most frequent issues of conscience and censorship—the chief concern of Adler in his *Art and Prudence*. Again, it should be said that the issue for the theorist is not that of the author's personal morals or philosophy. It may be true, as Hamm has asserted, that "a literary work can never be indifferent morally in its origins." It is certainly not true, as Adler has asserted, that "intrinsic" criticism of art is that which "regards the work in relation to the artist." We inquire now not about origins, nor about effects, but about the work so far as it can be considered by itself as a body of meaning. Neither the qualities of the author's mind nor the effects of a poem upon a reader's mind should be confused with the moral quality of the meaning expressed by the poem itself.

II

To take up the issue between poetry and morals at the cognitive level, it is to be observed that if Platonic proposition Ib, asserting the separability of poetry and morals, is not true, then one of two extremely unified and simplified views or claims will follow—or have followed at various times. Either (1) morals reaches over and claims poetry—not simply as superior to poetry but as defining poetry; or (2) poetry reaches over and claims to define morals. We have seen the second view in such romantic and postromantic statements as that of Shelley, "Poets are the unacknowledged legislators of the world," or in the system of Matthew Arnold, where poetry is a "criticism of life." "More and more mankind will discover that we have to turn to poetry to interpret life for us, to console us, to sustain us. Without poetry, our science will appear incomplete; and most of what now passes with us for religion and philosophy will be replaced by poetry." More recent psychological and anthropological theories of poetry have tended to continue in this direction. It is easy to see that a morality of this sort, determined by poetry, is not really a morality in the sense of a code, but a relative morality of almost indefinite diversity and flexibility—for such is poetry—and that hence what theorists of this school mean in the end is that they do not subscribe to a code. For these we may say that in the large sense the problem to be discussed in this essay does not exist, since there is no distinction between, and hence no need of explaining the relation between, poetry and morals.

Nor does the problem really exist for those of the other school, who deny Platonic proposition Ib for an opposite reason and make poetic value depend upon moral value: Sir Philip Sidney, for instance, when he answers Gosson with the argument that poetry is a "feigning notable images of virtues [and] vices,"[2] or Rymer and

[2] *The Defense of Poesy*, A. S. Cook, ed. (Boston, 1890), 11. In other passages Sidney is more inclined to make a Platonic distinction between poetic and moral power. "Poesy may not only be abused, but . . . being abused, by the reason of his sweet charming force, it can do more than any other array of words" (p. 38).

Dennis a century later, the school of "poetic justice," or the Earl of Roscommon in his couplet:

> Immodest words admit of no Defence,
> For want of Decency is want of Sense.

Among recent statements of the moral view the most extreme is perhaps that of Arthur Machen: "Literature is the expression, through the aesthetic medium of words, of the dogmas of the Catholic Church, and that which is out of harmony with these dogmas is not literature." Most moderately the late Irving Babbitt and other neohumanists have said that poetry gives ethical insight.

If the Arnoldian view, as we have seen, leaves morals in a bad way, it should be equally clear that the rigorous moral view not only leaves little to the critic of poetry in his own right (a loss which might perhaps have to be overlooked) but also makes a vast invasion into the usually recognized canon of the world's poetry—so much of it is in one way or another immoral. One cannot really refute Plato. Or to put this more moderately and without the unhappy implication that a great part of the world's best literature is substantially evil, let us say that a moral code must be by its nature too rigid to accommodate, or at least too rigid to account for or specifically sanction, the widely heterogeneous concreteness of the world's recognized poetry. There is no religion or philosophy that will embrace Homer's heroes and gods, the fatalism of Greek tragedy, the atomism of Lucretius, the Heaven, Purgatory, and Hell of Dante, the Senecan Stoicism of Shakespeare, the occultism—what has seemed to many the diabolism—of Milton, the world soul of Wordsworth, the flowers of evil of Baudelaire. The choice between poetry and morals is not specifically a Christian one—though today in the Western world it may be felt most acutely by a serious Christian. It is the choice which appears for any moralist—for Plato banishing the poets from the city, for Tolstoy in his old age repudiating all of his own work except two of his simplest short stories, for the totalitarian Marxist—except that for the Marxist there is no nice problem. He simply rejects—almost everything.

III

This essay is an attempt to express the point of view of one who, accepting a moral code, would yet save poetic value—not as superior to moral value but as different from it. And it is not easy—in a full and thoughtful way—to affirm Platonic proposition Ib and escape between the relaxed simplification of the Arnoldian and the severe one of the moralist. A long tradition, beginning with Plato and with the separation by Aristotle of his *Poetics* from his *Ethics,* testifies to the utility of the distinction between poetry and morals. Today the moralist will often make the distinction quite casually:

> Just as an engineer may not construct and approve a bridge, the durability of which he doubts for the load he knows his clients will attempt to transport over it; and just as a chef may not serve food which he knows is even partially on the way to corruption and which might presently cause distress or worse to the consumer,—so also the poet or writer may not express anything, however beautifully, which both he and his critics have reason to believe will be subversive to thought or action on the part of him who reads it.[3]

Yet it is not easy, especially when the moralist phrases it, to see how this distinction can be seriously maintained. The bridge which was destined to fall might look well when inspected, but looks are surely not a profound test of a bridge. The bridge would simply be a bad bridge. The food might taste well before making the eater ill, and here is a more plausible resemblance to what is maintained about beautiful but dangerous poetry. The food answers one important (if specious) requirement of good food. But how can poetry, which concerns good and evil, which is an intellectual art and which exists and has quality only in being understood, be both beautiful and morally destructive? Here one must indeed agree with Hamm: "Language, unlike marble, pigments and musical sounds, is immediately and essentially expressive of ideas . . . The literary artist

[3] Jerome Kobel, "Literature and Morality: A Prefatory Essay," in *The Franciscan Educational Conference,* XXII (1940), 267.

expresses implicit moral judgments."[4] Few, if any, important poems are simply imagistic. The late Dr. Temple, Archbishop of Canterbury, in a lecture on literature found "Hardy's great masterpiece, 'Tess of the D'Ubervilles' " to be "among the worst books ever committed to paper." He was unable to yield "to the undoubted artistic power that is displayed by Hardy in that great artistic achievement." Upon which a writer in the *Times Literary Supplement* observed: "The relationship of truth and beauty makes it impossible to accept that . . . a 'great masterpiece' can be numbered among the 'worst books ever committed to paper.' A masterpiece is not made by phrases, decorations and patterns; these qualities are imposed by the wisdom in their content." This, one might say, is a pronounced step in the Arnoldian direction. Yet the point of it cannot be overlooked. The problem has been made more acute in our day by schools of psychological criticism and of exhaustive rhetorical exegesis which have taught us to find the beauty of poems by sifting them to their minutest scruples of meaning. What Plato saw as the evil of poetry, the mixture of its emotions and the confusion of its advice, has become now, under such names as ironic "tension" and "synaesthesis," the richness of aesthetic value.

A hint at a solution was offered by Aristotle in his *Rhetoric* when he said that imitation is pleasant "even if the object imitated is not itself pleasant; for it is not the object itself which here gives delight—the spectator draws inferences ('That is a so-and-so') and thus learns something fresh." And the notion has been reiterated in diverse places—for example, in Plutarch's essay *How A Young Man Should Study Poetry,* in the *Summa Theologiae* of St. Thomas ("Imago dicitur esse pulchra, si perfecte repraesentat rem, quamvis turpem"), in Boileau's *Art Poétique,* in a *Spectator* on Imagination

[4] "It would seem," says Adler, "that the excellence of a work of art is due only to a technical mastery of materials by the artist and is unaffected by the direction of his moral character toward good or evil." *Art and Prudence* (New York, 1937), 443. But on the next page: "In the case of the fine arts, the situation is complicated by . . . the fact that for most of the fine arts, poetry and music certainly, the object of imitation is human action, the moral life."

by Joseph Addison ("The Description of a Dunghill is pleasing . . . if the Image be represented to our Minds by suitable Expressions"). Today the same notion is invoked to justify the historical study of literature: the scholar, says Professor H. N. Fairchild, "can admire a fine statement of a detestable fallacy in the spirit of a surgeon who speaks of a 'beautiful tumour.' " A refined version of the theory is thus defined by Maritain:

> The artist takes for stuff and substance of his work whatever is most profound, most exalted and most vile, the moral life of man, the heart of man "hollow and full of filth"—and the rarest passions and the life of the spirit itself, nay, the Gospel and sanctity, everything; but with it all an absolute prohibition, upon pain of committing a sacrilege against art, against pursuing any other end than the pure delight, order, richness, tranquillity and rapture, which the soul ought to savour in the work. This is no longer art *on nothing* as in the theory of gratuitousness in its first form; but art *for nothing,* for nothing but art's sake.

Maritain does not subscribe to this view, but in another place he himself has said: "Art . . . comes into the midst of our hierarchies like a moon prince whom etiquette has not foreseen, and who embarrasses all the masters of ceremonies . . . It can be mad and remain art." This is all very well. It should be obvious from what has been said so far that the argument of this essay tends rather in this direction than in the opposite. Yet such an explanation certainly runs the risk of leaving the poem in a posture of serious embarrassment. If poetry can say what is vile and full of filth as well as what is exalted and sacred—if it can even be mad—then it would seem to make no difference what poetry says. The theory must be another version of imitation for the sake of imitation—of art as sheer form—a theory of external rhetoric.

IV

The main thesis of Plato's *Phaedrus* is that an ideal rhetoric or art of using words would by dialectic and a certain inspiration rise to the level of philosophy—that is, would deal with truth. Actual rhetoric, that of the sophists, what was known to Socrates, was not an art—had no contact with truth—for it could be put to purposes of deception. This view of rhetoric and implicitly of poetry followed from the Socratic ethic, where virtue was wisdom. If to know was to do, then that which did wrong (rhetoric) did not know. The ethic of Aristotle was, on the other hand, a step away from the ethic of sheer wisdom, and accordingly Aristotle is able, both in his *Poetics* and in his *Rhetoric,* to say more than Plato in favor of verbal art as it was actually practiced. Rhetoric is a power which, like all other powers except virtue itself, can be misused. The misuse lies not in the art but in the moral purpose. Book III, chapters 1–13, of Aristotle's *Rhetoric,* on the devices of verbal style, is the natural complement of this basic view.

An idea of verbal rhetoric as distinct from the pith and worth of what is meant by words is thus from the start intrinsic to the theory of separable poetic and moral values which we have sketched so far and which we are struggling to improve. And something indeed may be said on the score of merely verbal rhetoric, and should be said here, though with the distinct reservation that such rhetoric must be far from enough to permit any important or profound distinction between poetic and moral values. It is possible to name certain formal levels of expression which, though intimately bound up with and deriving their value only from their relation to the stated meanings, are yet not parts of this meaning in the sense that they always add to it or in their absence subtract from it. Under this head come the various forms of syntactic and phonetic support of statement (the *parisosis* and *paromoeosis* of Aristotle), to some extent the intimations of what is called prose rhythm, and for certain kinds of writing and within limits, even correctness of diction —much, in short, though not all, of what is commonly thought of as "style." This might include the kind of values one may see in the prose of Edgar Allan Poe, where, though the message is often meretricious and merely lurid, yet a kind of cogent swing or rhythm of logic is felt. It might include what critics have alluded to as more music than sense in many lines of a decadent poet like

Swinburne or Dowson. But if the nonmoral value of poetry lay only here, it would be a trivial thing, worth the contempt of Socrates. "The style is excellent," says Pope, alluding to the judgment of a certain kind of critics; "the sense they humbly take upon content."

It is at deeper levels of meaning that more important distinctions must be sought. And if we understand the depth, subtlety, and indirectness of the total and many-dimensional meaning which modern criticism rightly discerns as the poetic object, we shall not despair of distinctions.

We may first of all make short work of a case often described with approval by the moralist, where evil is represented as evil—in the novels, for example, of Graham Greene (if so simple a statement does them justice, or if so simple a case ever really occurs). Here, of course, there is no moral evil, and no problem. The effects of the presentation may be unhappy for this or that reader (a moral, not an artistic, issue), but the meaning itself, the interpretation, is moral. Whatever literary quality is present, it has its moral basis. If the theory of gratuitousness means vileness of this sort, the theory is really no different from that of the moral critic. The moral judgment fits the matter or the situation. If the theory is to be different from a moral theory, vileness must be vileness represented as attractive, vileness with an apology, or vileness recommended. In short, the poem must be vile.

There are two main ways in which a poem may approach vileness—that is, in which it may be ethically defective: (1) by asserting an unacceptable philosophy; (2) by approving, commending, or inviting an immoral choice or passion. It is perhaps easier to see that the first way will rarely of itself be incompatible with some wisdom and with some or even a great deal of poetic value. One may agree with T. S. Eliot that poetry does not characteristically state philosophies. "In truth," says Eliot, "neither Shakespeare nor Dante did any real thinking—that was not their job." Poetry does not think, but presents the feelings connected with thinking, or thoughts as the grounds of feeling. It is perhaps true that, as Professor Norman Foerster says, Wordsworth's "Tintern Abbey" expresses a degree of "unwisdom." But then this unwisdom—the fusion of teleological naturalism, associationism, and pantheism which pervades the poem and without which indeed the poem would not be—is unwise simply in that it is not enough, it comes short of being an acceptable philosophy. Indeed we know this deficiency not so much through the poem itself as through our knowledge of its philosophic antecedents in Hartley or in Cudworth. As a philosophy it is better than no philosophy, or better, say, than dialectical materialism—because it contains much larger elements of truth. As an idea in a poem, a semi-metaphoric notion of a spirit pervading a landscape, it need be no more of a philosophy than one chooses to make it. It is one way of being inspired by a landscape, one approach, we may easily say, toward God. Poems, on the whole, as dramatic and specific utterances, here and now, tend to escape the defect of philosophic incompleteness. The philosophy need only be adequate to the situation in hand—or reach beyond that by symbolic extension.

A harder case is the second of the two named above, that of a poem which embodies a clear approval of an evil choice and its evil emotion. An answer to the question, how we are to find poetic value in such a poem, may be suggested in the statement that on the assumption of a Socratic ethic we might have more difficulty in doing so. On the Christian grounds of an ethic of will, we may find the distinction easier. The fact indeed that it seems to us possible to distinguish this class, the simply immoral, from the other, the philosophically wrong, marks the great difference between an ethic where the virtuous man is he who resists temptation and that where the virtuous man is he who is never tempted. But once admit temptation, and much is open to us—a wide realm of motives which may be profoundly moving and sympathetic though falling short of the morally acceptable. We have a question of how much good can be the cause of sin. Here I would be strictly Thomistic and would accept Maritain and Adler for a certain distance as my guides. The human sinner, so we are instructed in the classic explanation, does not choose evil *qua* evil—a contradiction, since *bonum* is defined as *terminus appetitus*. He chooses a lower good or one inappropriate to the moment—*quod non est vel nunc vel hoc modo bonum.* But of lower and inappropriate goods there are many levels, lower and higher, and in the gamut of human goods which in some situation the virtuous man foregoes, there is room for an indefinite range of complexity, richness, and sympathy.[5]

As a ground on which to explore this principle I choose the *Antony and Cleopatra* of Shakespeare. "The tragedy of Antony and Cleopatra," said Benedetto Croce, "is composed of the violent sense of pleasure, in its power to bind and to dominate, coupled with a shudder at its abject effects of dissolution and death."[6] If this is so, then of course there is no problem. *Antony and Cleopatra* is simply one of the easy cases, already alluded to, in which evil is represented as evil: the implications are basically moral. Again, there is the explanation of the theologically-minded critic S. L. Bethell, according to which *Antony and Cleopatra* celebrates "affections rooted deep in the sensual nature," intuitive, spontaneous, and positive, with all their "moral and aesthetic corollaries." The antitype is Caesar, the cold politician whose heart is set entirely on the passing world. In the tragic denouement the "element of self-giving inherent in the sensual nature" is "purged of selfish fear" and "revealed in its eternal significance."[7] It is not my purpose to deny the availability of such views to the interpretation of *Antony and Cleopatra* or in general of other poems which present similar moral problems. The solution of Bethell may, in fact, appear to differ only by a twist of emphasis from what I myself propose. The difference

[5] "Dans toute forme ou toute espèce d'art il y a comme un principe ou un germe secret d'immoralité," Ferdinand Brunetière, *L'Art et la Morale* (Paris, 1898), 15.

[6] *Ariosto, Shakespeare and Corneille* (London, 1920), 241. Antony and Cleopatra, says Dryden, were "famous patterns of unlawful love; and their end accordingly was unfortunate." *Preface to All for Love, Essays of John Dryden,* W. P. Ker, ed. (Oxford, 1929), I, 191.

[7] S. L. Bethell, *Shakespeare and the Popular Dramatic Tradition* (Westminster, 1944), 128–31.

is that I seek a formulation which will enable us to say frankly that a poem is a great poem, yet immoral.

What is celebrated in *Antony and Cleopatra* is the passionate surrender of an illicit love, the victory of this love over practical, political, and moral concerns, and the final superiority of the suicide-lovers over circumstance. That is a crudely onesided statement which makes the play as plainly immoral as it can be made. There is, of course, far more—the complex, wanton, and subtle wiles of the voluptuary queen, her infinite variety which age cannot wither nor custom stale, the grizzled and generous manhood and the military bravery of Antony—the whole opulent and burnished panorama of empire and its corruptions. Such intricacies and depths surely at least add to the interest of immorality and—without making it any more moral—yet make it more understandable, more than a mere barren vileness, a filthy negation. It is to be noted that the reasons on the side of morality are so far as possible undercut, diminished, or removed from the play. The politics from which Antony secedes are not a noble Roman republicanism, the ideals of a Brutus or a Cato, but the treacheries and back-stabbing of a drunken party on a pirate's barge. The victimized Octavia is a pallid and remote figure, never (as in Dryden's version) made to appear as a rival motive to the Egyptian seductions.[8] The suicides which provide the catastrophe have at least the subjective palliation that they are within the Stoic code which is the standard of the whole scene.[9]

> Give me my robe, put on my crown; I have
> Immortal longings in me; now no more
> The juice of Egypt's grape shall moist this lip.
> Yare, yare, good Iras; quick. Methinks I hear

[8] "Though I might use the privilege of a poet, to introduce her into Alexandria, yet I had not enough considered, that the compassion she moved to herself and children was destructive to that which I reserved for Antony and Cleopatra." Dryden, *Preface to All for Love,* I, 192.

[9] "Shakespeare nowhere approves suicide outside the Roman plays, but in them he seems to accept it, along with the pantheon, as data." Bethell, *Shakespeare and the Popular Dramatic Tradition,* 129.

> Antony call; I see him rouse himself
> To praise my noble act; I hear him mock
> The luck of Caesar, which the gods give men
> To excuse their after wrath: husband, I come:
> Now to that name my courage prove my title!
> I am fire and air; my other elements
> I give to baser life.

There is no escaping the fact that the poetic splendor of this play, and in particular of its concluding scenes, is something which exists in closest juncture with the acts of suicide and with the whole glorified story of passion. The poetic values are strictly dependent —if not upon the immorality as such—yet upon the immoral acts. Even though, or rather because, the play pleads for certain evil choices, it presents these choices in all their mature interest and capacity to arouse human sympathy. The motives are wrong, but they are not base, silly, or degenerate. They are not lacking in the positive being of deep and complex human desire. It is not possible to despise Antony and Cleopatra. If one will employ the classic concept of "imitation," the play imitates or presents the reasons for sin, a mature and richly human state of sin. Imitation, on this understanding, is not prior to and exclusive of interpretation, but follows it. The interpretation and judgment are taken as presented objects. This is the meaning of the defense repeated in every generation by the poet. "I moot," says Chaucer, "reherce Hir tales alle. . . . Or elles falsen som of my mateere." "Art," says William Butler Yeats, "is a revelation, and not a criticism."

V

Poetic value, though different from moral value, cannot thereby be considered as something autonomously remote from the rest of human experience. In the total of any concrete human situation— even that of the anchorite in his cell—there are multiple values inviting recognition or choice. The moral value in any given situation, what is right, is abstract; it is known by rule and conscience. By necessity it excludes. Neither a right nor a wrong choice, however, excludes the awareness of many values, some interrelated and supporting, some rival, some sacrificed by a choice, some in some situations held in ironic balance or entering into unresolved tensions. Poetry, by its concreteness and dramatic presentation of value situations, whether it inclines to a right answer or to a wrong answer—by the very fullness and hence imaginative power of its presentation—has the meaning and being which makes it poetry. This is the poetic value. It is a rhetorical value only inasmuch as the nuances of rhetoric, the symbolic complexities of a rhetorical unity, are the counterparts of the psychological complexities which make the meaning of a poem. Rhetoric, except in the most superficial sense, does not exist unless in a meaning of a certain stature.

It would seem to follow from what has just been said that there could be virtuous choices and right philosophy—or at least verbal descriptions of these—which would be too simple, severe, and abstracted from living reality, to have poetic interest. Certainly there can be verbal presentations of evil which are too simply negative or too naively mistaken to have this interest.

As the husband is, the wife is: thou art mated with a clown,
And the grossness of his nature shall have weight to drag thee down.

He will hold thee, when his passion shall have spent its novel force,
Something better than his dog, a little dearer than his horse.

The young man in *Locksley Hall* who muses thus is not only a bad young man but a callow one. There is a shallow simplicity about this poem that is expressed even in its rhythm. No irony or other tension advises us that we are not to share the young man's experience to the full and approve it. This kind of evil, one may suppose, is not what the theory of gratuitousness means. One will be hard pressed here to explain the "pure delight, order, riches, tranquillity and rapture, which the soul ought to savour."

The areas which are to be defined by such a conception of poetic badness will be at higher levels of course much disputed. It is with no thought of expressing an opinion about the poetry of Shelley that I cite here another of Eliot's delicate adjustments to the balance between poetry and doctrine. In his essay on Shakespeare and Seneca he believed it was not the job of the poet to think. Yet in his Harvard lectures on *The Use of Poetry and the Use of Criticism* he finds himself, for something like a philosophic reason, unable to accept the poetry of Shelley. For there are some beliefs which are acceptable (in these obviously a poetry can be grounded), others again which if not acceptable yet correspond so well to some large area of human experience that we may call them "tenable" (the Stoicism of Seneca, for instance, or the atomism of Lucretius)—but again others which are neither acceptable nor tenable. The poetry of Shelley, one would gather, is inextricably wound up in beliefs of the third class.

One of the faults which Plato found with poetry was that in imitating the actions and feelings of men, poetry discovered the lack of unity in their lives, the strife and inconsistency. Recent schools of criticism, as we have said, have likewise noted the importance to poetry of the elements of variety and strife in human living and have seen the poem as a report made under tension or an ironically suspended judgment rather than a commitment to solutions. And this view would seem to put the poem clearly in the realm of the amoral or premoral. But again, recent criticism has noted with approval the Coleridgean doctrine of a resolution or *reconciliation* of opposites, a doctrine which may not read so well with the ironic. To the present writer it would seem that though poetry is inclusive, it is also exclusive in the sense that a poem has a presiding idea, attitude, and coherence and thus at least a tendency to an assertion. As certain critics of a theological leaning have recently been saying, poetry, though it is not dogma and cannot take the place of dogma, yet finds in a frame of beliefs its "ultimate character" and "latent presuppositions."[10] If it is possible, as it has been the main burden of this essay to insist, that a poem, even a great poem, may fall

[10] Roy W. Battenhouse, "Theology and Literary Criticism," in *Journal of Bible and Religion,* XIII (1945), 21.

short of being moral—or to put it another way, if it is true that starting with the fixity of dogma we cannot hope to define the content of poems—it is yet true that poems as empirically discovered and tested do tend, within their limits and given the peculiar *données* or presuppositions of each, to point toward the higher integration of dogma. The Christian critic, if he cares to insist to the full at all moments on his Christianity as well as on his critical discernment, may without doing violence to the latter follow the direction recently pointed out to the poet: "Christian dogma will aid the artist not by giving him a privileged and special subject-matter but rather by defining for him a perspective from which 'full light' can be had on all subject matters."[11] Perhaps it follows that in this light the greatest poems for the Christian will never be that kind, the great though immoral, which it has been our labor to describe. *Antony and Cleopatra* will not be so great as *King Lear*. The testimony of the critical tradition would seem to confirm this. The greatest poetry will be morally right, even though perhaps obscurely so, in groping confusions of will and knowledge—as *Oedipus the King* foreshadows *Lear*. All of this is but the consistent capstone which completes but does not contradict a system of values in which poetic is distinguished from moral and both are understood in relation to the master ideas of evil as negation or not-being, a gap in order, and of good as positive, or being—in the natural order the designed complexity of what is most truly one or most has being.

[11] Battenhouse, 20.

Part IV

BELIEF AND FORM: THE PROBLEM OF CORRELATION

Preston T. Roberts, Jr.

A Christian Theory of Dramatic Tragedy*

MY CONCERN IN THIS ESSAY is to consider the nature of dramatic tragedy as a literary form from the point of view of what I understand to be the heart of Christian theology. The most famous theory of dramatic tragedy was set forth by Aristotle in his *Poetics*. Aristotle was a Greek. He deduced his theory—directly or indirectly—from the premises of Greek theology and on the basis of his acquaintance with the concrete models of Greek literary history, the plays of Aeschylus, Sophocles, and Euripides.

I shall attempt to speak as a Christian. As a Christian, my concern is to exhibit that the *Poetics* of Aristotle requires transformation in light of the differing and, I think, more searching premises of Christian theology and on the basis of an acquaintance with a more profound—or, in any case, a generically different—body of Christian literature: the Gospels, Chaucer's *Canterbury Tales,* Dante's *Divine Comedy,* Shakespeare's *Hamlet* and *King Lear,* Milton's *Samson Agonistes* and *Paradise Lost,* Hawthorne's *The Scarlet Letter* and *The House of the Seven Gables,* Melville's *Billy Budd,* and Dostoevski's *The Brothers Karamazov* and *The Idiot.*

Apart from the *Poetics* of Aristotle and the *Dialogues* of Plato, there are few outstanding prototypes for a Christian theory of literature in general or of dramatic tragedy in particular. Augustine

* Reprinted by kind permission of the author and the *Journal of Religion.*

for the most part followed Plato's aesthetic doctrines, Aquinas Aristotle's. To my knowledge no formidable work in literary theory or criticism has ever been written from the point of view of Protestant theology. In a sense and to a degree both Kant and Hume attempted to provide a philosophic basis for such an effort. Kant is to be remembered for his stress upon the creator and his motives, the ferment of genius before the work; Hume, for his emphasis upon the audience and its reactions, the impression forcible and lively after the work. By reason of this stress upon the author and the audience, I have found both Kant and Hume to be misleading. I think Protestant theology must recur to Aristotle's emphasis upon the inner content and structure of literary compositions in constructing a Christian theory of literature.

I

By virtue of the fact that Aristotle's *Poetics* is still the best work in literary criticism in the West, a Christian theory of dramatic tragedy must begin with an attempt to state dispassionately those aspects of Aristotle's work which are normative for Christian theology and those which are not.

In the first place, I do not think that Christian theology can presume, express, or imply any sweeping irreverence for Aristotle's *Poetics*. The very fact that it is his work which requires transformations is sufficient testimony to its greatness. Aristotle provides the point of departure from which any constructive Christian effort must start. His *Poetics* provides the text, for which Christian theology can provide the emendations. Christian theology is to my mind not at its best when it seeks to deprive the Greeks of this, their primordial and consequent character. Christian theology must start *in medias res,* in the midst of Aristotle, not *de novo* or *ex nihilo*.

Second, I do not think that a Christian theory of dramatic tragedy—or any theory of dramatic tragedy, for that matter—can be constructed apart from many of the formal terms and principles introduced and formulated by Aristotle in his work. What is formal and abstract in his *Poetics,* in so far as it is exhaustively clear and general, should prove to be as relevant "here and now" in Christendom as "there and then" in Greece. For example, no theory of dramatic tragedy can fail to make the general Aristotelian distinctions between the intent or motive of the creator, the inner content and structure of the work composed, and the effect or demands upon the audience. This triangle of poet-work-audience provides the formal setting within which any theory of literature must work. Nor can any theory of dramatic tragedy fail to distinguish dramatic tragedy as a literary form from the lyric and the epic, on the one hand, and from discursive or systematic works in history, philosophy, and the sciences, on the other. Similarly, any discussion of dramatic tragedy must recognize something like Aristotle's six formal elements: character, plot, thought, diction, melody, and spectacle. These are elements apart from which a dramatic tragedy cannot exist—elements apart from which it becomes some other kind of literature or some other kind of symbolism and discourse. The genius of the Greeks was this capacity for discerning recurrent formal structures, indifferent to and disengaged from any particular time, place, person, faculty, or belief.

Third, I do not see any good reason for supposing that Aristotle exhausted what can be said about literature from a purely formal point of view. Some of Aristotle's crucial terms and principles have not turned out to be either clear or general; for example, mimesis, referring to the intent or motive of the dramatist, and catharsis, referring to the effect or demand upon the audience. Moreover, many new terms and principles have proved to be both possible and necessary in modern literary analysis: theme or motif, "point of view," "focus of narration," atmosphere, tone, setting, scale, and pace. Just as Aristotle's substance-quality metaphysic has proved to be only one among several possible metaphysics, his fixed genus-species hierarchy only one kind of biology, his faculties only one form of psychology, his syllogism only one form of inference and reasoning, and his subject-predicate sentences only one form of statement—just so his *Poetics* has demonstrated itself to be only one among several possible theories of literature.

Fourth, I think that Christian theology must insist that the *Poetics* of Aristotle was constructed from the point of view of Greek theology. Directly or indirectly, consciously or unconsciously, Aristotle concretely interpreted many of his formal terms and principles with some of the basic insights and ideas of Greek theology and religiousness in his head. For example, the bare concept "intent or motive of the creator" is abstract and general. But the principle of mimesis—the imitation of life and nature—is a concrete interpretation. Mimesis may suggest the realistic ideal to a modern mentality. But by formal definition and in the context of Aristotle's *Poetics* mimesis in fact embodies a highly allegorical ideal concerning the best way of telling a story. By nature, literature is concerned with stating eternal truths, just as are science and philosophy. Literature is cognitive, not just expressive, in status, and the function of literature is to purify the emotions by the understanding and to transform subjectivity into objectivity. This general theory concerning the nature and purpose of literature follows, directly or indirectly, from the dominant and characteristic motifs of Greek theology: the notion of God as an ideal rather than as an actual entity, the divine spectator alone with himself thinking about thought, viewing the course of events without passion from above and beyond and apart; the notion of man as a primarily intellectual and sensitive as opposed to a passionate and wilful being, a being whose inherent nobility is imprisoned within a bodily and emotional frame; and an emphasis upon the aesthetic and intellectual as opposed to the moral, the political, and the religious virtues. Similarly, "effect upon the audience" is formal. But catharsis—the arousal of pity and fear and their purgation—is informal. Pity and fear are the appropriate reactions to a specifically Greek kind of dramatic tragedy. We feel pity because the consequences of the tragic deed are felt to be in excess of any specifiable moral guilt or religious sin. We feel terror because the consequences of the tragic deed are nonetheless stubborn, remorseless, and irreversible. And we feel the catharsis or cleansing of these emotions because the tragic hero in his nobility either defies or accepts the elements of generality and necessity in his fate. Just so, "tragic hero" is a concrete interpretation of character, suggesting and embodying as it does a highly aristocratic view of human excellence and its reverse. Moreover, Aristotle's specific interpretation of the *hamartia* or tragic flaw is Greek: he interprets it as an error in judgment, an intellectual mistake, or a failure to take thought and be prudent, rather than as a moral weakness or a religious sin. The very concept *hamartia* is in fact of itself Greek in flavor, implying a slight imperfection in a creature otherwise perfect. Just so, Aristotle's specific renderings of the anagnorisis and the peripeteia —the recognition scene and the reversal of fortune—are very Greek. Aristotle stresses the tragic hero's ironic and pitiful entanglement in circumstance, his movement from the complacency of ignorance to the bitterness of truth, and the general Greek theme of man's suffering innocence and nobility.

Fifth, I do not think that Christian theology is the only possible theological standpoint from which Aristotle can be emended. It is possible, for example, to ask for qualifications from within the premises of Greek theology itself. Aristotle does not render full justice to either the theological content or the literary structure of Aeschylean or Euripidean dramatic tragedy. Aeschylus foreshadows many of the motifs of Hebraic-Christian theology in his compassion for man's *hybris* or spiritual pride and in his awe before divine nemesis or judgment; and Euripides is an almost perfect prototype for modern skeptical literature in his perception of the way life begins with vivid memories and dreams and ends in boredom and in violence. One can infer from the *Dialogues* of Plato that he would make much less sharp divisions between the literary genres of which Aristotle speaks—the lyric, the drama, and the epic—and that he would mingle tragedy and comedy in principle, much as Shakespeare later so profoundly mingled them in fact. Similarly, many of the premises of pre-Socratic, Stoic, Epicurean, and Neo-Platonic kinds of Greek theology can give rise to sharply divergent interpretations of what the ideal Greek tragic hero and plot should consist of. The *Poetics* of Aristotle is thereby specifically as well as generically Greek. Moreover, many kinds of modern skeptical theology—humanist, agnostic, or nihilistic—can also ask for emendations.

In summary, the *Poetics* of Aristotle has two general implications for Christian theology, the one negative and the other positive.

Negatively, it means that what is informal in Aristotle's work may or may not be valid from the point of view of Christian theology. In fact, there are good reasons for the belief that what is informal is invalid. For example, the very concept "tragic hero" is in itself somewhat unfortunate from a Christian point of view. To speak of a Christian tragic hero is in a way immoral and profane. The very idea offends Christian morality and religiousness, for humility, the touchstone of Christian morality, disowns the ideal of a restlessly heroic life as consciously or unconsciously aristocratic and self-defeating. And faith, hope, and trust, the touchstones of Christian religiousness, affirm that the meaning of man's life can be and is something much more than the merely tragic. The notion of a tragic hero thereby of itself expresses the characteristically aristocratic theme of Greek theology—the theme of man's suffering dignity.

Positively, it means that Aristotle's general *sort* of literary criticism provides a genuine prototype for a Christian poetics. In basing literary criticism upon essentially theological events and meanings, no radical departure from Aristotle's general kind of literary analysis is involved. Aristotle was definitely not a "pure" or "formal" critic in the modern sense. In this connection the modern Neo-Aristotelians who seek to banish theology from literature and its criticism are the heretics from Aristotle, not the Christians. These Neo-Aristotelians fail to recognize that the *Poetics* of Aristotle represents a studied and profound deduction from wider theological, philosophic, and scientific as well as aesthetic principles. Like a Christian poetics, it is an integral part of a whole theological cosmology or world-view.

II

There are three general requirements a Christian theory of dramatic tragedy must fulfill. First of all, it must demonstrate the need for a specifically Christian poetics. Second, it must specify the marks of a specifically Christian play. Third, it must employ certain great pieces of Christian literature as models of itself.

By the first requirement, I mean that a Christian poetics must exhibit that it is possible to construct a play that is at once Christian and a tragedy, and that it is not possible to render fuller justice to the Christian story as a story or to dramatic tragedy as a literary form in any other way.

By the second requirement, I mean that a Christian poetics must define with a really clear and disciplined generality precisely what properties enable us to recognize a dramatic tragedy as specifically Christian rather than as specifically modern skeptical or Greek.

By the third requirement, I mean that a Christian poetics must be able to employ certain familiar and well-known works of literature as concrete models of itself in the same sense and to the same degree as Aristotle employed the plays of the Greeks.

The necessity for the first requirement arises out of the fact that many theologians and literary critics apparently do not believe that it is possible to construct a play that is at once fully Christian and fully a tragedy. They feel that there is a contradiction in principle between Christian theology as a story and dramatic tragedy as a way of telling a story. Moreover, they seem to feel that it is possible to tell the Christian story much more profoundly in some other way and that other kinds of theology are more intimately related to the native genius of dramatic tragedy as a literary form.

The necessity of the second requirement arises out of the fact that many theologians and men of letters claim to have written or to have read Christian plays that do not stand up under objective theological or literary analysis as fully Christian dramatic tragedies. The bare fact that a dramatic tragedy appears to be Christian to the sentiments of a reader or the bare fact that a man of letters sincerely claims to be constructing or to have constructed a Christian play does not suffice. The impressions of the audience and the intent of the dramatist may be necessary. But they are not sufficient. "The play's the thing." We must be able to specify the properties of a Christian dramatic tragedy in a formal and dispassionate way apart from the motives of the man of letters or the impressions upon the audience.

The necessity for the third requirement derives from the fact that it is not possible for a Christian poetics to defy the intuitive wisdom of mankind without a demonstrably good cause. Those works of literature which have commonly been recognized as Christian must receive a peculiarly vivid, forceful, and general interpretation, no matter where or when the poetics is competently employed. And no such work must prove incapable of such interpretation. This requirement does not mean that a Christian poetics has to accept all plays commonly recognized as Christian or all aspects of all the plays it specifies as models. But it does mean that it must endeavor to accept some aspects of any play and all aspects of some plays commonly recognized as Christian. Nor does it mean that a Christian theory of dramatic tragedy cannot employ epics, novels, short stories, and even lyrics among its models, in so far as they are interpretable as dramatic tragedies. As Aristotle correctly observed and reasoned, dramatic tragedy encompasses the epic and the lyric and is in a sense and to a degree the ultimate theological and literary form.

III

The question as to whether a Christian dramatic tragedy is possible raises perennial issues in the domains of theology and literary criticism, both among the living and among the dead.

The theological argument against the possibility of a Christian dramatic tragedy is that God as revealed in Jesus Christ transports life beyond tragedy. Life appeared to be and was in fact merely tragic for the Greek; life became merely tragic for the Jew; and life remains merely tragic for the skeptic. But in the light of the Christian faith and revelation life is much more than merely tragic. And life can become more than merely tragic for the pagans, provided they are moved to repentance and to faith. Before Christ tragedy was all there was. The very meaning of life was in doubt. But in Christ the meaning of life became clear, certain, and complete. The tears of tragedy were caught up in victory. Men saw through a glass darkly and then face to face. For those who have faith to trust in the revelation that is the Christ, evil, sin, the devil, death—in short all that is cursed, wretched, and miserable about this life—becomes redeemable in principle and redeemed at certain points and moments in fact. The essential pattern of life is no longer from hope to despair. The essential movement is from the despair of the Cross to the fulfillment of the Resurrection that is Easter, from tragedy to peace, from sin to grace, and from judgment to forgiveness. Dramatic tragedy may have provided a perfect literary expression for Greek or modern skeptical theology in the plays of the Greek tragedians, the neoclassic drama of Corneille and Racine, Melville's *Moby Dick,* Goethe's *Faust,* Joyce's *Exiles,* and in the drama of Ibsen and Shaw. But, in the light of Christian theology, there is a grace, a joy, and a goodness at the heart of life that dramatic tragedy as a literary form is likely to keep remote and dim. A Christian dramatic tragedy is therefore not possible, because it contradicts the whole theme and point of Christian theology.

A Christian dramatic tragedy is not necessary because there are other familiar and well-known literary forms which have and can render fuller justice to the Christian story as a story—from the Book of Job and the Gospels to the present day. Dante did not compose a dramatic tragedy. He composed a *Divine Comedy.* The movement is from the Inferno, through the Purgatorio, to the Paradiso. And Chaucer fashioned his *Canterbury Tales*—surely tales of light. And if Milton composed a *Samson Agonistes* and a *Paradise Lost,* he also conceived a *Paradise Regained.* Similarly, Dostoevski's greatest novel, *The Brothers Karamazov,* moves from the tragedy of the major plot centering around the brothers and their father to the Hallelujah Chorus of the subplot centering around the children. Finally, Herman Melville, at the end of one of the greatest of all theological odysseys recorded in the form of literature, came full circle from the skeptical and Faustian defiance of *Moby Dick,* and the piteous abnormality of his Oedipus-like *Pierre,* to the full and actual Christian glory of his *Billy Budd.*

The literary argument against a Christian dramatic tragedy is that a Christian play cannot be fully tragic in the literary sense. If God's grace, wisdom, and power are in fact the law of life, there really is and can be no tragedy. Life is no longer dark and pitiful. The Greek theme of man's suffering nobility and its feelings of pity and terror are banished from the stage. And the modern skeptical theme of man's piteous abnormality, inertness, and weariness becomes equally impossible. A Mass, a mystery or morality play, an oratorio, or some very elevated kind of tragi-comedy like *The Tempest* can be Christian. But a pure dramatic tragedy which seeks to be both Christian and a tragedy is bound to fail. It will become, in literary language, a deception, a fake, and a cheat. The Christian element becomes a *deus ex machina,* an unwonted minister of poetic justice. If God is in fact the Lord of life and history, the deep wound of tragedy is no longer deep.

These are powerful arguments, and certainly in some sense and to a degree they are true. Yet I do not think that they are completely true or the whole truth. They are not insurmountable. There is a larger and more important Christian truth.

To my mind the theological argument rests upon a misunderstanding of Christian theology, or at least of that kind of Christian theology that I think is most true and important and in which I believe. And the literary argument rests upon a misunderstanding of dramatic tragedy, or at least of that kind of dramatic tragedy I consider to be most desirable and profound.

The kind of Christian theology in which I believe mitigates but does not simply deny or cancel out tragedy. It shifts the locus of tragedy from God, nature, others, or our own essence to an aspect of ourselves and others—an aspect which is rendered sufferable, meaningful, and transformable by virtue of a conjunction between God's freely given grace and our freely received faith. Chance, necessity, and judgment remain, and yet there is also the great fact of man as forgiven and as forgiving. The consequences of sin are not erasable or completely reversible. Yet there is always the real possibility of a new creature and a new life. There is always the generic contrast between what might have happened and did not happen and what may or can still happen—for, by, and to others or our own future selves. No man falls so far as to be cut off from all possibility of salvation, and no man rises so high as to be beyond all possibility of reversion, stasis, or further ascent.

Just so, and by the same line of thought, a great dramatic tragedy is not simply and purely tragic. The meaning of a really great dramatic tragedy is not all despair and doom. Despair and doom are characteristic of certain kinds of dramatic tragedy, namely, the Greek and the modern skeptical. Their plays are stories of man's doom at the hands of caprice, necessity, and other things that are remorseless and senseless within the nature of things, both within and without. But some of the greatest of dramatic tragedies—namely, Christian dramatic tragedies—turn upon the theme of man's idolatry and pretension rather than upon the theme of man's suffering nobility or piteous abnormality. They move from fate to freedom, from defeat to victory, from doom to grace, and from tragedy to peace. This is the whole Christian point and meaning of Hamlet's "readiness is all," of Edgar's "Ripeness is all!" of Finnegan's "Look, look, the mist is rising!" and of Jesus Christ's "Forgive them, Father. . . ."

From this theological and literary point of view, the events and meanings of which Christian theology consists and to which it refers are not simply and purely beyond tragedy. And a great dramatic tragedy is not simply and purely tragic. A Christian tragedy therefore becomes both possible and necessary. It becomes possible because there is no inner contradiction between Christian theology as a kind of story and dramatic tragedy as a kind of literary form. It becomes necessary, for there is no other way whereby both

Christian theology and dramatic tragedy can rise to their full and proper heights. Dramatic tragedy deepens the deeper side of Christian theology, and Christian theology deepens the deeper side of dramatic tragedy. Very pointedly, this means that the Christian story itself may best be understood as a certain kind of dramatic tragedy, because, theologically speaking, the Gospels are not simply beyond tragedy and because in literary terms they are not simply tragic.

IV

If a Christian dramatic tragedy is at once possible and necessary, by what marks can we distinguish a Christian dramatic tragedy from the Greek and the modern skeptical? What requirements or conditions in the way of properties must a play fulfil in order to be called specifically Christian? In short, of what events and meanings must the inner world of a play consist if it is to exhibit the kind of world of which Christian theology speaks and to which it refers?

If the general properties of a Christian play are to be specified with some precision and scope, answers to the following set of questions must be provided. What is the motive or intent of a Christian dramatist? Is he trying to "hold as 'twere a mirror up to nature"? Is he trying to represent the eternal verities? Is he trying to contrast this actual world with some other possible or impossible world? Or is he trying to move the human heart with a vision of this life as redeemable and in part redeemed? What happens in a Christian play? And what does it mean? Is it fundamentally the story of man's fate and doom, dark and deep and pitiful? Or is it the story of man's freedom, guilt, sin, and redemption? What is the nature of the tragic hero? Is he just like us? Or is he better or worse? Of what does his tragic flaw consist? Is it simply an intellectual error in judgment, a mistake, a failure to take thought and to be prudent? Does it involve some kind of perversion, obsession, fixation, inertness, weariness, or melancholy? Or does it follow essentially from some kind of specifiable moral guilt and religious sin like pretension or idolatry? What is the relation of the protagonist to the other characters? Are they simply foils? Or are they real individuals, standing out in their own right and undergoing their own little tragedies? In what sense is the tragic hero free, and in what sense is he determined? When things go wrong, who or what does the tragic hero accuse? Does he accuse himself, others, nature, or God? What is the theme of the play? Does it concern man's suffering nobility, man's piteous abnormality, or man's guilt and sin? What is the nature of the plot? What happened before the play begins? What is the relation between what happened before the play begins and what happens within it? Is the play in a sense over before it begins? Or is it really open at the beginning? What happens at the beginning, in the middle, and at the end? What happens after the play ends? Is the end something after which there is nothing, as Aristotle said? Or is there some kind of continuity of life with life, some sort of rebirth of life out of death? Is the plot simple or complex, open or closed? Is the plot determined by fate and chance or by freedom and providence? In the anagnoris, or recognition scene, does the tragic hero move from ignorance to knowledge, from normality to madness, or from knowledge through temptation to sin? And in the peripeteia, or reversal of fortune, does the tragic hero move from happiness to misery and from high to low estate? Or does he not move from judgment to forgiveness and from tragedy to peace? Finally, what is the effect of a Christian play upon its audience? Is the audience depressed or exalted? Does it feel pity and terror or judgment and forgiveness? Does the play purify the emotions by the understanding, or the understanding by the emotions? Does the catharsis, or cleansing action, transform subjectivity into objectivity, or objectivity into subjectivity? In short, of what events and meanings do the intent, the inner content and structure, and the effects of a Christian dramatic tragedy consist?

V

The properties a play must exhibit in order to be called specifically Christian are to my mind relatively simple in character and limited in number. Apart from the mystery involved in any event and in every meaning, I think that they are specifiable in principle, and I should specify them as follows in fact. And yet I am humbly, if not apologetically, aware that these properties represent my own concrete decisions on controversial theological and literary issues. Moreover, I have been forced to employ certain theological and literary assumptions I lack space to argue: that the Christian story as a whole and in all its parts is wholly concerned with something within this given and actual world and does not involve any essential reference beyond life and history to another possible or impossible one and that the Christian kind of play may best be defined in generic contrast to plays of the other two classic types: the ancient Greek and the modern skeptical.

The most general property of a Christian play is that the motive or intent, the inner content and structure, and the sensory, emotional, and intellectual effects or demands upon the audience are symbolic rather than realistic or allegorical. As a symbol, a Christian play brings together the events and meanings realism and allegory would keep apart. Realism is likely to play favorites with events at the price of meanings. Allegory is likely to play favorites with meanings at the cost of events. The genius of Christian symbolism resides in the way it can mingle the events and meanings of which life and history consist. A Christian play is not just a realistic mirror or a set of eternal allegorical truths. Nor is it a fantasy—a recollection or a dream concerned with some possible or impossible world other than this given and actual one. A Christian play presents what is actual in this life with what is possible for it and what is possible for this life with what is actual in it. There is a real fusion and discrimination of events and meanings in such a way that the meanings of this life are represented as illustrated within the events of this life and in such a way that the events of this life are presented as exemplifying the meanings of this life. By virtue of this mingling of events and meanings in a symbol, a Christian play can purify the understanding by the emotions even as it purifies the emotions by the understanding. Just so, a Christian play internalizes objective and external facts even as it externalizes subjective and internal facts. Objectivity is transformed into subjectivity, and subjectivity is transformed into objectivity. The hopeless dualism between subject and object, mind and body, appearance and reality, and this world and another world at the heart and center of Greek and modern skeptical theology is overcome. This general property follows from what a Christian means by the radical character of God's immanence and transcendence; by the radical character of man's freedom, guilt, and sin; and by the radical character of the redemption and the damnation which occur within life and history. A harmony between the events of life and the meanings of life is possible in principle by virtue of God's immanence, is sometimes lacking in fact by virtue of man's capacity for guilt and sin, and yet is realized in fact at certain points and moments by virtue of that redemption which can come of conjunctions between the transcendent working of God's grace and man's faith.

A Christian tragic hero is a more or less constant subject of changing qualities and relations. Unlike a Greek tragic hero, he is not a simple substance, requiring nothing but himself in order to exist and be great. A Christian tragic hero endures in a manner that is ever more vivid, complicated, and deep if and only if he becomes more and more essentially qualified by and related to the course of events and meanings within life and history. He is internally related to and essentially qualified by other individuals, from the simplest of foils to God—including his former and future selves. He is only derivatively above and beyond these qualifications and this relatedness. His process *is* his character, and his character *is* his relatedness. And yet at certain crucial points and moments he stands out for and by himself alone—a solitary *causa sui*—uninfluenced and uninfluencing, internally determined and externally free. At these points and moments he is radically free: free to betray or to serve his former and future selves and free to regard or to disregard others, nature, and even God. Such radically autonomous freedom is of course only intermittent and in any case is always conditioned by the general metaphysical situation within and without to which God as well as he is subject. Nor can a Christian tragic hero completely disengage himself from the specific situation from which he has come and into which he will issue. And yet, apart from the data which have been given and the issues which are about to be suffered and done, something is left over that is open and remains to be decided. By virtue of this openness and freedom, the lives of others and even God's life are at his mercy. By virtue of the radical character of this freedom, a Christian tragic hero has rights and duties as well as pleasures and utilities. And by virtue of this freedom a Christian tragic hero is capable of moral guilt and religious sin.

A Christian tragic hero's *hamartia,* or tragic flaw, is a function of his abuse of this radical freedom. The flaw issues from his moral guilt and religious sin rather than from his ignorance or finiteness, as in a Greek play, or from his perversion, inertness, or weariness, as in a modern skeptical play. He is subject to all these other flaws —Greek and skeptical. But at certain crucial points and moments both his existence and his excellence or their reverse are functions of his freedom and of his moral guilt or religious sin. He is free to respond to God, to others, and to his own conscience. But he in fact responds to something less than God, others, or his own conscience. This is idolatry. Or he claims to be responding more completely and unambiguously to God, others, or his better self than he in fact is. This is pretension. He therefore moves in the anagnorisis, or recognition scene, from knowledge, through temptation, to sin, and in the peripeteia, or reversal, he moves from judgment to forgiveness. He is judged because he has identified his creaturely purposes with God's purposes. He is forgiven because God's immanence presents him with the basis for a new life and because God's transcendence can redeem the old life he has forsaken despite and even over against his guilt and sin. A Christian tragic hero's opening situation is filled with possibilities, ordered in relevance and determinately good and evil because of God's immanence, and yet he is free to regard or to disregard them. Even if he disregards them, they are presented to him again and again, for no finiteness or ignorance, no perversion or weariness, and no guilt or sin can cut him off completely from the patient kindness and power of God's grace. He is never so perfect as to be beyond the need of further perfection or the capacity for stasis or reversion, and he never falls so far as to be beyond the possibility of transmutation in the direction of a new creature and a new life. At certain points and moments this is precisely what happens in fact. Even if he resists the good that is presented, the good is attained in part despite and even in direct opposition to his conscious efforts. He is delivered in spite of his goodness or badness, not simply because of them. He is therefore likely to move from the heroic ideal, through a tragic vision, to some kind of religious longing and peace. In the recognition scene he can accuse God, others, nature, or himself. But he finally accuses himself: "Ahab, beware of Ahab." "The fault, dear Brutus, is not in the stars, but in ourselves, that we are underlings." And yet, in accusing himself, he does not accuse his own essence—something which could not have been otherwise before the event and something which remains unalterable after it. He accuses a contingent and relative aspect of himself which can be and is forgiven even as it is judged in grace and power by virtue of a conjunction between God's act of revelation and his own acts of repentance and faith.

The plot of a Christian play is to some extent open at the beginning, at the middle, and at the end. By being open, I do not mean that the course of events is unconditioned. It arises out of a definite, given, and limited situation; and it issues into a definite, given, and limited situation. I mean that at certain points and moments all individualities implicated in a Christian plot are internally determined and externally free; that their tragedy is a function of freedom and of character rather than of fate and of circumstance; and that a Christian play begins, moves through, and ends in something more than the simply tragic. I also mean that the plot of a Christian play has a real beginning, a real middle, and a real end.

By a real beginning, I mean that there are relevant possibilities and real alternatives in the initial situation. This can happen or that can happen. Something is there to be decided. Moreover, the possibilities are orderd in relevance by God. They are not a mere chaos. Some are compatible and some are incompatible. Any course of events will have to select from among them, deciding for *this* alternative rather than for *that* or *that*. But the possibilities are really there; some are more interesting and important than others, and some are clearly good and some clearly evil. The tragic hero's problem is not primarily one of knowledge. Just so, there is no entity making the worse appear as the better cause. Or at least the devil is not an actual entity in the same sense and to the same degree that God is an actual entity.

By a real middle I mean that the individualities involved in a Christian plot begin as effects facing the past and end as causes facing the future. Creativity rather than fate is the ultimate entity to which both God and the tragic hero are subject. Between the beginning and the end there is real freedom, real choice, and real guilt and sin. There are real causal efficacy and a real sense of direction. The causal lines are separable, and yet they are also related and intertwined. No individuality is vacuous, unqualified, and unrelated. Each stands out at some point and moment to make real decisions. Every decision arises out of a decided situation and issues into a conditioned situation, and yet decisions are made *by* every entity as well as *for* it or *to* it. That is, there are points and moments wherein every entity takes the whole of life into his own hands—including God's life and the lives of others. For the most part the tragic hero is at God's mercy, but in these points and moments God is at his mercy.

By a real end I mean that there is an appropriation of the dead by the living. What is divested of living immediacy becomes immortal by presenting itself to what follows as a final or persuasive cause and by determining what is to follow as an efficient or coercive cause. In this sense every beginning is an end, and every end is a beginning. Life must be described in terms of death, and death must be described in terms of life or rebirth. Therefore, the past before a Christian play provides as well as limits. It is a blessing as well as a curse, and the future after a Christian play is in a sense implicated in the present of the play. There is real continuity of life with life. The end is therefore more than a denouement or something after which there is nothing. In losing his life, the tragic hero finds it. After the Cross there is Easter, and after Easter there is the Holy Spirit, and after the Holy Spirit there is a community of the forgiven and the forgiving. In this way the Christian life takes on an intensity and a massiveness derived from the "before" and issuing into the "after" of which life and history consist. This is the "communion of the saints" and the "mutual ministry" of past, present, and future believers. No man is an island. We are members, one of another.

The effect of a Christian play upon its audience is a sense of judgment and forgiveness rather than a sense of pity and terror, as in a Greek play, or a sense of poignance and despair, as in a modern skeptical play. We feel judgment because the tragic deed has involved moral guilt and religious sin and because the consequences of the tragic deed are often less than this specifiable guilt and sin. We feel forgiveness because a conjunction between God's grace and man's repentance and faith in part redeem that which has been betrayed and forsaken.

These are the events and meanings of which a Christian's faith in God's revelation of himself in Jesus Christ consists. These are the properties a play must exhibit if it is to present the kind of world of which Christian theology speaks. And these are the properties I find to be fulfilled in the concrete models of Christian literary history.

VI

I shall now attempt to document these properties in some detail by means of a final summary appeal to theological and literary history, namely, to the generic contrast between the story of man's fate and suffering nobility as told by the Greeks and as deepened by the modern skeptics in their theme of man's melancholy, weariness, and piteous abnormality and the story of man's freedom and conscious or unconscious idolatry as told by Christian dramatists. The meaning of Greek and modern plays is despair, virtually complete and unmitigated, whereas the meaning of a Christian dramatic tragedy is that life and history are redeemable in principle and are in part redeemed at certain crucial points and moments in fact.

The protagonists on the stage of Aeschylus, Sophocles, and Euripides are Greek tragic heroes, exemplifying many of the fundamentally negative patterns of Greek theology, whereas the protagonists on the stage of Shakespeare, Chaucer, Dante, Milton, Melville, Hawthorne, and Dostoevski are in a very deep sense Christian tragic heroes, reenacting the Passion of Jesus Christ and illustrating some of the more affirmative patterns of Christian theology. Of course, I do not mean to imply that Shakespeare's tragic heroes are ideal or even conscious Christians, any more than that the Greek tragic heroes are conscious or model Greeks. I simply mean that the essential patterns of their lives, respectively, exhibit and fulfil the crucial motifs of Greek and Christian theology. Nor do I presume that either Shakespeare or his audience were self-conscious Christians—Catholic, Protestant, or otherwise. Nor do I wish to overlook Shakespeare's wondrous catholicity as a dramatist—his capacity for setting forth all the ultimately conflicting intuitions to which mankind is subject without deciding unambiguously among them. I simply mean that the full significance of a central aspect of Shakespeare's plays—especially when placed over against Greek and modern skeptical plays—cannot be fully understood apart from some reference to the nativity, the life and teachings, the Passion, the death, and the Resurrection of Jesus Christ and to some of the profounder insights of Christian theology. The tragic heroes in the novels of Hawthorne, Melville, and Dostoevski are Christian tragic heroes in the same sense, whereas this cannot be said so quickly or so justly for the plays and novels of Ibsen, Shaw, Hardy, Proust, Kafka, and Joyce. Modern skeptical tragic heroes are tired and sick rather than pretentious or blind. They are in love with something less and other than truth or beauty. Some obsession or perversion drives them this way and that and down and down until they destroy both themselves and others. They remember things they cannot possibly reenact and dream of things they cannot possibly realize. Their story begins in zest and ends in boredom or violence. Modern skeptical dramatic tragedy is, with few exceptions, an echo or a deepening of what is generically Greek—in the sense that its tragic heroes are in no need of redemption by virtue of their nobility or are incapable of redemption by virtue of their piteous abnormality. In the recognition scene, as they move from normality to madness, they are likely to accuse the very character of life and history—cursing the wretched loneliness and misery of their lives. The only resolution of tragedy of which they are capable was best expressed by Sophocles in his picture of Oedipus putting out his eyes—namely, in the violence and weariness of self-mortification or in death. Greek tragic heroes are creatures of ignorance, finiteness, and mortality. Modern skeptical tragic heroes are victims of obsession, perversion, fixation, inertness, weariness, and melancholy. Christian tragic heroes are creatures of freedom, guilt, and sin.

A Greek tragic hero is a simple and substantial entity who could be real and excellent on his own, requiring no other entities to exist or to be great. He happens to be qualified by and related to his situation by his body and emotions within and by fate and chance without. He thereby becomes implicated in other characters, things, and the caprices and necessities of nature, life, and history. What is substantially good and great about him is his "character" or persona, an essentially dispassionate and uninvolved essence it is his ideal abstractly to sustain. This essence or persona involves certain very formal kinds of external relatedness to other individuals and to the general course of events within life and history but no real or constitutive internal relations. He is primarily a self-sufficient, unmoving and unmoved entity, apart from certain qualities and relations he accidentally and derivatively is forced against his desire to take on. He is essentially defined by mind—by the entertainment of ideal meanings apart from perceived or enacted events. He is at his wisest and his best when alone with himself thinking about thought, indifferent to or defiant of what in fact comes to pass or is done. His tragedy arises because he is in fact not so completely disengaged from the course of events as he might wish. By virtue of finitude, bodily passion, and mortality, he unwittingly destroys that which he most loves and ironically attains the opposite of what he intended. In the anagnorisis, or recognition scene, he moves from the complacency of ignorance to the bitterness of truth, suffering a peripeteia or reversal of fortune that is undeserved, remorseless, and irreversible. His only consolation finally lies in his devotion to eternal forms of truth and beauty, forms in terms of which he can defy circumstance, and disembodied meanings that he should have known from the beginning to have been essentially incapable of complete expression in the form of events or deeds. His persona or "substantial form" suffers no radical change or development in the process. All change is subjective, not objective; physical, not mental; apparent, not real. Other individualities—God, man, or the plants and animals—are not real causes. They are not members of him, and he is not a member of them. As a tragic hero, he is alone with himself, unaffected at the beginning, the middle, or the end. He is independent of any real interpenetration of or by others.

By virtue of this transcendence, a Greek tragic hero is envisaged under the image of the Greek divinity. The Greek deity is similarly above and beyond the course of events, contemplating meanings that are separable from, externally related to, and only derivatively capable of exemplification within the course of events in nature, life, and history. His immanence arises out of, is expressed within, and issues into his transcendence. The Greek God is essentially alone with himself, the "unmoved mover" who "thinks about thought" and views the course of events from above and beyond and apart. Only incidentally is he related to others and to the course of events in life and history. He also refuses to yield his memories and his dreams to fateful chance or necessity. He is simple, substantial, devoid of parts, and unqualified by and unrelated to his former or future selves. Oedipus is thereby the perfect Greek tragic hero by virtue of the way he mirrors the divine element in the world. His life is haunted by a beauty in principle which is never realized in fact. He recollects things that were and dreams of things that might be which he, others, and God are powerless to be or do. As a young man in *Oedipus the King* he becomes fixed and sightless; as an old man in *Oedipus at Colonus* he is still heroically defiant; cursing the broken wretchedness and misery of man's mortal life. In both recognition scenes he accuses the very character of life and history rather than himself, others, or God. There is, moreover, no guilt or sin in him. He is the picture of man's suffering nobility, falling from lack of satisfaction within, understanding of, and influence over the events of life and history.

A Christian tragic hero is a concrete and existentially involved individual, internally complex with a flux of experience that is alive —bodily and emotional as well as mental—with all kinds of physical feelings, emotional perceptions, thoughts, hopes, fears, memories, and dreams derived from other individualities and issuing into other individualities. Greek theology and literature stress the abstract structure a character formally sustains; Christian theology and literature, the concrete and living process in which a character is implicated. The process is in fact his reality, and the relatedness is his character. He is internally related to his own past and to the past of others at the beginning of the play, and at the end of the play he is in some sense internally related to the future of both himself and others. *In medias res,* there is real freedom, whereby the tragic hero is internally determined and externally free. But this freedom arises out of and issues into the joust of life and history—the process of influencing and being influenced—and is radically qualified by moral guilt and religious sin. In the recognition scene and at the reversal there is thereby much more than the Greek movement from the complacency of ignorance to the misery of knowledge and from a high estate to doom. The tragic hero is transformed in his whole being, moving from knowledge to sin and from sin to judgment and from judgment to forgiveness. The theme is not simply the theme of man's suffering innocence and dignity. The theme is the theme of man's idolatrous indifference or pride. By virtue of the radical character of this immanence, a Christian tragic hero is projected in the image of the Christian divinity—essentially immanent within life and history and only derivatively transcendent. This is the whole point and meaning of the basic themes at the heart of Christian theology—the sovereignty of God over the course of events within life and history, justification by faith alone, the sacrificial character of love, the forgiveness of sins, and the redemption of tragedy.

The flaw or *hamartia* in a Greek dramatic tragedy is a purely intellectual error in judgment. Reason is what is wisest and best in man's nature. Tragedy is born of the erring judgments made within the imperfections and limitations of this bodily, emotional, and mortal world. The anagnorisis or discovery in a Greek play is therefore likely to come after the tragic deed rather than before it. In a Christian play, as in *Macbeth,* the recognition scene usually comes before the tragic deed, because the tragic flaw is not simply an error in judgment and because the problem of the tragic hero is not simply one of knowledge. In a Christian play the flaw involves moral guilt and religious sin. Moreover, the error can be conscious and witting as well as unconscious and unwitting. Just so, a Christian tragic hero is likely to blame an aspect of himself or others rather than his own essence or the very character of life and history. His reversal can thereby involve a movement from tragedy to peace as well as from happiness to misery.

Concerning foils and the Chorus, the great fact is that a Greek tragic hero always stands out solitary and alone, above and beyond and apart from all the rest. He only is "round." The minor characters are likely to be "flat," and there is no real interplay between the tragic hero and the other characters. In a Christian play all the characters, great and small, become terribly real and moving at some point and moment, undergoing their own tragedy and finding their own peace. The most incidental figures in Chaucer, Shakespeare, or Dostoevski are given a remarkable touch of life. Moreover, the foils are essentially qualified by and related to the tragic hero, and he is essentially qualified by and related to them. For example, in Shakespeare the highly aristocratic function of the Chorus in Greek tragedy is transformed in a Christian and democratic way. The Greek Chorus, apart from its more technical dramatic functions of handling the problems of exposition, foreshadowing, and atmosphere, is either an ideal spectator viewing the course of events and meanings without passion from apart—in short, a mirror of the Greek divinity—or else it is a common spectator who becomes too passionately and meaninglessly implicated in the course of events. In the first instance, the Chorus is above and beyond the tragic hero, even more like and closer to God than he. In the second instance, the Chorus is a picture of human imperfection, weakness, and frailty, less noble and great than the tragic hero because they are even less detached and disengaged than he. But in Shakespeare the many minor figures and groups who perform the choral function in a Christian play are given their own touch of life—the porter in *Macbeth,* the fool in *Lear,* the gravediggers in *Hamlet,* and the common soldiers in *Henry V*. The ordinary and the common man—the little man of small or no account—is pictured as in a sense more extraordinary, wise, and kingly than the exceptional and kingly man. This is not simply a social or a political contrast between an aristocratic and a democratic order. There is something wider and deeper here than the contrast between the Athenian *polis,* with its hierarchy of classes based upon the slavery of men and women, on the one hand, and the broadening democracy of an Elizabethan England evolving out of a feudal into a mercantile order. It is the contrast, the generic contrast, between Greek theology and Christian theology and between a Greek dramatic tragedy and a Christian dramatic tragedy. In a Greek play the key to a man's existence and the measure of his excellence—aesthetically, intellectually, morally, politically, and religiously—is a function of the one as over against the many, whereas in a Christian play both a man's existence and his excellence are a function of the many who are of small account. The common, the ordinary, and the familiar are peculiarly children of God. And they are children of God because they are essentially qualified by and related to the course of events and meanings of which life and history consist.

The plot of a Greek play is essentially closed at the beginning, at the middle, and at the end, whereas the plot of a Christian play is essentially open at the beginning, at the middle, and at the end. In this sense a Greek tragedy is a function of circumstance, fate, and doom, whereas a Christian tragedy is a function of character, freedom, and redemption. A Greek tragedy is almost all end in the sense of being closed before or very shortly after the play begins. Part of the deep irony of a Greek play derives from this fact that the initial situation may appear to be open—with a penumbra of alternatives, some right and some wrong—when in fact the situation is closed, and the distinction between good and evil is at best vague and ambiguous. At the middle of a Greek play the tragic hero is internally free but externally determined. His inner freedom thereby comes to naught. He is forced to destroy that which he set out to conserve and to create. And the end of a Greek play is all end. As Aristotle said, the end is something after which there is nothing.

The plot of a Christian dramatic tragedy has a real beginning, a real middle, and a real end. The beginning is real because the initial situation is filled with relevant possibilities both for good and for evil. They are ordered in relevance by God, and, by virtue of this fact of divine ordering, some are determinately good and others are determinately evil. There is a real middle because at certain points and moments the tragic hero is internally determined and externally free. And there is a real end in the sense that the end is also a new beginning. In a Christian play a new life always arises out of the old life. There is a datum, a transition of decision, and an issue. At the beginning of the play the past dies and is reborn in the present. At the middle the present stands out for its own sake, in part an effect facing the past, and in part a cause facing the future.

What happens in the present is radically a function of a cause internal to the individual. In a Greek play what happens is in large part a function of a cause external to the individual, and there is no new life arising out of the old life. Aeschylus' transformation of the Furies into the Eumenides at the end of the *Oresteia,* with its transmutation of the old order of blood feuds into a new order of peace within the *polis,* is rare in Greek tragedy. It is striking because it is rare. The despair of Oedipus at Thebes and the fury of Oedipus at Colonus are more typical. The real God of life and history in Greek tragedy is fate, and fate is man's enemy, not man's friend. The ideal God is a transcendent God. He is either a void, as in Euripides, or a powerless ideal, as in Sophocles. Oedipus thereby dies defiant and unreconciled to the real God of life and history, and a modern skeptical tragic hero also dies defiant, weary, and melancholy, cursing the day wherein he was born or "squandering his life wantonly as if it were immortal." There is no notion of rebirth, of restoration, of a new creature and a new life, or redemption within life and history, or of any essentially good news at the heart of Greek or skeptical dramatic tragedy. There is no real before and no real after that are a part of life and history. A Greek tragic hero does not even have one real chance to live. A Christian tragic hero has at least one real chance, and in a sense he can sin and sin and yet be born again. In fact, in Christian theology the life of mankind constitutes the shifting character of God's life itself. The beginnings, the middles, and the ends of our lives are the beginnings, the middles, and the ends of God's life. This is the real thing, not an image or a copy of the real thing. God's process *is* his reality, and God's relatedness *is* his character. In Catholic theology the emphasis is upon the last part of the temporal process. The beatific vision comes when all has been said and done. This is the Greek element in Christian theology. Protestant theology is more Hebraic. The emphasis is upon the sense of heroic calling and mission within the very center of life and history. The struggle is to get beyond the tragic visions which overwhelm heroic ideals within history. And yet both Catholic and Protestant interpretations of

Christian theology stress that there is and can be something beyond tragedy within life and history. The final living fact is not a relapse into matter, as in modern skeptical plays, or in elevation beyond life and history to some other possible or impossible world, as in Greek plays. There is an embrace of this life, an enchantment of the heart to this world, and a sense of peace here and now even as one stands deep in tragic misery. This is the force and meaning of both the Cross and the Resurrection. Grace and power, mercy and justice, judgment and forgiveness, are conjoined as intimately related aspects of one event or a series of events and of one meaning or a series of meanings. *Finis* and *telos,* efficient and final causality, events and meanings, come together. Every beginning is an end, and every end is a new beginning. Someone dies in order that you may be born, and you must die in order to be born again. Therefore, there is much more than a denouement at the end of a Christian play. There is real continuity of life with life and a re-creation of life out of death. We are internally, not just externally, related both before and after.

Perhaps the most pointed way to deepen this generic contrast between a Greek and a Christian dramatic tragedy is to compare the ultimate emotional, sensory, and intellectual effects they have upon their audiences. As Aristotle correctly observed and reasoned, the effects of a Greek play are pity and terror, because the consequences of the tragic deed are always in excess of any specifiable moral guilt or religious sin and yet at the same time are remorseless and irreversible. The effects of a Christian play are judgment and forgiveness, for the reason that the consequences of the tragic deed are often less than the specifiable guilt and sin and at the same time are rendered sufferable and transformable by virtue of the transfiguring and redemptive working of God's grace and man's faith. Moreover, the catharsis, or purification, of the emotions by the understanding of which Aristotle spoke is shifted in a Christian play from the audience to the inner and rising purgatorial movement within the soul of the tragic hero himself. Moreover, the understanding is cleansed by the emotions as well as the emotions by the understanding. In this sense and to this degree, a Christian tragic hero can witness his own salvation and his own tragic beauty. By virtue of this fact, a Christian tragic hero can forgive himself as well as others even as he is forgiven, whereas a Greek tragic hero first accuses nature, then others, then God, and finally brings the whole insufferable burden of tragic misery down upon his own unalterable essence. A Greek play thus ends upon a note of hopeless and unmitigated doom—deep and dark and pitiful—whereas a Christian play ends upon a note of faith, hope, and trust. There is Easter and the reassertion of the heart to new life. There is peace in the midst of tragedy by virtue of the transforming light and power of grace, both within and without.

VII

In summary, Greek tragedy presents life as unredeemable in principle and as unredeemed at every point and moment in fact. The flaw of the tragic hero is rooted in the very nature of things, within and without. The nemesis of doom is something from which there is no escape and something over which neither man nor God has complete control. The movement in the recognition scene and the reversal is from the complacency of ignorance to the bitterness of truth and from the heroic ideal to the tragic vision: but there is no peace. This fact of doom is variously interpreted by the Greek tragedians. Aeschylus stresses the heavy hand of the past, the inherited propensities to moral, political, and religious evil, and the working-out of a curse relentlessly by means of the inherited *hybris* or spiritual pride of a ruling family. Sophocles stresses the ironic and pitiful conjunctions of man's suffering nobility within and the blind caprices and necessities of nature without. Sophocles also stresses the tendency of the human spirit to have memories and dreams too vivid, too complicated, and too deep for life to express them and maintain its order too. And Euripides focuses upon the subrational vitalities at the heart of human motivation, restless energies that twist and drive the human spirit this way and that and down and down, apart from any specifiable order. But all the Greeks and the moderns agree upon the essential helplessness of the human spirit and of its God. God is either a fateful enemy, a powerless ideal, or a meaningless void. In either case, what is given or discoverable within the nature of things does not suffice to answer the cry of the human spirit. At its extreme this note of doom at the heart of Greek and modern tragedy leads to the pessimistic conclusion that it is better for a man never to have been born or that "no man is happy 'till he die." Or it can lead to the banal counsel of prudence—"Nothing too much." It can also lead to the violence and despair of Prometheus' "I am wronged!" or to the vision of Oedipus standing fixed, sightless, and maimed. Only by drawing what Whitehead has termed the "long bow of mysticism"—Platonic or Neo-Platonic—can the senselessly transient events and meanings of this life be transmuted in the name of another nature, another life, and another history wherein there "is no unrest, no travel, no shipwreck: 'There shall be no more sea.' " But the plays of Shakespeare and the novels of Dostoevski are in a profound sense Christian dramatic tragedies. Their tragic heroes come to trust the character of this life, God's life. There is a movement beyond tragedy to some "brave new world" and to a new God who is neither enemy, void, or ideal but a friend and suffering servant. This is the shift from Lear's "What cause in nature makes these hard hearts?" and "more sinned against than sinning" to Edgar's "Ripeness is all!" The movement is not from ignorance to the bitterness of knowledge but from knowledge to sin and from sin to judgment and forgiveness. Their tragic heroes are summoned to something much more than defiance, acquiescence, or resignation. They are summoned to the good news that is revelation and faith. Even as they stand deep in tragedy, they come to love the tenderness of life itself, transported by joy even as they suffer terribly in the face of agony. They come to a sadness and to a peace that is beyond transient pain or transient pleasure and beyond the prudent sobriety of fact or reason. They are summoned to come full circle from the suffering nobility of Greek tragedy or the piteous abnormality of skeptical tragedy, through the conscious or unconscious idolatry of Christian tragedy, to the peace and forgiveness that can come of contrition, repentance, and faith. They are summoned to reenact something more than the passion and doom of Oedipus or Socrates. They are summoned to re-enact the Passion and the Resurrection of Jesus Christ.

Christopher Fry

Comedy*

A FRIEND ONCE TOLD ME that when he was under the influence of ether he dreamed he was turning over the pages of a great book, in which he knew he would find, on the last page, the meaning of life. The pages of the book were alternately tragic and comic, and he turned page after page, his excitement growing, not only because he was approaching the answer but because he couldn't know, until he arrived, on which side of the book the final page would be. At last it came: the universe opened up to him in a hundred words: and they were uproariously funny. He came back to consciousness crying with laughter, remembering everything. He opened his lips to speak. It was then that the great and comic answer plunged back out of his reach.

If I had to draw a picture of the person of Comedy it is so I should like to draw it: the tears of laughter running down the face, one hand still lying on the tragic page which so nearly contained the answer, the lips about to frame the great revelation, only to find it had gone as disconcertingly as a chair twitched away when we went to sit down. Comedy is an escape, not from truth but from despair: a narrow escape into faith. It believes in a universal cause for delight, even though knowledge of the cause is always twitched away from under us, which leaves us to rest on our own buoyancy. In tragedy we suffer pain; in comedy pain is a fool, suffered gladly.

Charles Williams once said to me—indeed it was the last thing he said to me: he died not long after: and it was shouted from the tailboard of a moving bus, over the heads of pedestrians and bicyclists outside the Midland Station, Oxford—"When we're dead we shall have the sensation of having enjoyed life altogether, whatever has happened to us." The distance between us widened, and he leaned out into space so that his voice should reach me: "Even if we've been murdered, what a pleasure to have been capable of it!"; and, having spoken the words for comedy, away he went like the revelation which almost came out of the ether.

He was not at all saying that everything is for the best in the best of all possible worlds. He was saying—or so it seems to me—that there is an angle of experience where the dark is distilled into light: either here or hereafter, in or out of time: where our tragic fate finds itself with perfect pitch, and goes straight to the key which creation was composed in. And comedy senses and reaches out to this experience. It says, in effect, that, groaning as we may be, we move in the figure of a dance, and, so moving, we trace the outline of the mystery.

Laughter did not come by chance, but how or why it came is beyond comprehension, unless we think of it as a kind of perception. The human animal, beginning to feel his spiritual inches, broke in on to an unfamiliar tension of life, where laughter became inevitable. But how? Could he, in his first unlaughing condition, have contrived a comic view of life and then developed the strange rib-shaking response? Or is it not more likely that when he was able to grasp the tragic nature of time he was of a stature to sense its comic nature also; and, by the experience of tragedy and the intuition of comedy, to make his difficult way? The difference between tragedy and comedy is the difference between experience and intuition. In the experience we strive against every condition of our animal life: against death, against the frustration of ambition, against the instability of human love. In the intuition we trust the arduous eccentricities we're born to, and see the oddness of a creature who has never got acclimatised to being created. Laughter inclines me to know that man is essential spirit; his body, with its functions and accidents and frustration, is endlessly quaint and remarkable to him; and though comedy accepts our position in time, it barely accepts our posture in space.

The bridge by which we cross from tragedy to comedy and back again is precarious and narrow. We find ourselves in one or the other by the turn of a thought; a turn such as we make when we turn from speaking to listening. I know that when I set about writing a comedy the idea presents itself to me first of all as tragedy. The characters press on to the theme with all their divisions and perplexities heavy about them; they are already entered for the race to doom, and good and evil are an infernal tangle skinning the fingers that try to unravel them. If the characters were not qualified for tragedy there would be no comedy, and to some extent I have to cross the one before I can light on the other. In a century less flayed and quivering we might reach it more directly; but not now, unless every word we write is going to mock us. A bridge has to be crossed, a thought has to be turned. Somehow the characters have to unmortify themselves: to affirm life and assimilate death and persevere in joy. Their hearts must be as determined as the phoenix; what burns must also light and renew: not by a vulnerable optimism but by a hard-won maturity of delight, by the intuition of comedy, an active patience declaring the solvency of good. The Book of Job is the great reservoir of comedy. "But there is a spirit in man . . . Fair weather cometh out of the north . . . The blessing of him that was ready to perish came upon me: and I caused the widow's heart to sing for joy."

I have come, you may think, to the verge of saying that comedy is greater than tragedy. On the verge I stand and go no further. Tragedy's experience hammers against the mystery to make a breach which would admit the whole triumphant answer. Intuition has no such potential. But there are times in the state of man when comedy has a special worth, and the present is one of them: a time when the loudest faith has been faith in a trampling materialism, when literature has been thought unrealistic which did not mark and remark our poverty and doom. Joy (of a kind) has been all on the devil's side, and one of the necessities of our time is to redeem it. If not, we are in poor sort to meet the circumstances, the circumstances being the contention of death with life, which is to say evil with good, which is to say desolation with delight. Laughter may seem to be only like an exhalation of air, but out of that air we came; in the beginning we inhaled it; it is a truth, not a fantasy, a truth voluble of good which comedy stoutly maintains.

D. S. Savage

Truth and the Art of the Novel*

"*In the beginning was the Word . . .*"

TOLSTOY, WHO HAS BEEN WELL DESCRIBED as the most truth-loving writer in Russian literature, wrote in later life a pamphlet entitled *Bethink Yourselves!* in which he called on all his readers to halt in whatever they were doing, to detach themselves from whatever functional position they held in society, and seriously and radically to ask themselves *who* they were, *what* they were doing, and whether what they were doing was in conformity with their ultimate destiny as human beings. The call was to change a sleeping for a waking state. Now, it is not only the general life of society which is subject to a perpetual condition of habitual automatism; this condition affects even the production and the consumption of literature, so that in this field also the necessity arises from time to time for someone to rise up and issue a similar call to *Bethink Yourselves!* and in so doing to let loose the unpredictable dynamic of *the idea* in the midst of a mass of unquestioned assumptions, fixed opinions and established reputations. Why do we read novels and what are we really doing when we indulge in that habitual recreation? What *is* a novel, and—more largely—what is *art?*

The attempt to formulate a theory of the nature of a work of art resembles the attempt to formulate a theory of the nature of a man. Everyone knows what a man is, and likewise everyone knows what a work of art is—until he comes to think about it and to investigate

* Reprinted from *The Withered Branch* published by Pellegrini and Cudahy Inc., 1952, by permission of Farrar, Straus and Company, Inc.

what others have thought, when it transpires that there are endless theories, both of the nature of man and of the nature, purpose and meaning of artistic activity. These are not idle questions. Misconceptions of the nature of man may have disastrous consequences in human life, and it is the same with art. The two questions are quite closely related, and as it helps an argument to rest in the first place upon an axiom, I begin with the assertion of the close and organic dependence of art upon life: that is, upon human experience. Art is personal, being rooted in the existence of a concrete and particular individual, the artist. An artist, more particularly a literary artist, and specifically a novelist, must create out of the particular situation in which he finds himself, and to which he has been brought by the interaction of his character (and all that goes to form it) with the circumstances of his time and place. His work will bear the stamp of all these factors. Every novel has a pattern which is imposed upon it by its author's essential being—and this applies no less when the work has the quality of universality. Of all art forms the novel is the most patently personal: it is always autobiographical in its origins. Autobiography itself is merely the simplest form of fiction; the autobiographical novel, so called, is in turn the simplest form of the novel proper; but the more complex forms are no less personal in their foundations. In the simple autobiographical narrative the author presents himself to himself as the central character, in whom the action meets and has its meaning. Complexity enters first of all with dramatization, which reflects an advance in objectivity consequent upon an apprehension of the inter-personal mutuality of living. Implicit in the dramatic form is the avowal of the interdependence of all human destinies, where the meaning of the action is centered not in one character but in each severally, according to his capacity.

To begin with, the general problem which confronts the novelist is that of transmuting the chaos of experience into the order of significant form. Experience in its raw state is incommunicable: that which is communicated is never experience but a mental construct which stands in a symbolic relation to it, mediating between writer and reader, and the craft of fiction consists in discovering and presenting such a construct. Writer and reader must meet on a ground which is objective in its presence to both, and it is the novelist's technical task to prepare it. Somehow he must translate his intrinsically incommunicable experience of reality into a reversed mirror-writing which will be reflected back again, right side up, in the mind of the reader, and first of all in his own mind as his own reader. The novel, that is to say, grounded in subjectivity, aspires towards objectivization—not in the sense of alienation from the subjective, but of its embodiment in apprehensible form. It is objectivization of this kind which alone can set the novelist free from a helpless and inartistic identification with his experiencing self, making possible a form of self-transcension.

What is the operative factor in this interchange, which transforms the raw material of human experience into art? The American critic Mark Schorer follows a familiar course, which stands in need of examination, in calling it "technique." In an essay entitled "Technique as Discovery," he writes forthrightly: "The difference between content, or experience, and achieved content, or art, is technique." This he elaborates as follows:

> When we speak of technique . . . we speak of nearly everything. For technique is the means by which the writer's experience, which is his subject-matter, compels him to attend to it: technique is the only means he has of discovering, exploring, developing his subject, of conveying its meaning, and, finally, of evaluating it. And surely it follows that certain techniques are sharper tools than others, and will discover more: that the writer capable of the most exacting technical scrutiny of his subject-matter will produce works with the most satisfying content, works with maximum meaning. [This writer goes on to define technique as] any selection, structure, or distortion, any form or rhythm imposed upon the world of action; by means of which . . . our apprehension of the world of action is enriched or renewed.

In accordance with this definition, he speaks of Defoe's failure, in *Moll Flanders,* to distinguish his own values from those of the heroine, as a *technical* defect: "Because he had no adequate resources of technique to separate himself from his material, thereby to discover and define the meanings of his material, his contribution is not to fiction but to the history of fiction, and to social history." Discussing *Sons and Lovers,* he points to D. H. Lawrence's inability to separate himself as a writer from his experiential material—to sufficiently objectify his situation for the purposes of art; and this again he describes as a technical failure. "All this, and the character of a whole career, would have been altered if Lawrence had allowed his technique to discover the fullest meaning of his subject."

Clearly, in this dizzy elevation of "technique," something has been left out of account. Misgiving is roused in the first place by the very inclusiveness of "technique" as the word is here used; for something which means nearly everything may come frighteningly close to meaning almost nothing. The error, however, is so common that it indicates the importance of making a clear distinction between technique and a much more primary and fundamental activity, which I propose to call *vision.* In order to create the artistic entity which shall adequately objectify his subjectivity, the novelist must, of course, employ a technique, but his job will be not to make use of some impersonal instrument lying indifferently to hand, but to discover the method which is exactly suited to himself and to his subject, and this means in practice that he must *create* a technique for his always unique and particular purpose. As his vision penetrates the substance of his experience and subjects it to itself, it projects the *idea* of the form of the finished work, and the rest is a matter of experimental verification, of discovery and elimination in the chosen medium. No writer can possess himself of a technique for a creative purpose except through an act of imagination, and this applies even when a technique is apparently borrowed from another writer. Seen in this light, it would appear that Lawrence's difficulty lay on a far profounder level than that of technique; it was an interior, personal one—as common sense readily perceives. *Sons and Lovers* is an imperfect work of art not, at bottom, because of a defect of technique, but because of a failure of artistic imagination. Undoubtedly this deep defect is manifested in the structure and texture of the work, but to nominate it a technical fault is implicitly to deny depth to the novel and to misunderstand its nature.

So far we have two terms of the artistic synthesis, the subjective and the objective. It is in the simple opposition of these factors that two paths to artistic failure reveal themselves: the loss of balance which follows when subjectivity is regarded as all but self-sufficient and the corresponding deflection when the structure of objectivity is sought for its own sake. The first, which is the romantic error, leads to a formless expansiveness; the second, which is the classical, to an empty constructivism. But an integrated work of art contains within itself a resolution and equilibrium of the personal with the impersonal, the subjective and the objective meet and fuse to illuminate and to concretize each other, forming a third entity, a diamond of compressed carbon. There has been a qualitative transformation. In order, therefore, to understand the nature of the artistic synthesis we must put our finger on the third term in which these disparate parts may be drawn together and resolved into unity. That term is Truth. I use the capital initial to emphasize that truth is an absolute.

All art arises from the creative need to raise content into its proper form. Form is that which orders content into significance; the "significant" is that which has meaning, and meaning consists in a relation to truth. The artist—not the craftsman, the entertainer or the dilettante, but the authentic creator—is one who confronts his experience with a passionate and inflexible question as to its meaning, its inherent value, and who, working in his chosen medium, utilizes a particular technique to present the meaning he discovers, in symbolic form, to himself and to others. The discovery of meaning and its embodiment in the concrete artistic work is his justification and his triumph. To uncover the pattern in the formless flux, that which is meaningful in the midst of the sordid and the banal: to lay hold on this and to give it corporal, symbolic expression is the creative mission of the artist.

Truth, the absolute, forms in every integrated work of art the invisible center around which everything in it coheres and in relation to which it becomes a communicator of value. Truthfulness is accordingly the first and absolutely indispensable prerequisite of all authentic art. There are degrees of truthfulness, and of authenticity: a novel may be constructed out of a secondary or a tertiary or even a negative relation to truth, but a great novel can be brought into being only as the outcome of a primary act of apprehension of truth. The apprehension of truth is *imaginative vision.* Imaginative vision is not a mere extension into nothingness, it is a vision of experience informed by meaning—in other words, it is a concrete perception of truth. For it is *truth* which performs the liberating act that lifts the novelist from immersion in his subjective states and enables him so to objectify his experience that it is communicable: to others, indeed, but first of all to himself. Art humanizes. Human life is that of personal movement and response, of communion, of communication, and thus of speech. Relationship is only possible through a mutual relationship to truth; speech is only possible through an avowal of and an aspiration towards truth. Art is speech.

The artist and the thinker are thus akin. "Literature," as John Peale Bishop acutely remarked, "is the criticism of ideas by life." While the novelist may well be devoid of the capacity for systematic abstract thought, there is no good novel which does not demonstrate in a highly concrete and complex state, a process of thought. The common factor between the thinker and the novelist is precisely their orientation to truth.

Truth being an absolute, a resolute personal orientation is an act of transcendence. The pursuit of meaning presupposes a vow, an act of dedication, and the acceptance of a vocation. It is here that life and art are most intimately drawn together. Before the novelist can embody meaning in his work, he must have discovered the pattern of meaning in experience. At its highest and most complete, his artistic task is secondary to and dependent upon a prior personal devotion to truth.

In the transcendent relation to absolute truth, the relative is imbued with meaning, the particular becomes fraught with universality, the temporal wears an aspect of the eternal. From this arises the permanence of great art and the perishability of the inferior work. Art draws its autotelic quality from its relation to the eternal. Great art is a vision of eternity, and the lesson it teaches is that life, in so far as it, too, embodies truth, is itself autotelic. Great art declares the inherent structure of the universe.

Orientation to truth is essentially a religious act. It implies an act of faith in the truth and of constancy in devotion to it. Accordingly, the interdependence of art and life is most clearly shown, in conditions of cultural unity and compactness, in religion, which is the very heart of culture. Religious dogma, cult and ritual are the communal concretion and consolidation of man's transcendent apprehension of truth. Religion in its primitive unity is both art-in-life and life-in-art. The elevation which it effects of men's experience into a unified archetypal pattern results socially in a drawing of the multiplicity of particular lives into symbolic or typical relation with the eternal, the universal and the absolute. In a condition of cultural unity, truth is thus represented, in however imperfect a form, in the beliefs and practices which are held and performed in common and which hold society together in relation to a single center in relation to which, in turn, each social function has a non-utilitarian meaning. In a condition of comparative disintegration, on the other hand, truth ceases to be represented in this unified and unifying way. This means that not only is the self-questioning modern man deprived of the inwardly and outwardly sustaining power of an established symbol of truth, but he lives in a world of manners similarly deprived of accepted significant patterns. Because the life of western man stands inescapably in a relationship to the Christian faith which has provided the foundation for his culture and his civilization, so his art is, willy-nilly, positively or negatively, in a similar relationship. The disintegration in which the modern novelist lives and moves is that of a *Christian* culture; what meaning it has is, inevitably, a religious meaning.

In such a state of radical disorder and confusion the conscious individual must turn ever more inwards to seek out the foundations of his life. It happens that there is no more satisfactory way of presenting his own situation to himself in all its diversity and complexity than that provided by the art of the novel, and it is suggestive that the part played by this literary form in human life has increased in importance commensurably with the decay of religion and the subsequent disintegration of cultural unity, while simultaneously the novel itself, in its higher forms, has increased proportionately in scope and depth, accompanying, in its progress towards artistic self-consciousness, the increasing self-questioning of modern man. In order to substantiate this statement one has only to compare the seventeenth-century prose romance, still close to poetry, with the realistic narratives of the eighteenth-century writers, and those in turn with the increasingly rich and subtle novels of the nineteenth century, which gave us not only Scott, Dickens and Balzac, but Stendhal, Dostoevsky, and Henry James. No longer a running commentary upon contemporary manners, the novel increasingly centers upon itself, accentuating its inherently autotelic quality. At the same time it compensates by greater richness, subtlety and elaboration for the essential impoverishment of the modern man's life consequent upon his alienation from the larger world.

In the latter part of the nineteenth century the novel would appear to have reached its apogee. Although since then the writing of fiction has expanded almost into a branch of industry, the effect of yet further cultural disintegration has been to isolate the artist from his milieu, with the consequence that "creative" fiction has ceased directly to portray the social scene and has come increasingly to concern itself with the inner predicament of the individual. Since, as a man, the alienated novelist cannot in practice live in a state of pure flux, and since the very act of composition does in itself presume a search for intelligible form and thus for personal meaning, a situation arises in which the novel comes ultimately to be shaped by the novelist's human predicament, which, in a disintegrating culture, unavoidably takes the quite primitive and fundamental form of an absence of and a need for faith. It would be vain, and a misunderstanding of the novelist's role, to look to him for positive leadership in this matter. But by reason of the indirect relation to truth which obtains in the practice of his art, we may with assurance look to him for articulation of the condition in which he is enmeshed. It is here that the critical function finds its justification. As the novelist presents life to itself as art, so it falls to the critic to present art to itself as thought, drawing out its concealed meanings and tracing them to a common center, and relating his findings to the general cultural situation.

Like the arts of thought and of fiction, that of criticism presupposes a disciplinary orientation to truth on the part of its practitioner, and like them its power is immeasurably reinforced when this orientation is not only artistic but first of all existential. The creative critic must have at command an uncommon admixture of faculties. Standing midway between the novelist and the philosopher, he must have something of the former's sensitiveness to the particularity and multifariousness of human experience, together with not a little of the latter's capacity for abstraction and generalization.

And here, once again, it is necessary to distinguish between an inadequate subjective or objective critical attitude and an approach which is an integral combination of both. To suppose that there can be a form of criticism which is entirely personal and subjective is as fallacious as to suppose that there can be brought into being a foolproof critical discipline which is impersonal, objective and automatic; and yet we do find critical theory to oscillate in great part between these two misconceived extremes. As with every other art, that of criticism is fundamentally personal, but the critic's purely subjective perceptions, responses and insights are endowed with objective quality, through the rigour of his relation to truth. It is out of such strict and inflexible orientation that critical theory establishes its principles and formulates its disciplines, which, once more, cannot be mechanically appropriated, but have to be possessed from within.

Granted such a rigorous personal self-orientation on the part of the ideal critic, it follows that there can be no essential discontinuity between the mind he brings to his critical work and that which he takes to the rest of his human concerns. The same difference is effective here between the creative and the merely academic or popular critic as between that artist whose relation to truth is circumscribed by the specific discipline of his art, and that other whose orientation to truth is both artistic and existential—or, in other words, *religious*. It follows that the work of the creative critic will be powerfully affected by the *ideas* resulting from a relation to truth; it cannot be either impressionistically "personal" or studiously unbiassed and colourless, like the popular forms of criticism which are encouraged and exalted by reason of the fear of ideas which animates the general mind.

In the six studies of modern novelists which compose this book* an attempt has been made in every case at a sympathetic penetration to the heart of the work, and a consequent intuitive discovery of the underlying pattern which has shaped the sequence of the writer's novels. It will perhaps seem strange that I should use the word "sympathetic" in connection with studies which will appear severe and even harsh, but that word nevertheless expresses my primary approach, and I use it to indicate that, doubtless with many failures, I stand not in an exterior but in an interior relation to the writers with whose work I deal. In the great number of cases I had submitted myself more or less passively and at random to their influence over a long period of time before finding it necessary to my own development to separate myself from them in order to relate their work with increasing strictness to my own apprehension of truth. To the charge of a destructive negativeness, therefore, which may be brought against my treatment of them, I would reply that the severity towards a particular attitude or idea expressed must be considered in some degree as severity towards that part of myself which inclines or has inclined to the same direction.

But in a time of general laxness, severity is its own justification.

* Mr. Savage's reference is to his book, *The Withered Branch* (London, 1951), which includes studies of Ernest Hemingway, E. M. Forster, Virginia Woolf, Margiad Evans, Aldous Huxley, and James Joyce.—*Ed.*

In the words of Blake, Establishment of Truth depends on Destruction of Falsehood continually. I have little doubt that these novelists reveal in their work several distinguishable varieties of Falsehood which, taken together, indicate an acute stage of spiritual malaise, as well as of cultural disintegration.

Just here another objection must be met. It will be charged that in concerning myself with the underlying formative forces which determine the novelist's work, I am overstepping the rightful terrain of criticism and raising issues which have little or nothing to do with literary values. The critic, runs this type of argument, should concern himself only with the purely literary qualities of the work before him, leaving the novelist to enjoy his personal vagaries as he pleases. The fact is, of course, that there are no such purely literary qualities which are not deeply connected with the inner movements of the novelist's personality. Flaws in the surface of a work are the outcome of a disrelation to truth, and disrelation to truth is a part of a more general disorientation of being. As, being an independent writer, I am not compelled to observe that rigid departmentalization of "subjects" which is enforced by educational institutions, I see no reason why I should accept a widespread critical convention and draw an arbitrary line at the point where literature passes over into life. I can therefore state candidly that the typical modern novelists considered in this book reveal in their work several varieties of disorientation of being (or dehumanization) parallel with the deflection from truth which determines the structure of their work as a whole.

The varieties of slavery inherent in the human disposition which wait upon any such disorientation of being have been distinguished with great insight by Nicholas Berdyaev in his book *Slavery and Freedom*. Without in any way attempting to imitate Berdyaev's analysis, or to "apply" his findings to the modern novel—a procedure which would in my view show critical insufficiency and bad faith—I am bound to say that my penetrations into the work of the writers dealt with in the ensuing pages confirm just such an insight into the conditions of inner subjection. Thus in the writings of

Ernest Hemingway there is displayed a clear form of the slavery to war and to violence, in those of E. M. Forster there is marked slavery to the bourgeois spirit and to society, in Margiad Evans can be distinguished a pronounced form of slavery to passion and to nature, in Aldous Huxley the erotic lure is prominent, and in Joyce the aesthetic lure dominates everything, while in Virginia Woolf we see the elementary bewilderment of a mind incapable of formulating a clear view of her world of experience consequent upon inability to establish foundations in belief of whatever order. The lesson of the modern novel, as displayed in these figures, is that of the disintegration of the consciousness of modern man, resulting from his divided and depolarized being, sundered from its absolute centre. But while as a thinker I am interested in the organic manner in which, in these examples, one form of disorientation is connected with another, as a critic I note above all that each path here traced leads to a condition which may fitly be described as *the impossibility of speech.*

I began with a declaration of the dependence of art upon life. In order to understand this relationship in its larger sense it is necessary to make a formal distinction between two levels of life. Life and art, in the context of culture, are engaged in a continuous cyclic interchange, to comprehend which we must discriminate between the "lower" level of the primary experiential flux and the "higher," i.e. the distinctively human life of values, of meaningful action and significant relationship. Between the two stand those transforming agents of which art is not the least important, which perform their function by reason of their specialized relation to truth: in a state of cultural unity it is religion which performs this office. The lower life is transformed into the higher by means of the aspiration towards and the embodiment of truth. Thus art is born out of life, and the values it reveals again drawn into the current of social living, to fertilize and once more give birth. Culture is the result of ths process, or rather, it is the process itself. It has two faces, being at once a triumph—of form over the chaos of raw, undifferentiated "life"—and a failure—the failure to achieve and to *incarnate* truth in existence, and thus to effect the real, and not merely the symbolic, transfiguration of life. Yet without this transcendent endeavour towards the transfiguration of life in the truth, culture itself would be emptied of meaning, would shrivel and cease to exist.

Art is speech, and speech is ultimately impossible when there is no absolute existential relation to truth. The relation to truth which is implicit in the practice of art cannot be permanently sustained when truth is withdrawn from existence. Not only will life, disorientated completely from truth, succumb to chaos, but art which originates from a life which is chaotic will eventually also crumble from within. The instruments of technique will perish, the structure of the artistic work will collapse, drama will give place to a monologue which will end in the disintegration of language, of the sentence, even of the unitary word. The word has meaning only in relation to the Word.

In its cultural aspect, indifference to truth has the effect of upsetting the cyclic interchange of art and life, so that they become confused, merge and lead to a common debasement. The tendency towards this appears in artistic theory beforehand in the forms of *vitalism* and *aestheticism*—the broken halves of an entity formerly united by the aspiration towards truth. I consider them here first of all in their theoretical form. As a theory of art in its relation to life, then, vitalism is a despair of art which demands its subordination to the service of some utilitarian aim on the level of society and nature; while aestheticism is a despair of life which exalts art into a sterile and vacuous self-sufficiency. The vitalistic heresy may be either directly naturalistic and "pagan," as with D. H. Lawrence, or may take a sociological form, as in the varieties of Marxism. Poetry and the novel must lead to *more life*—either to a heightened sense of biological vitality, or to an intensified social activism. In any case its goal is no longer transcendent, but is displaced to the level of the primary experiential flux. The aesthetic theory is the converse of this, in its elevation of art at the expense of life. Life it sees as intrinsically meaningless and degraded; the revulsion it evokes can be alleviated only by retirement into a compensatory realm where all is refined, elegant and unsullied. Life is a deplorable reality, art a desirable dream. Both are linked with hedonism—truth being replaced by the pleasure-principle; and in each case there is a Utopian tendency in the final conclusion of art and life, the one being linked to notions of an idyllic state of nature, while the other inclines towards the aristocratic or plutocratic luxury of an artificial paradise. The vitalistic debasement of art to a functional purpose clearly leads to its extinction in a condition of sensational immediacy. The aesthetic denial of life progressively deprives art of content, forcing it ever further into insubstantiality.

To pass beyond the abstract theory to its emotional foundations, we find in E. M. Forster and in Margiad Evans a very plain substitution of ethical vitalism for spirituality, vitalism in this form being the quantitative valuation of life without regard to the qualitative distinctions which would be introduced by a relation to truth. On the other hand, the aesthetic attitude has profoundly conditioned the work of James Joyce and Virginia Woolf. It is of the greatest interest to see how in these cases an artistic sentimentalism is forced to give place at the last to a particularly gross vitalistic animality—a reduplication of the course of an earlier aesthete, W. B. Yeats. Thus art and life descend together to the level of undifferentiated "lower" life, where the human image is dissipated in the phenomenal stream.*

It would be mistaken to condemn these novelists for their failures, not simply because their condition is also ours, but because of the real contribution which is made by the mere articulation of their situations, in their contributions to speech, which are contributions to our understanding of ourselves—even when it can be clearly shown that the course they have taken terminates in speechlessness. That man is inconceivable whose life stands in no relation to truth;

* The "evidence" which Mr. Savage is prepared to offer in support of these contentions is, of course, marshaled in *The Withered Branch,* in which this essay forms the Introduction.—*Ed.*

every human thought, word and action stands in such a relation, but it may be at a multiple remove, to the furthest degree of automatism, or it may be wavering and negative and infirm, or contradictory of preceding and succeeding movements. These novelists, in the works which have grown from their searching of experience, have declared themselves and spoken their meaning, and it behoves their readers not to submit passively to the spell, but to examine that which is spoken and to relate it to their own understanding of life.

Martin Turnell

Poetry and Crisis*

I

We are often warned by historians against the practice of dividing literature into movements and periods, and labelling them as though these divisions were absolute. But this does not alter the fact that European literature does tend to divide into two distinct sections—medieval and modern—though these include sub-divisions and "periods." At the Renaissance, one world comes *finally* to an end and another begins. The new world and the new poetry possess qualities undreamed of in the pre-Renaissance world, and our first duty is to recognise the fact. We also have to recognise another fact—the fact that it was precisely the disappearance of other qualities, other beliefs, that made modern poetry and the world it presents possible.

Before going on to discuss the poetry of the two periods, there are one or two reservations to be made. The distinguishing characteristics of the two periods appear to be the presence of religion in medieval literature and its absence from modern literature. Now though the Renaissance seems to be the point at which the change took place, human nature did not of course suddenly change at a given moment. The Renaissance was simply the culminating point of changes which had been going on beneath the surface for generations and were suddenly accelerated. We must remember, for in-

* Reprinted with permission of the author from *Poetry and Crisis,* London, Sands.

stance, that many of the qualities we most admire in medieval poetry—its freshness, its spontaneity, its faculty for going straight to the object— were due to the fact that it was the product of a civilization which was young in the sense that contemporary civilisation is old. There will be a good deal to say about introspection and self-analysis in modern literature; but though both have been encouraged by the break-up of Christendom and the decline of metaphysics, and all the social and ideological consequences, it is certain that literature would naturally have become more introspective and more analytical as civilisation grew up. The real trouble with modern literature, with the *Confessions* of Rousseau as opposed to those of Augustine, is not that it is introspective, but that there is no longer anything to balance the introspection. Maritain went to the heart of the matter when he remarked that in order to be healthy, the introspection of a Proust would have to be balanced by the spirituality of an Augustine.

When we look at history, more particularly the history of the Christian era, we see at once that it is not merely a period of time, of steady progress in the same direction. It is rather a continual fluctuation between periods of violent upheaval and concentrated development, and periods of calm and stability. The primary fact of Western civilisation is Revolution, which may be defined as *a sudden re-orientation of society caused by a common realisation of some new aspect of truth*. Revolution implies destruction, and it almost invariably entails a preliminary destruction of the existing order or a part of it, as a prelude to the foundation of a new order. In this sense, the Incarnation is THE REVOLUTION. It involved the destruction of what was rotten in contemporary society and the completion and fulfilment of what was good.

It is from the fact of the Incarnation that any consideration of European literature must start. For Christianity developed—developed in Newman's sense—and finally gave Europe a metaphysic and a *Weltanschauung* which are reflected in a greater or lesser degree in all subsequent literature, even in a negative way in the literature of our own time. If Christianity is in one sense "the destructive element," we must remember that down to the Renaissance it actually provided the poet with his outlook. It added a completely new dimension to existing literature—a whole new realm of experience—besides preserving what was already there. The periods of instability—the age of Augustine, for instance—were followed by periods of stability like the thirteenth century or the seventeenth century in France.

The modern, or post-Renaissance, period has also been dominated by the idea of Revolution. The Renaissance and the Reformation were both in a sense revolutions. Since then there have been scientific revolutions like the Cartesian, the Copernican and the Darwinian revolutions; and politico-religious revolutions like the French and Russian Revolutions. It is precisely these other revolutions that have provided the modern poet with his outlook. The point is that modern revolutions, as far as their effects on the spiritual life of Europe are concerned, have tended to be largely destructive. For "new truth" can only benefit mankind provided that it is incorporated into a living tradition. Revolution is the process of perpetual renewal without which tradition runs dry and degenerates into dogmatism, as we can see from the end of the middle ages; but without the directive force of tradition, mankind has no means of consolidating his findings and relating them to the totality of human wisdom. The result is that the destructive side of the revolutionary process gains the ascendancy and ends in anarchy or in a still narrower dogmatism. This is, in fact, what has happened. The new doctrines introduced by the modern revolutions instead of leading to a new order have simply attacked the roots of traditional civilisation and produced a *state of crisis*. They have reduced European unity to a welter of conflicting sects.

The development of culture is a dynamic process. Until the Renaissance, the power behind it was religion. The genius of Christianity, considered as a cultural factor, has always consisted in its power of assimilating and transforming the diverse elements furnished by the surrounding world. This process of assimilation and transformation is Tradition. Now tradition can be used in a variety of senses. We speak of the public school tradition or the English tradition, meaning little more than the *continuity* of certain institutions. When I speak of tradition, I mean the European tradition, and the European tradition is the continuity of a way of life that was largely destroyed at the Renaissance. Its continuity as well as its characteristics were the creation of Christianity and as soon as Christendom broke up, the guarantee behind the European tradition was removed. It would be tempting to discuss the nature of the European tradition, but here it is not possible. Questions of this sort must be left in order to deal concretely with the differences between medieval and modern literature in so far as they are the result of religion.

II

I shall begin by setting out the traditional view of poetry, then try to show how it has been modified by circumstances over which the artist has no control. The best description of the "old" as opposed to the "new" poetry occurs in Claudel's *Positions et propositions*.[1]

"The object of poetry," he writes, "is not, as people often make out, dreams, illusions and ideas. It is that holy reality (*sainte réalité*) which was created once for all and in which we ourselves are placed. It is the universe of visible things to which Faith joins that of invisible things. It is everything which sees us and which we ourselves see. All that is the work of God who creates the stuff of the greatest poet and of the humblest bird. And just as the *philosophia perennis* does not invent, as great novelists who had mistaken their vocations like Spinoza and Leibnitz invented, abstract beings which no one had seen before their inventors, but is content with the terms provided by reality . . . so there is a *poesis perennis* which does not invent its themes, but takes what creation offers in the manner of the liturgy."

[1] Pp. 165–6.

In short, man was living in a clearly defined universe with a heaven above and a hell beneath. The poet was a member of a community united by a common faith. He had a common subject-matter—the visible world as given in sense-experience and the invisible world defined by faith. It is precisely the certainty not only about the existence, but also about the goodness of the created world, that accounts for one of the principal differences between medieval and modern poetry. The point becomes clear if we compare the following passages from representative medieval and modern poems, the opening of *The Prologue* and the opening of *The Waste Land*.

Whan that Aprille with his shoures sote
The droghte of Marche hath perced to the rote,
And bathed every veyne in swich licour,
Of which vertu engendred is the flour;
Whan Zephirus eek with his swete breeth
Inspired hath in every holt and heeth
The tendre croppes, and the yonge sonne
Hath in the Ram his halfe cours y ronne,
And smale fowles maken melodye,
That slepen all the night with open yë,
(So priketh hem nature in hir corages):
Than longen folk to goon on pilgrimages
(And palmers for to seken straunge strondes)
To ferne halwes, couthe in sondry londes;
And specially, from every shires end
Of Engelond, to Caunterbury they wende,
The holy blisful martir for to seke,
That hem hath holpen, whan that they were seke.

* * * *

April is the cruellest month, breeding
Lilacs out of the dead land, mixing
Memory and desire, stirring
Dull roots with spring rain,
Winter kept us warm, covering
Earth in a forgetful snow, feeding
A little life with dried tubers . . .

The first difference is the contrast between Chaucer's spontaneous joy in "the visible sweating universe," and the mixture of horror and disgust with which Eliot regards it. In one, harmony and stability: in the other, immense uncertainty and unrest. Chaucer rejoicing in something possessed, Eliot overwhelmed by a sense of something irrevocably lost. This is apparent from the details of the passage. Both writers are describing changes that occur in nature with the coming of spring. It is a time of awakening and for the medieval poet awakening means an *increase of life,* a joyful release from the bondage of winter. April showers are "sweet" and their virtue is to break up the winter-bound earth. They bring flowers and the fruits of the earth. For Eliot, on the contrary, April is "the cruellest month," precisely because it is the end of winter and the beginning of change from insensibility to awakening. Winter is not, as it was for Chaucer, a time of death but of pleasant numbness and insensibility. It is an awakening from which the poet would gladly escape. All that the earth produces is a few flowers. The roots are "dull," unwilling to grow. Chaucer is sensible enough of the effects of spring. Birds sing and cannot sleep. Men are revived by the stimulus of the season, are restless and feel the need to travel to foreign lands or to go on pilgrimages after being shut up all winter. In Eliot the effects of spring are narrowly sexual. It brings memories which stir our sluggish desires, but is essentially an unpleasant, morbid state. Whereas Chaucer's is a poetry of acceptance, Eliot's by comparison is a poetry of refusal and as such represents the modern outlook as Chaucer's represents the medieval. This does not mean of course that Eliot is not a great poet, or that he is in any sense an "escapist." He is a great poet and his greatness consists precisely in the unflinching honesty with which he faces a tragic situation. It is this honesty, indeed, which gives his finest work its peculiar strength and toughness.

Perhaps the most striking fact about the two passages is the difference of focus. The medieval poet is interested primarily in *things*—a point to which I shall return—and his poem is a record of reactions to them. The balance of the poem comes from the close correspondence between emotion and the object which evokes it. In the modern poet, the process is reversed. The poem is the analysis of a state of mind and the connection with spring and the use of a vocabulary drawn from spring are in a way fortuitous and subjective. In other words, the poet is not describing spring nor even his sensations in spring: he is equating spring awakening with a certain mood, and simply uses terms drawn from spring in order to exteriorise certain very personal feelings. For instance, I take the lines:

> mixing
> Memory and desire . . .
> Winter kept us warm, covering
> Earth in a forgetful snow . . .

to refer to a state of mind which has been made impossible (so the poet implies) by the advance of knowledge and the decline of religious belief, or what Dr. I. A. Richards calls "the neutralisation of nature." Thus the desire for new life is "mixed" with a wistful memory of a former state of ignorance described as "winter."

The whole point is that for the medieval poet, whether he was aware of it or not, the goodness of the natural world consisted in the fact that it was God-given. The natural presupposed the supernatural from which it sprang. Now one of the functions of religion —of the supernatural—is to *conserve* the natural world and natural human instincts. We therefore find that once the supernatural is denied, as it was, for example, by the French naturalist school in the nineteenth century, the natural withers and dwindles into an unnatural, inhuman materialism. This leads to one of the central problems of criticism.

The disappearance of the common outlook and the inevitable division of contemporary culture into a vast number of tiny independent cells, forces the literary critic into a distinction which looks at first sight like the old distinction of form and content, but in reality is nothing of the sort. The critic begins his study by an examination of the poet's language and style, but it is a mistake to think, as people are sometimes disposed to think, that his work ends there. He has to go on to criticise the poet's outlook and his choice of subject. There is no greater fallacy than to assume that subject-matter is of no importance, for this is simply to admit that there *is* a difference between form and content. The poet's subject, his outlook, his range of feeling are all functions of his sensibility; and his sensibility in turn is determined by the condition of culture and the poet's beliefs.

The problem of the place of belief in poetry arises in its acutest form in studying medieval poetry. I think we can say that the value of Dante or Chaucer or Villon, different as these writers are, lies chiefly in the feeling of stability, the belief in a fixed, unchanging order of nature that they succeed in communicating to the reader, whereas the appeal of the modern poet lies precisely in the felt absence of these things, in the sense of tension from which his work springs. The recent controversies over poetry and beliefs started from the assumption that a definite belief on the part of the poet was an obstacle which the reader has to overcome, and that an absence of belief is the most favourable condition for writing poetry. Actually, it seems to me that the reverse of this is the truth. The real issue is not whether the *reader* needs to share the poet's beliefs in order to enjoy his poetry to the full, but whether a belief, a system, enables the *poet* to write better. In his remarkable paper on "The Absence of Religion in Shakespeare," Professor George Santayana, who can scarcely be suspected of partiality, comes to the conclusion that it does:

> Shakespeare . . . is remarkable among the greater poets for being without a philosophy and without a religion. In his drama there is no fixed conception of any forces, natural or moral, dominating our mortal energies. . . . Those of us, however, who believe in circumnavigation, and who think that both human reason and human imagination require a certain totality in our views . . . we can hardly find in Shakespeare all that the highest poet could give. Fulness is not necessarily wholeness, and the most profuse wealth of characterisation seems still inadequate, if this picture is not somehow seen from above and reduced to a dramatic unity . . .

For what is required for theoretic wholeness is not this or that system but some system. Its value is not the value of truth, but that of victorious imagination. *Unity of conception is an aesthetic merit no less than a logical demand.*[1]

"Fulness is not wholeness"—this is the most penetrating criticism of post-Renaissance poetry that I know. It is precisely this "wholeness" that the medieval poet had to give. When Dante wrote the celebrated line:

e la sua voluntate è nostra pace

he was not making an isolated statement. Still less was he producing the line of "pure poetry" for which Arnold seems to have taken it. His line has behind it the *whole* of *The Divine Comedy*—the whole force of a clear, consistent and coherent attitude towards the universe is packed into the line and gives it its tremendous power.

We may not care much for the sort of experience Dante has to offer; we may perhaps prefer other forms of intensity. But these personal preferences ought not to blind us to the fact that "wholeness," which is always the outcome of "some system," of some beliefs, is an aesthetic value. Nor should they lead us to assume that *objectively considered* "wholeness" is necessarily inferior to "fulness."[2]

[1] *Interpretations of Poetry and Religion,* London, 1900, pp. 163–4. (Italics mine.)

[2] Professor Santayana's contention that Shakespeare is "without a philosophy and without a religion" is, of course, open to criticism in certain respects. I find it difficult to believe in the complete spiritual neutrality which the Professor seems to attribute to him. I think we have to distinguish between a philosophy in the sense that Epicureanism was Lucretius's, or Thomism Dante's philosophy, and a *Weltanschauung* or "philosophy of life" in the sense that some of Shakespeare's tragedies are thought to present us with a "philosophy." The strength of Lucretius and Dante lies in the fact that their philosophy and their *Weltanschauung* are identical, or to be more exact, that their outlook is the outcome of clearly apprehended principles. For the modern poet, one feels, the *Weltanschauung* exists without any corresponding philosophical system and may actually become a substitute for a system. The outlook behind ancient poetry is on the whole *intellectual* and the outlook behind modern poetry *emotional.*

III

At the Renaissance, the stability, which pervades almost every line that Dante wrote, was finally destroyed as far as a large section of European society was concerned. The old world comes to an end and the new world begins. It is true that the Renaissance led to discoveries about man, about the outer world; but the enormous delight of the Renaissance in nature and in man involved a sundering of God and man who had been joined in the Incarnation, of nature and the supernatural as defined above. There is a sense that nature and man are both independent of anything outside them, and consequently a failure to relate experience to unchanging principles which had become perfectly natural to the medieval mind.

It is easy to see how it was that the Renaissance inaugurated a period of doubt. Man was no longer a member of a community united by a common faith. He was independent—an isolated individual with no authority save his own experience. He began to doubt the existence of God and God's interest in his destiny, until finally he came to doubt the existence of the visible world and even his own identity. Now, the great paradox of the Renaissance is that in spite of its worship of the world, it marked the beginning of a movement away from this world—not a spiritual or ascetic movement, but a definite *retreat* inwards. Underlying the traditional world-view was the classical metaphysic with its emphasis on *being* and its confidence in the findings of the *sensus communis*. But this, too, disappears and is replaced by one or other of the idealist systems with their supposed antithesis between *idea* and *reality*. The theory that we can have no conceptual knowledge of the real leads to the conclusion that individual experience is the sole reality. The only thing of which man can be certain is his own experience, and all his speculations begin from the data of consciousness. We get, in fact, that endless and inordinate speculation about man's mental process which is registered in modern poetry. In other words, we get first a thorough-going subjectivism, and secondly a cult of experience, or more correctly of unrelated sensation, for its own sake which culminates in the work of a diarist like Amiel or a novelist like André Gide.[3]

Middleton Murry insists, in an essay which I shall have to discuss, that Shakespeare is the first "modern poet."

"At the beginning of the epoch stands Shakespeare, who comprehends within himself . . . the whole movement of which lesser men were to manifest the phases after him."[4] "We are bound," he continues, "ever and again and finally to return to Shakespeare in our pursuit of the spiritual history of man since the Renaissance. Up to Shakespeare the spiritual history of man—I speak of the West alone—is comprehended within the Church; with him it passes outside it."[5]

It is true that Shakespeare's work marks the breakup of Christendom and that in it we detect the sounds of tottering beliefs. It is the product of a society which was in the process of losing the faith and itself disintegrating, and the agony involved becomes, in greater or lesser degree, the subject-matter of modern poetry as stability was of medieval poetry. Shakespeare, however, does not belong wholly either to the medieval or the modern worlds. The heart of his poetry is the battle between the medieval mind and Renaissance sophistication. In Shakespeare there appears perhaps for the last time in English poetry the primitive folk-element which, though transformed and raised to the first intensity, was present in all medieval art—in Dante and Chaucer as well as in the carvings at Chartres—*and stamped it as the work of the people as an undivided whole,* as the expression of an experience in which every section of the community had its part. This element appears most clearly in *Henry the Fourth,* Part I, in the contrast between Falstaff and the Bolingbrokes; but it is also clear that the old social solidarity has gone and that divisions are growing within society. Shake-

[3] This is interestingly discussed by Professor Saurat in *Modernes,* Paris, 1935, and by Daniel-Rops in *Les Années tournantes,* Paris, 1932.

[4] *To the Unknown God,* p. 182.

[5] *Ibid.,* p. 186.

speare's loathing for "the multitude" would have been incomprehensible to Chaucer, who was at once the aristocrat and a man of the people, and so would his concern for the tragic hero.

But Shakespeare is too great to serve as an example for a purpose like our own, and it is to another poet, to John Donne, who also in a sense "comprehends within himself . . . the whole movement of which lesser men were to manifest the phases after him," that we must turn. Why Shakespeare will *not* and why Donne will serve as an instance is excellently put by T. S. Eliot.

"Donne, Corbière, Laforgue," he writes,[6] "begin with their own feelings, and their limitation is that they do not always get much outside or beyond; Shakespeare, one feels, arrives at an objective world by a process from himself, whoever he was, as the centre and starting point. . . . With Donne and the French poets the pattern is given by what goes on in the mind rather than by the exterior events which provoke the mental activity and play of thought and feeling."

Donne is a modern poet because we hear in his verse that instability, that anxiety and unrest which are peculiarly modern. A writer in *Determinations*[7] puts the matter in a nutshell when he remarks:

> Dante, Lucretius and Chapman are disciples rather than metaphysicians themselves; that is, they make no independent approach to reality, but only through another man's work. . . . Dante [he is comparing the *Paradiso* and *The First Anniversary*] presents us with the *fait accompli;* he and Beatrice are at the end of their mystic journey, and it does not trouble him now. Donne, on the other hand, tries to follow Elizabeth Drury point by point: the problem of how the journey was possible interests him at least as much as the fact that it was made.

It is true that Donne's dialectical subtlety is the outcome of the absence of a philosophy. Donne was a metaphysician trying to come to terms with the new world in which he found himself. He

[6] *A Garland for John Donne,* Cambridge, Harvard University Press, 1931, pp. 15–16.

[7] James Smith in a paper called "On Metaphysical Poetry," pp. 41–2, 43–4.

was a Christian—Mr. Eliot's criticism is not altogether fair—but he was a Christian in a very different and less assured sense than Dante or Chaucer. The famous passage on the "new philosophy" is a concrete expression of the modern outlook.

> And now the Springs and Sommers which we see,
> Like sonnes of women after fiftie bee,
> And new Philosophy calls all in doubt,
> The Element of fire is quite put out;
> The Sun is lost, and th'earth, and no man's wit
> Can well direct him where to looke for it.
> And freely men confesse that this world's spent,
> When in the Planets, and the Firmament
> They seeke so many new; then see that this
> Is crumbled out againe to his Atomies.
> 'Tis all in peeces, all cohaerence gone;
> All just supply, and all Relation. . . .

What is patent and plain in this passage is that the poet no longer has a ready-made philosophy which he can translate into emotional terms. He is on the contrary trying to find his way himself, and poetry is being called upon to perform a fresh function. It is being used by the poet as a substitute for philosophy, or rather the poet is trying to combine the office of poet and metaphysical thinker. What we must be quite clear about is that the poet is neither a professional philosopher nor a follower embodying the thought of another in verse; he is actually thinking, speculating as he writes. The emotion is generated in the process of thought in such a way that thought itself can never be pure in the sense in which St. Thomas's thought was pure: intellect is being led by the emotions.

If Donne was one of the most important poets of his century, it was because he was at once the last scholastic and the first of the moderns. In him two worlds meet with a difference. The best of Donne's critics, Eliot and Professor Bredvold, have emphasized his uneasiness and this uneasiness is closely connected with Donne's religion. For Donne lived in an age of transition, of change from the medieval to the modern world. It is a change from a state of spiritual unity to the dualism of the contemporary world. A critic, from whom I have already quoted, speaks of his work as "the battle-ground between the difficulty of belief and the reluctance to doubt."[8]

This puts the matter extremely well. Donne was one of the first great poets to find himself obliged to choose between conflicting outlooks, for whom in short a choice of outlook was a major issue. There had been differences of opinion in the middle ages, but differences within a single philosophy. From Donne onwards a difference of opinion means a complete difference of outlook.

The sort of perplexity and anguish this produced is apparent from Donne's standpoint in the religious dissensions of his own time. Donne was born a Catholic and became a Protestant. "On both sides," wrote Gosse,[9] "he was sprung from Catholics by the staunch old stock, animated by a settled horror of reform, by a determination to oppose it." Donne had Catholicism in his blood and he did not find it easy to throw over the inherited habits and ways of feeling of innumerable generations. He himself was conscious of the difficulty. In 1615, only a few months after his ordination, he said in a remarkable letter to Sir Henry Godere: "You shall seldom see a coyne, upon which the stamp were removed, though to imprint a better, but it looks awry and squint. And so for the most part do mindes which have received divers impressions."

From this we can turn to a famous sonnet written three years later:

> Show me, deare Christ, thy Spouse, so bright and clear.
> What! is it She, which on the other shore
> Goes richly painted? Or which rob'd and tore
> Laments and mournes in Germany and here?
> Sleepes she a thousand, then peepes up one year?
> Is she selfe truth and errs? now new, now outwore?

[8] *Determinations,* p. 17.
[9] *Life and Letters of John Donne,* I, p. 4.

> Doth she, and did she, and shall she evermore
> On one, on seaven, or on no hill appeare?
> Dwells she with us, or like adventuring knights
> First travaile we to seeke and then make Love?
> Betray kind husband thy spouse to our sights,
> And let myne amorous soule court thy mild Dove,
> Who is most trew, and pleasing to thee, then
> When she' is embrac'd and open to most men.

In speaking of Donne, we must remember that we are dealing with a poet, with one in whom the dissensions of the time were felt as an *experience* and were never merely speculative questions. Donne's mind was formed by a study of the great scholastics and I believe that the secret of his work is the dramatic conflict between the intellectual and spiritual unity of the middle ages and the spiritual multiplicity of the Reformation. The Reformation was not something that was going on in the outer world: it was a spiritual struggle that was working itself out *inside* the poet.

It should now be possible to draw conclusions. When I said that the value of medieval literature lies in its power of communicating *a feeling of stability and confidence,* I was not forgetting that Dante lived in a divided world and that Langland was Chaucer's contemporary. There was tension enough in the middle ages and an instance nearer home—Hopkins—shows us that Catholicism does not exclude tension, though it might seem to in the writings of Claudel and Sigrid Undset. We have to distinguish between writers who were *outside* the tension and those who are *inside* it. Beneath the clash recorded by Dante, beneath Villon's lament for lost beauty and perhaps even the apparent disunity of Hopkins, there is an underlying unity. Their unrest is related to a background of harmony in a way in which Donne's is not. With Donne we meet, perhaps for the first time, certainly in its most radical form, that divided self which is characteristic of modern poetry. In Hopkins, poet though he was of the age of Baudelaire, there is not the same kind of division, or rather the division and perplexity are related to something outside him which provides a solution and in a sense resolves the conflict. Donne's significance is different. He means so much to us because *he expresses for the first time the poet's awareness of living in an age of spiritual crisis,* and it is this that dominates nearly all the most important poetry written since his period. The scene shifts, there are variations, apparent changes of emphasis, but at bottom the crisis is the same. Donne's work is more intense because he is at the point at which the break took place. The unity that was destroyed was real for him, not simply an inherited memory as it is for a contemporary poet.

IV

These inferences are reinforced by a study of Donne's method. Here his relations with scholasticism are illuminating. Donne was soaked in Aquinas, and though he borrows freely from scholastic terminology, he does so not in order to describe a common experience nor to enunciate metaphysical propositions. The language of the schools, the language of cultured Europe, which as Eliot has pointed out helped to make of Dante a European poet, becomes in Donne a private language to express Donne's own love experiences. His approach is very well brought out in the lines:

> In some close corner of my braine:
> There I enjoy and there kisse her,
> And so enjoy and so miss her.

What Donne did—and it is here that he is essentially modern—was to dissociate *experience* from *things*. Life no longer consists in doing something, in action. It might just as well consist in sitting in one's study analysing and speculating about one's own feelings. Imagining takes the place of living. It is as good to enjoy one's mistress in thought as in bed.

In one sense Donne increased the scope of poetry enormously. His work is an intimate record of the workings of consciousness, he is the forerunner of a line of poets who have attempted to explore the whole of the mind and to integrate it in poetry *unchecked by any theological or metaphysical assumptions.* In his closeness to thought, in his power of expressing the simultaneous and often conflicting impulses of the mind, he looks forward not simply to living poets, but to the stream-of-consciousness novelists like Mrs. Woolf. *The Sunne Rising* is a notable example.

> She's all States, and all Princes, I,
> Nothing else is.
> Princes doe but play us; compar'd to this.
> All honor's mimique; All wealth alchimie.
> Thou sunne art halfe as happy'as wee,
> In that the world's contracted thus;
> Thine age askes ease, and since thy duties bee
> To warme the world, that's done in warming us.
> Shine here to us, and thou art every where;
> This bed thy center is, these walls, thy spheare.

Here the analysis of love, the sense that the whole world is transfigured by human love and all else nothing, is mingled with the fantastic reflections on the contraction of the world and the sun's old age.

Donne's century was also the century of Descartes and Spinoza, authors of the first modern treatises on psychology. It does not seem unduly fanciful to hold that the discoveries of these philosophers about the "passions of the soul" are paralleled by Donne's own discoveries. *The Prohibition,* one of the best examples of his analytical power, is a good illustration.

> Yet, love and hate me too,
> So, these extreames shall neithers office doe;
> Love mee, that I may die the gentler way;
> Hate mee, because thy love is too great for mee;
> Or let these two, themselves, not me decay;
> So shall I, live, thy Stage, not triumph bee;
> Lest thou thy love and hate and mee undoe,
> *To let mee live, O love and hate mee too.*

This passage reveals Donne's strength and his weakness. He is not simply reproducing Catullus's *odi et amo.* The poem, with its profound realisation of the interaction of love and hate, is a representative example of the way in which modern writers feel about love. We are already a long way from the simple though powerful desires of Chaucer's time: the mind is definitely being used to intensify the pleasure which comes through physical acts. It was against such an attitude, which was carried to its extreme limit by Marcel Proust, that the whole of D. H. Lawrence's writing was directed. Donne's strength, as seen in these lines, lies to a great extent in his psychological insight, in his power of analysing emotions and situations which is one of the heritages of a Catholic psychology. He is revealing human nature to itself in a new way.

It also reveals in a very striking way Donne's weakness. One of the effects of a Catholic psychology and a Catholic presentation of man is to guarantee a certain round of emotions. With a disappearance of these sanctions, however, the guarantee disappears too. The body of principles to which Donne should naturally, automatically relate experience has already grown blurred and dim. The poet no longer knows what love is; he has burrowed so far into himself that he has got beyond all the traditional categories. Instead of trying to relate his particular experience to something outside it, he decomposes it into its component parts. It is whittled down to a balancing of the sensations of love and hate, or attraction and repulsion, against one another—anticipating, it seems to me, some of the more sensational findings of psycho-analysis. Thus Donne appears as the father of modern psychological poetry, of the unrelated analysis of emotion. He inaugurates the cult not of experience, which must always to some extent be the function of the poet, but of *unrelated* experience which becomes indistinguishable from a cult of sensation.

We can sum up Donne's contribution to poetry by saying that with him the intellect abandons its traditional role. For the middle ages the intellect was creative, was the principle of synthesis; for the moderns it tends to be the principle of destruction. It is no longer, as it had been for Dante, as it will be for Racine, the faculty of vision and synthesis; it is purely analytic. It is turned inward in order to analyse the poet's sensations without any attempt to organise or systematise them. Inevitably the intellect ends by destroying its own object, for in *The Prohibition* the analysis of emotion is pushed to the point at which emotion is destroyed.

V

It would serve no useful purpose to pursue the subsequent history of English poetry in detail. The position I am putting forward can be made clear by summarising the changes that have taken place in poetry since the middle ages. English poetry divides into three phases.

1. The medieval period when religion was an integral part of everyday life and religion and poetry complementary.

2. The post-Renaissance period when there is a sharp division into religious and secular poetry. There are two main streams: the poetry of doubt and spiritual unrest on one side, and on the other a poetry which is religious in a very restricted sense. After Milton, there is no English *Christian* religious poet who can truly be considered a major poet until we come to Hopkins.[10]

3. The third period is the Romantic Movement, which is an attempt to build up a religious poetry on a basis which is completely independent of the Christian tradition. The poet becomes a seer and claims, in Shelley's words, to be regarded as one of the "unacknowledged legislators of the world."

The whole trend of significant contemporary poetry has been away from the Romantic Movement and back to the seventeenth century. The modern poet has taken over and developed the spiritual restlessness of Donne and his successors. But it would be a mistake to treat the Romantic Movement as something isolated and detached. For it was precisely the weaknesses that came into poetry at the Renaissance—an extreme individualism and an ex-

[10] There is, of course, the problematic figure of Blake. But it seems to me that Blake is too obscure, and his experience too chaotic, for him to be regarded as a major poet in the full sense of the term.

treme subjectivism—that account for the failure of the Romantics.

The Romantic Movement had its origin in a genuine desire of God; it was a genuine spiritual revolution caused by the fact that impulses, which had been driven underground and stifled in the eighteenth century, now demanded satisfaction. But instead of availing themselves of the resources of the great Western spiritual tradition, the Romantics rejected it entirely and the Movement ended inevitably in a thorough-going spiritual anarchy. The nature of the failure is apparent not only from the cloudy theology of the Romantic poets, but also from their inability to order their perceptions and translate them into words, which is one of the faculties of intellect. Nowhere is this more apparent than in the famous passage from the third book of the *Prelude:*

> To every natural form, rock, fruit or flower,
> Even the loose stones that cover the highway,
> I gave a moral life: I saw them feel,
> Or linked them to some feeling: the great mass
> Lay bedded in a quickening soul, and all
> That I beheld respired with inward meaning.

The tell-tale words are the repeated "feel" and "feeling," and curiously self-conscious phrases like "moral life," "quickening soul," "inward meaning." They are bad because they are blurred, because there is no longer any correspondence between the intellect and its object. The poet is unable to express what he feels and sees, and, instead, juggles with counters. He can only tell us vaguely that he does feel and does see.

Although this may seem at first sight to be remote from the criticism of Donne's use of intellect, in reality it is not. It simply marks the culminating stage in a process which sets in as soon as the mind turns away from *things* in order to concentrate on its own *reactions* to things. It means that feeling becomes completely divorced from things, as Wordsworth's feelings are really divorced from the flowers and the stones. The poet—it is a romantic trait—is simply exploiting the outer world in order to reveal fresh aspects of his own personality. From Wordsworth onwards, this tendency becomes more and more evident, and we witness the gradual submerging of the intellect in the emotions.

Finally, we have to estimate what poetry has gained and what it has lost by the break-up of Christendom. It would be absurd to deny that the human mind, and therefore poetry, has become in many respects subtler and more complex with the passing of time, even if the gifts have not always been made good use of. If modern poetry has lost that feeling of solidity and stability, at least it is richer and more varied, more profound in its knowledge of the human heart. The position has been well stated by Eliot in his essay on Dante:

> From the *Paradiso* [one learns] that more and more rarefied and remote states of beatitude can be the material for great poetry. And gradually we come to admit that Shakespeare understands a greater extent and variety of human life than Dante; but that Dante understands deeper degrees of degradation and higher degrees of exaltation. . . . Shakespeare gives us the greatest *width* of human passion; Dante the greatest altitude and greatest depth.[11]

Mr. Eliot's distinction between the "altitude" and "depth" of Dante and the "width" of Shakespeare does not leave a great deal to add. The medievals were occupied in plotting the degrees of the spiritual life, the moderns with the complexity and variety of human passions. In none of the great Catholic poets, neither in Dante nor Chaucer, for all his insight, neither in Villon nor Racine, master psychologist though he was, nor in a prose-writer like Boccaccio, is there anything resembling the *psychological novelty* of the successors of Shakespeare and Donne. The loss is as clear as the gain. It is not merely that we have lost all that the close of the *Paradiso* means to us, that other dimension added by Christianity; it is that there has been a breach between poetry and the Christian tradition.

The implications of this breach with the Christian tradition are very far reaching. I have already pointed out that nearly all Chris-

[11] *Selected Essays,* pp. 238, 251.

tian religious poetry written since Milton is minor poetry; but the matter does not finish there. The serious thing is that *all* religious poetry—the poetry of the great Romantics as well as of Herbert, Vaughan and Smart—becomes a special department of poetry. Instead of bringing the whole span of human existence within the poet's compass as it had done in the middle ages, religion seems to be turned against life and to have the effect of narrowing the poet's horizon. The conventional criticism of the Romantics—that there is a lack of human interest in their work—is only too true; and it is a criticism that applies to the greatest of them all, to Wordsworth, as much as to anyone. From whatever angle one looks at it, to be a religious poet in the modern world means to exclude a large part of life, as large a part as the unbelievers who leave out the supernatural altogether.

In the nineteenth century the processes inaugurated at the Renaissance reach their logical conclusion. The poet has no common outlook. He is completely deprived of the discipline provided by the Christian system and by the classic submission to things outside him. Thus the poets who were remarkable for their discoveries about the human mind like Donne, and the poets who were rich in religious intuitions like Wordsworth, failed alike to consolidate their findings and to integrate them into a scheme. They remained to a great extent unrelated experiences. The result is that the presentation of emotion grows more and more disorderly as the century progresses. The great difficulty of writing poetry at all in a civilisation like our own comes from the fact that the poet is faced with problems which could not arise in a healthy society. Instead of being able to use his powers *as a poet,* he is obliged to hunt for a fresh common outlook which is the only alternative to complete unintelligibility. This is illustrated by the work of W. H. Auden. There is no doubt that the author of *Poems* is possessed of natural endowments of the first order. What he might have achieved in a civilisation that gave him any help can only be a matter of conjecture. What happens in a civilisation that doesn't can be seen from his later work. It is a choice between the waste and confusion of *The Orators* and the impoverishment due to a materialist philosophy which is apparent in *The Dance of Death*.*

The tragedy is that modern poets are cut off from their spiritual heritage. It has unfortunately been a matter of sheer gain and sheer loss, a failure to combine what was already there with what the modern poet had to add, or what he might have added, without relinquishing his heritage.

* Mr. Turnell's comment on Auden should be read in the light of the fact that this essay was first published in 1938.—*Ed.*

Gabriel Marcel

The Finality of the Drama*

I AM FULLY AWARE of the ambiguity associated with the term finality in English. It is self-evident that I shall use it here in its strictly philosophical—or theological—meaning. Does a dramatic work have a finality? And if so, what is its nature? We shall have to see why the question in this context presents any significance or special relevance to contemporary theater. I shall approach the question as it applies to myself both as a playwright and as drama critic. And clearly also, I shall never lose sight of what can be called the philosophical horizon of the problem.

Let us notice, to begin with, that this question can be answered and solved by the near invalidation of itself. This answer would consist in saying that the theater exists only to entertain, to fill time, or even, if you wish, as a way of killing time. It is all too obvious that a great number of plays actually do nothing else, and it is also true that a large number of theatergoers ask only that a play provide them with this kind of diversion. I have even gone so far as to say that the plays which we call in Paris *pièces de boulevard* can be treated as branches of gastronomy, the predominant characteristic of such plays being that they digest easily and that they even speed along the digestion of the dinner which preceded them.

But to ask oneself whether or not the art of the drama has a

* This essay was originally delivered by M. Marcel as a lecture at the University of San Francisco, late in 1961. Reprinted from *Ramparts*, 1962 by kind permission of the editors and the author.

finality is precisely to ask oneself whether or not it reduces itself to being anything else than a diversion of this kind, and one can honestly say that the whole history of the drama before compels us to reply negatively.

Yet immediately a question comes up which requires us to use precise terms: philosophers and, in particular, Kant, have instituted a fundamental distinction between an internal finality and an external finality. There is external finality each time one finds oneself in the presence of an object that has been conceived and manufactured so as to fulfill some definite purpose. An instrument or a utensil of any sort whatever are instances of this. On the contrary, it is generally acknowledged that a living organism bears an internal finality which stems from the fact that the links which unite the organs and the functions are subordinated to a certain unity, which is the unity of the living body itself. In principle, there is no need here for the manufacturer, who has conceived the tool so that it will be able to fulfill some function, or for anyone like him, to intervene.

What could the external finality of a dramatic work be? It is immediately apparent that in each and every instance it would lie in the didactic bearing of the work. A play intended to illustrate a certain practical truth, of which the playwright wants his audience to be made aware, implies an external finality. I have said *practical* truth rather than a speculative one, because the playwright wishes to alert the spectator to some danger and to influence his behavior thereby. I shall mention two pertinent instances which serve here as extreme examples. There was in France at the beginning of the century a playwright by the name of Eugène Brieux, who was, moreover, an extremely fine and worthy man, a man who was naively convinced that his calling in life was to devote his creative talents to the service of what he considered to be the good purpose. And so he wrote a play called *Les Remplaçantes* in order to make the women of the middle class realize that they were wrong to delegate the feeding of their infants to wet nurses called in from the provinces. In another play, *Les Avariés*—it has been named

Damaged Goods in the English translation which is enthusiastically prefaced by George Bernard Shaw—he alerted young people against venereal disease and undoubtedly intended to demonstrate the utility of a pre-marriage medical certificate. One wouldn't dream of challenging the wisdom of these counsels and recommendations, but, today, almost everyone would agree that he degraded the theater to a certain extent by mistaking it for a public pronouncement or a type of pamphleteering. Moreover, we shall have to ask ourselves, why this is so?

It would certainly be a serious mistake to think that the play with a thesis has disappeared today: it triumphs indeed in the work of Brecht, who, in the "Lehrstück," consciously uses the art of the drama to abet the cause of the Revolution. This last sentence must, moreover, be understood in an extremely broad sense. For this service actually consists in helping to form a new man, one freed from all the prejudices and from all the wrongs which vitiate capitalist society. On this subject Friedrich Heer, the playwright in charge of the Burgtheater in Vienna, wrote:

> Man must learn to recognize his mortal enemies, to designate them as such and to arraign them. But above all else he must think that he moves and acts a-fresh. The theater will be conceived here as a moral institution in the strictest and most rigorous sense, as a place where new men take form. . . . Thus it is immanently a theater of war: on the stage, the lines will be spoken which will induce him to arms against the enemies of the people, enemies from without and from within.

This didactic bearing is clearly discernible in all of Brecht's works, at least in all of those which are fully meaningful, and it is very strange to see how the French theatergoer, who usually detests feeling that he is being indoctrinated, is held very strongly under the domination of Brecht's work, even if he is in no way attracted by Communism. This was especially true in a play, quite mediocre in itself to my way of thinking, called *The Resistible Rise to Power of Arturo Ui*. Here, Brecht undertook to show in a sort of parabola the causes of Hitler's success. Yet one cannot imagine anything more misleading, anything more arbitrarily designed than this play which puts a gang of cauliflower dealers on the stage. The responsibilities which fall to the German people in its entirety are quite simply ignored here, as if only the traffickers had been guilty. But this work *does* illustrate the serious shortcoming which taints all theater of this *genre:* it implies a one-sided representation which is the servant of a partisan outlook, and by this very fact, it is a representation untrue to human reality. This is the same as saying that the author of the drama in such an instance commits the mistake, I should say even the unpardonable sin, of himself abetting the party adherent.

But I think it proper to give the problem some deep consideration and to ask oneself what *is* the basic objection which any didactic theater raises. I fully realize indeed that I am expressing my personal opinion here, that these are the fundamental ideas to which not only my own theatrical works must answer but which, furthermore, are the bases for the evaluations I make of the plays that I see each week, and about which I must make a professional assessment.

But here, it is fitting for me to anticipate an objection which cannot fail to present itself to the minds of the listeners. It is a fact, one might say to me, that you are limiting yourself here to issuing a personal opinion or preference which does not seem necessarily to have to be a consideration for some one who seeks to define the essence of bearing of a dramatic work.

To this I must reply that the word "preference" is deceptive here. Assuredly, we move here in the realm of freedom, and the reason that one might invoke would not prevent some others from rallying over to the Brechtian conception, or if it were the question of a Christian theater, from rallying over to a didactic or apologetic conception of religious drama. But what is important to understand is that the matter of different standards for evaluation which we are discussing here can in no way be reduced to the matter of a difference of taste.

First of all, it cannot be unimportant to know that from the very beginning, not only in Greece, but also in the Far-East, the art of the drama was linked with religion, and it certainly does not suffice to say that this initial link was purely and plainly broken. When we consider certain masterworks of the theater, great plays, both ancient and modern, we cannot but acknowledge that these works still retain this element of the sacred within. However, this element of the sacred cannot exist except where a transcendence affirms itself with respect to the passions and to the ways of thinking which are inseparable from it. Three examples from the Greek theater have an illuminating importance for us here: Aeschylus's *The Eumenides,* and Sophocles' *Oedipus at Colonna* and *Antigone.* It is self-evident that nothing will prevent the philistines, who are abundant today, from declaring that these works no longer affect them, and that as a consequence they challenge the testimonial which is in some way contained therein. But in adapting this attitude, they place themselves outside a certain great living tradition, and it is permissible to believe that a man cannot disown this tradition without to some extent disowning himself. Now, what is especially significant about such works of art is that they manifest a certain transcendent justice which upon reflection appears to be inseparable from Order or from Truth.

Here again, it is truly fitting to anticipate a possible objection. To subordinate the dramatic work to the manifestation of a certain justice or a certain truth, *is* this not, once again, to utilize it as an instrument, to use it as the agent of a precept which one intends to make accessible to the spectator? Does there exist, one will ask, an absolute difference, for instance, between this last didacticism and the previous one whose legitimacy you have challenged in Brecht? But I think that this parallel or similarity is unwarranted for the following reason: there intervenes in the "Lehrstück" of Brecht—let us think for example about the Prologue to the *Caucasian Chalk Circle*—a party stand both social and political along with the willful use of propaganda for the sake of the party line. And we cannot fail to perceive the presence of an author or, more exactly, of the party which has enlisted the author into its own service, whereas in the works of art that I have evoked there is a universal principle which must reveal itself from within the very movement of the dramatic action without at any moment the intervention of this foreign presence. Moreover, this is not only true for the Greek tragedy, but for great modern works, whether we look at Shakespeare or Racine, the great German tragedians, or Ibsen, or, in a very different register, even Chekhov.

And although there may be something a bit improper and even slightly ridiculous about bringing up one's own personal experience in a context such as this, I should like now, in order to illustrate what I mean when I speak of the finality of a dramatic work, to recall the conditions under which, it seems to me, a realization of the need for dramatic expression grew up in me.

At the very roots of coming to this knowledge was my loneliness as an only child who did not feel on a level with the adults around him, a loneliness which felt the need to populate itself from within, with the result that my first creations were undoubtedly the brothers and sisters whom I invented for myself as partners. However, another matter was even more decisive. From a very early age I painfully sensed, at first in an indefinable way, then later much more consciously, that I was living amidst people whose views on basic issues opposed one another. Let me mention one of many examples: at the time of the Dreyfus case, which so sharply divided the French, I noticed that there was a total schism between the opinions of my father and those of my aunt, who, since the death of my mother, had been a second mother to me. Whereas she was passionately for the Dreyfus cause and believed that the issues should be cleared up at all cost, my father, who was extremely conservative politically, was above all aware of the serious damage that this case was doing to French society as a whole, and, without asserting that Dreyfus was guilty, he deplored, that for the sake of a man who had no exceptional merit of his own, the French were coming to the brink of a civil war. Although I was scarcely ten years old at the time, I am sincerely convinced that my direct contact with a debate such as this one fostered in me the need to reach a sphere wherein such conflicts might be transcended.

Still more significant and determinative was an event of a private nature which happened a few years later within my own family. I am referring to the divorce of one of my uncles, a brother of my mother. This divorce caused distressing differences of opinion between two of my closest of kin, my grandmother on my mother's side, and my father. Although my father was not at all friendly with his brother-in-law, he had cultivated a friendship with my uncle's wife, based on their mutual love of music. On the other hand, my grandmother, as was to be expected, took the side of her son. This situation upset me all the more since my uncle and my aunt had a daughter of whom I was very fond and whom I knew would suffer from the consequences of the divorce. I am certain that I am not mistaken when I say that this experience strengthened my need to reach a certain level where I might somehow escape from myself and from my own self-enclosedness. At this level, I would be able to perceive reality simultaneously from several contrasting points of view, which in life are excluded.

One might be tempted to say that thought, and especially philosophy, has as its goal a many-sided understanding. But I believe, in fact, that this is an illusion, and that philosophy, to the extent that it attempts to elaborate syntheses, risks always losing contact with the individual as such. I think, as far as I can tell, that the reason dialogue held such a magic sway over me as a small child is that it seemed to confer to its author the magical gift of being at once himself and another person. It is true that there has existed ever since Plato the philosophical dialogue which is absolutely different from dramatic dialogue: dialectic seemed to me to be faulty, to be a sort of dummy, in so far as it is a process used as a means to demonstrate a way of thought that is headstrong and anxious to assert itself. Dialogue as I conceived it then, and as I conceive it to this day, has a completely different nature. It supposes that the author, that the playwright, removes his own personality in some way in order to provide a place for autonomous beings and their intercourse.

I have since frequently emphasized that it is possible to recognize or discern better the characteristic features of a dramatic work from the theological point of view. I am referring to the act by which God the creator is believed to leave a margin of room within which individuals can appear and develop freely. I am convinced that a similar *kenosis* is inherent in the phenomenon one must call the dramatic action.

It is easy, however, to see how this radically excludes any didacticism. For didacticism conflictingly implies the active and essentially indiscreet intervention of the author, and in an even more pernicious way, the intervention of that advocacy for which the playwright is but the mask.

But what it is most important to grasp in the view which I am attempting to clarify is that the finality or end of a dramatic work is in a kind of inward promotion which in no way reduces itself to the development either of learning or of a purely intellectual understanding as is the case in the philosophical dialogue which differs from a treatise only by virtue of its form. In a sense, it is truly an encounter which the playwright must bring to life.

One might ask whether this encounter is with others or with oneself? Astonishingly, indeed, this conflict between oneself and another is transcended here. The playwright worthy of this name commands the ability to make the spectator recognize himself in the confrontations of the persons presented to him, and who live before him. And by the same stroke, the spectator is raised to a superior level of being, because in this specially invested spot which is the theater, the barrier, which separates people from each other, finds itself overturned. And thus the spectator is wrenched from himself, so to speak. But let us notice that this alone would not be complete. There is, for instance, a superficial and indeed vulgar pathos which implies that one is torn away from oneself. But authentic tragedy sharply differs from this pathos, because it implies, just as much as the going beyond the self of which I have spoken, the arrival to a superior level of consciousness. I stress the fact, however, that this superior consciousness does not necessarily grow into discursive thought: this is extremely unusual indeed. Let me mention that in this respect there is a profound similarity and affinity between the type of theater to which I have myself been devoted and about which I am thinking, and music, which establishes itself on a level much higher than the pure impressions of the senses, but yet cannot be translated into intellectual formulae. This is true, I think, for instance, of works such as Beethoven's late String Quartets or Schubert's Quintet with two violoncelli, or, in another register, of Fauré's last works, which seem to me to be the high points of French music.

The term transcendence, which has been recently so much abused and has so regrettably deviated from its meaning, conveys to my mind, very correctly, the process which lifts man's thought above the sphere of desire and of ownership, which is the sphere of immediate conflicts, in order to reach a superior serenity. But let us be careful that this superior serenity not be cold and far away, as could be termed that of the ancient sage, for this serenity retains within itself something of the fevers or the sufferings over which it has triumphed, and this is the same as saying that it is, in the strongest sense of the word, *compassion*.

This should not, I believe, be lost from sight, if, as it is proper for us to do here, we put stress upon the bearing of the dramatic work as a liberator.

I should add, perhaps, that this liberation must take place in two different ways: first of all, it is to permit the individual to extricate himself from the *social* pressure exerted upon him by the various groups to which he belongs. This pressure expresses itself in a conformity whose characteristics would closely approximate those of automation if it were not that very often the individual finds himself stretched between conformities which pull him in several directions at once. Confusion is the most frequent result of this situation. The work of art, and specifically the dramatic work, can effectively help him to step out of this confusion and thus to become himself.

There exists, on the other hand, another much less tangible condition of servitude which is constituted by the psychological conditions: it can be said at the start, each one of us is the prisoner of his own tendencies. Moreover, these tendencies are rooted in the distant past. The unquestionable merit of psychoanalysis has been to bring this to its full light. The drama, in this same sphere, projects an indirect light upon these, our shadowy depths, and thereby helps us to reach a state where the personality ceases to identify itself with the initial ego.

From this point of view, it is not surprising that some playwrights, such as Lenormand in France and O'Neill in America (especially in *Strange Interlude*), have devoted their talents toward the ends of psychoanalysis. A play such as Lenormand's *Le Mangeur de Rêves* seems to be literal commentary upon Freud's early works. One must also recognize that both of the authors just mentioned successfully avoided what I consider a very tempting mistake. One will ask, why a mistake? A mistake because the author of drama here again is alienating to some extent his own freedom if he can no longer prevent himself from casting his own characters directly from the moulds of psychoanalytic thought. One sees that the basic danger is always the same—and a bit of thought reveals that it must be extremely difficult indeed for the playwright to resist the temptation to look for a foothold outside of his own imagination. In my play, *Le Coeur des Autres,* the playwright, Daniel Meyrieux, says that he envies the scholar because his purpose is to deal with a reality which will answer his questions. In other words, he envies the scholar because he is engaged in a search which will legitimately admit of verifications. It is certain, too, that the author of drama needs some confirmation, and moveover, I have found this to be true in my own experience as a playwright. I have always experienced great joy when someone, after seeing or reading one of my plays, has said to me: I know a situation which corresponds exactly to what you have shown on the stage: or, I would believe that you knew him. And inversely, if I conceive of persons and situations which in their uniqueness, are of such a nature that the spectators not only do not know any analogy, but even are truly unable to give credence, then I should not fail to feel a certain uneasiness.

Given these conditions, one will undoubtedly say, would it not be best to recommend that the playwright invariably choose as starting points situations known to him from his own experience?

If I am to judge from my experience and from whatever I have been able to observe in other authors of drama, I find it necessary to beware of viewing this as an imperative or a foolproof method: it seems clear, although it is impossible to generalize in all certainty, that the imagination of the playwright tends to be stimulated more by something of which he has been given a glimpse in a kind of penumbra, and which leads him on to conjecture and to divine, rather than by the people whom he has come to know as such. I shall go so far as to say the following: even if real situations as such do not directly paralyze the imagination, the paralyzing action of more or less arbitrarily modifying reality must of necessity constrain it. And modifications must be performed in order to avoid having the persons concerned recognize themselves, so that there be no risk of scandalous consequences on the practical or even the judiciary level.

The essential question still remains the same: How, then, *does* the playwright succeed in bringing people to life on the stage? It is all too obvious that this question will not, strictly speaking, admit of a solution. There are no tricks of the trade for bringing a person to life. It can be said without the slightest exaggeration that the use of any technique *per se* in this realm would be self-defeating. It is certainly more reasonable to point out the obstacles which almost inevitably confront the beginner. As in so many other instances, the primary danger seems to me to be to comply with one's own desire to use one's own creations purely as vehicles for the pretty words in which one luxuriates. Therefore, to speak negatively first, the playwright must be on guard against this temptation. Making positively constructive suggestions, I agree with the classics in the belief that the author of drama must above all be observant. Truly, he must be a careful observer, yet his observations differ sharply from those of the scholar. Some naturalistic playwrights made the mistake of being insufficiently sensitive to this difference. I feel very strongly that no genuine observation can be made without Love. For, in a sense, Love is mingled with the art of poetry itself. On the contemporary scene, I think that the Irish playwrights, above all Synge, but also Sean O'Casey, are among those who have most successfully done this. Another example among contemporary playwrights is the Lorca of *Blood Wedding* and *The House of Bernarda Alba*. These are, to my mind, extremely significant examples for the following reason. Spain as well as Ireland are countries whose people have maintained their identity. In these countries, the native traditions are still alive; in short, the people have resisted the leveling or depersonalizing forces which large cities impose upon those who are compelled to live in them. It is impossible for me to see any one of the works to which I have just alluded without having the sensation that a fountain of life bursts forth before me, and the secret of the poetry lies in the fact that even without ever having lived in Ireland or Spain, and I might add, in Chekhov's Russia, we experience inside ourselves a deep concern for this world of people, so alive and vivid, which is set up before us. At the extreme, this feeling can ally itself to a kind of unconscious recollection, which it is superficial to dismiss as illusionary. For here, we have crossed the frontier between truth and illusion.

In matters which concern me, since I have undertaken to refer to my personal experience as much as possible, I will admit that both in my experience and in my plays, I am distressed to feel the absence of this nourishing soil which has given birth to so many of the dramatic creations which I admire. And indeed, I am tempted to ask myself by what indirect means I have attempted to compensate for its absence. After thinking about it, I should dare say that it is music, the experience of music which goes back to the very roots of my life, which has held the place of a ground soil for me. For the sidewalk of a big city and even the gravel of a public garden, contain nothing whatsoever of what can be truly called a ground soil. But music can be one. It seems to me that music can be an inner soil, fertile with nutrient sap.

I confess that what seems perhaps the most disappointing thing about the so-called "avant-garde" theater, is that it is totally bereft of ground soil. One nearly always has the impression that it is conceived from a café table. I say café and not a pub—which is another thing altogether. This is exactly what I recall having said about the world as Sartre sees it. I said that I thought that it was the world as seen from a café. I think that he heard this remark, and he replied "Why not?" Well, why not? I shall take care not to underestimate the merit of Sartre's best plays, especially *No Exit* and *The Dirty Hands*. He *has* achieved the remarkable feat of reconciling dialectic with life to some extent. And in this achievement, these particular works of his are, in my opinion, perhaps unequaled. But there is the ever-present danger that in the final result, life may be sacrificed for the idea, as it is in *The Devil and the Good Lord,* and as it also tends to be in his most recent play, the *Condemned of Altona*. For this reason, I should say that Sartre, even in his best works, sets us a dangerous example, because he tempts the man who would imitate him to sacrifice individual beings for the Idea.

I should express myself in a slightly different manner on the subject of the plays of Beckett, or Ionesco, or of the large number of young playwrights who seem to want to follow in their footsteps, and I must confess that, on the whole, I am much more critical of them. While I admit that *Waiting for Godot* is based upon an experience that is real and tragic, I deplore that one finds in it nothing that resembles a discernible structure. And let me add that I find elements of sadism in the scene of the clown, which are personally distasteful to me.

Concerning Ionesco, I confess that I find what I should truly call theatrical material only in the last part of *The Killer* and in *Rhinoceros*. It is true, at any rate, that in all this theater, I deplore the total absence of music, and by that, I mean, as you must have realized by now, the total absence of a sense of the warmth between persons and in their attachments to each other.

A *genre* of theater such as this brings me neither the entertainment which I find in the real comedies, so rarely written today, nor the kind of spiritual sustenance and elevation which I have tried to define, and which abounds in the work of Ugo Betti whom I believe remains under-recognized on the contemporary scene.

Let me say a word about the contemporary American playwrights, without even discussing O'Neill, whose achievement seems to me to be of primary importance, particularly the works of his which were published after his death. I greatly admire Arthur Miller, and also Tennessee Williams, although about the latter, I am skeptical of his complexes which seem to me to paralyze his inspiration ofttimes. But, in any case, I am convinced that on the whole, the works of playwrights such as these indicate that they have been true to the ideals which I have taken upon myself to evoke in this talk.

Harvey G. Cox

Theological Reflections on Cinema*

MOST THEOLOGICAL WRITING on cinema has concerned itself with thematic criticism. The perceptive reviews by Sidney Lanier and Tom Driver are good examples. I wish, however, to approach the film art somewhat differently and to discuss two questions of a more structural character. I want first to ask, what is the responsibility of the theologian *as theologian* in view of the sociological role played by the cinema in shaping the modern consciousness? Secondly, I wish to venture a suggestion as to *why* the film is structurally more capable of dealing with the unique theological problem of our generation than are the other artistic media. In the course of discussing the second question I shall also suggest what seems to me a legitimate division of labor between stage and screen.

I

What role does the film play in forming the modern mind? The answer obviously cannot be found by counting the number of people lined up outside the Brattle or the Beacon Hill. We can only begin to answer by looking for the sources of the germinative ideas, the "dangerous" thoughts and embryonic gropings of our society. If we look carefully we shall find this source in the film.

In December, 1953, a noted American artist named James E. Davis wrote the following:

* Reprinted from *The Andover Newton Quarterly* by kind permission of the editor and the author.

After thirty years as a painter and sculptor I have come to the conclusion that the only recording medium with which a visual artist can express the ideas of our time adequately is motion picture film.

Davis was convinced that the venerable media of sculpture and painting had become entirely too limited to capture the sweep and verve of modern life. An artist who clings to outworn media, he argued, "dooms himself to repetition of ideas better expressed in previous cultures or to regression into the primitive, or to being so subjective he ceases to communicate with anyone but himself." Just as the Renaissance artists abandoned a flat, two-dimensional style and turned to a revolutionary three-dimensional depiction of reality, so today the film artist, according to Davis, sets aside the static forms and concepts of the nineteenth century and plunges into the new space-time media of our era.

James Davis was not alone in his estimate of the film. Two years earlier, in 1951, the English translation of Arnold Hauser's important book, *The Social History of Art,* had appeared. Hauser premised his view of the history of art on the idea that changing sociocultural forms evolve disparate artistic expressions, and he excited considerable comment when he called our period "The Film Age." What Hauser meant was not that we could no longer produce paintings or other non-filmic works of art. What he did intend to say was that, given the social structure, cosmopolitan culture and mass populations of our epoch, and given the technological artifices that have been developed, the cinema is the characteristic art form of the mid-twentieth century. All other art forms, from ballet to ceramics, live in the film age and are influenced by it.

All art illuminates the mystery of human existence. But just as not all paintings or statues are art, likewise, very few of the thousands of films produced each year are art. Very few of today's films convey fresh visions of reality. Most convey sentimental clichés. Our disadvantage today in judging the proper importance of the cinema is that we have such a glut. Civilization has preserved for us from the Italian Renaissance the paintings of Titian, Leonardo, and Tintoretto. It has mercifully laid aside the thousands of less worthy paintings that were dribbled and dabbed during those years. How many hacks were scribbling books in 19th century New England? Yet today we stick pretty much to Hawthorne, Emerson, Thoreau, and Melville. We have forgotten their dwarfish confrères. Today the number of classic films is so small we often lose sight of them in the surfeit. In any given year there are sometimes only a handful of new films that even deserve to be seen. But he who misses them, and he who misses the established champions as they reappear in festivals and at film-series programs, misses the artistic recreation of existence and thereby suffers an impoverishment of his own life. As the characteristic art form of the twentieth century, the film not only mirrors, but also *forms* our spiritual outlook.

But there is an even more important reason why the theologian *as theologian* should develop the skills prerequisite to a thoughtful evaluation of the film. If theologians are to be testing the spirits and discerning the signs of the times, then inattention to the phenomenon of cinema as a serious cultural and artistic force amounts to at least a venial if not a mortal sin against the theological calling. The film is a part of what the young German critic and essayist Hans Enzenberger has called the *Bewusstseinsindustrie* (the consciousness industry). By *Bewusstsein* Enzenberger means what in American social scientific parlance might be called "identity," as the term has been employed by the Harvard psychiatrist-sociologist Erik Erikson. The difference is that "consciousness" is a more inclusive term. It signifies not only an answer to the query, "Who am I?" but an implicit answer to the other elemental questions of human existence at the levels of collective order and ethical meaning. For both Enzenberger and Erikson the style of consciousness characteristic of any given epoch (the "spirits" to be tested?) cannot be extricated from the socio-cultural matrix in which human consciousness arises.

This insight is not new. Three pioneers of modern social science, Émile Durkheim, Karl Marx and Sigmund Freud, all recognized it. In 1846 Karl Marx wrote in his *German Ideology,* "The consciousness is always and above all a product of society, and it remains so just as long as man exists." In his *Primitive Forms of Religious Life,* Durkheim pointed out how the symbols and rituals through which peoples represent their history and destiny are closely intertwined with the social structure of the tribe. Freud's work focuses on the manner in which the individual introjects the meanings and goals of his race as they are mediated to him through his relationships to the super-ego of his parents. All three reject the idea of an untrammelled self formed from within, a homunculus only latterly related to socio-cultural nexuses. Such an inner self-superstition is a creation of a kind of philosophy symbolized by Descartes but now very much passé. Descartes may have earnestly believed that he had crawled into the dark lair of his "inner self" and then reconstructed a world *de novo* from a few "clear and distinct ideas" (including "I think, therefore I am"). But even Descartes could not crawl away from his own consciousness, a consciousness that, in his case, was formed, at least in part, by the brave but futile ideology of bourgeois civilization and its insistent individualism.

But what do we do with the "self" concept?

In recent years a theoretical frame of reference has emerged that corrects the one-sided emphases of the nineteenth-century founders of social science. It acknowledges that the person, the society, and the culture *influence each other.* We can talk about an "identity" mediated by the culture, but we recognize that individual personalities share the cultural identity that is so mediated. From this point of view the "consciousness industry," of which the film industry is a part, can be said to *influence* but not *create* the mentality of our age.

But its influence *is* enormous. It is, says Enzenberger, the "characteristic key industry of the twentieth century." He supports his case by reminding us that whenever a highly developed country is occupied today, whether by an external foe or an internal revolution, the new regime busies itself immediately, not with mopping up the streets or with changing the managers of the heavy industries, but with replacing the people who control the press, radio, TV, films, and theater. Indeed, the heavy industry personnel can often be kept on, but the leadership of the consciousness industry must always be changed.

The consciousness industry ostensibly does its business in goods and services, but the books and airwaves it handles are merely its material media. Its real product is meanings, values, judgments—the consciousness in all its forms. It operates in both capitalist and communist societies, and in both it tends to legitimate and hallow the existing power relationships and myths that guard them from criticism. The consciousness industry has a marked proclivity to be conservative, bland, uncritical, and soporific. It drones a perpetual liturgy celebrating the symbols on which the societal power rests. The neat flannel suits of its practitioners are the sacral robes of a new prelacy. The symbol-manipulators of the consciousness industry are the priests of our new cultural religion.

But not all of them are. It is precisely my point that here and there an artist arises who dares, like the child in the story of the king's invisible clothes, to tell the truth. At that moment the artist serves a prophetic function. Since we all have a certain aversion for truth (see Calvin's *Institutes,* Book I), an artist, a film-maker, for example, is faced with the tricky decision of whether to tell the truth or to make money (or in some places to be around to make another film next year). To the vast majority, for whom film-making is a way to make money, the response of the biblical faith is clear. Such people cease to be artists and become charlatans. They are ordained in the cultural priesthood. To make money by lying to people when one is in the consciousness business is a particularly serious perversion. It constitutes the breach of a whole handful of commandments. To lie with an art form is all at once to have another god, to make graven images, to steal, and to bear false witness. The theological judgment on such efforts as *Ben Hur* and the *Ten Commandments* should find its inspiration in the reaction of Moses to the Golden Calf.

But with those who are trying to tell the truth, our relationship is one of appreciation, even when we disagree with the vision they express or the way they express it.

I should like to cite two examples of truthful cinema and to suggest a theological response. The first is the so-called American Film Group. The second, to which I shall come in the second part of this essay, is the new Italian school.

The "American Film Group" is made up of young and talented directors, working in New York and San Francisco, whose films are, by and large, not shown at neighborhood theaters and not recommended by *Together*. The group includes John Cassavetes (*Shadows*), Shirley Clarke (whose *The Connection* made a great impression at the Venice Film Festival in 1961), Robert Frank (*Sin of Jesus* and *Pull My Daisy*), and Jonas Mekas (*Guns of the Trees*). In the words of Mekas, the main objective of this group "is not the question of films being good or bad artistically. It is a question of . . . a new understanding of man."

These films can be understood within the tradition of prophetic criticism. But two questions immediately come to mind. First, why have they not been seen as widely as, for example, *King of Kings?* The answer to this would involve a complicated analysis of the economics of film distribution and the ruthless discrimination faced by theater managers who are bold enough to screen such non-Hollywood films. It may come as an uncomfortable surprise to many Americans to learn that, just as post-Stalinist conditions in the USSR are beginning to allow a young generation of Soviet film-makers such as Andrev Tarkowsky (*A Summer to Remember*) some critical scope, their counterparts in America must work with hand cameras and tape recorders, do their splicing in Greenwich Village attics, and then discover that theater managers cannot use their films due to tie-in clauses with Hollywood distributors. We continue to stone the prophets. (But this is too long a story to take up at this time.)

The second question is this: If these non-Hollywood directors, whose work seems to be appreciated everywhere but in the USA, are really concerned with a view of man, how could anyone believe that this is an irrelevant or peripheral consideration for the theologian? Writing in *Film Culture* about the American Group, Edouard de Laurot says, "Their questions are those of the Psalmist, Socrates, Ecclesiastes, Job, Hamlet. What is man? What is justice? Why do the evil prosper? To be or not to be?" Jonas Mekas calls his *Guns in the Trees* "a meditation on Love and Death in an age of rebirth." Robert Frank's *Sin of Jesus* is a bittersweet re-telling of Isaac Babel's tale of the love-starved widow who prays to Jesus for a new lover. She is granted her request, but then squeezes her angel-paramour to death in her too-long-stifled embrace. As opposed to *King of Kings,* the *Sin of Jesus* represents precisely the prophetic as opposed to priestly film art. Yet, while Sunday School classes by the droves were herded into *King of Kings* and its monotonous teammates in the neo-De Mille stable of "biblical" epics, the churchly response to the *Sin of Jesus* was only a superior sniff at its dangerous juxtaposition of sex and the Saviour. (The orgy scenes in the epics, which reoccur with deadening regularity, are apparently acceptable, since it is the baddies who are being orgiastic.)

Prophetic films probe the soft spots of a culture's claims to ultimacy, whether the culture makes such a claim on the blasphemous basis of a "Christian West" or on the equally false if less idolatrous basis of "scientific socialism." Prophecy is always critical. It always unmasks, reveals, undercuts. Its word of hope is always closely juxtaposed to threats against the groundless self-assurance of men and nations. And prophecy always leaves a mark. When a Polish director takes advantage of a cultural thaw to make a critical film, as Andrzej Wajda did with *Ashes and Diamonds* in 1958, the country is never quite the same again. Repression may return, but the monolithic consciousness the regime constantly seeks to secure will always bear a crack that no amount of plaster can repair. In Communist countries film-makers will find ways to criticize Marxist orthodoxy, if only by depicting human situations that cannot be reduced to formulae. In the West, the truly critical films will tend to become more and more anti-clerical. This is natural and right. It will bother the church only where the church forgets that biblical faith itself is anti-clerical, only where it has allowed itself to forget the creative history of Christian anti-clericalism and to become encumbered in the rigmarole of cultural orthodoxy. In short, we should applaud every effort to challenge the pervasive phariseeism of our culture and its perversion of biblical faith into a crutch for our own values, just as we applaud criticisms of Marxist orthodoxy. We should applaud even when the criticism is anti-religious. Faith is purified and strengthened, not by hot-house protection, but by hearing the deepest and frankest criticisms the world has to offer. Protestantism's capacity to absorb and even welcome radical criticism may well determine whether it has any future in our age.

So far we have been speaking of the prophetic style of some films. We have noted the hope of the so-called "American Group" to frame a new view of man, their struggle with the meaning of death and life and love, their willingness to be profoundly anti-clerical if the occasion demands it. But having affirmed the intention and the courage of this group, we can now raise a question about their success. This is a question at quite another level. A lie in wide-screen cinerama remains a lie. Truth remains truth with a hand camera and make-shift lighting. We stand by those who try to tell the truth in art, even when they do not always succeed. But our standing by them requires us to criticize them.

A theological criticism of the American Group must not be "religious" or "moralistic." It is precisely our inherited morals and religions that these young artists are calling into question. Rather, our criticism should suggest that their artistic mastery of the film art falls short of the demands laid on that art by the power of the ideas they seek to express. When Jonas Mekas says film-making "is not a question of art . . ." he is of course wrong. The ghost of Aristotle returns to haunt even the beatniks. The most passionate truth turns pallid when expressed without the discipline and unity of an artistic form. The form of the film medium lends itself to realism and to selection. We shall have more to say of this in a moment when we discuss the contribution of the Italians to modern cinematic art. The trouble with the American Group, for example, is either a certain propensity toward uncritical documentation (versus selection), *or* what one critic has called an "inchoate distortion" (versus realism). In the "new wave" school of modern French cinema—which bears some close resemblances to the American Group—Jean-Luc Godard suffers to some extent from the first (see his *Breathless*), while the second problem finds a supreme example in the technically brilliant but artistically scrambled work of Alain Resnais and Alain Robbe-Grillet (*Last Year at Marienbad*).

But, to repeat, our theological conversation with such filmmakers as these (I say "conversation" figuratively, since I know of nowhere where this conversation is taking place) is on a completely different level from our response to the box-office spectaculars. Dialogue is possible only where serious statements about the meaning of human existence are made or implied. This is the cleft that separates "entertainment" from "art." Camus is art. Françoise Sagan is entertainment. Cassavetes is art. De Mille is entertainment. I have no objection to entertainment. But when entertainment *pretends* to be art, especially when it masks itself as "religious," then we should object. The orgy in the *Ten Commandments* does not bother me half so much as its re-tooling of Moses into a mixture of superman and Daniel Boone. Jesus was quite clear that prostitutes get into the kingdom of God with relatively little difficulty. It is the Pharisees, the self-righteous religionists, who seem left out. As Paul Tillich says, the first word of religion is always a critique of religion. Our response to the people who use religious themes in the film to exploit human sentiment, make money, and tranquilize the masses, is all too clear. It differs radically from our response to honest criticism of our society and its institutions, including its tribal cultus. It is precisely because the cinema does play such a role in the consciousness-forming influences of our time that we decry its perversion into pabulum, and we honor its few artists by disagreeing where necessary with the ideas they express, or by pointing out their inability to express them with the clarity and precision they deserve.

The responsibility of the theologian *vis-à-vis* the cinema is not to spy out sensual footage or irreverent treatments of clergymen. His responsibility is to understand the cinema as an authentic art form, to expose the frauds for what they are, and to assist the artist to perform his indispensable function by criticizing him appreciatively and by helping him to get a hearing.

II

I have so far dwelt largely on the place of cinema in the formation of the modern consciousness. I should now like to go one step further and point out why, from a theological perspective, cinema is particularly suited to an airing of *our* characteristic theological problem in the second half of the twentieth century.

First, then, why cinema and not theater? The first answer is a sad one. Theater, alas, is sick. It has not yet learned to live in the "film age," and until it does it will remain sick. Broadway has become a circus of musical comedies and star vehicles, some of them good entertainment—but hardly more than that—and some of them merely bad and boring in every respect. The little theaters live out threadbare existences on the tattered remnants of nineteenth century dramatists and on a few of their early twentieth century epigones. Since Eugene O'Neill died, the American theater has been strangely barren of anyone willing to probe below the levels of sexual and political aberration, below the lock-step shallowness of business culture, to the center of our beings where caged panthers still lurk and snarl. And if the theater cannot find our depths, then how can it hope to effect catharsis or hold out a vision of hope? When Big Daddy's earthy wife in Williams' *Cat on a Hot Tin Roof* points to a bed and says to her daughter-in-law, "If there's any trouble, that's where it starts," she reveals in one comment the utter bankruptcy of the stage. We cannot emerge cleansed and quickened from the ritual of drama if we have gone no deeper than between the sheets of the post-Victorian couch.

So celluloid has rushed in where footlights cannot illumine. Such modern writers and directors as Alain Resnais, Ingmar Bergman, Federico Fellini, and Michelangelo Antonioni have delicately lifted the torch of a badly staggering muse. They know that the problem goes deeper than sex. In their work we catch a glimpse of what Aristotle once boldly called "the universal." After all, Tennessee Williams' sexual drifters and Arthur Miller's functionalized salesman can hardly lead us to the universal dimension in man. Of course, in a great artist they *could*. The sexual disaster of Emma Bovary and the political disaster of Richard III become translucent to something universal, something for which the vehicle is itself just that—a vehicle. But on the modern stage we somehow never get past the accidental roles and ripostes through which the universal seeks to show its face. We behave at the theater too much like those memorable communicants at the church in Corinth to which the apostle Paul once wrote a letter. They gluttonously devoured the bread and wine to the point of drunken stupor, without discerning in it the Body of the Saviour. That O'Neill never permits us to do this, though he deals in sex and savagery, is to his credit. But O'Neill is gone, and in his place has emerged a swarm of lesser lights who dawdle so long in some shady sexual or sociological nook along the way that they never guide us to the journey's objective.

But the artists among the film-makers do better, and there is a *structural* reason. The starkly *visual* character of the film allows it to include much more of the superficial trivia without dwelling on them. We catch it all, as it were, out of the corner of our eye. Perhaps it is precisely because of their visual richness that movies have altered so markedly the situation in which the dramatist does his work. We have become so accustomed to a certain optical fullness in the cinema that plays on the stage tend always to appear spare and abstract. A playwright cannot seem to be realistic and profound at the same time, while a film-maker can. Perhaps that is the heart of the matter. A film-producer can assume a certain *given ambience,* a visual reality that is simply *there,* especially in films made on location. He can, if he knows what he is doing, simply get on with the job, making certain to utilize the natural provision in whatever way is most helpful with the camera. Not so the playwright. He writes a play, which then falls into the hands of any and all set designers and directors. They must bring the visual accouterments of the world *to* the play. In even the most "theatrical" or epic productions they still must do this; they simply do it in different ways. The decision to do a play, for example, a Pirandello, on an absolutely bare stage is still a decision about sets. It is an effort to lend a *kind* of reality to the statement. The problems created are almost too much for even the best playwrights and directors. The result is that, although we can still be moved by productions of the work of pre-contemporary dramatists—man will be moved by Oedipus as long as he is man—nevertheless, the reason is that these writers, from Sophocles to O'Neill, had a certain confidence in their medium that had not yet been shaken by the appearance of cinema. Of no contemporary playwright can this be said. The world-view of every one of us has been in some sense ineradicably "cinematized," and we now bring to the writing, and more importantly, perhaps, to the production of modern plays a problem that neither Marlowe, Chekhov, nor even Lorca ever faced. The last named died, after all, only a few years after "talkies" had been introduced. The coming of the "Film Age" has precipitated a crisis for the stage that will end only when a clear division of labor emerges.

At the moment films focus the human scene, its passions and predicaments, better than theater. But why in this new art form of our time are the Italians clearly so much better than anyone else?

Immediately after the war, when we were treated to a succession of so-called "neo-realist" films, it became evident that the Italians were to cinema what the Japanese are to flower arrangement. *Open City, La Strada,* and *The Bicycle Thief* remain unsurpassed in their genre. More recently, in the work of Federico Fellini (*The Nights of Cabiria, La Dolce Vita*), Vittorio De Sica (*Two Women*), and Michelangelo Antonioni (*L'Aventura, La Notte, L'Ecisse*), we have witnessed a whole new chapter in film history as the Italians have turned from their searching social critiques to a direct confrontation with the crisis of post-modern man. As he plays a few bars from a Bach fugue, Steiner says to Marcello in *La Dolce Vita,* "Listen! It's like a sound from another world, a world we can no longer hear." Why, even in comparison to the carefully plotted symbolism of a cerebral Bergman and the daring camera artistry of a Truffault, do these Italians still stand in a class by themselves? Why are they able so to shape a glaringly realistic cinema tradition that in their skilled hands it becomes a luminous chalice for the bitter-sweet nectar of contemporary man's own problems?

The answer is obviously not that the Italians had a richer dramatic and theatrical tradition on which to draw. They did not. I think the answer lies in the cultural memory of Italy and in the special place Italy holds for the consciousness of Western man. Fellini and Antonioni live in a land of empty vessels, vessels which were once full to overflowing with the substance of Western Christian civilization, a substance for which we can now feel only perhaps a nostalgia. In Antonioni's *L'Aventura,* the fickle Roman architect, Sandro, stands on a bell tower in Sicily overlooking a colossal Romanesque church, baptistry, and school—all somehow empty of life and activity. He turns to his woman companion, Claudia, a fellow-Roman, and says, "What a stage setting!" He is right. And he is reminding us that Antonioni already has in hand in making a film what not even the most highly skilled scene-designer could accomplish on a stage. And because he cannot accomplish it, the playwright must somehow make up for it. If he attempts to do this by out-stripping the cinema in naturalism, or by trying to, he will always come off second best. If he does it by resorting to theatricality—to stylized sets, masks, and epic procedures—then he must be very good indeed. And here comes the theological point.

The Italians are able to lead modern man through all the diversions to the terrible nub of the problem precisely because modern man's question *must* be posed first of all against the disappearance of Christian civilization. Perhaps we should say, not its "disappearance," since its appurtenances and monuments are still among us, but rather its apparent irrelevance. Christian culture is the stage setting on which post-Christian man plays out his puzzled existence. The characters in *L'Aventura* walk around and through the silent reminders of a world-view to which they seem to bear no relation. The backgrounds used by Fellini and Antonioni, and even De Sica, are selected with elaborate care. They are part of the action itself, so intimate a part, in fact, that to call them "backgrounds" becomes downright misleading. Christian culture is there, brooding, heavy, silent. The past is *there* in De Sica's *Two Women,* in the broken and empty church in which a mother and daughter are raped under the motionless eyes of the Virgin. It is *there* in *La Dolce Vita,* in the awkward swaying statue of Christ suspended over the city of Rome with no living connection between it and the teeming populace below. It is *there* in the strange empty churches and monuments of Sicily, through which the listless search in *L'Aventura* goes on. It is *there.* But it no longer seems to offer sustenance. We no longer pray at its altars or drink at its fountains. It is there as a pervasive presence to which we no longer have access. The pathos of a post-Christian plot unfolds itself on a stage constructed with another Drama in mind. The result is, and must be, irony.

The Italians capture the fleeting query of post-Christian man by placing him in a setting that asks him questions, even when he is unable to ask them himself. They picture man flitting fitfully here and there without direction. But they picture him against the backdrop of a religious culture that has never had a Reformation, that has never managed to institutionalize secularism as the Protestant countries have succeeded in doing. Modern neurotic Romans drive their hopped-up Fiats and copulate in sterile modern apartments, but all within the somber shadow of St. Peter's. No one is ever very far from the sound of monastery bells, and the church is curiously present even for unbelievers in a way that people who live on 187th Street rather than on Via Sancta Trinita could never understand. It is this irrepressible presence of the ghost of the Christian past that gives Italian films such weight. This strange "presence" suggests a moral intensity that the action itself lacks, a quality for which Bergman must rummage through the lockbox of Jungian symbols or return to a surrealist reading of the Middle Ages, as in *The Seventh Seal* and *The Virgin Spring*. It is a quality that sings a kind of silent descant to the thin melody of the action and provides a recurrent dramatic tension where the story itself no longer can.

The Italians know we must hear that inaudible Word again if we are to be truly human in our time. But they know, perhaps better than Bergman, that we must hear it in a fresh and decisive way, unencumbered by the antique luggage of the dying era of Constantine. The Word that comes to us today must affirm both our modernity and our humanity in an age of radical secularity.

Italian film-makers do something else. They provide a clue that will illumine the future both of the theater and of the cinema. The clue is that they are different artistic media and are at their best when they remain such. Before the movies it was proper for the theater to engage in a flirtation with realism. Now it is not. Theater must be theater—and since Brecht, Pirandello and Beckett, we really ought to know that. The audience for which the dramatist writes can no longer be won by the rickety realism of the stage. Cinematization has done its work. Conversely, the cinema is at its best when it is cinema. It is not a play that is photographed. It is a medium superbly fitted to a selective celebration of man in his real-life setting. I say "selective," because in the cinema the art enters not at the point of elaborate sets and costumes but in the magical movement by which the camera is able to construct a unified experience through a creative recombination of commonplace elements. The act of willing disbelief by which I enter into the make-believe of the drama and that by which I identify myself with the space and time of the camera are related, but different. So let theater be theater; let it bear us up on wings of fancy to that place from which we can see ourselves from afar, and therefore more closely than we dared to look before. And let cinema be cinema; let it hold before us the shattered pieces of our everyday world, until they take a shape that allows us to see ourselves as we are, and therefore, perhaps, to see beyond.

Part V

THE "SILENCE, EXILE, AND CUNNING" OF THE MODERN IMAGINATION

Elizabeth Sewell

The Death of the Imagination*

I

In the north side aisle of Hereford Cathedral there hangs that wonderful old document, the *Mappa Mundi*. Whenever you go there, turning into the cool nave from the long line of rose-filled and swan-patrolled gardens down the Wye (for each cathedral city seems to have its appropriate weather and for Hereford it is midsummer), there is always a group of people to be found in front of *Mappa Mundi,* gazing at that work of the cartographer. Jerusalem stands there in the center of the earth, a little citadel surmounted by spire and cross, and one can amuse oneself by considering the very odd shape of Spain or Arabia, or the monsters lurking in the corners. If you look in the right place, not very far from Inde, you will find a territory labeled Paradise Terrestre, the Earthly Paradise.

Anyone who knows about the mind knows that time and space inside it are quite different from time and space outside it, and the further into the mind one gets, the queerer do they become, as dreams will testify. For the thirteenth-century map maker, the Earthly Paradise was contemporary with himself. It was no relic of an ancient tale dating back to God knows when, but something existing at the same time as himself, though considerably removed in distance. We need for the present this same frame of mind, for it is an imaginative one. This is our first step into the imagination, which is its own *Mappa Mundi.* There will be others to follow, for one can only study the imagination by consenting to it, in part at least. Reason will do what it can, but the only entry to this world is by affirmation of its ways; and if this seem already to you like the death of reason, it has to be accepted in faith as no more than a sleep in a darkness which, after all goodnights, is not a final one but merely this world turning itself in its proper hemispheres of day and night. Without your consent, we can advance no further and Paradise will be Lost for good and all.

What an image the Earthly Paradise gives the mind! There are those who claim to know what it is like. "Men say that Paradise terrestre is the highest lande in all the worlde, and it is so high that it toucheth nere to the cyrcle of the Mone . . ."[1] That is Sir John Mandeville, but he adds, with a curious pathos in so noble and full-blooded a liar, "Of Paradise can I not speake properly for I haue not bene there." Milton, too, is a rather odd mixture of sobriety—"A happy rural seat of various view"[2]—and subtropical exuberance. Each soul would image it for himself, one asking one thing and one another: a stretch of black and white squared marble tiling, between box hedges and rose borders; water in small stone fountains; wild rocky streams down open valleys full of tumbled boulders and birds sailing; sunflowers along the edge of a wood. Yet we know this country when we meet it in others, "a most pleasant Mountainous Countrey, beautified with Woods, Vinyards, Fruits of all sorts, Flowers also, Springs and Fountains, very delectable to behold."[3] All park and garden images, from the Song of Songs to Elizabethan emblem books and the rose garden in *Alice in Wonderland,* have this familiarity about them, as if we knew this place and had only to remember it with an effort of concentration. It is this too which makes the image of the defiled garden so powerful. A ragged wilderness where once was cultivation and abundance brings home to the imagination the vision of what Paradise might

1 *Travels,* Chapter CII.
2 *Paradise Lost,* Book IV.
3 *Pilgrim's Progress:* Christian is shewed the Delectable Mountains.

have grown into after the Fall, as if at the very moment Eve sank her teeth into the apple the weeds began to germinate and grow, as though the hair of the ground rose slightly, and now

> The rusted nails fell from the knots
> That held the pear to the gable-wall . . .[4]
>
> . . . the wild brier.
> The thorn and the thistle grow broader and higher,[5]

as they grew, lush and rank, over the calcined ground of Hiroshima.

Paradise Terrestre, then, this island in the sky, walled in with a great wall as the Hereford map and Mandeville insist, is a country of the spirit, which haunts the imagination under various forms. Fairy tales know of it, and you may get there by going up a beanstalk or find it under the water. Its shadow lies faintly behind the Abbaye de Thélème, behind Atlantis, behind the land True Thomas visited and Kilmeny saw. Science fiction has impounded it to some extent, and you may catch a glimpse of it in Jules Verne and his successors. With its double character, a land at once fair and befouled, a place which seems real and unreal, it will serve as our image here. It will not be, however, an image from which we start, but one which we work toward, with Adam and Eve waiting for us somewhere and no doubt the serpent as well in this spiritual continent, the *Mappa Mundi* of mind and heart.

It is not long after the Fall that imagination is first spoken of in the Bible. "And God saw that the wickedness of man was great in the earth, and that every imagination of the thoughts of his heart was only evil continually" (Gen. 6:5). Practically every time the word occurs in Scripture it is in a derogatory sense. St. Paul talks of "casting down imagination and every high thing"; the Magnificat says, "He hath scattered the proud in the imagination of their hearts." It is as if only the thorns and brambles were to be seen, and the note continues down through literature. Shakespeare's speech on the lunatic, lover and poet who "are of imagination all

[4] Tennyson, *Mariana*.
[5] Isaac Watts, *The Sluggard*.

compact" has a distinct note of reserve. A contemporary of his[6] speaks of it as "uncertain, inconstant, fleeting, deceitful, a very ill and dangerous guide." Later comes another magisterial voice, "*Imagination:* C'est cette partie décevante dans l'homme, cette maîtresse d'erreur et de fausseté . . . cette superbe puissance, ennemie de la raison."[7] The chorus is unanimous enough to remind one of the endless fulminations against Woman in the Middle Ages, and suddenly one wonders if there may be any connection between them, remembering a curious little thought of Valéry's, in *Suite, Tel Quel II,* where he likens Adam to the brain and Eve to the sympathetic nervous system. That is to suggest that the latter, which is intimately related with the imagination, is particularly likely to fall into the snares of the serpent. "The frontiers between sense and spirit are the Devil's hunting grounds."[8] Paradise, ruined and overgrown, yet still one of the high places of the earth, still lifted in some blind arrogance toward the stars, is likely to be a dangerous place. For that reason we had better go forward as simply as possible, making no claims for the imagination at present, but trying to see what it is and what may be expected from it.

"The Imagination then I consider as" . . . it is a famous opening, but Coleridge will not greatly clarify our path with what follows it. We shall probably do better to take a remark or two of St. Thomas on the subject. According to him, the imagination is a corporeal faculty, a power of the sensitive soul; and the nature of a form in the imagination, which form is without matter but not without material conditions, stands midway between the nature of a form which is in matter, and the nature of a form which is in the intellect by abstraction from matter and from material conditions.[9] This puts us down where we need to be, in a border region where mind and body join. That is only an approximate and clumsy metaphor,

[6] Pierre Charron, *Of Wisdom.*

[7] Pascal, *Pensées.*

[8] Coventry Patmore, *The Rod, the Root and the Flower.* Aphorisms and Extracts.

[9] *Summa Theologiae,* Part I, Q. 57, Art. 4. Q. 77, Art. 8, Q. 55. Art. 2.

however. It should be clear that they join here not by contiguity but by fusion. Because reason requires it, we tend to think of ourselves as divided into separate powers and faculties of mind and body, memory, say, or intelligence, and at times we deal with these mentally as if they could be isolated. In one sense they can, but in another equally valid one they cannot. Soul is not added to body, it is infused into it, and informs the body in every part; but yet we need to distinguish in order to employ our powers of rational thought. From now on we shall have to accept both these ways of working, agreeing where necessary to divide, since reason must stay with us in this inquiry, but agreeing, too, to unification, for that is how the imagination works. This will not be a successive process, now one and now the other; it will be an attitude of mind which, quite calmly and simply, adopts both at once, realizing they are contraries. This is important partly because it will be the only way of understanding what we are about, but also because this is again one of the normal methods of the imagination, which is always ready to affirm two contraries simultaneously. By such maneuvers we shall make our methods conform to the nature of our subject matter and so—an extremely important thing in all research and one which is not generally understood—create a formal mental analogy with the object of research from which much may be learned.

If this seems to us like confusion, we must reorder our thinking a little, for it is not the nature of the imagination to muddle but to order. Its order, however, will be different from, perhaps at first sight opposed to, the order which rationality imposes on the facts of experience and on our consciously directed thought. We have to discover something about the order of the imagination, for upon that order its freedom must depend. If the imagination is pure chaos, one can have no freedom in it at all. There is no liberty in chaos, and no possibility of those accompaniments of liberty—life, action and fruitfulness. Anarchy is bondage, and if the imagination is anarchical we as imagining beings are in the same state as that described by Dryden,

> When nature underneath a heap
> Of jarring atoms lay,
> And could not heave her head . . .[10]

But we must not let reason lay down beforehand the conditions of order, as if she had a monopoly of order and only her laws were valid in every sphere. For in the imagination the body must have its rights, the senses and the heart as well perhaps—see how in the Bible, the phrase runs "the imagination of the thoughts of man's heart." One remembers a much later voice, questioning whether Fancy be "Or in the heart or in the head."[11] Body and mind have somehow to find freedom here in the imagination, and because of that, the conditions of free activity will be different from those of the reason alone.

II

"The height of feeling intellect"—that is a poet's phrase (Wordsworth's in Book XIV of the *Prelude*) in connection with the imagination, and we shall turn to the poets as we proceed for help and corroboration, because there are a number of difficulties ahead. For one thing, this is not well-explored country. Even Blake, who knows perhaps more of it than almost any other being, says, "The Nature of Visionary Fancy, or Imagination is very little known";[12] and if that seem too long ago, here is another voice within the past twenty years, speaking of "the imagination, a very mysterious faculty, not yet pinned down or labelled."[13] Then because the body is involved, we have to forego simplicity, which is attainable only at the level of abstraction. Most difficult of all, some of this territory is not well provided with words. Since at this point the going cannot be easy, I shall here put aside any general considerations about freedom in the imagination, and concentrate upon its nature as

10 *Song for Saint Cecilia's Day.*
11 Shakespeare, *The Merchant of Venice.*
12 *A Vision of the Last Judgment.*
13 J. B. Priestley, *Midnight on the Desert.*

such. You may ask, Why should the poets be likely to help? Partly because, according to Shakespeare, they have the freedom of this country and may prove more reliable guides than lovers or lunatics if we have to make our choice among such shady company. Dante for the darkest part of his journey was accompanied neither by saint nor sage nor theologian but by a poet whom he loved. Poets understand by the nature of their art the combination of opposites and how a thing can be simple and complex at one and the same time. Lastly, they have the task of reducing the areas of human experience where language has not yet penetrated; and though much here is without words, it seems to struggle toward speech.

What we need to know is how the imagination thinks. Or, to turn it another way, how the human being thinks with his imagination; how he thinks in pictures.

What pictures are at our disposal? Turning again to St. Thomas for a moment, we find him saying that imagination apprehends only the images of bodies, and is the storehouse of things received through the senses.[14] So it seems as if the imagination's primary material is any one of the myriad objects of creation or of man's handiwork, people, animals, things perceived through any of the five senses, and our own selves so perceived, for we are partially to ourselves "images of bodies received through the senses." We can begin, perhaps, by thinking about already organized languages of pictures, consisting of series of images of bodies. Three such occur to me: the signs of the Zodiac; heraldry; and playing cards, particularly the Tarot.

I wish here that I could burst into colored illustrations, and string across my page three rows of little squares in which should appear Ram, Bull, Heavenly Twins, Virgin Scales, a pageant of medieval blazonings and a reproduction of a number of Tarot cards, so that they might speak for me. Take the Zodiac first—twelve signs through which the sun and the year move, each an image and related to a constellation, part of the enormous picture

[14] *Summa Theologiae,* Part I, Q. 57, Art. 1, Q. 78, Art. 4.

language of the stars, joining with astrology and alchemy which also has a hermetic picture language of its own:

> De ward ein roter Leu, ein kühner Freier,
> Im lauen Bad der Lilie vermählt . . .
> Erschien darauf mit bunten Farben
> Die junge Königin im Glas . . .[15]
>   these bleared eyes
> Have waked to read your several colours, sir,
> Of the pale citron, the green lion, the crow,
> The peacock's tail, the plumed swan.
> *Mammon:* And lastly,
> Thou hast described the flower, the sanguis agni?[16]

From here it seems only a step either to the Tarot or to heraldry, as if picture languages were all interconnected, as perhaps they are. Here is heraldry's equivalent: "Azure semée of fleurs de lys, a lion rampant guardant argent . . . Argent a dance gules in chief three leopards heads sable . . . Azure three sunbeams issuing from three clouds gules (sunbursts) crowned with three imperial crowns."[17] With the Tarot cards also, one has only to name their names for the imagination to be stirred into activity—the suits of Wands, Cups, Swords and Pentacles, and the Greater Trumps, among them the Hermit, the Tower, the Sun, the Lovers, the Chariot, the Hanged Man, the Star, Death, the Fool. All three of these languages had a practical or near-practical use, but they move beyond this, almost as if their users had desired not merely to employ them for immediate ends but to enlist the imagination, to bind it to their service as well, realizing that this might greatly increase their scope especially in the case of alchemy where the aim was akin to magic and in the Tarot which were used for divination. It is characteristic of images in the imagination that they may appear strictly practical and yet not lose their imaginative currency. Take the names of inns, for example—a case of simple identification one would say, and yet

[15] Goethe, *Faust,* Erster Teil, Vor dem Tor.
[16] Ben Jonson, *The Alchemist,* Act II, Scene I.
[17] From Antony Wagner's *Heraldry in England,* King Penguin Books.

one has only to collect a few together to find them also beginning to make a language of their own: The Green Man, the Ring of Bells, the Three White Pigeons, the Little Rose, the Bee-hive, the Elephant and Castle.

Having called these picture languages, one ought presumably to go on and inquire just what they are saying. No single answer to that is possible. To give one would be to turn oneself into those dream books which will tell you exactly what each element of your dream means, a particular object standing for financial gain, let us say, or a change of residence; but one knows this is pointless, "For the phenomenon of dreaming is not of one solution, but many."[18] It is the nature of this kind of language to say a great many things at once. How else can one explain the mind's surprised and excited response? "The amazement is, I think," Maud Bodkin says, "the result in consciousness of relations felt though not explicitly recognized."[19] The response is probably the same to any series of pictures which are assembled with intent to produce this mysterious conviction of relatedness and significance:

> The lily, the rose, the rose I lay,
> And through the glass window shines the sun,
> How should I love and I so young?
> The bailey beareth the bell away.[20]
>
> Nine for the nine bright shiners,
> And eight for the April rainers,
> Seven for the seven stars in the sky
> And six for the six proud walkers.[20]
>
> From the bronze of the maple, from the sap in the bough:
> Lianor, Ioanna, Loica,
> By the stir of the fin,
> By the trout asleep in the grey green of water;
> Vanna, Mandetta, Viera, Alodetta, Picarda, Manuela,
> From the red gleam of copper,
> Ysaut, Ydone, slight rustling of leaves,

[18] Christopher Smart, *Jubilate Agno.*
[19] *Archetypal Patterns in Poetry.*
[20] English traditional.

Vierna, Jocelynn, daring of spirits,
By the mirror of burnished copper,
O Queen of Cypress . . .[21]

Höhenzuge, morgenrötliche Grate
aller Erschaffung,—Pollen der blühenden Gottheit,
Gelenke des Lichtes, Gänge, Treppen, Throne,
Räume aus Wesen, Schilde aus Wonne, Tumulte
stürmisch entzückten Gefühls und plötzlich, einzeln,
Spiegel:[22]

The names of the angelic orders stir this response; so do the Names of God, or the titles given to Our Lady in her litany—Mirror of Justice, Mystical Rose, Tower of Ivory, House of Gold, Ark of the Covenant, Gate of Heaven, Morning Star. This is one of the few places in contemporary life where this language is left to us, apart from poetry. In other days there was far more to-and-from between these worlds. Thus the unicorn, for instance, wounded but blissful, penned into its little pen on a flowering sward and chained softly round its neck by a gold chain to a pomegranate tree, was at once the symbol of Christ (as was the phoenix or the pious pelican) and of spousal love, and no one cried incongruous or irreverent. One is reminded also of the additional magic lent to *Les Très Riches Heures du Duc de Berry*—a devotional work after all—by the Zodiac figures which head the designs for each month. Nowadays if you look for them you will find them only as charms to hang on a bracelet, or in "What the Stars Say This Week" in popular Sunday newspapers; but it is interesting that they are still with us, even in debased forms. Heraldry too, which used to flower so wonderfully, along with color and pattern, in churches, is reduced now to the little wooden shields you can buy at Oxford and Cambridge in the cheaper souvenir shops, though we still occasionally hang up regimental colors in church, and flags speak this language also: "fair as the sun, clear as the moon, and terrible as an army with banners."[23] All illuminated books speak this language as well as

[21] Ezra Pound, *The Alchemist:* Chant for the Transmutation of Metals.
[22] *Rilke,* Second *Duino Elegy.*
[23] *The Song of Solomon* 6:9.

their own, as if their scribes would not be content to be restricted to one form of communication alone, and set foliage or grotesques curling in and out of the lines of writing, and perched tiny odd figures in the loops of capital letters, as in the Book of Kells. A great many alphabets were, after all, picture-writing by origin, and children retain the capacity to see letters as pictures. I remember that when learning to read and write I had a special affection for the face of the letter *e* and was sorry that I distorted it by my own clumsy efforts at reproducing its portrait. "Une page est une image,"[24] and it is interesting that the art which knows this and works upon it, typography, should be one of the healthiest and most flourishing arts in England today.

Ordinary picture books or works that are illustrated are generally too rational nowadays and too clearly divided into letterpress and illustration to speak this language, but it is not extinct, though it has taken refuge in curious places. Cigarette card collections, collections of stamps, playing cards, shop catalogues, children's books of transfers, books of samples of wallpaper or figured materials, scrapbooks, perhaps even cookery books (which children love to read)—all have the potentiality of producing inward meanings for the mind.

The sense of significance in the imagination may arise not merely from pictures of objects, but from patterns of colors, as is the case in so much of heraldry. This is curious because a pattern is almost entirely formal, and, one would have said, intellectual; yet it looks as if patterns too can speak to the imagination by their form as well as their color. I know myself that I am unable to look at a simple crisscross of black lines on white, or alternating black and white squares, no matter where it appears—the tiling lines round the bathroom, marble floors, wire netting, squared paper—without the imagination teasing, because the pattern seems to be a picture of the world (as perhaps Carroll knew when he made Looking-Glass world squared into checkers) or a picture of the mind ("Le fond de

[24] Valéry, *Pièces sur l'art.*

la pensée est pavé de carrefours," says Monsieur Teste).[25] It is partly this that makes a mirror image so compelling, the retention of elements and colors but a neat precise formal reversal of their order. Children certainly, and those who do not lose their childhood insights, feel that they have to master patterns, in figured wall-papers for instance or carpets or curtains, exploring them thoroughly to see what they may have to say. The word "figure" in this connection is interesting, for it suggests first geometry and then number, which are originally concepts of pure intelligence, but then bundles in the human form (in French it also means "face"), a movement in a dance, and a device of language in the figure of speech. You may regard this as the impurity of language; but if you agree with Owen Barfield you will see in it a profoundly poetical and hence imaginative insight, showing that all these are imaginatively united and interrelated. Barfield gives the example of *spiritus,* subsequently differentiated into spirit and breath, but originally fusing both notions. Puns on the other hand are words where the joint meanings are quite fortuitous and so are objects not of poetic illumination but play.

Our picture languages have brought us back in the end to word language. We still have not answered the legitimate question, "What do they say?" but we are nearer to it than we were. If we were to ask now why certain collections of pictures (at a gallery, for instance), or certain types of enumerative poetry, such as Whitman at his least satisfying, call up no excited sense of significances in the imagination, we can say that the relationship between them is simply that of a collection of units, each distinct from the other, and the whole collection quite separate and detached from the apprehending mind, so that their relationship is an intellectual and not an imaginative one. Where, however, a group of images suggests to the mind that it is interrelated in some way, the imagination immediately rushes out to meet it, establishes its own relationship with it, draws it into itself. Why? Perhaps we can say that in that complex of relations and cluster of images the imagination

[25] Valéry, *Quelques Pensées de Monsieur Teste.*

recognizes and gives a loving welcome to itself as a whole self, mind and body. Then all exploration of these images and their relationships, and all further images and relationships which they may engender in the mind, will be applicable in some way to the self and will throw light on the nature of the self and the world, not separately and successively but at one and the same moment.

Coventry Patmore in his collection of aphorisms, *The Rod, the Root and the Flower,* says this: "Adam's naming of the animals in Paradise was his vision of the nature, distinction, and purpose of each of his own instincts and powers: for he *was* Paradise."[26] Here is the suggestion that the world, which was then the Earthly Paradise, is fused with the self which was then no less glorious than its surroundings. And if this were so, the self was united with Paradise in detail, not merely with the spreading geography of its contours but with everything in it, the animals and all the living things and the trees and plants, down to the pebbles in the small streams and the way the airs moved and the rain fell. This is important, for this is one of the chief ways in which the imagination works. It is its nature to put together, as Coleridge points out in his discussion of *Einbildung*. It is its nature to multiply relationships in every possible way, and to accept contradictions. And so there is no reason to be surprised if we see that it requires the self to unite and identify itself with whatever it may be contemplating, in fact or in image. If this sounds reprehensibly egocentric, I can only say that all questions of right and wrong have to be left on one side for the present. We do not blame ourselves, and rightly, because our "dreams are absolutely egotistic,"[27] as Freud asserts and as any dreamer can testify.

This union of the self and the object it is contemplating may seem strange at first sight, but it is the essence of poetry, perhaps also of prayer, certainly of all children's games of make-believe. It is as if the imaginative self had only one approach to everything: to stand before it, saying, with what Mother Julian would call a soft

[26] *Aurea Dicta,* XCI.
[27] *The Interpretation of Dreams,* Chapter VI.

dread, "Lord, is it I?" By the imagination we have this relationship, quite unlike any other in the mind, with the world around us, people, things, anything the senses can perceive. By an ever-increasing number of transformations, during which, however, identity is never wholly lost (and therein lies one of the proper contradictions of this process) the self will be made one with whatever it is in contact with, provided only that it allows the imagination to operate.

> There was a child went forth every day;
> And the first object he looked upon, that object he
> became;
> And that object became part of him for the day, or a
> certain part of the day, or for many years, or
> stretching cycles of years.
>
> The early lilacs became part of this child,
> And grass, and white and red morning-glories, and white
> and red clover, and the song of the phoebe-bird,
> And the third-month lambs, and the sow's pink-faint
> litter, and the mare's foal, and the cow's calf. . . .
> And the tidy and fresh-cheeked girls, and the barefoot
> negro boy and girl.
> And all the changes of city and country, wherever he
> went . . .
> The horizon's edge, the flying sea-crow, the fragrance
> of salt marsh and shore mud;—
> These became part of that child who went forth every
> day, and who now goes, and will always go forth
> every day.

The whole of that poem (Whitman's *Assimilations*) is a beautiful illustration of the point. If we do not know what it might feel like to be a cabbage or an umbrella (open or shut) or a cedar of Lebanon or a bird, it is time we began, or began again. Now here is someone who knows about becoming a bird.

He felt his toes shooting out and scratching on the floor. He felt his heels rise and stick out behind, and his knees draw into his stomach. His thighs got quite short. A web of skin grew from his wrists to his shoulders, while his primary feathers burst out in little soft quills from the end of his fingers and quickly grew. His secondaries sprouted out along his forearms, and a charming little false primary sprang from the end of each thumb.[28]

Do not misunderstand this; it is not an invitation to an infantile and dilettante game of whimsical make-believe. It is an invitation to the universe.

It all depends upon mind-and-body, working jointly in the imagination, being keenly alive to every possible sense impression, feeling and intuition, observing passionately and with joy by means of its five senses everything that is going on inside and outside itself, and ready always to relate sensations, feelings and images, not just out of a vague experimentalism but because of a realization that this is a wonderful means of discovering new significances. Many of the analogies and likenesses will not be fruitful, just as much of what we dream is apparently useless to the mind; but it is the process which matters, for it will offer the reason material which reason cannot itself perceive, though if it is friendly-disposed as it should be, it will receive it most gratefully at the imagination's hand. It is impossible to overemphasize the importance of acute observation for the health of the imagination and hence of the whole organism, and of a lovingly retentive memory. If one's body is merely a thing one drags around, grudgingly feeds and puts to sleep, whose lumpishness and poor face one is ashamed of; if one is afraid, in some strange, absolute sense, of the tiger which is passion, keeping it mangy in a cage till it breaks out in an orgy of destruction until it can be beaten back into its dark hovel again; if this is so, then the imagination is bound to be mortally sick, "for that call'd Body is a portion of Soul discern'd by the five Senses,"[29] The imagination cannot work and the wholeness of the human being will be ruined if mind wars against body in this way, for since the imagination is a unifying agent in all its operations it needs body and mind together in a reasonable prelimary harmony before

[28] T. H. White, *The Sword in the Stone,* Chapter 8.
[29] Blake, *The Marriage of Heaven and Hell.*

it can proceed with the rest of its work, the multiplication of unitive relations between that harmony and all external things.

I might begin with suggestions about this loving imaginative unity between mind and body, for it is the first step of all, and without it the imagination cannot live. In Paradise this unity must have been natural, but this is not so now, and it has to be learned (and, indeed, taught) and practiced nowadays like any other skill and rule of health. (I shall keep till later a discussion of contemporary conditions of life and how these may affect the imagination.) I wish I could speak more clearly here, but these are matters for which language as we have it today has very little vocabulary. What is needed is the patient cherishing of one's own flesh and blood and bones (not confounding this with indulgence), the listening to what it has to say, the faithful helping of the body to think and to contribute all it can to the life of the mind, the long-suffering with its weaknesses and obstruction. If this sounds like a conscientious and solemn Narcissism, I have put it badly. It is not in the least solemn, and one has to set oneself idiotic tasks, like saying, "Some day I am going to learn how to think with my big toe," or trying to discover how one's left hand feels like from the inside. (I set that as a task to my Narrative Writing class last year, and we had much amusement and profit from it.)

A few areas one can be a little more explicit about. Two of these are pain and movement. In this body-and-mind world of the imagination, each of these constitutes a kind of sublanguage or dialect, but one has to learn to decipher it.

> Here's pain, here's pain!
> See by that impress, wind-mark, signature,
> By inmost spirit fretting the mind and flesh,
> By nature made articulate . . .[30]

So too Valéry-Teste has a word on the subject: "Une douleur que nous pourrions considérer nettement et comme circonscrire deviendrait sensation sans souffrance—et peut-être arriverions-nous par là

[30] Alan Porter, *The Signature of Pain.*

à connaître quelque chose directement de notre corps profond—connaissance de l'ordre de celle que nous trouvons dans la musique. La douleur est chose très musicale, on peut presque en parler en termes de musique. Il y a des douleurs graves et d'aigües, des andante et des furioso, des notes prolongées, points d'orgues, et des arpèges"[31]. . . . This coincides partially with something Suzanne Langer says in *Philosophy in a New Key,* where she speaks of music as "a morphology of feeling";[32] the idea that anything as vague as a "feeling" can have a morphology is an intensely imaginative one, suggesting as it does a closer union between body and mind. It is possible also to turn pain into pictures. One experiments with this oneself, wondering what will serve for the one that starts at the base of the neck and curls up and forward round one's left frontal sinus. This can be met with in other places too: "the headache stood away from her, something hard and knobbed, outside. It turned into a stick; it turned into Alxenor; it turned into a ship, one could watch it turning, quite calmly."[33]

The other area is movement, and here the body can have and invent for itself a complete language of its own. The Indians with their study of *mudra,* the symbolism of gesture, know incomparably more about this than we do, and it is this that makes their classical dancing stimulating to an imagination which may find European ballet curiously frigid in comparison. It is not just any movement, or any serenity, but the understanding that from particular movements significances may arise, not necessarily by direct imitation, which is relatively unimportant, but by analogy, as if there were certain bodily attitudes which may be accepted or discovered as being peculiarly suited to the complex of a particular being, object or situation which one desires to represent imaginatively. Dancing belongs here, mime and ritual; so does magic, and mind and body in the imagination consent to all of them. I have found that those who are unable to obey the suggestion that they "act a part," that

[31] *Quelques Pensées de Monsieur Teste.*
[32] Chapter VIII.
[33] Naomi Mitchison, *Cloud Cuckoo Land.*

they should "be" trees or a ship sailing or the sun in the sky, are also those whose imagination is as stiff and clumsy as the way in which they hold their bodies, too self-conscious to undergo such submission. Because they do not love themselves they refuse to have those selves transformed out of themselves. In the same way it is possible to apprehend, in oneself and others, an imaginative bodily response which is appropriate to certain situations. Standing before a painting, for example, one is nearly always aware, even if barely consciously, of a certain stance or gesture or holding of oneself which might make an appropriate response to it, at least if the picture moves one (look at the word—moves) at all. One recalls with love and gratitude the Rilke lines in the Fifteenth of the first *Sonnete an Orpheus: Tanzt die Orange*—dance the orange! It is a curious and significant fact that before most contemporary abstract art such a response is impossible, and the imagination, as body, senses its deprivation and resents it, realizing that all the artist can be asking from the body as distinct from the mind is that it should be annihilated. Its only gesture could be to go bang and vanish, and this it refuses, very properly, to do.

It is by means of this imaginative connection and fusion of ourselves with other things (children go in for it wholeheartedly and, if suddenly addressing a child, one is very likely to be warned, "Don't talk to me—I'm a goods train—chuff chuff chuff") that we give the outer world a plasticity which our reason tells us it does not possess. Caudwell says that in dreams (which is one of the fields of the imagination though not the freest one), we make experiments with matter.[34] Chesterton says much the same thing in *All Things Considered:* "To be at last in such secure innocence that one can juggle with the universe and the stars . . . that may be, perhaps the real end and final holiday of human souls."[35] Magic takes the process one stage further by denying the distinction between what happens in the mind and what happens in the world outside. So a rain dance will bring rain because the dancers are the rain:

[34] *Illusion and Reality,* Chapter IX.
[35] Essay 11.

Far as man can see,
Comes the rain,
Comes the rain with me. . . .

From the Rain-Mount.
Rain-Mount far away.
Comes the rain,
Comes the rain with me . . .

Through the pollen,
Through the pollen blest,
All in pollen hidden,
Comes the rain,
Comes the rain with me . . .

Here is another of the same kind:

Comes the deer to my singing,
Comes the deer to my song,
Comes the deer to my singing . . .

From the Mountain Black,
From the summit,
Down the trail, coming, coming now,
Comes the deer to my singing.

Through the blossoms,
Through the flowers, coming, coming now,
Comes the deer to my singing.[36]

There are strange powers behind this sort of thing. In *A Pattern of Islands* there is a firsthand account of porpoises summoned in such a way; and they come. Similarly Geoffrey Gorer in *Africa Dances* tells of how he saw the panther-fetish men summon fifteen full-grown panthers out of the bush and how they moved about among the worshipers. Among stories of the saints, too, there are those which tell of extraordinary friendships between holy men and beasts.

We must leave such things on one side (since it is not our busi-

[36] Navaho chants, translated by Natalie Curtis.

ness to inquire into them), but not in any spirit of superiority or of disassociation of ourselves from them. Magic and madness may not be our concern, but in this world there are endless possibilities of strangeness, and unless the imagination accepts this, it cannot do its job. And such acceptance means readiness to be united with magicians and madmen, to think as they think, as doctors and saints must. They are merely following the imagination to extreme conclusions, though in different directions. The magician is applying to the world of fact the techniques of the imagination and the dream, and so reaches Sympathetic Magic and all the developments this way of thinking draws from its perception of likenesses and extra-rational relationships. Those who are out of their mind, St. Thomas said, "hold fast to the images of things as to the things themselves, as is manifest in sleepers and lunatics."[37] In each case we need to be on open and friendly terms with them, for otherwise we shut them out, and that is a serious loss, a betrayal of others by the imagination, for the imagination must preserve a loving openness to all comers or it betrays humanity, in those whom it excludes and in itself.

We can move away from this world of ritual and dance and magic into more sober ones, but the processes of the imagination remain unchanged. We find a sober historian saying, "I plunge beneath the surface of my mind"—he is speaking of professional method—"and there live a life in which I not merely think about Nelson but am Nelson, and thus in thinking about Nelson I am thinking about myself . . . If what the historian knows is past thoughts, and if he knows them by re-thinking them himself, it follows that the knowledge he achieves by historical enquiry is not knowledge of his situation as opposed to knowledge of himself, it is a knowledge of his situation which is at the same time knowledge of himself. . . . He must be, in fact, a microcosm of all the history he can know."[38] In literary criticism we find the same suggestion. "The great source of character creation is of course the novelist's own self. . . . *Know thyself* is the novelist's first maxim, and the novelist

[37] *Summa Theologiae,* Part I, Q. 54, Art. 5.
[38] R. G. Collingwood, *An Autobiography,* Chapter X.

with the widest range as a creator of character is he who contains within himself the greatest variety of potential selves."[39] Both statements are direct appeals to the imaginative approach. Within the last year two books have been published which have stated explicitly that they were accounts of journeys not merely through earthly places but through the mind as well: Professor Day Lewis' long poem, *An Italian Visit,* which opens with a quotation to the effect that to explore Italy is to explore the self, and Laurens Van der Post's *Venture to the Interior,* prefaced by Sir Thomas Browne's remark, "We carry with us the wonders we seek without us: there is all Africa and her prodigies in us." It is once again the ancient vision of Microcosm and Macrocosm: "we justly call each silly man/A little world."[40]

Between one microcosm and another, too, between human beings in fact, there are communications in the imagination to be established, imaged often in objects, the imagination's rightful material, but working in exactly the same way. In such a way, the phrase "My true love hath my heart and I have his" becomes a little more than a conceit, and one recalls Donne's spheric geography of his mistress in the Elegies. "O my America! my newfound-land!" Sometimes the being concerned finds the object of his affection inextricably fused with everything around, almost to the point of obsession,

> Since I left you, mine eye is in my mind . . .
> For if it see the rud'st or gentlest sight,
> The most sweet favour or deformed'st creature,
> The mountain, or the sea, the day, or night,
> The crow, or dove, it shapes them to your feature.[41]

The lunatics and poets we have already met; here are the lovers. It is not merely the beloved, however, who has to be admitted to the world of imagination. It is also the traitor, the criminal, the crabbed and timorous and petty, whose universes wait our imaginative

[39] Robert Liddell, *A Treatise on the Novel,* Chapter V.
[40] Donne, *Heroicall Epistle,* Sapho to Philaenis.
[41] Shakespeare, *Sonnet* CXIII.

union, our sympathy and compassion in a literal sense. Keats talks about this in his letters and the way in which it affects the poet, but it is not a professional matter. We all have this laid upon us by the sheer fact of possessing an imagination. It is not at all a case of saying "There but for the grace of God go I," which always looks like smugness masquerading as humility. It is to say, always, "Lord, is it I?" for, as you may remember, the one to whom the answer "yes" was finally given was Judas, and though the other eleven were not yet actual traitors, their desertion was only a few hours away from them. In such cases also, if we refuse to admit these universes to our own we shall find ourselves impoverished and belittled.

There are other functions of the imagination which ought to be explored, the perception of relations, for instance between one object and another, or one being and another, sensed through the medium of the self—dream and poetry are active here: the function of words in the life of the imagination, and so on; but these are more specialized questions, and enough has already been said to give a general idea of the workings of mind-and-body. To sum up: Imagination may be considered as that power, half spiritual, half fleshly, essentially unitive and all-embracing, which operates by transforming the self into, and by means of, images of bodies, and perceiving or generating complexes of relations between its images which may bear analogy to other such complexes exterior to itself or apprehended in a different manner, as for instance by the intellect or the soul.

III

The imagination has been much condemned and much exalted; there, in a sense, we have again that double image of Paradise Terrestre, the evil jungle and the lovely innocence of green secluded proliferation. We have now to balance the one against the other, and with that in mind, let us glance at the dwellers there, Adam and Eve. It is the teaching of the Catholic Church that in these two the whole of mankind was comprehended and resumed. With their Fall, every succeeding human soul is tainted, not to total corruption (that is Protestantism) but wounded by what is now disorder in the proper human splendor, so that by no effort of his own could Adam or any of his descendants return to that original state of innocence, beauty, and harmony with God and with creation. Its chief effect within man and woman was and is that the due ordering of soul, mind, passions and body to one another was disturbed. The lower obtained the power to overthrow the higher, and the result was an element of anarchy within man himself, reflected mysteriously in a corresponding sickness throughout the external creation.

The imagination is a normal faculty of body and mind, one of the gifts of God, and as such was present in our first parents. To speculate on the nature of this faculty in them would have no point, but clearly in a paradise of harmony the imagination could only have been a free and joyful power, binding together body and mind, and allowing each to converse in the imagination's language with one another and the external world, supplying the intellect with material, enlightening the spirit. Imagine the gropings I have tried to suggest here magnified and perfected, and you will have some glimpse of that liveliness and, with it, a terrible homesickness at the heart.

Mais le vert paradis des amours enfantines,

L'innocent paradis, plein de plasirs furtifs,
Est-il déjà plus loin que l'Inde et que la Chine?
Peut-on le rappeler avec des cris plaintifs,
Et l'animer encor d'une voix argentine,
L'innocent paradis plein de plaisirs furtifs?[42]

Happy those early days when I
Shined in my angel infancy! . . .
O how I long to travel back
And tread again that ancient track![43]

[42] Baudelaire, *Les Fleurs du Mal,* Moesta et Errabunda.
[43] Vaughan.

But very rightly that is called *The Retreat*. The longing is not to be denied; it is in every imagining heart, every artist, every poet—how often explicitly in these last: "The Nature of my Work is Visionary or Imaginative; it is an Endeavour to Restore what the Ancients call'd the Golden Age";[44] "C'est vrai, c'est à l'Eden que je songeais";[45] "Oh, from wide circuit shall at length I see / Pure daybreak lighten again on Eden's tree?"[46] It is no use pretending, however, that with the Fall behind us the imagination is not, like all man's other powers, liable to corruption and disease and death. If this seems terrible, as it does to me who love the imagination dearly, and who over the last few pages have given myself the happiness of imagining its working as if it were free of itself to grow and blossom, this pain has to be accepted, with the knowledge that one cannot any more traverse *Mappa Mundi* and jump up so that one's chin overhangs Paradise wall and one can see what is there; or if one did, one would see the nettles because they would be in one's own envisioning sight.

The wall round Paradise—it is there now to keep us out; but it may have lasted from Adam's time, giving him originally his necessary circumscription, for he was human and not angelic or divine and so would have needed the reassuring sense of due and freely chosen limitation which all human liberty and activity require. His ejection from the walled garden into the wastes and infinities of space was not a liberation.

> Adam lay yboundin, boundin in a bond,
> Foure thousand winter thought he not to long,

and anyone with an imagination, born where he was mentally and spiritually to fend for himself, knows all those four thousand years, the attempts to tame the imagination in league with the body and the passions against his bewildered spirit, trying everything by turns, total suppression, magic, appeasement, license, in an effort

[44] Blake, *Vision of the Last Judgment.*
[45] Rimbaud, *Une Saison en Enfer,* L'Impossible.
[46] Walter de la Mare, *The Exile.*

to bring his disintegrated inner universe to order. The imagination has its martyrs—Rimbaud surely among them—just as it has its abjurors and its hedonists; but none of these are what we are after. For the imagination has every right to ask, not for annihilation or cosseting, but for conditions in which it may take its proper place in the human *Mappa Mundi*. Integrity, that truly heavenly quality, can only be found if the body, the imagination, the mind and heart and soul are not merely at peace but actively loving and cooperating with one another. It is Emerson who says "Imagination is not a talent of some men but is the health of every man."[47] I am not claiming that one must be perfected in all natural parts before one can get to heaven; the sick and the halt and the maimed and the blind will, one knows, get there safely. Yet given this talent—and surely most people are imaginative, for how rare it is to find a completely unimaginative child!—one has a responsibility toward it.

So far I have been discussing the general conditions of imaginative processes. No imagination, however, can in fact operate except in the given conditions of its day and place, and we had better consider next the conditions in which our imaginations have to work here and now. I shall deal only with the countries I know, England and the United States; they make a reasonably well-matched pair to handle, since they are related in culture and background, share more or less of a common language, exchange their productions culturally and commercially, have the same general ideas in politics and education, and are both predominantly Protestant. Where does the imagination stand in these two places, and is it free, happy, and doing its job?

At once a rather strange thing happens. One has the impression that the imagination has vanished. Where on earth can it have gone? Into the practical world of hard fact, buying and selling, real estate, weekly wage-earning, stocks and shares? Into the acts and speeches of party politicians, into foreign policies, the British or American Way of Life? Into churches, so many, so sober and so socially minded? It is hard to see it at work in any of these. One

[47] *Letters and Social Aims:* Imagination and Poetry.

goes on to the sexy advertisements (which, though they are creeping into Britain, still astound the traveler arriving in America for the first time), to television and radio, comic strips and books, popular songs, the things people read—magazines, Westerns, love stories, thrillers, science fiction; the books English children read, about nothing but horses or gangs of children acting as detectives and recovering the stolen plans, etc.; I'm not sure what they read in America—Hopalong Cassidy? Baseball stories? At the end of it all one asks oneself what the imagination can be doing in the midst of all this.

The answer is, I believe, that the imagination is at present in a very bad way indeed. It receives no direct and disinterested encouragement from anyone, no proper food, no love. The fields in which it should be most at home, education, scholarship, art, some religious forms, are either arrayed against it or are suspect in the eyes of the general public. An idealist nowadays is "starry-eyed"; art is an "ivory tower," poetry is "sissy" or, in England, vaguely indecent as is religion—which is "all right if kept in its proper place." In America those who pursue the intellectual life are likely to be called "eggheads"; in England they are "highbrows." The word "academic" is a derogatory epithet in English Civil Service parlance, while in academic circles themselves a scholar showing a developed imagination may find himself labeled "unsound." Now look at all those terms. They are all imaginative, metaphors, thinking in pictures. In such a way the imagination is taught to decry itself in its own terms, as if the image in the mirror were taught to spit at the living face it reflects, so that those who exploit the imagination by easy metaphor (compare "the Iron Curtain" with its complacent acquiescence in division between East and West, and all the devices of propaganda and persuasion) can continue to do so unchallenged.

The progressive abandonment of the imagination begins in childhood. In England if a child is to have the "grammar school" type of education, there will be neither time nor place for imaginative occupations or ways of thought. They will be crowded out by irregular verbs, the terms of the Treaty of Cateau Cambrésis or the Statute of Praemunire, logarithms, the missionary journeys of St. Paul, the overwhelming need to prepare for and excel in a series of examinations. There will be organized games in the afternoons, school prayers in the mornings, and, at boarding school, chapel probably twice on Sundays. Art, singing, dramatics will be a half-casual distraction from real work, and time for them will decrease as the pressure of examinations increases. Dancing and music will be extras, and a large number of parents will be unable or unwilling to pay for them. There are brighter moments; one may be encouraged to read the Bible, and if one is lucky, the teaching of literature may be a refreshment. The worst of the system is that nothing connects, and nobody minds provided the school successes in University entrance and in interschool matches are kept up. The University can then carry on with the process, caring for nothing but the detached intellect and developing this in isolation from the whole of the rest of the personality, with results unfortunate in men but disastrous in women. In other types of schools the process is a little different. At experimental schools the child will probably be delayed far longer at the level of "constructive play" with water, sand and so on, with reading and writing postponed, and activities are likely to be emphasized rather than scholarship, as in many American schools. In other types of secondary education, you may learn your trade, or be engaged on Projects—"Our Town," perhaps, or "Parliament—How It Works"—but there will be no connection, no realization that the perfunctory prayers and the carpentry and homemaking and the odd spells of elementary biology and literature can join up.

I am obviously much less familiar with American education, and can only speak here from general impressions. These lead one to suppose that many schools are principally concerned with turning out a nation of young extroverts, boys and girls who are socially adept and popular, who can speak up for themselves, are independent, practical and friendly. The value of schooling seems to be assessed largely on "social cooperation" or "extracurricular activities" and "leadership." Noise, movement, excitement and a busy social life leave no opportunity whatever for the individual to have any solitude, and the desire for it is regarded as a bad sign.

I am generalizing, of course, and all generalizations are to some extent distortions, but it is near enough to the mark for my purpose. The results in each case are interesting. The English system turns us, as Newman points out,[48] into beings who are proud, bashful and reserved, whose sense of self-respect leads them "to paint a smooth and perfect surface, so as to be able to say to themselves that they have done their duty." The American system produces the apparent contrary, beings who are externally self-confident, ready to rush in anywhere, hail-fellow-well-met, worshiping youthfulness. It is our apparent oppositeness which makes us so often intensely irritating to one another. Yet despite this irritation we draw closer and closer together, bound not by love and understanding of our proper differences but by a perhaps unconscious recognition of our similarity, our common need, the need to stanch somehow the thirst and vacuum of the imagination we both suffer from. This is our real meeting ground, a great vacuum of intellectual and spiritual resourcelessness.

There is something immensely pathetic and touching in the way in which we mutually attempt to satisfy one another's thirst in the imagination, though in ways which can only be unsatisfying. (The fact that these ways are also commercially profitable is part of the judgment upon us both.) The United States sends us Hollywood movies, nearly all our popular songs, jazz and musicals, types of television programs and styles of advertising. We send the United States our best ballet and Shakespearean companies, old silver and antique furniture, and the Royal Family news and the Coronation. Put in more general terms, America sends us her own concept of Romantic Love, as false to reality as it is to the truths of mind and heart; and we export to America relics of a splendor which was once a living part of our national existence but is now little more

[48] *On the Scope and Nature of University Education,* Discourse VII.

than a carefully preserved artificiality, and as foreign as America's product to genuine feeling and thinking.

It is the same story over again—nothing connects. But the imagination cannot live upon disconnection. Naturally any part of the human organism suffers if it is isolated, but body and mind can get along in a state of civil war, though it is a fearful drain on their energy and life. The imagination, however, can work only by putting together; it has no other mode of operation. Consequently all the food that is offered to it which splits mind and body is useless to it, and under pretense of nourishment merely increases the hunger, as, I believe, do certain types of rat poison. De Rougemont in *Love in the Western World* says, "When the distinction between mind and body took the place of the separation of mind from believing soul, the result was to divide a human being into intelligence and sex." This is exactly what seems to have happened to us.

Let us take a general look at the American product first. Romantic love is used as the cover for sex in nearly every case. Where products are to be sold, the advertisers will do their best to link them with an appeal to sex, but will do it by suggesting that "love" and marriage will never come the way of those who do not employ the product in question. The most suggestive movie poster will usually claim to be advertising a "love" story, and Hollywood itself has become the center of this cult of "love" and "marriage," promiscuity being covered up by a would-be respectable facade of divorces and remarriages. In magazine writing, romantic love is practically the only acceptable theme—"boy meets girl," "she married her boss," the tabloid plots. There is no connection in these fields between the mind and the body; the former is excluded, and the imagination, which is thus deprived of half its proper orientation, is left only with sentimental "feelings" which are not satisfying to it, or with the suggestions of bodily passion to which it is only too liable to succumb. It fares no better with science fiction and thrillers. These make some slight claim to engage the intelligence, the former with technical detail, the latter with the detection. In each case, "love interest" will almost certainly be added, and there will be equally certainly a great deal of violence, which is, after all, only bodily passion assuming a slightly different form in its desperate isolation; for in stories of this type the faculties of mind and body do not really coalesce at all. Science fiction with its obsession with brutality and its complete divorce from normal life is merely De Rougemont's intelligence and sex in another form. The healthy imagination does not work with supermen and space ships and robots with electronic brains; it has to work very humbly, with its own halting brain and its own unglamorous limbs and the little circle of the world it can see and feel. The passion of science fiction for superhuman strength and power and speed, for scientific mastery over the elements and over space itself is diabolical, a temptation to the imagination to launch into those high places in which it has no place, in a megalomaniac arrogance which destroys itself, as is evident in the essential paucity of invention or originality in this class of work. It is also dangerous for the young. One sees how this and the other types of communication we have been discussing connect with the problem of juvenile delinquency, and the growing suggestion that it is closely linked with illiteracy. A sense of mental inadequacy and a frustrated imagination are appallingly dangerous, and the consequences of both in self-assertion at the level of sex or violence are before our eyes.

This violence, working much of the time behind a stalking horse of sentimentality, is particularly characteristic of America, and springs in part at least from her excess of vitality. In England our ways are on the whole more gentle, and this, like America's violence, is both weakness and strength. We seem to offer at present the curious spectacle of a traditionalism which, aesthetically and externally, retains its outward splendor, yet is sapped of the vigor of life, of mind and body, necessary to sustain it. At the moment the Monarchy is the principal export in this class. I mean no disloyalty, but it is significant how many English people at the moment feel some profound if inarticulate discomfort about it. There are very queer undertones—the way the popular women's magazines dwell to saturation point on details of the Queen's private and married life, the really distasteful intimacy (distasteful when directed toward anyone, not merely royalty) of tone in which she is written or spoken about in public; the way in which she is mobbed, reminding one of the crowds of hysterical women who wait hours in the rain to gloat over the bride at a big Society wedding. All this talk of "New Elizabethans" has the same curious flavor, like an old man regretfully remembering the wild oats of his youth but supposing that his collection of keepsakes and tokens can compensate him for his unwelcome old age. The intellect has no part here, which is perhaps why no good poetry has been written on the Coronation, nor is likely to be, and the imagination is fed upon hollow ceremony and fine words.

It is a strange situation on both sides. The Americans call us decadent. We call the Americans crude vulgarians. Yet each laps up the other's product, Hollywood fills our screens and Radio City comes out of our wireless half the day, while the Coronation sweeps America. Yet each is a mockery as far as the imagination is concerned, a travesty of true love and true splendor, and, since mind and body cannot work together in either, the imagination hungers still.

The same disconnection, baffling the imaginative powers, can be seen in poetry, painting and music. Blake calls those "the three Powers in Man of conversing with Paradise, which the flood did not sweep away."[49] Are we, through these, conversing with Paradise? In each we see, at the top of the scale, an extreme cult of the abstract and intellectually difficult, naturally inimical to the body—which to sheer abstraction is an obstacle and a burden. Think of the intellectual nature of most modern music, the obscurity of modern poetry, the profusion of abstracts in painting and sculpture. Then at the other end of the scale consider what there is. I do not mean Surrealism which is only intellectualism in a mirror, but the art people really live with. In art the other end of the scale is pin-up girls, postcards, comic strips, and in poetry and music it is the cur-

[49] *Vision of the Last Judgment.*

rent popular numbers on the radio and phonograph. The logical response to the Museum of Abstract Art is the collection of smutty books one can buy for a dime or a quarter a time in the next-door drug store, or its equivalent in little stationers and railway bookstalls in England. The response to Bartok and Schönberg is the crooner, and the response to the obscure poetry is one after another of the monotonous little ditties which go with the sensual and sentimental music:

> Night and day
> You are the one;
> Only you beneath the moon and under the sun . . .[50]

> When the poppies bloom again,
> I'll remember you . . .[51]

> You must realize,
> When your heart's on fire,
> Smoke gets in your eyes . . .[52]

(Forgive me, my knowledge of popular songs is twenty years out of date; but the genre does not change.) This is what the imagination finds itself stuffed with, false images that mock heart and mind, and lead only to boredom. How significant it is that the cry of "ennui" as a perpetually recurring sickness to be fought off comes first, in European literature, from Voltaire, in that eighteenth century which really began to see the results of the division into the scientific intellect and sensuality, with the cult of sensibility in the middle. Boredom, false sentiment, and both a thin skin over some profound imaginative and bodily malaise—you find this also in the imaginative works in literature during the last century or so, with a few exceptions such as *Moby Dick*. The sickness is there in Hans Andersen, and children smell it out and are frightened by his work. It is there in the *Hunting of the Snark*. You can sense it in Oscar

[50] Copyright 1932 by Harms, Inc.

[51] Copyright 1936 by the Irwin Dash Music Co., Ltd. by permission of Shapiro, Bernstein & Co., Inc.

[52] *Smoke Gets in Your Eyes,* Copyright 1933 by T. B. Harms Company. Used by permission.

Wilde's fairy tales, it is stamped all over *Peter Pan* and the cult of childhood, and lurks in a darker form in the imaginative works of C. S. Lewis and the poetry and novels of Charles Williams. De Quincey, Poe, De Nerval, Baudelaire, Lautréamont, Nietzsche, Kafka—the list could go on and on. No matter at what level, the starved imagination is likely to run after aberrations. Among the literary it has tended to be drugs, alcohol or madness, as compensation or illusory satisfaction for the imagination's thirst for the love and splendor which are denied it except in ersatz form. Among ordinary people the imagination runs in a different direction, and because it is deprived of the exercise of love and splendor within itself it will pursue those who seem in themselves to embody it. The only types it knows, however, are those false types we have discussed above, and so you find what you might expect and what you can deduce from the pages of any popular newspaper, a cult, which may become hysterical, of the Royal Family, stars of stage, screen, radio, and television (and those of sport which has its *mystique* in both our countries, founded on bodily and strictly vicarious glory) and spectacular criminals of the violent type.

If we draw breath here to see what has brought the imagination to such a plight and how its world, inside and out, has come to be broken into such an array of fragments, I think of one or two things.

In the second *Studierzimmer* scene of *Faust,* Part I, Goethe puts into Faust's mouth a great curse on all those things which in his eyes falsely enmesh the spirit, keeping it from the heights of power and knowledge. The curse ends so:

> Fluch sei der Hoffnung! Fluch dem Glauben!
> Und Fluch vor allen der Geduld!
> (Accursed be hope! Accursed be belief!
> And accursed above all be patience!)

There follows immediately a chorus of spirits, bewailing Faust's action, for they say that he has destroyed the beautiful world—"Ein Halbgott hat sie zerschlagen"—a demigod has broken it to bits. They then adjure him to build it again, better and more beautiful than before, in his own breast. Faust is one of the great types of modern man (he is sixteenth-century, remember), and here is W. H. Auden commenting on this very destruction from which so much was hoped: "When the break came, it was drastic. Luther denied any intelligible relation between Faith and Works, Machiavelli any intelligible relation between private and public morality, and Descartes any intelligible relation between Matter and Mind. Allegory became impossible as a literary form, and the human Amor seemed no longer a parable of the Divine Love but its blasphemous parody."[53] Renaissance and Reformation have produced vast achievement: these are to be held in mind if we talk about the imagination and the Church, for polemic is never the task of the imagination, and I hold in mind these achievements too, as well as the Church's failings. Yet the sober historical fact remains—our current imaginative disintegration has to be accounted for, and from the Renaissance and Reformation we emerged "every man his own priest"; divided into nation states; art and learning secularized; the seven Liberal Arts abandoned for increasing specialization; art and science severed, religion and science regarded as hostile to one another; and analysis the great and approved method of all investigation, till we end by being able to split the atom asunder, and are now afraid. There is no need here to apportion blame. All that is necessary is to know to what an extent secularism and Protestantism carry analysis and subdivision within themselves as their special method.

I have repeated one essential thing about what I conceive to be the true life of the imagination, that in it the life of the mind depends for its liberation upon a kind of submission to the life of the body (and the human), and that the two must live together, according to the way of man and not of angels or demons. This submission is, superficially, a scandal, but, more profoundly viewed, it is a way of freedom. We might say the same thing about the

[53] Anthology: *Poets of the English Language,* Introduction to Volume I.

Church. It too is a body, it too a very precise and determined one, which requires a lofty submission of the mind.

Just as with the body, here too one can make no conditions, present or future—conditions which would give us the kind of infinite and shapeless body that would allegedly not get in the way of the free imagination. In both cases, with the human reality and the Church, one has to take one's possibilities of intellectual and imaginative development with an act of trust. Some of those who wish to stand outside of both these bodies probably wonder whether either may not prove to be an intolerably strict disciplinarian, in matters intellectual and moral. It may easily seem so from the outside, and some would regard any talk about intellectual and imaginative freedom inside any such limitation as so much cant (they regard the Church as primarily an agent of repression, negativing man's right to free thought and free living).

What must be finally stressed is that we cannot re-enter the old Paradise, and this must not be our dream. The terms we now face are doubly new: a body with a wounded sensitivity and the divine Body of Christ, two things that can be put together in the Church only, leaving out nothing of either, of man or God. Surely this new Eden is a superb act of unity, most complex and fascinating, something that will be acceptable to neither hedonist nor Puritan. And seeing that unity is the great business of the imagination, it will desire to play at least some humble role, cooperating with the intellect as a wonderful instrument for research into the new Paradise which it was not given to Adam, in the old, to know. Many of those who will flout this task will be drawn from those who have catastrophically flouted the place of the body and the human in the life of the imagination, and have already terribly separated the body and the mind—as it has been the purpose of these pages to relate.

Charles Moeller

The Image of Man in Modern European Literature*

DELPORTE'S BOOK, *La naissance de l'esprit laïque à la fin du moyen âge,* describes in detail the stages of man's growing awareness of the dimensions "creation" and "world" in the sense of the work of art emerging from the hands of God. Jesus' words, "Render to Caesar the things that are Caesar's, and to God the things that are God's," come into the argument. Only, this birth of the "secular spirit" has come progressively to mean an emancipation of man, sometimes even a revolt against God, the Father and the Creator of the world. The English term "secular" well expresses this profane aspect which increasingly appeals to the modern man; it does not exclude, but neither does it clearly imply, the element of refusal in our Lord's words. Fifteen years of reading around this theme have inspired the reflections which follow. They may be too schematic, but their purpose is precisely to stress the ambiguity of the term "secular" when it is applied to some modern writers. Three features mark the face of man in this literature: autonomy, contingency, and guilt. Merely to enumerate is to reveal a sort of inconsistentcy, for, as we shall see, the sense of autonomy does not lead to a revolt against God but to a total indifference, whereas the experience of contingency and guilt, which should lead to religious enquiry, stays on this side of it, in *l'humain, trop humain.*

* Reprinted from *The Student World* by kind permission of the editors and the author.

Autonomy

Sartre's characters, for example, are always seeking in some sense to create themselves, to be dependent upon nobody. The world appears to them to intimidate. For example, we may recall the famous description of the "root" which leads the hero of *La nausée* to an almost physical experience of being *de trop: de trop* in the square, *de trop* in the town, *de trop* in a viscous, slimy, crowded world, which holds nothing in store for him, which insidiously threatens him in his liberty, in his consciousness. Admittedly, the world "obscenely present" that Sartre evoked in the "within oneself" throughout *L'être et le néant* (1943) has disappeared from the later works. But the threat of it is no less omnipresent. It is human relationships, within society, which by a sort of counter-shock or boomerang action cause human liberty to be made captive. Thus the passengers queuing for the bus at St. Germain des Prés in Paris are entirely at the mercy of the logic of numbers. The time they have to wait is in direct proportion to the number of passengers, the number of empty seats, the number of buses passing every hour. This captivity in the *sériel* Sartre also calls the *practico-inert*. Intimidation slips also into the most reassuring faces of life. It would seem that the more tenderness and affection surround the Sartrian heroes, the stronger is their impression that there is something false somewhere, that, for example, parents, friends, or lovers are "playing" at love, just as the café waiter, moving a little too fast, recovering the balance of his tray a shade too late but still just in time, is acting his part of waiter so well that it is impossible not to detect his acting. Woman, in particular, appears in Sartre's works—but this could also be demonstrated in the work of Paul Valéry—as a snare, a permanent hazard, a sort of treacherously disguised ridge causing men to stumble, to trip, to fall into an ambush. Love between man and woman is never, it seems, communion, communication of a life, knowledge in the sense of the biblical word, in other words, "living union of the living spirit," but facing in parallel the truth about life, which is to say the horror of life.

We spoke at the outset of the aspect of intimidation, for I think that the *sentiment premier de la vie*—in the sense of Max Scheler of *Grundgefühl*—of many of our contemporaries is of the danger of alienation. What is bestowed, given gratuitously, seems to be destructive of autonomy, of self-consciousness. There is in this a radical absence of the meaning of the "gift," of grace, of the disponibility necessary in the presence of the gift. The capacity to welcome, in confidence, in total hope, in a "credit," a sort of "signature on a blank cheque," what Gabriel Marcel in other words calls "the mystery," is identified with a passivity which is negative, amorphous, unworthy of a free man.

In the face of these threats, this alienation whose ghost haunts all the avenues of existence, it is necessary to pursue the affirmation of oneself in absolute autonomy, just as much in solitude as in the reciprocity of human relationships. Thus the group, of which Sartre speaks in *La critique de la raison dialectique* (1960), should achieve the fusion of individuals who are lost in the *sériel.* A sort of "common individual" is formed, for example, in the revolutionary teams who captured the Bastille in 1789. When, after victory has been achieved, the cohesion of the group is threatened, the "oath," in a sort of secular Pentecost, comes to the rescue to fuse together the members of the group. In the oath, nobody owes anything to anybody else; each depends on all and all on each; there is a radical *do ut des,* a sort of give and take, a perfect equality. The Terror Fraternity compensates moreover by mutual fear, within the group, for the diminution of the external purpose when this is once achieved. Thus equilibrium is attained. Men create themselves, they are "their own sons," they form themselves "out of the primeval slime of necessity."

In all this, Sartre is thinking above all of the revolutionary groups which accomplished the overthrow of the regime in Cuba under the leadership of Fidel Castro. Only, the autonomy thus pursued also appears in the work of Bertolt Brecht, for example in *Der Ja-Sager*. At the same time we discover an aspect of autonomy as it is pursued in the Marxist *kolkhozes* and *sevkhozes;* there too the liberty of the individual is compensated by the requirements and supervision of the rest; only each one knowing exactly what he contributes, and expecting from the other the exact counterpart in duty and collaboration, the group affirms its autonomy in the presence of a world requiring radical transformation.

A characteristic note of the affirmation of autonomy in this literature is that it no longer appears in a context of Promethean pride. The myth of progress, the kind of "liberal" philosophy which presented human history as a sort of triumphal march beneath triumphal arches, adorned with optimistic banners, has been put away in the attic with the children's toys. The pride of Faust in confronting nature is absent. There is instead an explicit awareness of each individual's responsibility towards the world; since we no longer believe in God, we cannot "share" this responsibility with him; we cannot share it with the universe either, for even if this depends on man, it shows itself at the same time to be so "inhuman" that the individual feels himself lost, isolated, alone in a "desacralized" world. The human being can no longer do anything but assume in the rather terrifying seriousness of an interminable task—for all victories over the universe are Pyrrhic victories, "the plague" always invading the "fotunate cities" all over again—his duty as a "workman" in the presence of nature. He can certainly share, with others, in reciprocity, in collaboration, in solidarity, but the autonomy of the individual will never be corrected by a true communion.

Confirmation of this first point—the most important, moreover—is to be found in the ideas of Simone de Beauvoir on the position of woman. Too often, it is true, woman is still treated as a "second sex," inferior to the first. Only, instead of replying to this situation by a demonstration of woman as "the other" sex, as the complementary pole of the "human existing"—that of "being with," in disponibility, in welcome, in a "dependence" which is also activity of a superior type, liberty in the gift—she tries to make woman into a sort of "conforming copy" of the "first" sex; she gives exaggerated importance to the qualities of autonomy, of affirmation, which she hopes to discover in the woman of tomorrow. Human and true as this requirement is, this way of understanding it almost exclusively in terms of radical autonomy, as beings "without fathers or mothers," displays an obsession with liberty cut off from all relationship with a nourishing soil, even more from a God who gives a basis to this very liberty.

If the first mark of the image of man is then liberty, which represents progress in relation to the positivist vision of a man who is only the "mathematical resultant" of social and physiological determinisms, it loses this positive value as a result of a manifest exaggeration of the affirmation of radical autonomy. This liberty "for nothing" comes very near to being an autonomy devoid of all meaning.

Contingency

St. Gregory spoke of life as of a *quaedam prolixitas mortis,* as a sort of display, of anticipation of death within life itself. Curiously, those who today preach the "best sermons" on death are no longer the Christian writers but such as Camus, Simone de Beauvoir, Sartre, Bataille, all witnesses to the vanity of the world. They describe physical death, the living death, too, which characterizes our "social" relationships as much as our vaunted self-knowledge.

The theme of the death of man was first of all, in Camus' work, a background which heightened by existential contrast the mystique of happiness to be seized in the present moment. In the works published later, death has come into the foreground; it becomes a *gros plan,* a cinematographic close-up. Thus the agony of dying becomes the "true" face of men, and not the reasonable mask which they wear over their faces. Jeanine of *La femme adultère* (1954) discovers one night that if she could overcome her dread of dying she would be happy; only she overcomes nothing at all and "she was going to die without being set free." In the same way, the loss of faith, in Simone de Beauvoir, was accompanied by a dread of personal death which caused her, one afternoon when she was alone in her parents' study, to "scream and scratch the red moquette" and wonder "what other people did when their end was approaching." At the end of *Les mandarins* (1954), Anne Dubreuilh, hearing her husband talking to friends about the political future of France and of the world, suddenly wonders what meaning this all has in the silence of the galaxies; she herself no longer thinks of anything but a smile which revealed love to her, during her visit to America, only she knows at the same time that this smile can disappear when the heart of her lover stops beating. Man in truth is tied to death; he is *zum Tode,* as Heidegger puts it. There is no point in transforming this "for" into an "against" with André Malraux; this struggle against death is in the nature of things useless, since no hope of survival in God is available to relieve the anguish of living.

Death anticipates itself, precedes itself in a sense, in our very life. We are dead men reprieved, not only because every morning brings us nearer the final term, but still more because we are not sure of really existing. What are we? Who are we? Are we at least something? Among all the masks that the interior comedy continually lays over our incoherent abyss of desires and fears, which is true? Is there even one which can ever be true? Alain Guimiez, in *Le planétarium* (1958) by Nathalie Sarraute, does not know who he is: he thinks he is an artist, for he is researching in Roman art; he builds an essential part of his life around a woman's recognition of the fact of his being an artist, a woman who has the reputation of being an artist herself. But what is this Germaine Lemaitre herself? Is she not also a caricature of the artist? When at the end of the book the patiently constructed edifice of his face in the eyes of the admired woman collapses, for it is revealed that Germaine Lemaitre is a pretentious and empty blue-stocking, Alain falls back into interior chaos, into the void. All the "new novels," by effacing the points of reference and systematically avoiding any indications that might recall Madame Tussaud's waxworks, or those of the *Musée Grévin,* will plunge the reader into the obsessional vision of interior chaos. Butor, Duras, Robbe-Grillet, Claude Simon, Samuel Beckett, present us with a universe in which man, mixed up with things—tables, apartments, chairs, a crossroads, an armoured car during the war—no longer knows who he is, nor even whether he is something. The French heroine of *Hiroshima mon amour* does not know who she is: her "name" is "Nevers" as her Japanese lover's name is "Hiroshima," for she is so mixed up with the events of the war, so emptied of her personal substance, that she no longer exists, literally, so that she is nothing more now than a girl in love, whose love has been brutally broken by war; she is nothing more than "the impossibility of loving": at the moment when she "loves" her Japanese friend, she "lives" this love as though it had been already lived, at Nevers, as though it is already dead, dead at the very heart of apparent life.

At the same time, the contingence of social relations is suggested. The life of society is comedy, parallel monologues, and no real understanding ever occurs. The theme is not new, but in the theatre of Adamov, of Ionesco, of Pirandello, of Diego Fabbri, it takes on a burlesque and tragic form. Thus, in *La cantatrice chauve* (1956) by Ionesco, there is neither a singer nor a bald woman, but a series of characters who think they know each other, who recognize each other, but who still are lost in a maze. Monsieur and Madame Martin, who in the eyes of the spectator are husband and wife, seem to have forgotten the fact; then, by degrees, they observe that as they live in the same town, the same street, the same house, the same floor, and, finally, the same room, they must be husband and wife; the little girl they have is apparently the proof of it; only, the one that each "knows" is not the same; there is a mistake over the person, for *à chacun sa vérité*. Similarly in Robbe-Grillet's novel-film, *L'année dernière à Marienbad,* the characters who "meet" do not know whether they have really seen each other or recognized each other, if they really talked to each other last year. "To be known as one is," said the pastor in Gabriel Marcel's *Un homme de Dieu,* "or else die": not one of the characters of the social comedy is known as he is; they die, not from suicide, but from this insidious death that Beckett described in *Fin de partie.* In this looking-glass game, this hall of mirrors which extends into our intimate selves, as into society, where is the true face of friendship, of love? Where is the authentic encounter? Where shall we find the resources to overcome the feeling of interior emptiness, of the *vacio,* of the *insustancialidad,* of the metaphysical insubstantiality of personal life and of life in society, which haunted Unamuno? *La vida es sueño,* life is a dream, by Calderón, besets the "new novel."

Guilt

These same "modern" characters know themselves to be guilty. Not only has the sense of the responsibility of each for all made its entry into the universe of the novel, even to the point of dethroning concern for the "interior" life for the sake of a generous but simplist social exteriority, but the feeling of guilt has grown out of it. Beyond the dialectics of "master and slave" central to Marxism, was revealed the dialectics of "the judge and the judged." Clamence in *La chute* (1956) by Camus, Temple Drake in Faulkner's *Requiem for a Nun* (1952), Franz von Gerlach in Sartre's *Les séquestrés d'Altona* (1960) are all three haunted by a sense of guilt all the more devastating because accompanied by the certitude that there is no transcendent judge, no heavenly father, who, while "proclaiming" law and judgment, can restore life and reconcile. Franz von Gerlach at once objects to his father as judge, and requires him to judge him.

Man is a creature haunted by values before he is haunted by the play of instinctive forces. Now, among the values which shape the person, the sense of guilt appears inevitably. These morbid forms, too frequent, according to a witness like Dr. Hesnard, must not let one forget the need to be responsible for this situation. The need for law, consequently also the need to encounter "a judge by whom one would consent to be judged," as E. De Greeff says in *Le juge Maury* (1955), and so the need to find a father who judges and restores life, are written into modern literature like a very legible watermark. There is no question, indeed, of "diluting" personal guilt in the "so-called deluge" of general guilt, as Clamence and Franz von Gerlach do. One must take responsibility for one's situation. As there is no divine judge, nor any valid human mediator, nothing remains but to destroy oneself. Kafka's characters do this: they rush of their own accord into the machine of *La colonie pénitentiaire* (1922) which will write their sentence upon their skins. The moment when the text of the sentence is fully inscribed upon their living flesh is the moment of the maximum pleasure and the maximum pain; it is the moment of death; but of a death for no purpose because it brings you before no heavenly judge; it only transforms you, it *metamorphoses* you—whereas faith in God judges, transfigures—into a cockroach, a giant vermin, according to Kafka's frightful parable in *La métamorphose* (1913), or the horrible pachyderm horn in *Le rhinocéros* by Ionesco.

Strange Ambiguity

Thomas Mann, Kafka, James Joyce, had in some way "prophesied" this final situation of modern man, wishing to be autonomous, knowing himself to be contingent, to be vanity and nothingness, seeing himself to be guilty, seeking for a judge, a father, and finally a God, but rejecting him.

In *Doktor Faustus* (1947) Mann showed that, in order to save humanism, this Goethian balance between the appeals from below and the appeals from above, it was necessary to go beyond secular humanism itself and to appeal to the categories of sin and grace. Kafka, in his *Lettre au père* (1919), as in the whole of his work, was the "secular Moses," pointing to the entrance to the promised land—wife, children, paternity, soil, and law—without entering into it himself. At least, though he remained this side of any attachment to religion, including the Jewish religion, he "never liquidated the paternal values": he did not condemn his own father, in his view the enigmatic idol of paternity, arbitrary and paralysing; he did not deny his existence, an old greybeard who'd seen better days; he condemned himself, continuing to proclaim that the promised land did exist, even though he himself could not enter in.

It is Joyce, perhaps, who is the most explicit "secular" witness.

The central idea of his books is that man is ceaselessly in search of himself and others. Thus Daedalus, the new Telemachus, in *Ulysses* (1921), is looking for his father, in order to find out who he himself is, the son of Bloom or a bastard, in order to find out if he is, what he is. Bloom, on the other hand, the new Ulysses, is looking for his son; he is also seeking to find again "the bond of love" with his wife Molly, the Penelope of the atomic age. But neither Daedalus nor Bloom will ever know whether they have found each other, whether even they have ever been anything more than shadows. If they wander thus in an Odyssesy which never reaches the point of return, it is because somewhere in immemorial time, but leaving an impression on the present in depth, a link has been broken, deliberately, that of the engendering of the son by the father, that of filiation, with its origin in a love which has joined two beings. This ontological break can be felt in the page of onomatopeia with which Joyce opens the "vicio-cyclous-monster" of *Finnegans Wake* (1939). This cascade of sounds, wherein allusions to more than twenty-six world languages are heard in puns and allusions, is devoid of meaning; it makes one feel chaos, not the chaos over which brooded the spirit of God, making it fruitful, giving it form, bringing to birth life, love, and the knowledge of love, but the chaos which is created by man, proceeding from the rupture of the bond of paternity. The world of art remains the only outlet for man. But he is shut in upon himself. Art will never succeed in concealing the fact that this muttering, this enormous rumbling, which opens the drunkard's reverie in *Finnegans Wake,* is a caricature, a sort of inversion of the creative and revealing "Word" which resounds through the opening of Genesis and St. John's Gospel.

Conclusion

Let there be no mistake: these three writers who unveil the substructure of the man without God are unbelievers. The most fundamental mystery is, indeed, that this sense of contingency and guilt which, logically, should lead to the search after the living God, turns back upon itself, in hopeless captivity. Further, this contingency and this guilt inspire an increasing mistrust of any intercession, any mediation which, coming from Another, would at once be denounced as a threat, as a risk of alienation. In other terms, the sense of the absolute autonomy of man wins. This man, like Ugolin, devours his children, his own offspring: the radical vanity of life, the irremediable guilt of man, alone, autonomous, without father or mother. So man withdraws into himself. Autonomous, solitary, gnawed at by death, forever causing suffering, forever doing evil, he receives upon his shoulders the whole weight of history, the whole responsibility for the unrolling of time, all the incoherence of encounters and collisions with his fellows.

So true it is that all knowledge of nothingness and of sin is not good. It is God who judges; in the last analysis it is he alone, in the revelation of his Word, who accuses, challenges, judges, and saves. Only thus can man have, in his condition as a sinner before God, the kind of knowledge which is also conversion.

There is thus in the secular literature of the present century planetary hope and cosmic fear, appeals from God and appeals to God, but buried in the sand like footprints on the sea-shore whose meaning is lost.

Amos N. Wilder

Art and Theological Meaning*

He is neither priest nor proctor . . .
It is a fresh spiritual that he defines.
—Wallace Stevens

JEAN COCTEAU CHARACTERIZES the subject matter of the modern arts as *le mystère laïc,* the "lay mystery" or "secular mystery." "Chirico," he says, "is a religious painter without faith," "a painter of the lay mystery." Cocteau holds that the modern artist must deal with the "lay mystery," that is, with secular experience understood religiously. Or, we can translate the phrase as "secular transcendence." Now we can recognize the importance of the theme for the theologian. We live in an age when any other kind of transcendence or mystery has lost its meaning. The old two-story world is a thing of the past. Dualistic metaphysics and ontologies can still speak to us through Plato, Dante, or Wordsworth; but a poem or a novel written today with this presupposition must be put down as a flashback, as an archaism. To build a new Gothic church in today's life is like disinterring the dead or opening a time-capsule out of a remote past. In an American city of today the average man walks by such a building without seeing it. It is not there for our sensibilities. We have no antennae for it.

If we are to have any transcendence today, even Christian, it must be in and through the secular. If we are to have any mystery it must be the lay mystery. If we are to find Grace it is to be found in the world and not overhead. The sublime firmament of over-

* Reprinted from the *Union Seminary Quarterly Review* by kind permission of the editors and the author.

head reality that provided a spiritual home for the souls of men until the eighteenth century has collapsed. But this need be no loss. I take it that we have been learning this from Bonhoeffer and Gogarten among others. We must take the world more seriously, nature and our nature more seriously, history more seriously.

But all this means that the artists and the poets are more important to us even than before. Not because they preserve for us—as was at first thought—a refuge for the dreams and ideals threatened by materialism. But because the artist properly deals with the givens, the primordial givens, of the senses, the affections and the passions. These still have their transcendence; even in a one-story world these still have their theological import. And in the modern situation this becomes all the more significant; now the believer and the artist are dealing with the same single reality, and the artist is freer in handling it. By virtue of his craft and his embattled autonomy, he presents the voices of nature more directly. The theologian cannot enter so freely into the modern reality, nor can the conventional religious artist identified with the *art sacré* of the past, for they suffer the curvature and the stiffness of an ancient dualistic gesture. Here is the context of Cocteau's phrase. Protesting to the theologian Maritain, Cocteau says that the artist must deal with the lay mysery and that to deal with it he must be free. But this does not mean that such art will be immoral or amoral, for, he writes: "I believe that art reflects morals, and that one cannot renew oneself without living dangerously and attracting slander." That is, the artist must deal at first hand with life, beyond the fences of social or religious propriety.

It is something like this that Wallace Stevens means when he says of the poet or artist today:

> The ephebe is solitary in his walk.
> He skips the journalism of subjects, seeks out
> The perquisites of sanctity, enjoys
>
> A strong mind in a weak neighborhood, and is
> A serious man without the serious . . .

He is neither priest nor proctor . . .

It is a fresh spiritual that he defines . . .

. . . .

The actual landscape with its actual horns
Of baker and butcher blowing, as if to hear,
Hear hard, gets an essential integrity.[1]

In the case of Stevens we can talk about a lay sanctity, a "fresh spiritual," just as in the case of Cocteau we can talk about the secular mystery. We are familiar with Tillich's related views of the religious dimensions in modern painting. But we should not confuse what we are saying here with romantic or pseudo-religious ideas of nature or art; these interpreters speak as disabused moderns.

Let us say first, then, that the theologian can well put himself to school to the modern artist to free himself from hang-overs of old fashions in transcendence. He must do this not only with a view to better strategies in communication, but with a view to honesty: honesty of feeling as well as honesty of language. It is a question of where today Grace is actually to be found—in old habits and rhetorics or, as Stevens puts it, in

The actual landscape with its actual horns
Of baker and butcher blowing.

To avoid misunderstanding we might say that these horns of the butcher and baker relate us more directly to the ram's horns of the Exodus and the Seven Trumpets of the Apocalypse than do ecclesiastical electrical chimes or Christmas carols piped through loudspeakers in our shopping centers. The horns of the butcher and baker are not, of course, the Gospel, but they are real. Stevens is talking about the primordial givens of our human nature and experience, and these have "perquisites of sanctity," genuine coruscations of glory.

[1] "An Ordinary Evening in New Haven," in XIII, "*The Auroras of Autumn*," from *The Collected Poems of Wallace Stevens,* Alfred A. Knopf, 1955, pp. 134–35. By permission of the publishers.

Now we go one step farther. If the artist often calls theology and piety back to an "essential integrity," one can say that art as a whole, the aesthetic order, is always an indispensable corrective and nourishment to faith. Recurrently threatened by docetism and irrelevance, the Christian faith is in need of recurrent baptism in the secular, in the human, to renew itself. It has to be continually re-immersed in the vitalities of nature to be saved from a spurious and phantom Christ. Art mediates this order of creation to us.

The second Adam presupposes the first Adam. The Christian presupposes the man. Art gives us the first Adam, and if we lose sight of him and his true secular mystery and endowments we cannot rightly identify the second Adam or the Christian. To say all this with reference to literature: in the autonomy of the literary arts, precisely in secular literature, we come face to face with the reality of the first Adam, with the secular mystery, and only as we are open to this revelation can we rightly assess "theological meaning" in itself or in its various articles of belief. Theology and witness today will be impoverished unless they take account of secular man in all his dynamics, of the lay mystery that gives evidence of itself precisely in a desacralized world, of that new kind of transcendence that is made possible today when the category of the supernatural is gone.

The nourishment and provocation of our religious tradition by doses of paganism, nature, the aesthetic order, can be illustrated through many of its vicissitudes in the past. We may call to witness the fertility patterns of the ancient Near East as they became ordered by Hebrew cult-theology; the Wisdom tradition of Egypt and Edom as digested by Israel; the pagan vitalities of Hellenism, transubstantiated by the early church. In certain Biblical writings we can observe the process. In Job, a disabused look at the irreparable and immitigable occasions a new leap of faith. In John, Hebrews, and Ephesians we see Hellenistic Christianity absorbing and surmounting a far-flung pagan encounter with meaninglessness, beyond the horizon of the Jerusalem beginnings. For us today secular strains of the Renaissance, the Enlightenment, and the Romantic movement provide essential challenge, provocation, and nourishment. Without these our faith and our theology become cloistered and inhuman. We need ever-renewed exemplars of the first Adam in art and in life. What serves us best is the contemporary instance—more contemporary than Goethe, Nietzsche, or Walt Whitman—a Gide, a Yeats, a Rilke, or a Faulkner.

Art in the Church

Before proceeding, it is necessary to introduce a caveat against misplaced aestheticism in the Church. We should not encourage aesthetes in the pulpit, or "literary parsons," or liturgical revivals inspired by false views of beauty. We should safeguard the distinctions between the image-maker and the disciple, the creative talent and the religious calling, the spirit and the Holy Spirit. Granted our overdue reaction as Protestants against an ascetic or inhibited type, we should not go to excess on the other side into uncritical eros and a fetish of creative spontaneity without Christian norms. This would be to make the mistake of the Jewish youths of the time of the Seleucid rulers who were captivated by things Greek, who wore Greek garb, went to the circus and the amphitheatre, were ashamed of their circumcision:

> Whereupon [certain of the people] built a place of exercise at Jerusalem according to the customs of the heathen: and made themselves uncircumcised . . . (I Macc. 1:14–15; cf. II Macc. 4:9–17)

The temptation was great for the Jewish youths of the time in view of the attraction of Hellenic and Hellenistic achievements, and in the face of the inhibited image of man presented by the defensive tradition of the Second Temple. So today. We awaken to a sense of the stunted image of man widely current in the middle-class Protestant ethos; we recognize the immeasurable attractions of certain humanist and secular ideals identified with the arts—and we can easily become confused.

I see this awkwardness—a transitional awkward age among Protestants as they possess themselves of the gospel of the arts today—in two versions: In one case we have the man from a

Protestant pietism to whom a kind of subjective release in art is congenial. His aestheticism is a passage from pietism to Romanticism. I have a strong suspicion here of experimentation with the religious dance especially; but also of addiction to a kind of oracular-mystical poetry, such as that of Khalil Gibran; or of sentimental representations of Christ or religious subjects in painting which may have superficial aspects of modern style but are essentially governed by pathos or eros.

The other case is that of the man whose background is not pietism but some more dogmatically defined type of Christianity, a tradition involving a built-in asceticism or emotional barrenness. In his case the temptation is not to a Christian romanticism, but to some kind of Christian antinomianism, à la Nietzsche, shall we say. Or he may be attracted to some very sophisticated high-church symbolic traditionalism. The antinomian response may take the individual right out of the Church as in the case of an André Gide or a Robert Graves: salvation by the epiphany or magic of Beauty prevails over salvation by hearing. Some theological students have a prolonged struggle with this dilemma. The liturgical-aesthetic response, indeed, is an understandable awakening to the symbolic dimension of religion. It has it in its favor that Christian theological norms may be seriously recognized. But this too can pass into aestheticism. Even when it does not, the aesthetic emancipation identified with it becomes too easily identified with obsolete forms.

So much on the dangers of the new interest in the arts in the churches. In my appreciation of the secular arts expressed in the following paragraphs, I am aware of such misunderstandings. But I am more interested in the benefits of this new confrontation when it is wisely worked out by the Christian.

Those Who Are Not A Nation

Let me state the positive significance of our confrontation with the arts and the whole aesthetic order by using an analogy from Paul's Letter to the Romans, as he cites Deuteronomy:

I will make you jealous of those who are not a nation: with a foolish nation I will make you angry. (Rom. 10:19; Deut. 32:21)

Paul is saying that God's work among the Gentiles will give heart-burnings to Israel, will startle and anger them. Today can we say that God is using the essentially pagan reality of art—man's often sublime, unbaptized sensuous and imaginative talents and works—to provoke the Church, to needle it, to introduce a ferment into it? "I will make you jealous of those who are not a nation." Certainly the Bohemia of the artists is not a nation, not a called people; they are individualists, Ishmaelites. But they have uncovenanted mercies and even callings. Do we have here God speaking through people, perhaps with strange lips, through the pagan miracle, the secular mystery?

Can we say that God is on both sides in the war of the myths, the war of the historical myth of the people of God with the natural myths of Adam, that is, with the secular celebrations of art? For was it not precisely in the war of the myths that first Israel and then Christianity has often drawn the resources of language to define itself and communicate itself. Let us not be detoured here by the question of the Fall, of man's evil imaginations. For the arts and myths and creativities of unbaptized man have their sound aspects. Professor Mircea Eliade, speaking as a student of non-Christian cultures, observes that we Christians look too exclusively upon the darker side of their arts and ceremonies. Nevertheless, he observes, by these, great societies live.

We may see the nature of art as pagan, natural, representing the endowments of the first Adam. This is said in appreciation of art, not in disparagement. We should let art, poetry, etc., be autonomous and pre-Christian. We thus avoid parochialism, since we do not rule out the aesthetic activity of man in any culture—from the caves of the Dordogne or the artifacts of the paleolithic age to the latest compositions in electronic sonorities. We also avoid false dualism and spiritualization in our view of art. We do not obscure the basic human sensuous foundation of all art. We maintain the polarity of art and faith, and thus keep open that special reality which art represents. In theological terms we emphasize the doctrine of redemption. We may note, parenthetically, the same issue in the case of science. Christianity has most to profit, with respect (for example) to Biblical science or religious sociology, if it acknowledges in them their own autonomous methods and activity.

The great importance of the Church's encounter with art emerges only when we envisage the surpassing greatness of man's artistic endowments and achievements, with their transcending and breathless instances. It is good for Christians to have to make a place in their sometimes shrunken outlook for the formidable energies and realities evident in the arts. It represents a theological provocation which is good for us. In the first age of Christianity the mood and kerygmatic witness of the believers was of a pitch and level to encounter and master and to transmute to its own purpose the dynamic conceptions of pagan antiquity. Its language, its imagery, its symbol were equal to the pagan imaginations of the epoch, let alone the civil and political arts and rituals, all representing the prodigal exuberance of the Roman world. The lowly Christian cells lived by creative powers and community-building "ideology" that in very deed outrivaled the seven wonders of the world, and could battle on more than equal terms with whatever human greatness is represented for us by the names of Virgil, Horace, and the classics of the Roman *paideia*.

The arts of our time as indices of man's prolific and consummate powers—quite apart from whatever cultural instruction we may derive from them—should provoke the Church to have a life and a message and a lexicon of communications worthy of this mysterious contemporary Adam. When reading some of the best of our modern literature we cannot but feel that we have moved into another dimension in the grasp of our human condition than we find commonly in our theology. Even if our human lot is not seen in Christian terms it is evoked with a cruciality, a searingness that compels men to take a fuller account of themselves: on the one hand a communication of the fatalities that hem in and block the life-impulse at so many points; on the other hand evidence of man's paradoxical potentialities and incredible works. Fortunately a great deal of this modern literature is on the side of the angels. In all sorts of obscure ways it is shaped by Jewish-Christian and humanist legacies resident in western man. But it often towers above our institutional Christian patterns. And our Christian habits of mind and heart seem to inhibit if not cripple our resourcefulness so that we are not able to communicate with the secular mystery of the age.

The Problem of "The Sacred"

To illustrate the stature of art in our time let me take the field of poetry. Consider the special handicaps of the poet today, either with respect to his world and audience or with respect to the state of the English tongue. Culturally speaking it is an age of incoherence. Linguistically speaking, our media of discourse and communication are desacralized. The poets of the past worked in languages that had numinous overtones. I have observed that the chief difficulty in translating the New Testament into contemporary English lies at this point. Our English tongue today at its best—and I am not speaking of Journalese or the idiom of Broadway or of Madison Avenue—is practical, or abstract, in any case one-dimensional; it lacks a penumbra of magic or mystery. The translators of the New English Bible, therefore, are hard put to translate the Greek word *thlipsis,* which we know as "tribulation"; they translate it "trouble." *Mamonas* is translated "money." *Peirasmos,* the Greek term for the eschatological birth pangs, has to be translated as "test." *Anathema* takes the weak sense of "outcaste."

Now with all such handicaps note the achievements of certain modern poets. In face of the special aspects of cultural fragmentation and incommunicability present today, we have writers who have been able to go beneath and behind our modern anarchy and find images of meaning and order. They can say things for us, whether tragic or affirmative, by which we can enter into possession of our enduring humanity. I think of the marvelously controlled complexities of our modern experience in the earlier work of Eliot;

and of the ordering of both our psychological and political stresses in the work of Auden. I think of the perfection and invention beyond praise of much of the work of Wallace Stevens, whose supreme play with language went on year after year. I think of the crystallike miracle of a certain vein in Ezra Pound, who stands near the springs of life; as Hugh Kenner writes, he provides the "nutrition of impulse," he "incites humanity to go on living." In Pound's own phrase we have the "dance of the intellect among words." One cannot read in his *Cantos* without experiencing a cumulative awareness of the aesthetic miracle and wonder at the enigma of man's powers. I have reference to the Protean play, the modulations, the subtleties, the echoes and resonances, of a vast register of resources, both of the lexicon itself and of cultural symbol, both of rhetoric and of passion, both of private sensibility and of the fables of the tribe. If we speak of the secular mystery, we have it here, nature in a modern instance in an incandescence to evoke astonishment.

But we could go on to speak of other poets: of the magician-like shaping of our recalcitrant human speech by poets like Yeats and Valéry. And we could speak of St.-John Perse, Marianne Moore, Robert Graves and others. We have "lords of language" in our time too, and it evidences what I say about the too easily forgotten depths and dimensions of man and God's hand upon him. Nor would I forget the talents of many poets who are less well known: men and women who report significantly—that is by signs—on what it means to live in the wrestling today between conformity and freedom, the adjusted and the unadjusted, the even and the odd, the sodden and the sensitive, between custom and wonder. The true artist today is the man who has no armor, no secondhand buffers and blinders, and who is therefore exposed and vulnerable, and one therefore through whom the ancient hungers of man can speak, and speak by words and signs both timeless and contemporary.

In our desacralized world, what was once the religious dimension is opened up for many by artistic experience alone. As Robert

Spike has said, the symbols have widely lost their power in the Church but they still have power elsewhere, for example in the secular Protestant ethos, and in secular artists who quicken these and other potent legacies. A striking example of this secular quickening of Christian imagery is afforded by Beckett's *Waiting for Godot*.

"One of the thieves crucified beside Christ went to Heaven. Do not despair. The other thief went to Hell. Do not presume." It was from these sentences of St. Augustine's that Samuel Beckett, having rejected Christian belief but finding no meaningful aesthetic patterns outside Christian tradition, got the idea of *Waiting for Godot*.[2]

So far as contemporary art is concerned, then, we should be more humble before modern secularity in its creative aspects, and see what it can teach us even if we have to divest ourselves for the time being of our own inherited badges of authority. Here is where our thought links on with that of Bonhoeffer in his view of a world come of age and a naked Christ divested of dualistic titles. Our world explores the secular mystery in non-supernatural terms. It is possible for the Gospel to be lived and thought and imaged so as to speak to these presuppositions.

The Christian Imagination

Our topic, however, requires that we give attention also to the work of the Christian artist, to the Christian imagination, and to Christian imagery. This point should be made only after taking into account the foregoing discussion. We have separated the Christian from the artist deliberately and assigned autonomy to the artist, so that we can then find the fullest relevance of art to the theological world. We have let man as maker and image-maker give us the unbaptized human phenomenon in all its vitality and poignancy, its mystery and miscarriage. We understand better, then, the work of God with man, of redemption with nature, the meaning

[2] Cited from G. S. Fraser, "The Modern Poet and Christianity," *Frontier*, II (Summer, 1959), 106.

of election, calling, responsibility, judgment, guilt, expiation. It is not surprising that our fuller understanding of the Gospel today is opened up for us by a long line of secular artists, by outsiders, by scapegoats and prodigals and victims of the modern experience. We turn perforce to artists outside the camp who know modern man better than we know him ourselves, men who have belonged to the resistance of our time, the anti-Fascist battalions, the anti-totalitarian cells, the anti-bourgeois insecure, the outer or inner emigration of our world. They have had to sustain the struggle for man's moral freedom and imaginative freedom, often with error, in exposed situations, and in solidarity with their fellows in a way not so characteristic of the Christian. In doing so, as artists, they have restored to us an image of man, paradigms of man in depth, which rebuke our conventionality and expose the inadequacy of our speech.

It is at this point that the *Christian* artists of our time can enter into their labor and reap the benefits. We recognize that a painter like Rouault or poets like Eliot and Auden can speak out of the same depth and with an adequate rhetoric today because they have learned from secular art. Thus the Christian artist learns how to speak so that modern man can know himself directly addressed when he hears the Gospel today. Of course, there are only a few Christian artists of this stature; but the lesser Christian artists and the faithful preacher and apologist on all the many fronts of the Church today increasingly rediscover the stature of man in his secular mystery, in his enigma and in his dynamics, and increasingly repossess an adequate language, a new lexicon of faith, and a new manual of communication. To repeat what I have said elsewhere:

> The modern poets (and one could say artists) have awakened us to the power in our lives of ancient myth and ritual, ancient and yet contemporary. They have given us back a discourse adequate to the mystery of existence and we superficial Christians, intimidated by modern practicality and knowingness, are thus encouraged to communicate our faith imaginatively and dramatically at deeper levels. The poets know how to break up the crust and to make us know again in our own present what sin, hell, revelation, and new birth can mean.

The War of Myths

With the appreciation which we have expressed here for the arts and the modern arts, it should, nevertheless, be clearly understood that the obligation to test the spirits is always with the Christian. The world of the arts and the imagination is even more fateful for men than that of their ideas and philosophies. Art often takes the form of idols. There are false imaginations. If great societies and civilizations really live as they do by myths, in the sense of compelling world-pictures and their assumptions—and order their institutions and unwritten laws by them—it is evident how decisive a role is played for good and for evil by the artist, the image-maker. Christianity is, therefore, always involved in a war of myths for men's souls. This only suggests again how important it is that Christian faith in any epoch should have the dynamic to provide its own compelling images and potent art-forms over against the prolific and malific magics that every age produces. In one sense, one can say that Biblical faith throughout was a war against pagan myths. But it is also true to say that the emergence of the Gospel meant a renewal of mythical apprehension and communication. Only this kind of plastic conception could do justice to the depth of men's grasp of existence and destiny. But such imagery rose out of the drama of the Cross and was a kind of world-portrayal that inevitably contradicted the imaginations of Greece and Rome, even as it might borrow from them.

For the war of myths of today and the overthrow of the false icons of our Romes and our Corinths we can learn from the first believers. The Christian artist may learn where power of conception is born, at the zero point of the flesh which is at the same time the Alpha of a new creation, that is, at the Cross. He may also learn that the Christian speaks to every man and age in his present and in his current idiom, for there is no holy language. He may also find an apostleship in the realization that the Gospel prevails not by instruction and argument but by revelation, by bodying forth.

Selected Bibliography

This checklist, far from representing, or even aiming at, any sort of comprehensive notation of the literature in the field, seeks only to remind the reader of those works which broach the possibility of a Christian poetic in ways that permit the easiest commerce between a theological perspective and the general ethos of contemporary criticism and literary theory in the English-speaking world. In many instances, a given book or essay might well have been listed under more than one heading, and thus the manner in which the various titles are arranged may involve some measure of arbitrariness.

PART I

The Problem of a Christian Aesthetic

Berdyaev, Nicolas, *The Meaning of the Creative Act*. Trans. by Donald A. Lowrie. New York: Harper and Bros., 1955.

Bridge, A. C., *Images of God: An Essay on the Life and Death of Symbols*. London: Hodder and Stoughton, 1960.

Clutton-Brock, A., *et al, The Necessity of Art*. London: S.C.M. Press Ltd., 1924.

Dillistone, F. W., *Christianity and Symbolism*. Philadelphia: The Westminster Press, 1955.

Dix, Dom Gregory, *The Shape of the Liturgy*. Westminster: Dacre Press, 1945.

Every, Brother George, *S.S.M., Christian Discrimination*. London: The Sheldon Press, 1940.

Forsyth, Peter Taylor, *Christ on Parnassus*. London: Independent Press Ltd., 1959 (Second Impression).

Gilby, Thomas, *Poetic Experience*. New York: Sheed and Ward, 1934.

Glendenning, Frank, ed., *The Church and the Arts*. London: S.C.M. Press Ltd., 1960.

Hebert, A. G., *S.S.M., Liturgy and Society*. London: Faber and Faber Ltd., 1935.

Hildebrand, Dietrich von, *Liturgy and Personality*. New York: Longmans, Green and Co., 1943.

Jenkinson, R. S., "Towards a Christian Aesthetic," *The Downside Review,* Vol. 67, No. 207 (Winter, 1948–49).

Jones, David, *Epoch and Artist*. London: Faber and Faber Ltd., 1959.

Kegley, Charles, "Paul Tillich on the Philosophy of Art," *Journal of Aesthetics and Art Criticism,* Vol. XIX, No. 2 (Winter, 1960).

La Tour du Pin, Patrice de, *The Dedicated Life in Poetry*. London: The Harvill Press, 1948.

Lewis, H. D., "Revelation and Art," *Proceedings of the Aristotelian Society,* Supplemental Volume XXIII. Reprinted in Professor Lewis's *Morals and Revelation* (London: George Allen and Unwin Ltd., 1951).

Little, Arthur, *S.J., The Nature of Art*. New York: Longmans, Green and Co., 1946.

MacGregor, Geddes, *Aesthetic Experience in Religion*. London: The Macmillan Co., Ltd., 1947.

Maritain, Jacques, *Art and Poetry*. New York: Philosophical Library, 1943.

Maritain, Jacques, *Art and Scholasticism*. New York: Charles Scribner's Sons, 1943.

Maritain, Jacques, *Creative Intuition in Art and Poetry*. New York: Pantheon Books, 1953.

Maritain, Jacques, *The Responsibility of the Artist*. New York: Charles Scribner's Sons, 1960.

Maritain, Jacques, and Cocteau, Jean, *Art and Faith*. New York: Philosophical Library, 1948.

Maritain, Jacques, and Maritain, Raissa, *The Situation of Poetry*. New York: Philosophical Library, 1955.

Mascall, E. L., *O.G.S., Theology and Images*. London: A. R. Mowbray and Co., Ltd., 1963.

McCarron, Hugh, *Realization: A Philosophy of Poetry*. London: Sheed and Ward, 1937.

Murray, Rosalind, *The Forsaken Fountain*. New York: Longmans, Green and Co., 1948.

Pointing, Horace B., *Art, Religion and the Common Life*. London: S.C.M. Press Ltd., 1947.

Reinhold, H. A., *The Dynamics of Liturgy*. New York: The Macmillan Co., 1961.

Sayers, Dorothy L., *The Mind of the Maker*. New York: Meridian Books, 1956.

Scott, Nathan A., Jr., "Maritain in His Role as Aesthetician," *The Review of Metaphysics,* Vol. VIII, No. 3 (March, 1955).

Scott, Nathan A., Jr., "Faith and Art in a World Awry," *Motive,* Vol. XXII, No. 2 (November, 1961), pp. 22–28. Also published in *Student World,* Vol. LV, No. 2 (Second Quarter, 1962), pp. 196–210.

Van der Leeuw, Gerardus, *Sacred and Profane Beauty: The Holy in Art*. New York: Holt, Rinehart and Winston, 1963.

Watkin, Edward Ingram, *Catholic Art and Culture*. New York: Sheed and Ward, 1944.

Watkin, Edward Ingram, *A Philosophy of Form*. London: Sheed and Ward, 1938.

PART II

The Nature of the Christian Vision

Berdyaev, Nicolas, *Dostoievsky: An Interpretation*. New York: Sheed and Ward, 1934.

D'Arcy, Martin C., *S.J.*, "Literature as a Christian Comedy," *The McAuley Lectures, 1961*. West Hartford, Conn.: Saint Joseph College, 1962.

Dillistone, F. W., *The Novelist and the Passion Story*. London: Collins, 1960.

Driver, Tom F., *The Sense of History in Greek and Shakespearean Drama*. New York: Columbia University Press, 1960.

Fowlie, Wallace, *Paul Claudel*. New York: Hillary House Inc., 1957.

Frye, Roland M., *Perspective on Man: Literature and the Christian Tradition*. Philadelphia: The Westminster Press, 1961.

Hirn, Yrjo, *The Sacred Shrine: A Study of the Poetry and Art of the Catholic Church*. London: Faber and Faber Ltd., 1958.

Lloyd, Roger B., *The Borderland: An Exploration of Theology in English Literature*. New York: The Macmillan Co., 1960.

O'Donnell, Donat, *Maria Cross: Imaginative Patterns in a Group of Modern Catholic Writers*. New York: Oxford University Press, 1952.

Pfleger, Karl, ed., *Wrestlers with Christ*. New York: Sheed and Ward, 1936.

Sayers, Dorothy L., *Introductory Papers on Dante*. New York: Harper and Bros., 1954.

Sayers, Dorothy L., *Further Papers on Dante*. New York: Harper and Bros., 1957.

Scott, Nathan A., Jr., "Graham Greene: Christian Tragedian," in *Graham Greene,* ed. by R. O. Evans. Lexington, Ky.: University of Kentucky Press, 1963.

Scott, Nathan A., Jr., "T. S. Eliot's *The Cocktail Party:* Of Redemption and Vocation," *Religion in Life,* Vol. XX, No. 2 (Spring, 1951).

Scott, Nathan A., Jr., "The Poetry of Auden," *The Chicago Review,* Vol. XIII, No. 4 (Winter, 1959), pp. 53–75. Also published in *The London Magazine,* Vol. VIII, No. 1 (January, 1961), pp. 44–63.

Speaight, Robert, *The Christian Theatre*. London: Burns and Oats, 1960.

Watkin, Edward Ingram, *Poets and Mystics*. London and New York: Sheed and Ward, 1953.

Williams, Charles, *The Figure of Beatrice*. London: Faber and Faber Ltd., 1943.

Williams, Charles, *The Image of the City, And Other Essays*. London: Oxford University Press, 1958.

PART III

Moorings for a Theological Criticism

Abrams, M. H. ed., *Literature and Belief*. New York: Columbia University Press, 1958.

Battenhouse, Roy W., "The Relation of Theology to Literary Criticism," *The Journal of Bible and Religion,* Vol. XIII, No. 1 (February, 1945).

Bethell, S. L., *Literary Criticism*. London: Dennis Dobson Ltd., 1948.

Brémond, Henri, *Prayer and Poetry*. London: Burns, Oates and Washbourne Ltd., 1927.

Buckley, Vincent, *Poetry and Morality*. London: Chatto and Windus, 1959.

Chapman, Raymond, *The Ruined Tower*. London: Geoffrey Bles, 1961.

Claudel, Paul, *Positions et propositions*. Paris: Gallimard, 1929.

Connolly, Francis X., "Is a Christian Theory of Literature Possible?," *The McAuley Lectures, 1961*. West Hartford, Conn.: Saint Joseph College, 1962.

De Selincourt, Oliver, *Art and Morality*. London: Methuen and Co. Ltd., 1935.

Du Bos, Charles, *What Is Literature?* New York: Sheed and Ward, 1940.

Every, Brother George, *S.S.M., Poetry and Personal Responsibility*. London: S.C.M. Press Ltd., 1949.

Fowlie, Wallace, "Catholic Orientation in Contemporary French Literature," in *Spiritual Problems in Contemporary Literature,* ed. by Stanley R. Hopper. New York: Harper and Bros., 1952.

Gardiner, Harold C., *S.J., Norms for the Novel.* New York: The America Press, 1953.

Gardner, Helen, *The Business of Criticism*. London: Oxford University Press, 1959.

Hopper, Stanley R., *The Crisis of Faith*. Nashville: Abingdon-Cokesbury Press, 1944.

James, D. G., *Scepticism and Poetry: An Essay on the Poetic Imagination.* London: George Allen and Unwin Ltd., 1937.

Lewis, C. S., *An Experiment in Criticism.* Cambridge: University Press, 1961.

Lewis, C. S., *They Asked for a Paper: Papers and Addresses.* London: Geoffrey Bles, 1962.

Lynch, William F., *S.J., Christ and Apollo.* New York: Sheed and Ward, 1960.

Ong, Walter J., *S.J., The Barbarian Within.* New York: The Macmillan Co., 1962.

Pottle, Frederick A., *The Idiom of Poetry.* Ithaca, N.Y.: Cornell University Press, 1946.

Roberts, Michael, *The Modern Mind.* London: Faber and Faber Ltd., 1937.

Rooney, William J., *The Problem of "Poetry and Belief" in Contemporary Criticism.* Washington, D.C.: Catholic University of America Press, 1949.

Scott, Nathan A., Jr., *Modern Literature and the Religious Frontier.* New York: Harper and Bros., 1958.

Scott, Nathan A., Jr., ed., *The Climate of Faith in Modern Literature.* New York: The Seabury Press, 1964.

Scott, Nathan A., Jr., "The Realism of Erich Auerbach," *The Christian Scholar,* Vol. XXXVII, No. 4 (December, 1954).

Scott, Nathan A., Jr., "Poetry and the Crisis of Metaphysics," *The Christian Scholar,* Vol. XXXVI, No. 4 (December, 1953).

Scott, Nathan A., Jr., "The Meaning of the Incarnation for Modern Literature," *Christianity and Crisis,* Vol. XVIII, No. 21 (December 9, 1958), pp. 173–75.

Scott, Nathan A., Jr., "The Relation of Theology to Literary Criticism," *The Journal of Religion,* Vol. XXXIII, No. 4 (October, 1953).

Scott, Nathan A., Jr., "Art and the Renewal of Human Sensibility in Mass Society," in *Christian Faith and the Contemporary Arts,* ed. by Finley Eversole. New York: Abingdon Press, 1962.

Scott, Nathan A., Jr., "The Tragic Vision and the Christian Faith,"

The Anglican Theological Review, Vol. XLV, No. 1 (January, 1963), pp. 23–45.

Scott, Nathan A., Jr., "Allen Tate's *Collected Essays,*" *The Chicago Review,* Vol. XV, No. 1 (Summer, 1961), pp. 113–19.

Scott, Nathan A., Jr., "Religious Implications in the Humanities," *The Journal of Human Relations,* Vol. II, No. 2 (Winter, 1954).

Thomas, George F., *Poetry, Religion, and the Spiritual Life.* Houston: Elsevier Press, 1951.

Turnell, Martin, *Poetry and Crisis.* London: Sands, The Paladin Press, 1938.

Wilder, Amos N., "Protestant Orientation in Contemporary Poetry," in *Spiritual Problems in Contemporary Literature,* ed. by Stanley R. Hopper. New York: Harper and Bros., 1952.

Wilder, Amos N., *Theology and Modern Literature.* Cambridge: Harvard University Press, 1958.

Wimsatt, W. K., Jr., "Poetry and Christian Thinking," *The Verbal Icon.* Lexington, Ky.: University of Kentucky Press, 1954.

Wimsatt, William K., Jr., and Brooks, Cleanth, *Literary Criticism: A Short History.* New York: Alfred A. Knopf, 1957.

PART IV

Belief and Form: The Problem of Correlation

Auden, W. H., "The Christian Tragic Hero," *New York Times Book Review,* 16 December, 1945.

Auden, W. H., *The Dyer's Hand.* New York: Random House, 1962.

Auden, W. H., "Edtor's Introduction," *The Portable Greek Reader.* New York: The Viking Press, 1948.

Berdyaev, Nicolas, *Dostoievsky: An Interpretation.* New York: Sheed and Ward, 1934.

Brooks, Cleanth, *The Hidden God: Studies in Hemingway, Faulkner, Yeats, Eliot, and Warren.* New Haven: Yale University Press, 1963.

Eversole, Finley, ed., *Christian Faith and the Contemporary Arts.* New York: Abingdon Press, 1962.

Fairchild, Hoxie Neale, *Religious Trends in English Poetry*. New York: Columbia University Press, Vol. I, 1939; Vol. II, 1942; Vol. III, 1949; Vol. IV, 1957; Vol. V, 1962.

Gardiner, Harold C., *S.J.*, ed., *Fifty Years of the American Novel, 1900–1950: A Christian Appraisal*. New York: Charles Scribner's Sons, 1951.

Getlein, Frank, and Gardiner, Harold C., *S.J.*, *Movies, Morals, and Art*. New York: Sheed and Ward, 1961.

Greene, Graham, *The Lost Childhood*. New York: The Viking Press, 1952.

Heller, Erich, *The Hazard of Modern Poetry*. Cambridge: Bowes and Bowes Ltd., 1953.

Henn, T. R., *The Harvest of Tragedy*. London: Methuen, 1956.

Jarrett-Kerr, Martin, *C.R.*, *Mauriac*. New Haven: Yale University Press, 1954.

Jarrett-Kerr, Martin, *C.R.*, *Studies in Literature and Belief*. New York: Harper and Bros., 1954.

Lewis, R. W. B., *The Picaresque Saint: Representative Figures in Contemporary Fiction*. Philadelphia: J. B. Lippincott Co., 1959.

Luccock, Halford E., *Contemporary American Literature and Religion*. Chicago: Willett and Clark, 1934.

Lynch, William F., *S.J.*, *The Image Industries*. New York: Sheed and Ward, 1959.

Moeller, Charles, *Littérature du XXe siècle et christianisme*. Tournai: Casterman, Vol. I (*Silence de Dieu:* Camus, Gide, Huxley, Simone Weil, Graham Greene, Julian Green, Bernanos), 1953; Vol. II (*La Foi en Jésus-Christ:* Sartre, Henry James, Martin du Gard, Malègue), 1953; Vol. III (*Espoir des hommes:* Malraux, Kafka, Vercors, Cholokhov, Maulnier, *et al*), 1957; Vol. IV (*L'espérance en Dieu Notre Père:* Anne Frank, Unamuno, Marcel, Charles du Bos, Fritz Hochwalder, Charles Péguy), 1960.

Mueller, William R., *The Prophetic Voice in Modern Fiction*. New York: Association Press, 1959.

Paul, Robert D., "Theology and Detective Fiction," *Student World*, Vol. LV, No. 2 (Second Quarter, 1962), pp. 186–195.

Ross, Malcolm M., *Poetry and Dogma*. New Brunswick, N.J.: Rutgers University Press, 1955.

Savage, D. S., *The Withered Branch: Six Studies in the Modern Novel*. New York: Pellegrini and Cudahy, n.d.

Savage, D. S., *The Personal Principle: Studies in Modern Poetry*. London: Routledge, 1944.

Scott, Nathan A., Jr., ed., *The Tragic Vision and the Christian Faith*. New York: Association Press, 1957.

Slater, John R., *Recent Literature and Religion*. New York: Harper and Bros., 1938.

Stewart, Douglas, *The Ark of God: Studies in Five Modern Novelists*. London: Carey Kingsgate Press, 1961.

Stewart, Randall, *American Literature and Christian Doctrine*. Baton Rouge, La.: Louisiana State University Press, 1958.

Turnell, Martin, *Modern Literature and the Christian Faith*. Westminster, Md.: The Newman Press, 1961.

Ulanov, Barry, "The Rhetoric of Christian Comedy," *The McAuley Lectures, 1961*. West Hartford, Conn.: Saint Joseph College, 1962.

Ulanov, Barry, *Sources and Resources: The Literary Traditions of Christian Humanism*. Westminster, Md.: The Newman Press, 1960.

Wilder, Amos N., *The Spiritual Aspects of the New Poetry*. New York: Harper and Bros., 1940.

Wilder, Amos N., *Modern Poetry and the Christian Tradition*. New York: Charles Scribner's Sons, 1952.

PART V

The "Silence, Exile, and Cunning" of the Modern Imagination

Auden, W. H., *The Enchafèd Flood, or the Romantic Iconography of the Sea*. New York: Random House, 1950.

Bennett, Joseph D., *Baudelaire: A Criticism*. Princeton: Princeton University Press, 1946.

Bethell, S. L., *The Literary Outlook*. London: The Sheldon Press, 1943.

Coleman, Elliott, *The Golden Angel: Papers on Proust*. New York: Coley Taylor, Inc., 1954.

Eliot, T. S., *After Strange Gods: A Primer of Modern Heresy*. New York: Harcourt, Brace and Co., 1934.

Eliot, T. S., *Essays Ancient and Modern*. New York: Harcourt, Brace and Co., 1936.

Eliot, T. S., *On Poetry and Poets*. New York: Farrar, Straus and Cudahy, 1957.

Every, Brother George, *S.S.M., Poetry and Personal Responsibility*. London: S.C.M. Press Ltd., 1949.

Fowlie, Wallace, *The Clown's Grail: A Study of Love in Its Literary Expression*. London: Dennis Dobson Ltd., 1947.

Fowlie, Wallace, *Jacob's Night: The Religious Renascence in France*. New York: Sheed and Ward, 1947.

Fowlie, Wallace, *Rimbaud*. New York: New Directions, 1946.

Fowlie, Wallace, *Clowns and Angels: Studies in Modern French Literature*. New York: Sheed and Ward, 1943.

Fuller, Edmund, *Man in Modern Fiction*. New York: Random House, 1958.

Gannon, Edward, *S.J., The Honor of Being a Man: The World of André Malraux*. Chicago: Loyola University Press, 1957.

Hollis, Christopher, *A Study of George Orwell*. London: Hollis and Carter, 1956.

Hopper, Stanley R., "The Problem of Moral Isolation in Contemporary Literature," in *Spiritual Problems in Contemporary Literature*, ed. by Stanley R. Hopper. New York: Harper and Bros., 1952.

Hopper, Stanley R., "On the Naming of the Gods in Hölderlin and Rilke," in *Christianity and the Existentialists,* ed. by Carl Michalson. New York: Charles Scribner's Sons, 1956.

Jarrett-Kerr, Martin, *C.R., D. H. Lawrence and Human Existence*. London: Rockliff, 1951. (Published under the pseudonym, Fr. William Tiverton)

Killinger, John, *Hemingway and the Dead Gods*. Lexington, Ky.: University of Kentucky Press, 1960.

Marcel, Gabriel, "Rilke: A Witness to the Spiritual," *Homo Viator: Introduction to a Metaphysic of Hope*. Chicago: Henry Regnery Co., 1951.

Nicholson, Norman, *Man and Literature*. London: S.C.M. Press, 1943.

Noon, William T., *S.J.*, *Joyce and Aquinas*. New Haven: Yale University Press, 1957.

Noon, William T., *S.J.*, "God and Man in Twentieth-Century Fiction," *Thought,* Vol. XXXVII, No. 144 (Spring, 1962).

Noon, William T., *S.J.*, "Modern Literature and the Sense of Time," *Thought,* Vol. XXXIII, No. 131 (Winter, 1958–59).

Rougemont, Denis de, *Love in the Western World*. New York: Pantheon Books, 1956.

Rougemont, Denis de, *Love Declared: Essays on the Myths of Love*. New York: Pantheon Books, 1963.

Scott, Nathan A., Jr., *Rehearsals of Discomposure: Alienation and Reconciliation in Modern Literature*. New York: King's Crown Press of Columbia University Press, 1952.

Scott, Nathan A., Jr., *Albert Camus*. London: Bowes and Bowes Ltd., 1962.

Scott, Nathan A., Jr., *Samuel Beckett*. London: Bowes and Bowes Ltd., 1964.

Scott, Nathan A., Jr., "The Broken Center: A Definition of the Crisis of Values in Modern Literature," in *Symbolism in Religion and Literature,* ed. by Rollo May. New York: George Braziller, Inc., 1960.

Scott, Nathan A., Jr., "The Example of George Orwell," *Christianity and Crisis,* Vol. XIX, No. 13 (July 20, 1959), pp. 107–110.

Scott, Nathan A., Jr., "The Modest Optimism of Albert Camus," *The Christian Scholar,* Vol. XLII, No. 4 (Winter, 1959), pp. 251–274.

Scott, Nathan A., Jr., "The Recent Journey into the Zone of Zero:

The Example of Beckett and His Despair of Literature," *The Centennial Review*, Vol. VI, No. 2 (Spring, 1962), pp. 144–181.

Scott, Nathen A., Jr., "The Literary Imagination and the Victorian Crisis of Faith: The Example of Thomas Hardy," *The Journal of Religion,* Vol. XL, No. 4 (October, 1960), pp. 267–281.

Scott, Nathan A., Jr., "Society and the Self in Recent American Literature," *Union Seminary Quarterly Review,* Vol. XVIII, No. 4 (May, 1963), pp. 377–392.

Scott, Nathan A., Jr., "The Bias of Comedy and the Narrow Escape into Faith," *The Christian Scholar,* Vol. XLIV, No. 1 (Spring, 1961), pp. 9–39.

Tate, Allen, *The Forlorn Demon.* Chicago: Henry Regnery Co., 1953.

Weidlé, Wladimir, *The Dilemma of the Arts.* London: S.C.M. Press Ltd., 1948.

In the 4th century B.C., Aristotle charted a "poetics" for the pagan world, and Christians —although in other respects transfigured by a new vision—have not substantially added to it. Our idea of tragedy (despite the death and resurrection) is still largely Aristotle's idea of tragedy; our humanism (despite the incarnation) is seldom more than paganism-plus-optimism.

Yet individual Christians have had intuitions about art, and about the criticism of art, which have provided tantalizing glimpses and hints of a brand-new poetics. A critic here and a poet there have brought blazing new insights to the question — but almost always in the splendid isolation of post-reformation Christianity. Disunion has left us, here as elsewhere, with a hundred brilliant fragments.

Professor Scott has undertaken the aesthetically-ecumenical task of bringing these insights together. He deploys twenty-two well-known authors to achieve the effect of a single Aristotelian inquiry: what have Christians thought about art in general — and in what way does the Christian vision illumine art? What have Christians thought about literature in particular? Then, narrowing on his target, how do Christians go about criticizing literature? And–narrower yet—how do they unlock its various forms: drama, poetry, novels, movies? Finally, what is their relation in all this to the modern secular imagination?

The authors are nicely balanced between criticism and creation. There is none of the scholastic abstractness that has made Christian aesthetics one of the more obscure branches of metaphysics; there is plenty of the hard awareness of "the material" which is the artist's first concern, the thing he must struggle with before "aesthetics" even arises.

Aristotle's biology has long since been, respectfully but firmly, supplanted. His poetics are hardier, and remain a corner-stone. But they are not enough for a full Christian consciousness: the imagination has moved onto new ground. No one writer is master of this ground, but many have staked corners of it. THE NEW ORPHEUS assembles the fragments, and the outline of a new poetics begins to take form.